Pro SharePoint Solution Development

Combining .NET, SharePoint, and Office 2007

Ed Hild with Susie Adams

Apress®

Pro SharePoint Solution Development: Combining .NET, SharePoint, and Office 2007

Copyright © 2007 by Ed Hild, Susie Adams

ISBN-13 (pbk): 978-1-59059-808-5

ISBN-10 (pbk): 1-59059-808-3

Printed and bound in the United States of America 9 8 7 6 5 4 3 2 1

Lead Editor: Jonathan Hassell
Technical Reviewer: Sahil Malik
Editorial Board: Steve Anglin, Ewan Buckingham, Gary Cornell, Jason Gilmore, Jonathan Gennick, Jonathan Hassell, James Huddleston, Chris Mills, Matthew Moodie, Jeff Pepper, Dominic Shakeshaft, Matt Wade
Project Manager: Kylie Johnston
Copy Edit Manager: Nicole Flores
Copy Editor: Candace English
Assistant Production Director: Kari Brooks-Copony
Production Editor: Kelly Winquist
Compositor: Dina Quan
Proofreader: Nancy Sixsmith
Indexer: Brenda Miller
Artist: April Milne
Cover Designer: Kurt Krames
Manufacturing Director: Tom Debolski

Distributed to the book trade worldwide by Springer-Verlag New York, Inc., 233 Spring Street, 6th Floor, New York, NY 10013. Phone 1-800-SPRINGER, fax 201-348-4505, e-mail orders-ny@springer-sbm.com, or visit http://www.springeronline.com.

For information on translations, please contact Apress directly at 2560 Ninth Street, Suite 219, Berkeley, CA 94710. Phone 510-549-5930, fax 510-549-5939, e-mail info@apress.com, or visit http://www.apress.com.

The source code for this book is available to readers at http://www.apress.com in the Source Code/ Download section.

I dedicate this work to my family. To my wife, who supports my many dreams. To my son, who lost a lot of time with me for this book. And to my parents, who raised me with the work ethic necessary to see this through.
—Ed Hild

To my nieces and nephews: Alli, Zach, Connor, Matt, and Payton (Paytie-Moe).
—Susie Adams

Contents at a Glance

PART 1 ▪▪▪ Introduction

PART 2 ▪▪▪ Microsoft Excel Solutions

PART 3 ▪▪▪ Microsoft Word Solutions

PART 4 ▪▪▪ Microsoft PowerPoint Solutions

PART 5 ■■■ Microsoft Outlook Solutions

PART 6 ■■■ Microsoft InfoPath Solutions

PART 7 ■■■ Conclusion

Contents

PART 1 ▪▪▪ Introduction

PART 2 ■■■ Microsoft Excel Solutions

CHAPTER 6   Integrating Spreadsheets into the Enterprise. 101

PART 3 ■■■ Microsoft Word Solutions

CHAPTER 7   Merging SharePoint List Data into Word Documents. . . . 129

PART 4 ■ ■ ■ Microsoft PowerPoint Solutions

PART 5 ▪▪▪ Microsoft Outlook Solutions

PART 6 ▪ ▪ ▪ Microsoft InfoPath Solutions

PART 7 ■■■ Conclusion

About the Authors

ED HILD's first job after college was as a math and computer science teacher at Walt Whitman High School in Bethesda, MD. After upgrading the curriculum, he decided to practice what he was teaching and moved into consulting. Ed soon felt the teaching itch again and took a position teaching MCSD and MCSE courses for a technical education center as well as developing the software that would run all the schools. Ed gained most of his development experience at his next position, which was as the director of technology at e.magination (a Microsoft partner in Baltimore, MD). There he worked for several years building web applications for a wide variety of customers by using Microsoft technologies. He was then lured to Microsoft and now works as the collaboration technology architect in the Microsoft Technology Center in Reston, VA. Ed was published in *MSDN Magazine* in March 2006 and has spoken at several conferences, including Microsoft Developer Days and TechEd.

SUSIE ADAMS is an MTC Technical Director with Microsoft Corporation. She has over 20 years of application integration and development experience and is currently managing a team of senior architects at the Reston Virginia Microsoft Technology Center. She has contributed to several industry technical journals, was the lead author for *BizTalk Unleashed* (Sams Publishing), and was a contributing author for *Visual InterDev 6 Unleashed* (Sams) and *Microsoft Visual InterDev 6.0 Enterprise: Developer's Workshop* (Microsoft Press). She has spoken at several industry tradeshow conferences, including the Visual Basic Insider Technical Summit (VBITS), Microsoft Developer Days, and Microsoft TechEd.

About the Technical Reviewer

■**SAHIL MALIK** (www.winsmarts.com) is a Microsoft MVP (C#), International .NET Association (INETA) speaker and the author of a bestselling ADO.NET 2.0 book. He is a consultant, trainer, and mentor in various Microsoft technologies. His talks are high-energy, highly charged, and highly rated. Sahil blogs about various technical topics at http://blah.winsmarts.com.

Introduction

When we first proposed this book, we set a goal of writing a different kind of SharePoint book. We did not want a reference that repeated the software development kit, nor did we want a how-to book that explained how to configure the out-of-the-box functionality. Instead, we envisioned a book that helped developers apply the Microsoft Office platform to customer problems. Since Susie and I work at the Microsoft Technology Center in Virginia, we have a unique opportunity to work with a wide variety of customers, in both the commercial and public sectors, who are trying to realize a benefit from incorporating Office technologies into their enterprises. Many of these customers are not just seeking installation or configuration advice. The focus is on how the Microsoft Office platform will make their workers more efficient, their processes more repeatable, and their businesses more profitable. For these customers, the technology must be applied to their specific challenges.

With the release of Office 2007, Microsoft provides the developer with a complete platform (both client and server) for generating documents, automating processes, enhancing collaboration, and integrating line-of-business data. This platform not only includes the latest releases of SharePoint products and technologies, but also a new set of desktop applications. More importantly, these applications are more extendable by .NET developers than in any previous release. This book will walk through solutions to common customer challenges. It will utilize both the client and server technologies of the Office 2007 platform, including Microsoft Office 2007, Microsoft Office SharePoint Server 2007, and Microsoft Visual Studio 2005 Tools for Office SE.

Since we too are developers, we recognize that often you buy a book just for that one code sample or chapter you need to complete a project. Unfortunately, many books don't support that approach and have a huge example that builds throughout the book. As much as possible, we have designed our solutions to be self-contained within their own chapters. We anticipate that you will see something that you can immediately relate to or something that has a high priority for you. Go ahead and skip to that chapter and read that solution. Make sure you come back, though; the other chapters are just as interesting!

After the first few chapters, which introduce the technologies and outline the book, the remaining chapters each present a real-world customer problem and its solution. In every chapter we will introduce the problem, give you examples of customers who typically have this problem, provide you with an overview of the solution, and a complete walk-through. Accompanying this text is a download of completed solutions on the Apress web site (in the Source Code/Download section of http://apress.com). In each chapter we will also highlight some of the key concepts that you will likely use again and list extension points for enhancing the solution. Finally, each chapter contains a set of links for further reading on the topics included in the solution.

So what are we going to build? The solutions combine the familiar interface of the desktop applications with the server capabilities of SharePoint. The solutions include items such as custom web parts, Office add-ins, SharePoint features, forms, workflow, the Business Data

Catalog, Outlook form regions, Excel Services, and the Open XML file format. But that is not a complete list. In most cases, a solution is not just any one of these items, but a combination that meets the customer's needs.

Who This Book Is For

This book is for developers looking to apply the Microsoft Office platform (both client and server) to their own solutions. We did not set out to write a reference book; instead we focused on how the features and services of Office and SharePoint can be leveraged. Therefore, we assume the reader is already familiar with .NET code. Ideally the reader has also been exposed to some sort of development with Microsoft Office and at least used a SharePoint team site. We do provide a few background chapters for developers new to these areas or unfamiliar with the enhancements of the latest releases. If you are a developer who has always wanted to build solutions that dynamically build Office documents, automate processes, enhance collaboration, and integrate line-of-business data, then this book is for you. If you want to learn how to construct solutions that combine items like custom web parts, Office add-ins, SharePoint features, forms, workflow, the Business Data Catalog, Outlook form regions, Excel Services, and the Open XML file format, then this book is for you. If you ever wanted a book that focused on solutions and treated Microsoft Office 2007, Microsoft Office SharePoint Server 2007, and Visual Studio 2005 Tools for Office SE equally, then this book is for you.

Downloading the Code

The source code for this book is available to readers at `www.apress.com` in the Source Code/ Download section of this book's home page. Please feel free to download all the code there. You can also check for errata and find related titles from Apress.

Contacting the Authors

You can contact the authors by email. Ed Hild's email address is `edhild@microsoft.com` and Susie Adams's email address is `susiea@microsoft.com`. Additionally, Ed maintains a blog (`http://blogs.msdn.com/edhild`) that has more SharePoint code examples, best practices, and general collaboration information.

PART 1

■■■

Introduction

This section will focus on describing what this book is about, its intended audience, and the technologies we will utilize in our solutions. It will introduce the common business challenges for which we will construct solutions in the remainder of the book. Part 1 includes overviews of Microsoft Office SharePoint Server 2007, Microsoft Office 2007, and Visual Studio Tools for Office.

CHAPTER 1

■■■

Office Business Applications

It is sometimes difficult to remember the corporate office of the recent past. Think back 5 or maybe 10 years. For many of us, that isn't long ago. However, from a technology perspective, we are talking about an era that might seem as distant as the dark ages. Sure, personal computing was taking off and the Internet was in its infancy. Not every company had a web site, and the average business user in a corporate office had very little exposure to the technologies that seem commonplace today. Remember when only the technically proficient used spreadsheets? Remember when email was a productivity tool and didn't require labor-intensive filing and sorting? This trip down memory lane lends some perspective as to how far workers have come to embrace the technology solutions IT offers. Unfortunately, the amount of information that workers have to interact with increases daily, as does the proliferation of often-siloed software systems trying to provide work-related solutions. Today, many organizations find themselves in a state where information and labor are duplicated. Often, workers take more time finding and constructing information than analyzing it and making decisions. It is here that technology has an opportunity. The opportunity is to provide more-intelligent tools that focus on the work the corporate business user needs to accomplish. It is in this area that this book will explore common challenges and scenarios and their solutions.

Companies often believe the average business user isn't going to find new technologies or solutions easy enough to use. Though there is some truth here, history has shown us that the information worker will adapt if the solution delivers a true value. What is more interesting is to observe the behaviors of the next generation of workers. Recently we had the opportunity to perform some community service in the New Orleans area after Hurricane Katrina. Some of our team helped restore houses, others helped local services restore computer networks, and we got to visit area schools to do something similar to a career day for the students. Before we walked into classrooms, the principals told us that most of the families who had the means to do so didn't come back to the area and that we should not have high expectations about how much technology the students had been exposed to. Of course, we didn't listen and asked the same questions we always ask students we interact with:

1. How many of you have cell phones?

Almost every student had one. And most were comfortable discussing the phone as a multipurpose device. I quickly learned to turn off my Internet-browser access when the students were playing with my Treo. Most of the students had sent text messages and used their phones for music.

2. How many of you can type faster than you can write?

Again, almost every hand in the room was raised.

3. How many of you use a computer daily?

The hands remained raised. During our time there, many students asked us questions about their home networks. Even with middle-school kids, they were the ones setting up the networks for their families.

Our school experience is evidence that not only will the average corporate business user pick up a new technology if we can provide a solution that delivers value, but our workforce continues to get injected with users who have more exposure to technology outside of the office. However, we do have to be aware of the crowd that doesn't want to learn something completely new. Because they exist, this book will focus on solutions that customize tools that have been a staple on the corporate desktop. The solutions in this book will extend the most familiar Microsoft Office tools: Word, Excel, Outlook, and PowerPoint.

Why focus on Microsoft Office? For the information worker, Microsoft Office has a proven value that few other technologies can compare with. Word, Excel, Outlook, and PowerPoint have been on the corporate desktop for more than a decade and users are comfortable working with them. Microsoft itself is using this strength to address the needs of the enterprise around how they create, organize, and search information. At the heart of these enterprise application servers are Microsoft SharePoint Products and Technologies.

Specifically, the name SharePoint is attached to two applications: Windows SharePoint Services (WSS) is a Windows Server 2003 component (it is included in the R2 release of Windows Server 2003 and available as an add-on to the original release) that provides collaboration features focused on delivering Web-based sites for teams and groups of users. These sites provide a focal point for activities such as planning a meeting, reviewing a document, or completing a business process. Microsoft Office SharePoint Server (MOSS) extends WSS to provide enterprise-level features such as search, records management, content management, personalization, application integration, and so on. There is a reason that SharePoint carries the Microsoft Office designation—these products extend the Microsoft Office desktop applications to provide services that an organization needs beyond document creation. The server applications integrate seamlessly into the Microsoft Office desktop applications. As a result, organizations can connect information workers, service their collaboration needs, and help them locate information—all from within the same document, spreadsheet, presentation, or email that they are working on.

The latest versions of the Microsoft Office desktop tools and application servers provide an incredible number of features and functionality out of the box. They integrate more strongly than any previous release. However, as organizations apply these technologies to their business processes or to solve specific problems, there may still be some gaps because of the nuances inherent in the way a company wants to use them. This is where the application developer enters center stage. The mistake often made here is for the application developer to build a solution completely removed from the environment that the user is familiar with. Any solution needs to be highly integrated with the Office desktop tools as well as leverage SharePoint's services. There would be no reason to build a custom database application that stores documents and their metadata, and provides versioning capabilities. Such features are available from any SharePoint document library. In terms of interface, why ask the user to close the document they are working on to go to some other thick Windows client or custom web page?

Historically, developers have avoided customizing the Office tools for several reasons. The first is that such solutions are notoriously difficult to construct. This is in large part due to the lack of a sophisticated development environment. Developers focused on C++, Visual Basic, or C# are typically not exposed to VBA, the development model within Office, and therefore lack the comfort level needed to build effective solutions. Microsoft Visual Studio Tools for Office (VSTO) bridges this chasm. VSTO is a runtime library that provides a layer of abstraction between the .NET developer and the Microsoft Office primary interop assemblies. This layer helps hide some of the COM particulars from the .NET developer and enables them to build .NET solutions for Office using Visual Studio and focusing on their solution, not on interop plumbing. In addition to making the code simpler, VSTO provides a designer experience. For example, when building an Excel-based solution, Excel is loaded into Visual Studio and the spreadsheet becomes the design surface. This means the developer can drag and drop their well-known Windows forms controls right onto the spreadsheet, set their properties, and add a code-behind. This is the expected experience for the Windows or Web developer. Most of the examples in this book will utilize Visual Studio Tools for Office.

Another recent milestone that promotes new development opportunities is the switch from Office documents that rely on proprietary binary file formats to formats that are open and built on XML. The new Microsoft Office 2007 desktop tools rely on an Open XML format. Very often, developers find themselves in a situation where a solution requires the generation of a document, spreadsheet, or presentation based on data in a SQL database, web service, or other external application. Previously, most solutions relied on automating Office, which required the application to be installed on the server. Not only were these solutions extremely difficult to scale, but in most circumstances they were not supported by Microsoft. With the Open XML file format, developers will be able to build server-side document-generation solutions without having the Office application even present on the server.

So this book is about building solutions on top of the Microsoft Office platform. This means that the solutions will incorporate SharePoint, Office, and VSTO. This is a book for the developer community. We assume an average level of experience building .NET applications and some familiarity with Office and SharePoint.

The three chapters following this one (Chapters 2, 3, and 4) provide an overview of Share-Point, Office, and VSTO, as well as new features and enhancements present in the latest versions of these technologies. Almost all of our chapters have a "Further Reading" section at the end in case you want more information on the topics covered there. This book is not meant to be a reference manual that teaches you every feature of these technologies; instead it shows you common solution patterns through scenarios that could apply to any organization. If you are an expert in these technologies, feel free to skim the overview chapters or even skip them and jump straight to the scenario/solution ones (Chapter 5 and onward). We set out to make each of our solution chapters capable of standing on their own so you can read them in any order, focusing on the scenarios that most interest you.

You might think with all of this technology that we will be building solutions never dreamed of before. However, that really isn't the case. The solutions we will construct are ones that developers have been struggling to deliver for some time. The biggest differences are the ease with which we will construct them and the reduction in the amount of code required.

The solutions we will construct have their humble beginnings in custom VBA applications. Many VBA solutions are brought into businesses by a technology-savvy business user who loves to record macros and see the code they emit. Such users are able to put together a document or spreadsheet that turns into a mission-critical application. Unfortunately for the organization, this application becomes difficult to manage and deploy. Performance and security are hardly ever presented as a benefit. For the developer, debugging has always been largely a process of trial and error. Even though the VBA applications are rather primitive, these applications tend to be a huge success. The reason is that they are targeted to make the information worker's job easier and their time to deployment is rather quick. They are integrated into the Office applications and were built by someone intimately involved with the challenges faced in the workplace.

A layer above VBA applications are solutions developed using the COM interfaces exposed by Office. These tend to be application add-ins that run within an Office tool or applications that automate Office. An add-in is essentially a custom library that Office will load as the application launches. This add-in can then extend the Office tool to provide additional functionality. An example could be an Excel add-in that adds a button onto the toolbar that, when pressed, loads data from an external source onto the spreadsheet. The add-in model is a powerful one that continues into the managed code solutions created by VSTO. The biggest differences between COM and VSTO add-ins are the improvements in the development experience and the benefits of .NET code bases over COM.

Developers have also built solutions that rely on automating an Office tool. An example of this would be custom code that loads the application of Word (Word.Application) and automatically begins to construct the document based on a data source. These applications tend to be deployed on servers where this work can be done on behalf of the user. The main problem with these solutions is that they will not scale since automating Word in this manner is equivalent to each user logging on to the server and opening the application directly. Not to mention, the server-based automation of Office is something Microsoft has never been willing to support.

Smart documents were an application type that appeared with Microsoft Office 2003. The idea of a smart document was to solve the information-integration/duplication challenge. Smart documents took advantage of the task pane and Office 2003's support for XML. An example of such an application would be a Word document that, through a custom task pane, allows a user to select data from another application. That data is then placed appropriately into the document based on the document's XML schema. Smart documents were first presented as COM applications in which the task pane was HTML with an XML file detailing the controls that were to be loaded. Later the first version of VSTO for Visual Studio 2003 provided a .NET programming option, but only for Word, Excel, Outlook, and InfoPath. These types of applications got "smart" in their name because of their similarity to smart clients. In *smart client applications*, a thick client relies on external resources such as web services. This model has many appealing advantages, including deployment scenarios and support for disconnected clients. Visual Studio 2005 Tools for the 2007 Microsoft Office System continues to evolve solutions of this type and exposes this model to many more Office applications.

Solutions developed on the Microsoft Office platform are termed *Office Business Applications*, or *OBA*. The OBA team at Microsoft has documented common patterns that solutions incorporate to deliver integration, a rich experience, and data reduction for the information worker. These patterns can be grouped into the categories displayed in Table 1-1. As we introduce you to the scenarios in the book, we will describe which of these patterns the solutions implement. (Often there is not a single pattern used, but rather a combination.) For more information on these patterns and OBA, visit the OBA developer portal at http://msdn2. microsoft.com/en-us/office/aa905528.aspx.

Table 1-1. *Categories of Office Business Application Patterns*

Pattern Category	Description
Office Applications as a Reach Channel	Using Office to present data from other systems in an effort to simplify access or reduce duplication of effort
Document Integration	Automating the generation of documents with data from another system or processing the documents to extract data
Composite User Interface	Bringing together data from disparate resources into a single tool for the end user
Complementary Document Workflow	Providing the ability to incorporate ad-hoc workflow into other line-of-business processes
Discovery Navigation	Providing the ability to search and navigate through data of other systems
Collaborative Site	Using a SharePoint site to represent an instance of a structured process
Application Generated Tasks and Notifications	Consolidating task requests from systems into Microsoft Outlook

You've just read about the need for these solutions, the technologies we have access to, and how we may have built them in the past. Now let's focus on the information-worker problems we will solve in this book. We have arranged the solutions in this book by the Office application that we will leverage, and we've designed each solution not to rely on code presented in another chapter. Therefore, you will be able to read these chapters in any order depending on how appealing you find the problems.

Part 2: Microsoft Excel Solutions

Chapter 5: Maintaining Offline List Content from Multiple Sites—Windows SharePoint Services provides team sites to support collaboration for a particular team of users or in support of a business process. Often, users are members of several of the same type of site. As their membership to these sites increase, so does the burden of maintaining the site content. The user must visit each of these sites to make their content changes. In this chapter we will consolidate the maintenance of this content into a single Microsoft Excel workbook. A spreadsheet-based application will pull the data from the user's sites, present a single interface to make edits, and post changes back to the server. In addition, this application will support offline storage for working on the content when the user does not have access to the SharePoint sites.

Related OBA patterns: Composite User Interface, Collaborative Site

Chapter 6: Integrating Spreadsheets into the Enterprise—Information workers have become accustomed to modeling business calculations with spreadsheets in Microsoft Excel. Often developers take these spreadsheets and recode their logic into custom applications or line-of-business (LOB) systems. This usually removes information workers completely from the picture, leaving them unable to have any influence on the calculation without making changes to the application. In this chapter we focus on techniques to extend Excel so that it can participate with other enterprise systems; we do this by adding .NET code exposed as new Excel functions that can call web services, query databases, or perform calculations that are normally not available. In addition, we show you how the Excel Services feature in Microsoft Office SharePoint Server allows you to reuse the spreadsheet's calculation logic in your own applications while still allowing the information worker the ability to alter it.

Related OBA pattern: Office Applications as a Reach Channel

Part 3: Microsoft Word Solutions

Chapter 7: Merging SharePoint List Data into Word Documents—Organizations often have sets of document templates that are used throughout their enterprise. It is not unusual for several of these templates to share common data elements. At the same time, the list structures in SharePoint sites are increasingly being used to store records of data that might have previously been in local spreadsheets or Access databases. In this chapter we show you how to leverage the Open XML file format to insert a list item into a Word document so that its fields are displayed in designated locations.

Related OBA pattern: Document Integration

Chapter 8: Working Collaboratively with Document Fragments—By storing a document in a SharePoint library, users are able to collaborate and benefit from features such as versioning, metadata, and security. However, the document can be checked out by only one user at a time. What if an organization had a document that contained standard sections that needed to be completed by different users concurrently? In this chapter we will build a SharePoint library that is capable of breaking apart a document into separate files for each of its sections. Once these fragments have been generated, they can each be modified independently. Each fragment can also leverage the metadata and versioning features of the library. Once complete, our library will reassemble the sections into a single document.

Related OBA pattern: Document Integration

Part 4: Microsoft PowerPoint Solutions

Chapter 9: Extending PowerPoint to Build a Presentation Based on Site Content—Windows SharePoint Services provides team sites to support collaboration for a particular team of users or in support of a business process. Often the users involved with this process have to present their progress to the organization or to upper management. In this chapter we will extend Microsoft PowerPoint with a wizard that allows the user to have presentation slides containing site content inserted into their presentation automatically.

Related OBA patterns: Document Integration, Composite User Interface

Chapter 10: Building a Presentation Server-Side within a Web Part—When an organization uses a team site to represent an instance of a business process, it often has to report the status of that process in the form of a presentation. That presentation usually includes content from the lists within the site. For types of presentations that happen frequently, the organization has likely adopted a presentation template that is always used and ordered the slides and information in a specific manner. In this chapter we will build a web part that takes a PowerPoint template and populates the slides with content from a SharePoint site. This all happens server-side with a simple click of a button.

Related OBA pattern: Document Integration

Part 5: Microsoft Outlook Solutions

Chapter 11: Working with Email Messages and SharePoint—Microsoft Outlook already includes functionality to dissuade users from sending copies of a document as attachments in an effort to collaborate and gather feedback. When the authoring user sends the email with the attachment, Outlook asks them if they would rather create a collaboration site and send a link to their recipients. However, there is no such integration for an email a user *receives*. What if a user receives an email with attachments from an outside organization that warrants an internal site for processing? In this chapter we will extend Microsoft Outlook to enable these users to easily persist these messages to SharePoint repositories.

Related OBA pattern: Collaborative Site

Chapter 12: Surfacing Data from Line-of-Business Applications—Information workers are often put into an environment where they need several tools that contain silos of duplicate data. They often have to jump in and out of these tools, copying and pasting data from one screen to the next. In this chapter we will show you how to leverage the Business Data Catalog (BDC) functionality of Microsoft Office SharePoint Server to seamlessly integrate a line-of-business system with SharePoint. This will allow the data to be used in web parts and columns of lists, and will support search indexing. We will also show you how to extend the BDC's integration with a web service so that another application (Microsoft Outlook) can consume it. This limits the integration to a single authoritative point for the data.

Related OBA patterns: Office Applications as a Reach Channel, Discovery Navigation, Composite User Interface

Part 6: Microsoft InfoPath Solutions

Chapter 13: Taking InfoPath Forms to the Web—InfoPath was introduced with Office 2003 and information workers in the enterprise quickly realized its value in easily replacing the collection of data traditionally done with paper forms. However, the use of InfoPath was usually relegated to simple, departmental forms that never left the boundary of the company. This limitation was largely due to the fact that user who would need to fill out the form also needed to have InfoPath. In this chapter we will show you how the Form Services functionality of Microsoft Office SharePoint Server enables you to take InfoPath-designed forms and present them to a user in a browser-only interface. We will also tackle strategies for incorporating these forms into the enterprise, such as how to connect to data sources, security implications, and how to host the forms in your own application.

Related OBA pattern: Office Applications as a Reach Channel

Chapter 14: Incorporating Workflow into Forms Processing—Traditionally forms are used to collect data for a line-of-business application. The user fills out a form and the data is submitted into another system. However, many scenarios require a complementary workflow process to intervene before the data is stored in the LOB system. These workflow processes could be ad-hoc, requiring different routes of approval. In this chapter we will show you how to leverage SharePoint's workflow capabilities to complement the processing of forms to enterprise systems.

Related OBA Pattern: Complementary Document Workflow

Part 7: Conclusion

Chapter 15: Realizing the Vision—Finally, Chapter 15 will sum things up, revisiting the importance of the solutions and taking a look into the future of developing on the Office platform.

Development-Environment Requirements

There are many options for a development environment, but we are assuming that you are using either Microsoft Virtual PC or Microsoft Virtual Server to provide you with a sandbox to implement the solutions presented in the book. Our core development environment for the book consisted of two Windows Server 2003 R2 virtual machines running under Virtual Server. This does create quite the hardware requirement. If you are going to match our configuration, you should have a recent machine with at least 2GB of RAM, and an external drive for one of the virtual machines is recommended. One virtual machine was our domain controller (sample.com) and supported Microsoft Exchange 2003 and Microsoft SQL Server 2005. The second virtual machine was the Microsoft Office SharePoint Server and our development environment. The following products were installed there: Microsoft Office Enterprise 2007, Microsoft Office SharePoint Server 2007 (enterprise features enabled), Microsoft Office SharePoint Designer 2007, and Microsoft Visual Studio 2005 Team Edition. In MOSS we used separate web applications for the shared service provider, the My Sites (my.sample.com), and the portal (portal.sample.com). In addition to these core products there were many starter kits, SDKs, toolkits, and things we installed. Here is a summary:

- Visual Studio Tools for Office 2005 (included in VS.NET Team Edition)

- Visual Studio Tools for Office 2005 SE

- The .NET Framework (versions 2.0 and 3.0)

- 2007 Office System XML code snippets

- MSXML 6.0 parser

- Office SharePoint Server 2007 SDK (including ECM Starter Kit)

- Visual Studio 2005 extensions for .NET Framework (WCF & WPF) November 2006 CTP

- Visual Studio 2005 extensions for Windows SharePoint Services November 2006 CTP

- Visual Studio 2005 extensions for Windows Workflow Foundation

- Windows SharePoint Services 3.0 SDK

It is possible to do everything on one virtual machine, but in our experience it really does not lessen the hardware requirements of the machine you run on.

Note There is one solution (Chapter 5) that required us to have an Office 2003 Professional–based environment. For that solution, we had a Windows XP virtual machine with Microsoft Office 2003 Professional, Visual Studio 2005 Team Edition, and both Visual Studio Tools for Office editions. Since Chapter 5 is different from the others, we will repeat this information in a compatibility section in the chapter.

■ ■ ■

CHAPTER 2

SharePoint Products and Technologies: Overview and New Features

SharePoint Products and Technologies is a term that is used to describe Microsoft's collaboration platform widely. More specifically, this term today refers to two distinct applications: Windows SharePoint Services (WSS) and Microsoft Office SharePoint Server (MOSS). Windows SharePoint Services provides the foundation for the platform and is actually a component of the Windows Server 2003 operating system. It provides core functionality such as the ability to quickly provision collaboration sites, and a sophisticated document repository featuring collaboration necessities such as versioning, checkin/checkout, as well as a metadata system. Whereas WSS provides collaborative sites to facilitate teams of users, MOSS provides features to the enterprise. With MOSS, the focus is on distributing information, application integration, search, and content-management features targeted beyond basic document sharing.

History of SharePoint Technologies

To understand these products as they exist today, it is important to review their history. Each product has a different heritage and only recently have they been so seamlessly aligned and integrated. Before the term *portal* grew in popularity, developers sought to use Microsoft Outlook as a foundation to provide access to different systems and data, and most of the attention was focused on creating views that aggregated information from different applications into a single display. These views were made up of page components and were organized similar to the Outlook Today view. Microsoft provided SDK material and soon developers were building components to be loaded into the Outlook interface. This technique was referred to as building *digital dashboards*. It allowed developers to build reusable components that could be arranged on the dashboard to provide a view of data across the enterprise. These components were the beginning of the web parts we know today. Developers used them to query databases and to display charts, data, and other key information.

Early in the Web era, Microsoft released a FrontPage server application that ran on top of IIS (Internet Information Services) and relied on the FrontPage HTML-design tool for administration and customization. The power of the FrontPage server was that it shipped with web site templates. Therefore, an organization could quickly create new sites that automatically had some application functionality such as calendaring and task lists. These web sites would be ready for use after simply running a wizard. This removed the labor-intensive processes of web designers and application developers dramatically decreasing the time it took to deploy a web site. The result was especially powerful for a straightforward web site that was going to be used by a small number for users and usually for a small period of time. For many organizations, such a site was not worth the effort and cost of a full-blown web-development effort. These FrontPage sites eventually evolved into a product named SharePoint Team Services, or STS. This product was still based on Active Server Page (ASP) technology. With the .NET evolution, Windows SharePoint Services (v2) arrived and its features were released as a component of the server operating system. This led to a proliferation of organizations using this application's ability to create collaboration sites based on templates for teams of users.

Microsoft SharePoint Portal Server (SPS) 2001 was the first release of enterprise collaboration services that were to complement the agile team sites. This portal product was also based on ASP technology and focused on creating workspaces. With a workspace, the product provided a document repository as well as a web site where an organization could set up a site structure or taxonomy for organizing its information. The focus here was that documents should be categorized and that users would browse the category terms to locate their documents of interest. This category-based interface was a popular one for Web-based search engines such as Yahoo!. Included in this release was a search service as well as Web-based component platform supporting web parts. A major difference between this version and the ones that would follow is that SharePoint 2001 did not rely on SQL Server for its storage. Instead the repository was more similar to Exchange 2000 and was called the Web Storage System. This repository wound up being an Achilles' heel for scalability and was abandoned for SharePoint.

Like WSS, SharePoint Portal Server received a major facelift with the move to the .NET platform. Microsoft SharePoint Portal Server 2003 provided organizations with the ability to create enterprise portals. These portal sites relied on the WSS foundation for their document-repository needs and added new features for the enterprise. These enterprise features included a search that could index not only content stored within its repositories, but also other content stores such as file shares, web sites, and Microsoft Exchange public folders. SharePoint 2003 folded the workers of the system into the content mix as well. The services of My Sites and user profiles allowed the system to capture information about an organization's users and provided an application that let users view each other's profile from within the system, access documents that they shared, and locate users by attributes such as proficiency in a particular language. In fact, a user could be returned as a search result item along with documents and sites. SharePoint Portal Server 2003 also extended the web-part interface provided by WSS by incorporating a personalization service that allowed for a page to hide or show specific web parts to specific audiences of users. SharePoint's single sign-on service provided an application-development framework for translating security contexts between the logged-in user and that user's credentials to an external application whose data was used by a web part. Ultimately, SharePoint Portal Server 2003 completed the touch points a user would have with his organization's information. Whereas WSS answered the needs for teams of users, SPS provided the services to meet the needs of the overall organization, divisions, and even the individual.

Windows SharePoint Services v3

The newest version of Windows SharePoint Services (v3) is still geared toward providing collaborative sites for teams of users. It maintains its agility by providing an easy provisioning process. The sites themselves are still based on templates and composed of web parts. This version of WSS still provides the core document-repository functionality to the rest of the platform. So the bottom line is that v3 has the same goals as the previous version; however, there are significant changes. Many of these changes are feature enhancements, where functionality of the previous version has been extended to meet customer needs. Also, several enhancements are direct results of the fact that this version is built on the ASP.NET 2.0 framework as opposed to the 1.1 version. This section will explore some of the most important changes in Windows SharePoint Services v3 and their impact on you, the developer. This section is by no means a complete reference to WSS v3 and therefore we will include links to external content where you can learn more. We will also call out features that we will incorporate into the solutions in Chapters 5 through 14.

ASP.NET 2.0 Foundation

Windows SharePoint Services v3 is built on ASP.NET 2.0 and as a result, it has many advantages over the previous version. For example, in earlier versions of SharePoint it was very difficult for an organization to consistently brand its sites and reuse common user-interface elements. This was largely due to the fact that there was little separation of the layout of the page (web-part zones), page content, and the other look-and-feel elements. Therefore, designers often found themselves making the same change to dozens of ASPX pages so that the edit would be reflected throughout the system. The numerous changes were a by-product of WSS v2 storing identical ASPX pages in different site-definition folders. WSS v3 is able to reduce this pain by separating the content elements from the rest of the page's look and feel. Version 3 accomplishes this feat by relying on ASP.NET 2.0 master pages. Master pages are a part of the ASP.NET 2.0 architecture and are specifically designed so that content pages need only a reference to the master page to have their content merged with the appropriate layout, look, and feel. WSS v3 ships with a single master page called default.master, which is shown in Figure 2-1 from within SharePoint Designer 2007.

It is not recommended that you change the installed master page, but rather that you use it as a guide to build your own. There are two supported scenarios for customizing master pages:

- Copying the default.master page

- Working with SharePoint Designer 2007 to edit a master page

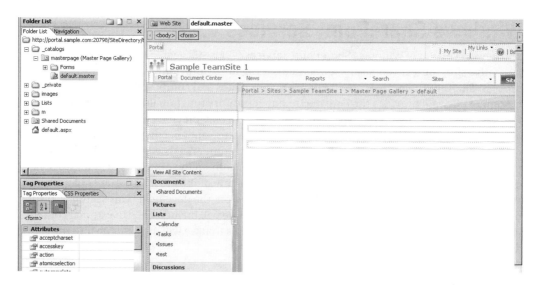

Figure 2-1. *Editing the default master page*

Master pages can reside in two different places in a WSS v3 solution. First, there are master pages that are deployed through the file system. These are located in the `C:\Program Files\Common Files\Microsoft Shared\web server extensions\12\Template\Global` directory by default. You can also deploy master pages for a specific site by uploading them to that site's master-page gallery. Once inside the gallery, the master page is stored in the content database for that site collection. When a new site is provisioned, the WSS site will initially use a cached version of the default master page from the file system. The designer can then use the master pages in the gallery to apply a new look and feel, or use a tool such as SharePoint Designer 2007 to edit a master page. The master pages that are in the file system also display in the gallery. This leaves open the possibility of a designer wanting to change the file-system–based master page for a specific site. This can be accomplished through the gallery, but the modified master page is then stored in the database as a customized page. This system is similar to the ghosted/unghosted techniques of the WSS v2 system, but is now called *customized* or *uncustomized*. A big difference in v3 is that a designer can use SharePoint Designer 2007 to revert any customized page back to relying on the file-system–based template. The following links provide more information on creating your own master pages:

- Master pages and Windows SharePoint Services 3.0:

    `http://www.codeproject.com/useritems/Glimpse_At_Master_Pages.asp`

- Discover Significant Developer Improvements in SharePoint Services:

    `http://msdn.microsoft.com/msdnmag/issues/06/07/WSS30Preview/default.aspx`

Another major component of ASP.NET 2.0 is its web-part infrastructure. Previously web parts were unique to SharePoint. However, the design pattern of building reusable components that maintain their own settings and support personalization and connections was far too valuable to be locked into a single application. Therefore, Microsoft decided to include the web-part infrastructure in ASP.NET 2.0. WSS v3 builds upon this infrastructure and therefore

SharePoint developers must adapt to a new base class and syntax for constructing web parts. The new base class is System.Web.UI.WebControls.WebParts.WebPart. This class should be the starting point for your new SharePoint web parts. This means that it is possible to build a web part that will run in SharePoint without even referencing the SharePoint assemblies. Listing 2-1 is a rather basic example of a web part with the new syntax.

Listing 2-1. *New Web-Part Syntax*

```
Public Class SampleWebPart
    Inherits System.Web.UI.WebControls.WebParts.WebPart

    Private m_message As String = String.Empty

    <WebBrowsable(), Personalizable(PersonalizationScope.Shared)> _
    Public Property Message() As String
        Get
            Return m_message
        End Get
        Set(ByVal value As String)
            m_message = value
        End Set
    End Property


    Protected Overrides Sub RenderContents(ByVal writer As ~
        System.Web.UI.HtmlTextWriter)
        writer.Write("Hello World")
        writer.Write("<br/>")
        writer.Write(m_message)
    End Sub

End Class
```

This sample web part includes a property, Message, that can be set for any particular instance of the web part that has been placed on the page. The message is scoped to Shared, meaning that all users will see the same output. The solution presented in Chapter 10 focuses on building a more complete web part and presents detailed instructions for deploying and debugging.

With a new base class to work with, you may think you have to go back and modify/recompile all your existing v2 web parts. Fortunately, WSS v3 includes the old SharePoint web-part base class for backward compatibility. This SharePoint base class is now derived from the ASP.NET 2.0 web-part class. This means that most v2 web parts will run as is when deployed to a v3 environment. However, when a developer's web part relies on features of the old environment that are not found in ASP.NET 2.0, the developer may have to rely on SharePoint's web-part base class even for new projects. Some examples of these features include

- Cross-page connections

- Connections between web parts that are outside of a web-part zone

- Client-side connections

- Data-caching infrastructure

- Asynchronous web-part processing using the WebPartWorkItem infrastructure

ASP.NET 2.0 also introduces a provider model in which certain web-site functions such as authentication, authorization, maintaining user profiles, and building site navigation are compartmentalized and abstracted from the rest of the site's functionality. This layer of separation allows for the ASP.NET developer to switch in different implementations of these providers without affecting the rest of the site. For example, authentication could be accomplished by examining the user's Windows Active Directory credentials, a user object defined in an LDAP repository, or even user names and passwords in a database. Site navigation could be constructed based on an XML file or a database query.

Since Windows SharePoint Services v3 is built on ASP.NET 2.0, it conforms to ASP.NET 2.0's provider model. This means that there are a set of SharePoint providers that plug in to the ASP.NET 2.0 provider extensibility points. That means you can switch these providers and even build your own. Figure 2-2 depicts the settings page where the administrator is configuring the authentication provider that should be used based on the URL the visitor is using to access the site (called a *zone*).

Central Administration > Application Management > Authentication Providers > Edit Authentication

Edit Authentication

Zone These authentication settings are bound to the following zone.	Zone Default

Authentication Type
Choose the type of authentication you want to use for this zone.
	Authentication Type
	  ○ Windows
	  ● Forms
	  ○ Web single sign on

Anonymous Access You can enable anonymous access for sites on this server or disallow anonymous access for all sites. Enabling anonymous access allows site administrators to turn anonymous access on. Disabling anonymous access blocks anonymous users in the web.config file for this zone.	☐ Enable anonymous access
Membership Provider Name Enter the name of the membership provider. The membership provider must be correctly configured in the web.config file for the IIS Web site that hosts SharePoint content on each Web server. It must also be added to the web.config file for IIS site that hosts Central Administration.	Membership provider name:
Role Manager Name Enter the name of the role manager (optional). The role manager must be correctly configured in the web.config file for this zone.	Role manager name:
Client Integration Disabling client integration will remove features which launch client applications. Some authentication mechanisms (such as Forms) don't work well with client applications. In this configuration, users will have to work on documents locally and upload their changes.	Enable Client Integration? ○ Yes ● No

Figure 2-2. *Specifying the authentication provider*

The providers focused on security are particularly important; in WSS v2, the system limited deployments to rely on users having Windows accounts in an Active Directory or simply accessing the site anonymously. This inflexibility restricted the options for an organization deploying an extranet. Now in WSS v3, you can tailor your authentication provider to different data sources. By default, the product will support Windows Basic, Digest, NTLM, Forms, and Kerberos authentication methods. An LDAP provider comes with Microsoft Office SharePoint Server 2007. Not only are different providers available, but they can be used in combination for access to the same site. A typical example where more than one provider is used is a site that is shared by users inside (intranet) and outside (extranet) the organization. Using authentication zones that relate the URL entered by the user with the necessary provider allows you to employ different providers on the same site. So in WSS v3, the internal users could sign in with their Active Directory credentials while external user credentials are stored in a SQL Server table.

The following URLs provide further reading on the providers:

- ScottGu's Blog: SharePoint 2007 — Built on ASP.NET 2.0

  `http://weblogs.asp.net/scottgu/archive/2006/04/30/444598.aspx`

- ASP.NET 2.0 Provider Model: Introduction to the Provider Model

  `http://msdn2.microsoft.com/en-us/library/aa479030.aspx`

- Configuring Multiple Authentication Providers for SharePoint 2007

  `http://blogs.msdn.com/sharepoint/archive/2006/08/16/702010.aspx`

Repository Enhancements

The repository is the foundation for information storage and is fundamentally made up of lists and libraries. Lists are the most basic storage structure and simply store items made up of columns of data. Contacts, tasks, calendar events, announcements, and threaded discussions are all examples of lists in the repository. Libraries are focused on a particular file or document. There are several different types of libraries: document, picture, and form are a few that existed even in the previous version. The library stores the file and the columns of metadata describing it.

WSS v3 provides many enhancements to the repository system. In the previous version there were several reasons why an administrator would decide to create additional libraries. Fortunately, a lot of the need to create additional libraries has been removed in WSS v3.

Security: In WSS v2, security control ended at the list or library level. This meant that if you had a set of documents and a subset of them needed to be secured differently, you needed to place them in a second library.

The lists and libraries in v3 support item-level security. This means that two files in the same library can have different access-control lists associated with them, securing them differently. In fact, if the user does not have read permission to a particular item, it will not show up in the interface. This functionality is often referred to as the *security-trimmed interface*. Security within the library works similarly to the way file permissions are maintained in NTFS. There is an inheritance model where items, by default, use the same permissions as their parent container. This means that folders in a library default to using the same permission as the library. Items in a folder use the same permission as that parent folder. At any point in the tree, however, the inheritance can be broken and permissions for that object and its children can be specified.

Schema and templates: In WSS v2, every file in the document library ended up having the same metadata schema applied to it. This meant that the user was presented with the same metadata form with the same validation controls regardless of the file the user was adding to the library. If a team site was storing two different types of files (contracts and proposals, for instance) whose metadata requirements were different, the administrator would be required to use different libraries.

Additionally, in WSS v2, each document library could have only one default template file. This template would be sent to the user when he clicked the new button. So if the organization had two separate Word templates representing a contract and a proposal, two document libraries would be necessary to provide them to the user.

In terms of schema and templates, there are two new concepts that will ease the burden of administrators. First, WSS v3 supports *shared column definitions*. This allows for the administrator to define a column (metadata field) once and then lists or libraries can reference that definition. This means that if the administrator later had to add an additional item to the choices for a shared column, he would have a single place to make that change. Content types are another enhancement for libraries. With a content type, an organization can define the metadata requirements for a logical file type. We use the term "logical" here because we are not necessarily referring to a physical file type. The previous example of a contract and a proposal could both be Microsoft Word documents physically, yet they would be implemented as different content types. This distinction would allow us to have different metadata schemas for each type, as well as different template files. And more importantly, these content-type definitions can be reused throughout the system. In fact, they could both be used in the same document library. As shown in Figure 2-3, this improves the user experience by providing options from the New menu.

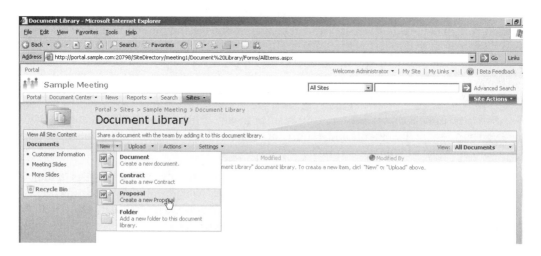

Figure 2-3. *Content types in the New menu*

Content types are incorporated into Chapters 7 and 8. The following URLs provide further reading on content types:

- Plan Content Types (Windows SharePoint Services):

  ```
  http://technet2.microsoft.com/windowsserver/WSS/en/library/
  267ab7e5-35f6-46c9-ba64-2c63d6a0dbc01033.mspx?mfr=true
  ```

- Using Content Types in Windows SharePoint Services (version 3) and SharePoint Server 2007:

  ```
  http://www.officezealot.com/downloads/moss/ContentTypesBeta2Conceptual.pdf
  ```

- Using Columns and Content Types to Organize and Manage Your Content in Windows SharePoint Services (version 3):

  ```
  http://www.officezealot.com/downloads/moss/
  ContentTypesandColumnsBeta2Conceptual.pdf
  ```

With WSS v2, developers could build event handlers for libraries. An event handler allowed the developer to have its custom code run in response to an action that the user initiated on a document. This system was a bit limited, however, in that it worked only within a document or form library and the custom code was run asynchronously in response to the action. There was no way to examine the action before it was performed. This limitation led to rather complex attempts at building a recycle bin–like feature in which the custom code wanted to cancel the deletion action. Since the event handler ran in response, the file was already gone by the time the code was invoked.

In WSS v3, the event-handler system is expanded beyond libraries to include lists and some limited Web and site events. The event model is also deeper in that it includes both *before* and *after* types of events. Before events are suffixed with "ing" and are raised synchronously before the action is performed. Some examples of events in the before set include:

- ItemAdding

- ItemCheckingIn

- ItemCheckingOut

- ItemDeleting

- ItemUpdating

After events are suffixed with "ed" and are raised asynchronously after the action has been performed. Some examples of events in the after set include:

- ItemAdded

- ItemCheckedIn

- ItemCheckedOut

- ItemDeleted

- ItemUpdated

With WSS v2, SharePoint's repository provided versioning capabilities for its document libraries. *Versioning* is the idea of capturing the way an item changes over time. In the previous version of WSS, versioning was limited to files in a library and relied on a simple numbering scheme. Each time the file was edited and checked in, the version number increased by one. In WSS v3, versioning functionality has expanded to support lists as well as libraries. It also provides a more sophisticated numbering system that supports major and minor version numbers. This allows for the editors to distinguish between an in-progress version (minor) and a published version (major). In addition, WSS v3 also supports policies as to how many major and minor versions should be retained for a given item. Cleaning up old versions was a manual process in the previous version, and that process was often left until the site hit its storage quota.

It is important to understand that the repository of WSS relies on Microsoft SQL Server databases for storing all of its list items and documents. By using databases, WSS is able to provide the collaboration features such as metadata, versioning, and checkin/checkout. This storage mechanism is more feature-rich than a file system where users are constantly renaming a file with "_1", "_2", etc. to try to create a versioning system. However, using databases for storage does complicate the backup and restore processes. This is because a single file is not as easily retrieved out of a database system as from a file share. This is because the file is now much more than a single item—it is a collection of records in related tables containing previous versions, metadata, and auditing information. Though it is possible to back up and restore databases, this task is often too labor-intensive for the frequency of an accidental single file deletion. For this reason, WSS v3 provides a recycle bin. In this version, each site has a recycle bin that stores files and list items that were deleted by an authorized user. This site-level recycle bin is available to the site administrator should he need to restore an item that was accidentally removed. If items are deleted from the site-level recycle bin, the administrator can turn to a farm-level recycle bin where items remain for a defined period of time. From here, a SharePoint administrator could restore a file that had been deleted twice without having to go to a database restore operation. There are also many additional backup and restore techniques available so administrators can adequately plan to meet their service-level agreements.

Deployment Model Based on "Features"

Developers will now be able to group custom code efforts such as web parts, list or library templates, content types, and event handlers into a single item that can be deployed and activated within a SharePoint environment. This grouping technique is referred to as a *feature*. Features can be scoped to a Web, site-collection, web-application, or even farm level. When one is turned on, the elements of that feature "light up" within that particular scope (for instance, a SharePoint site). This light-up could involve new web parts in the gallery; new list templates in the Create menu; or even a new action link in a toolbar, admin page, or item menu. Features can be deployed so that a site administrator may choose to turn them on, or they can be activated automatically. In fact, you will be able to write custom receivers that contain event handlers that can run your code when the feature is activated, deactivated, installed, or uninstalled. Figure 2-4 shows the user interface for maintaining a site's features.

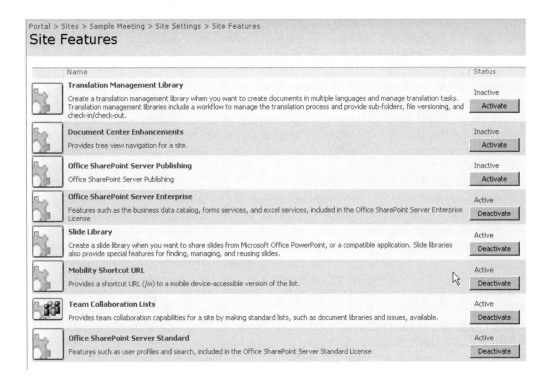

Figure 2-4. *Maintaining a site's features*

We'll use features in Chapters 7 and 8 for custom actions and customized administrative pages. The following links include more information on developing features:

- How Solution Deployment has Changed Development with SharePoint Technologies:

  http://blogs.msdn.com/cjohnson/archive/2006/09/11/749105.aspx

- SharePoint 2007 Features—Creating Site Columns and Content Types:

  http://sharethispoint.com/archive/2006/07/17/11.aspx

- How to: Create a Simple Feature:

  http://msdn2.microsoft.com/en-us/library/ms475286.aspx

- Working with Features:

  http://msdn2.microsoft.com/en-us/library/ms460318.aspx

Site Enhancements

Windows SharePoint Services v3 has many enhancements at the site level, as well. For starters, there are two new types of sites: wikis and blogs. A wiki is a site that allows users to easily create, edit, link, and restore an individual web page. A wiki site can be a useful tool for gathering information in a loosely structured manner from a wide audience. It is the type of tool that a team could use for brainstorming sessions. It supports the connection of ideas, tracking of contributions, and annotations. Blogs are more of a publishing mechanism, where an individual user or team posts articles or pieces of information. Blogs in WSS v3 support article postings, reader comments, and archive views. Both of these types of sites have gained in popularity on the Internet. With WSS v3, an organization can provide the same types of services to its staff.

In the previous version of Windows SharePoint Services, site content was locked into being displayed only on the site where it was created. Despite the presence of web services, there was no real easy way to simply present a site's content either in another site or a separate application. In WSS v3, the system gains incredible flexibility: every list, library, and search can now be presented as an *RSS (Really Simple Syndication) feed*. It defines an XML specification that allows the source content to be consumed by aggregating applications. If you have never experienced RSS, the best place to start is by looking at how most news sites use it.

Imagine that you visit five news sites regularly to check for new articles. What if you could have an application that visited these sites for you and displayed a list of article titles and abstracts of the news items on those five sites? The standard by which these news sites expose their content is RSS, and the application putting it all together for you is the *aggregator*. Microsoft Internet Explorer 7 and Microsoft Outlook 2007 both can aggregate RSS feeds, and there is a gadget in Windows Vista as well as a SharePoint web part that can be used to display content gathered through RSS. Additionally, numerous applications and tools are available on the Internet. The result is that WSS v3 content can be reused and displayed easily outside of the site it was created in. For more information on RSS in SharePoint visit http://weblogs. asp.net/jan/archive/2006/06/07/YASR_3A00_-RSS-In-SharePoint-2007.aspx.

Another feature enhancement of Windows SharePoint Services v3 is the increased support for email as a method of creating site content. Previously, it was possible to create email-enabled document libraries where email attachments would be stored. This functionality has been expanded to include list types where one could easily imagine email as a mechanism for content creation.

Take discussion boards for example. An item in a discussion board is really a message to a collection of users who respond with their own comments. Email messages are a natural way to create this content usually contained within distribution lists. However, simply relying on distribution lists often means that users are left to keep their own archive of previous messages and searching is rather difficult. WSS v3 fills this gap by capturing the threaded messages in a list that is integrated into search. WSS v3 creates content for each email sent to the list. It also is capable of automatically creating an Active Directory distribution list for the SharePoint list. In the future, this functionality will supplant Microsoft Exchange public folders, which are being deemphasized beginning with Exchange 2007. Now document libraries and lists can rely on email for content creation and with the MOSS Records Repository, described later in this chapter, provide an email-archiving story. For more information on email enabling Share-Point, visit http://www.combined-knowledge.com/Downloads/Moss07incoming_e-mail.pdf.

There are several other site enhancements that are gained by integrating Outlook 2007 with SharePoint. It is very common for teams of users to use a WSS team site to accomplish a goal. Whether it is constructing a document or preparing for a meeting, the team often keeps a list of tasks. These tasks are assigned to users and provide them information on what it is they are to do. Unfortunately, in the previous version of WSS, users had to first visit the site and subscribe to alerts for the task list if they wanted to be informed when they were assigned items. This meant that a user who never visited the site would never know they had work to do! To address this in WSS v3, tasks and alerts have been enhanced. Task notifications can now be sent automatically to the user who is assigned the task, regardless of whether that user has visited the site. In addition, SharePoint-based tasks now integrate with Microsoft Outlook 2007 and display along with Outlook tasks. This is not the only improved integration with Outlook. Outlook 2007 with WSS v3 gives users the following benefits:

- Read and write access to SharePoint items such as calendars, tasks, contacts, discussions, and documents

- Synchronization of offline support of document library and lists

- Ability to check out and edit documents when offline

- Roll-up views of calendars and tasks across multiple lists and sites

- A unified view of personal and SharePoint tasks in Outlook 2007

Figure 2-5 shows a Shared Documents library from a user's My Site being accessed when the user has no connection with the SharePoint deployment. Notice the preview pane displaying the PowerPoint presentation.

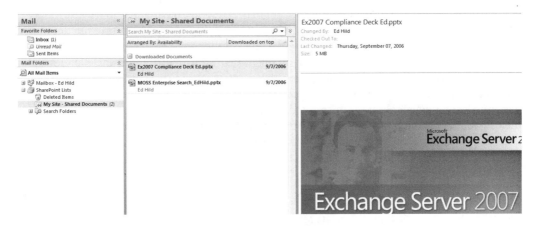

Figure 2-5. *Accessing a document library from Outlook*

User Interface

There are several significant improvements to the user interface of WSS v3 sites. First, the product and therefore its sites are more compatible with browsers other than Microsoft Internet Explorer. Though IE 6.0 or 7.0 are still preferred and provide the full experience, many browsers have made it into the Level 2 category. Level-2 browsers support the basic functionality, allowing users to read and write content as well as act as administrators. Level-2 browsers include

- Windows: Firefox 1.5+, Netscape 8.1+, Mozilla 1.7+

- Macintosh: Safari 2.0+, Firefox 1.5+

- Unix/Linux: Firefox 1.5+, Netscape 7.2+

In addition to browser compatibility, the user interface is more accessible and is also capable of providing an alternate experience for mobile devices. The SharePoint product's team blog has more information on this topic: `http://blogs.msdn.com/sharepoint/archive/2006/07/19/671735.aspx`.

The user interface is now *rights-trimmed*. This means that if a user does not have the ability to perform an action (like add a new document), the link or button that would trigger that action is hidden. This combats the experience in WSS v2, where a user would get a link to add a document and when the user clicked on it, he would get challenged for a different login.

The user interface of WSS v3 is also easier to navigate. The product has conformed to a natural set of menus, including a global navigation, local navigation, and bread-crumb links. More importantly, when sites are a part of a portal, the portal global navigation carries through to the team sites, removing the awkward transition of the interface from WSS v2.

Of course, not every organization will want its sites to have the out-of-the-box look and feel. Customization is important and v3 makes implementing new designs much easier than ever before. In the previous version, the look and feel of a site was controlled through site definitions and each had ASP.NET ASPX pages that provided all of the page content surrounding the web-part zones. The problem was that besides some shared CSS style sheets, there were not many ways of making sweeping and consistent design changes to the site. Removing a graphic or changing a table structure may result in the designer having to touch every ASPX page in every site definition. Combine that with the fact that editing the existing site definitions was not supported, and you end up with a real maintenance headache. The solution to this problem is the fact that WSS v3 is built on the ASP.NET 2.0 environment and therefore can take advantage of ASP.NET master pages (discussed earlier in this chapter). Simply put, a master page is a template. A designer can put all of the look-and-feel elements into the master page and leave a placeholder for the remaining content. Each ASPX page in the site definitions then assumes a relationship with the master page and defines only the elements and controls that are to be loaded into its placeholder. This layer of abstraction makes it much easier to make a single design change that cascades throughout the environment.

Workflow

Windows SharePoint Services v3 hosts Microsoft's Windows Workflow Foundation (WF). WF is a workflow engine and API designed to provide value to any application that requires workflow features. Though WSS v3 does support WF, it does not ship with any out-of-the-box workflow templates. MOSS provides templates containing the logic that dictates the workflow, conditions that are checked, and resulting actions. To incorporate workflow functionality into WSS v3 implementations, organizations will need to model their processes in SharePoint Designer or Visual Studio. SharePoint Designer provides a tool for building workflows by incorporating conditions with a set of actions. Figure 2-6 shows the tool being used.

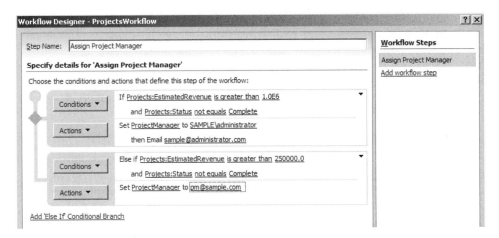

Figure 2-6. *SharePoint Designer's workflow tool*

By limiting the workflow to fixed sets of conditions and actions, SharePoint Designer can enable the workflow to be constructed and deployed without the user having to write a single line of code. More-complex workflow processes will require a developer to use Visual Studio and the WF project templates. Workflows in SharePoint typically rely on two site lists during execution: A task list informs users of actions that need to be taken, and a workflow-history list provides an audit log. We will focus on workflow in Chapter 14. The following links provide more information:

- Developer Introduction to Workflows for Windows SharePoint Services V3 and Share-Point Server 2007:

  http://msdn2.microsoft.com/en-us/library/ms406057.aspx

- Introducing Microsoft Windows Workflow Foundation: An Early Look:

  http://msdn2.microsoft.com/en-us/library/aa480215.aspx

- Getting Started with Windows Workflow Foundation: A Developer Walkthrough:

  http://msdn2.microsoft.com/en-us/library/aa480214.aspx

- SharePoint 2007 Workflow with Visual Studio 2005:

  http://weblog.vb-tech.com/nick/archive/2006/09/04/1753.aspx

Microsoft Office SharePoint Server 2007

Microsoft Office SharePoint Server 2007 (MOSS) builds upon the WSS foundation, adding enterprise features and services. It is appropriate that the word *portal* was removed from SharePoint's name. Such a term limits the expectation of the impact the product can have on an organization. The previous version of SharePoint was targeted toward intranet portals for organizing and distributing information. MOSS expands on the feature set to provide a single platform for all kinds of organization sites, including intranet, extranet, and even Internet deployments. This means that the product goes beyond document management and provides support for other types of content and their life cycle within the organization. Specifically, MOSS increases its area of responsibility to include web-content management, support for electronic forms, and a records-management solution. In addition, MOSS is loaded with new search features and functionality, supporting business processes and business intelligence. This section will explore some of the most important changes that appear in MOSS 2007.

Portal Enhancements

Even though MOSS goes well beyond delivering the portal functionality of its previous version, this product still includes these features (with some important enhancements and extensions). In SharePoint Portal Server 2003, a portal was a site that required special administrative attention and was dramatically different from a WSS collaboration site. Specifically, a portal site had to live in an IIS web site (called a *virtual server*) and that IIS site was limited to hosting only a single portal. This was in dramatic contrast to WSS sites, which could number in the thousands for a given IIS site. Whereas WSS sites had subsites, a portal had areas. Content targeting based on audiences worked only in the areas, leaving out key personalization options on WSS sites. The portal's security model was not as granular as WSS; it stopped at the area level. The portal's navigation controls were completely different than the top-level navigation bar in WSS. SharePoint 2003 portals also had the concept of *shared services*, where a parent portal would host certain services for other child portals, either in the same server farm or in a different one. Shared services included features such as the profile store of user data, My Sites, and search. Unfortunately, an organization had to decide whether to deploy a shared services model early in its planning stage because the choice was not reversible.

Microsoft Office SharePoint Server 2007 makes the SharePoint product more consistent with the rest of the platform. First, an IIS web site that hosts MOSS or WSS v3 functionality is now called a *web application*. This change was made to alleviate confusion with Microsoft's Virtual Server product. The special relationship between the portal and its IIS web site has been removed. A portal is now nothing but a new site definition that has the MOSS features enabled. This is a profound change. A portal in MOSS is simply a supercharged WSS site. That means that a single web application can host multiple portals. In fact, the MOSS enterprise features are also available to be activated on WSS sites in the same web application. So the MOSS install bits provide features that you can activate in any site collection. This will make development more consistent. Areas are now a thing of the past. Like WSS, a portal site simply has subsites. The security models of MOSS and WSS are identical and the global navigation of the portal carries through to its subsites.

The Shared Services model has also been re-architected to be more flexible. Instead of locking certain features into a portal site that must share them, MOSS uses the concept of *shared service providers* (SSPs). A shared service provider hosts a set of services that can be configured once and then consumed by sites in another web application. The shared service providers can even be in their own web application. The big difference from SharePoint 2003 is that a farm could have several SSPs, each with its own configuration of search, user profiles, My Sites, etc., and each site bearing web application partners with an SSP. This partnership is not a one-time decision. From the administration interface, a web application can join an SSP, leave an SSP, and even join a different SSP.

The profile store is one of the features of a shared service provider. Microsoft Office SharePoint Server 2007 maintains a profile store that captures information about an organization's users. In SPS 2003, this user-profile store was populated by importing data from Active Directory or another LDAP-compliant repository. Users could also enter additional data through their profile page for attributes that were not stored in another system. SharePoint Portal Server 2003 treated profile data as content and would include users as search-result items along with documents and sites. This provided an organization with a "find the expert" type of application. Unfortunately, there were a few features lacking that limited the effectiveness of these searches. Missing was support for multivalued attributes, controlled vocabularies, and integration to pull a user's attribute from a line-of-business (LOB) application. MOSS fills these gaps, increasing the effectiveness of the user-profile store.

Another SSP feature is Personal sites (also called My Sites). These sites were introduced as a feature of SharePoint Portal Server 2003 that allowed each user of an organization to have her own site. This site had a public and private view. The private view was a personal dashboard where the owner could add and configure web parts for information that needed to be readily available. Other users of the system could see the public view, and it provided them with the owner's profile data, access to their shared documents, and a list of workspaces that had been created under the personal site. New to Microsoft Office SharePoint Server 2007 is the concept of social networking where the public view of the My Site customizes itself to highlight relationships between the visitor and the owner. In MOSS, a public My Site is capable of showing a user a manager he shares in common with the My Site owner, distribution lists that they are both members of, and colleagues that they share. Also, the data on the public My Site supports privacy policies. These policies can control the amount of profile data that is displayed for different types of users, such as colleagues, managers, or the public.

Search

Just like SharePoint Portal Server 2003, MOSS provides Microsoft's enterprise search service. This version of the search engine takes advantage of the latest search technologies coming out of Microsoft Research. These same technologies are being leveraged in the new Internet search (`http://www.live.com`) that has been integrated into MSN, and are being used by the Microsoft Vista OS to provide desktop search. Though the technologies are similar, each space is dealing with a slightly different search challenge. MOSS's search is specifically targeted to the challenges of the enterprise and has been enhanced to provide better relevance, increased scale, and more features while simplifying administration. MOSS enterprise search can index several types of content sources by default:

- SharePoint content

- Web content

- File-share content

- Exchange-folder content

- Business-data content

- Lotus Notes (not installed by default but available on installation media)

New to MOSS 2007 is the business-data content. It refers to the new Business Data Catalog feature, which allows MOSS to integrate with other LOB applications without a need for custom code. For search, this means that MOSS can index data in external applications that are reachable through an ADO.NET connection or a web service call. The Business Data Catalog hooks right into the search scopes and tabs while providing the ability to create a search result details page. In the previous version of SharePoint, organizations would have required developers to custom-code protocol handlers for each application they needed to tie into search results. Now these applications can be registered with the Business Data Catalog through XML configuration files with no new developer created compiled code injected into the environment. There is more information on the Business Data Catalog in the "Business Intelligence" section of this chapter, and in Chapter 12.

The search engine within MOSS has a new ranking engine for determining relevance that goes far beyond simply examining how many times the keywords appear in the document. Though that is obviously important, many other factors need to be considered to deliver an effective enterprise search. Some of those factors include

- Click distance from an authoritative site

- Hyperlink anchor text

- URL surf depth

- URL text matching

- Automated metadata extraction

- Automatic language detection

- File-type relevance biasing

- Enhanced text analysis

In SharePoint 2003 and WSS v2, consistent ranking was a problem because each product relied on a separate indexing and ranking solution. In its previous release, WSS v2 relied on SQL Server full-text indexes. These often left users confused since results within the site would differ greatly from results within the portal. With the 2007 version, this experience is consistent—the WSS v3 search uses an implementation of the MOSS search engine, but the search is limited to within the site or site collection.

One of the more important items in the relevance list is *Click distance from an authoritative site*. This refers to the number of links between a search-result item and any of the high-authority sites. In the search configuration admin, administrators can define high- and low-authority sites. The farther away an item is from a high-authority site, the lower the relevance score.

Another important search feature in MOSS is the ability to generate reports detailing search activity. These reports will help an organization understand the types of information users are looking for and which sites are providing the answers. The reports included help-answer questions about the following:

- Query-volume trends

- Top queries

- Click-through rates

- Queries with zero results

Content Management

MOSS 2007 extends the product's area of responsibility for managing content to include web-content management and records management. Web-content management focuses on providing an environment for page authors to maintain and publish HTML content. This is new to SharePoint; the previous version provided features only around lists and document libraries. In SharePoint Portal Server 2003, only the content-editor web part supported the authoring of HTML content on a page. There was no workflow or publishing model to approve changes to HTML content and no ability for the organization to enforce styles or limits on the author. This type of functionality was previously shipped as part of Microsoft Content Management Server 2002 (MCMS) and this product often accompanied SPS 2003 in deployments to provide a more complete content-management platform.

With MOSS, a web-content management application is built on top of the SharePoint foundation. This application integrates seamlessly, taking advantage of the libraries, workflow, master pages, and other elements of SharePoint. Though this functionality can be enabled in different types of sites, it is best explored through the Internet Presence Web Site template. This template provides a top-level site for a web presence with publishing-focused subsites. The default site includes support for maintaining press-release pages. The pages of this site reside in a library and therefore take advantage of the item-level security, versioning, and workflow services that one typically associates with documents. Figure 2-7 shows the Create Page screen where the user defines the title and page file name and selects a page layout.

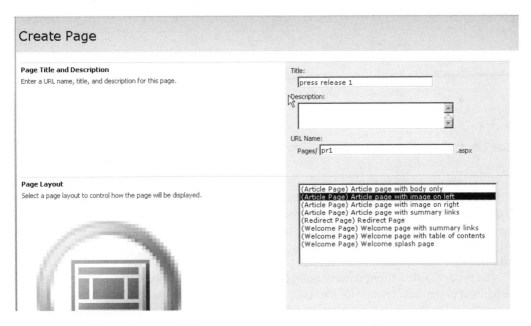

Figure 2-7. *Creating a new press release*

The Page Layout selection here is very important and is key to understanding how this authoring environment in layered on top of SharePoint. Each item in the Page Layout menu tells the author two pieces of information: The type of page (a content type within SharePoint) is displayed within parentheses and a specific layout is described afterward. As described in the WSS portion of this chapter, content types are a feature in WSS v3 that allow a defined set of columns to be created and used uniformly throughout a site collection. In this case, the columns of information are not used just to store metadata, but rather they describe the distinct page elements that the author will be able to edit. For example, the Article Page content type allows the author to enter a title, rollup image, page image, article date, byline, image caption, and page content. These columns are then placed as field controls in a variety of layouts to provide the authoring experience. Figure 2-8 shows the "Article page with image on left" Article Page layout.

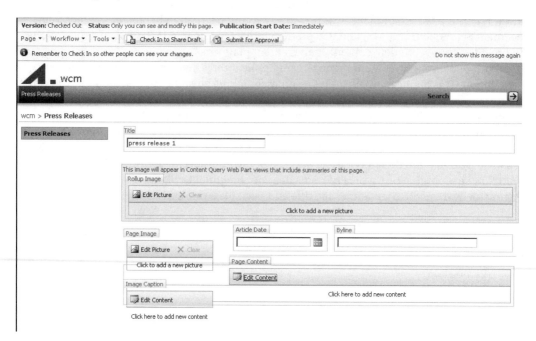

Figure 2-8. *Authoring a press release with an Article Page layout*

This technique is very similar to what a Microsoft CMS developer does today. Whereas MCMS has a template definition that describes the elements of the page in the database, MOSS relies on a content type to contain that information. Both MCMS and MOSS have ASPX pages that are physical representations of the template descriptions. In MCMS this ASPX page had placeholder controls organized in a layout. The ASPX page of MOSS is called a *page layout* and contains field controls.

The result is a structured environment for the authoring user. An organization can define the types of pages that it needs to maintain and the elements that make up those pages. The organization can then control the type of editing the author can do, placing limits in areas where there's a consistent style sheet for uniform look and feel. The following links provide more information on web-content management and content deployment scenarios in MOSS:

- SharePoint 2007 for MCMS 2002 Developers:

  http://msdn2.microsoft.com/en-us/library/ms406043.aspx

- Content Management Server and SharePoint:

  http://blogs.msdn.com/sharepoint/archive/2006/01/20/515564.aspx

- Compare MOSS 2007 WCM and MCMS 2002:

  http://www.sharepointblogs.com/jimyang/archive/2006/07/05/8914.aspx

- Content Deployment:

  http://blogs.msdn.com/sharepoint/archive/2006/05/02/588140.aspx

The other new area of content management in MOSS supports an organization's need to apply a disciplined approach to content that has evolved to apply to regulatory compliance guidelines or possible legal defenses. This area is referred to as *records management*. Once a piece of content is considered an official record, the organization typically is concerned about its level of control. Features such as retention and expiration schedules are necessary to make sure the content item is kept as long as is required, but not any longer. Once it is considered a record, the item is subject to increased auditing requirements. To match the electronic world or records with the physical world, MOSS also supports labeling and bar-coding.

An organization subject to legal defenses often needs to maintain holds and freeze content items that may be a part of litigation. These are features of the Records Repository within MOSS. In addition, MOSS can integrate with Windows Rights Management Services (RMS) to enforce these policies even if the document is taken out of the repository. RMS wraps a restriction policy with an encrypted version of the document. This policy details specific actions that the user can and cannot take once he has opened the document in an RMS-aware application. It requires a key exchange between client and server for at least the initial opening of the document and relies on Active Directory identities and groups. For example, Microsoft Word can restrict the user's ability to save a copy of the file, edit it, or print it. In fact, Windows will even keep the user from performing a print-screen operation. RMS techniques can also been applied to email and restricted in Microsoft Outlook to control the receiver's ability to forward your message to unanticipated recipients. RMS is about securing the accidental distribution of information. Its integration into the MOSS repository adds an additional layer of security for possibly sensitive records in an organization.

Business Process

For most organizations, business processes are very form-driven. Users enter data into a form, possibly combined with some data from other back-end systems, and then that form is transported among other users or even other applications. SharePoint Portal Server 2003 provided the foundation for an electronic forms-management platform. With SPS 2003, organizations could publish their forms using Microsoft InfoPath 2003 and centralize the collection of data through the use of SharePoint form libraries. These libraries included features focused on the collection of XML files that could be processed by custom code or another application. This solution had gaps, including a requirement for the user who completed the form to have InfoPath, and a lack of support for a human-oriented workflow-approval process. Microsoft Office SharePoint Server 2007 includes a new Forms Server application that makes it possible to design a form in InfoPath 2007 but allows the users to complete it in a browser-based interface. This is a design-once development model: the same form can be rendered in the thick InfoPath client, a web-browser interface, or even in a Microsoft Office 2007 application to capture metadata. Chapter 13 will include details on InfoPath and Form Server.

As described earlier in this chapter, Windows SharePoint Services v3 hosts Windows Workflow Foundation to provide workflow capabilities to SharePoint. Though the ability to have workflow services resides at the WSS layer, MOSS includes some out-of-the-box workflow application templates. These workflow templates address common reasons to route documents and information:

- Collect Signatures

- Disposition Approval

- Approval

- Collect Feedback

- Three-State Workflow (for tracking items in a list)

- Translation Management

These workflow templates obviously do not provide a solution for every business process. This is why workflow is one large area of extension for MOSS. The technique to build your own workflow falls into two categories: *custom code* and *no code*. With SharePoint Designer, users can describe a workflow process as a series of steps, conditions, and actions using a preset vocabulary. This results in a custom no-code workflow process, which does not require new code to be deployed. If you need a workflow that steps outside of this controlled vocabulary, Visual Studio.NET becomes the required tool and custom code must be written. Visual Studio .NET developers can build complete workflow solutions or deploy custom activities and conditions to be used in SharePoint Designer. Forms also have a role in this customization, as a developer can rely on InfoPath to generate the user touch points for the workflow. This would include gathering the initial parameters for the workflow, approval forms, and so on. Of course, these forms can be rendered with just a web browser. Workflow is a major part of the solution presented in Chapter 14 and InfoPath forms are detailed in Chapter 13.

Business Intelligence

Business intelligence is about exposing an organization's users to the right information so that they can make better business decisions. Microsoft Office SharePoint Server 2007 includes many features to display data from other applications into an easy-to-consume interface that takes little or no developer code to build. Earlier in this chapter we introduced the Business Data Catalog as a way to have MOSS search custom databases. Why is the Business Data Catalog so important? First, an organization is going to have other LOB applications and the data within them is usually of interest to a wider audience than the user base trained to use that piece of software. Take any customer relationship management (CRM) application as an example. Many organizations use CRM applications to track customers, accounts, sales, and opportunities. CRM applications are typically viewed as sales tools and maybe only users in the sales department have the necessary client software and/or licenses to access it. However, there is likely basic information such as customer contact information and corresponding account teams that would be valuable to the entire organization. Duplicating this data in another system could lead to inaccuracies and outdated information. The Business Data Catalog provides a way to display this data into MOSS.

In addition to integrating into search, the Business Data Catalog allows users to employ the LOB data in library or list metadata columns as well as user-profile attributes. MOSS also provides a set of business data web parts that require only XSLT to present the LOB data inline on a SharePoint page. All of these integration points would have required custom code efforts in the past. MOSS allows the organization to bring this data to its users without having to worry about testing and maintaining entire libraries of custom code. The Business Data Catalog is featured in Chapter 12. The following links offer more information on the Business Data Catalog:

- Business Data Catalog:

  `http://blogs.msdn.com/sharepoint/archive/2006/04/18/578194.aspx`

- MOSS BDC MetaData Manager:

  `http://www.sharepointblogs.com/tbaginski/archive/2006/07/16/9259.aspx`

- SharePoint 2007 Business Data Catalog (BDC):

  `http://geekswithblogs.net/sharepointless/articles/77923.aspx`

Another new way to display data to users is through published spreadsheets. With MOSS Excel Services, a user can publish a Microsoft Excel 2007 spreadsheet to the server so that other users can interact with it simply by using a web browser. This technique is especially useful for spreadsheets that rely on a large amount of data and perform heavy calculations or other business logic. Often such spreadsheets take a very long time to load on a desktop-level computer, and interaction (such as working with pivot tables and pivot charts) is cumbersome. By publishing these spreadsheets, server resources are used to do the calculations and visualizations. The end user simply is presented with a DHTML Excel-like interface. This DHTML application does have a limitation: It doesn't permit a user to add data and save it back to the server. This can be viewed as a feature for organizations that want to maintain a single version of the truth. MOSS Excel Services does provide a web-services model to allow other programs to programmatically send and receive data to published spreadsheets. Chapter 6 and the following link have more information on Excel Services: `http://msdn2.microsoft.com/en-us/library/ms517343.aspx`.

When most users think of business intelligence, they visualize the dashboard concept, with application data being rolled up and presented in a digestible form. The MOSS Report Center is a site optimized for organizing a company's dashboards. In addition to supporting the Business Data Catalog web parts and Excel Services published spreadsheets, the site has tools that help the organization manage their reports and data connections. The Report Center also provides enhanced levels of integration with SQL Server Reporting Services and SQL Server Analysis Services. This integration includes a scorecard solution for presenting key performance indicators (KPIs) that may rely on WSS lists, Excel workbooks, or SQL Server 2005 Analysis Services. Scorecards are an effective way of presenting data against an organization's objectives. (For instance, a red-yellow-green light interface is an example of a scorecard depicting the health of the organization in comparison to the objective's target value.) Since dashboard sites are densely populated with web parts that connect to other applications, the site contains a specific library where data connections are stored. By placing connection details to external applications in a library, MOSS provides a single point of maintenance as well as a reusable connection definition.

Further Reading

- Digital Dashboards: Web Parts Integrate with Internet Explorer and Outlook to Build Personal Portals:

  http://msdn.microsoft.com/msdnmag/issues/01/01/ddrk2/

- The Scalability of Digital Dashboards:

  http://www.outlookexchange.com/articles/stevebryant/bryant_p1.asp

- Gathering MOSS: New Dev-Centric Features In Office SharePoint Server Keep Your Apps Rolling:

  http://msdn.microsoft.com/msdnmag/issues/06/08/GatheringMoss/

- Differences between the 2007 Office System and Office 2003:

  http://technet2.microsoft.com/Office/en-us/library/
  a9189734-e303-4d7d-93eb-3584c358d1c91033.mspx?mfr=true

- Windows Rights Management Services:

  http://www.microsoft.com/windowsserver2003/technologies/rightsmgmt/
  default.mspx

■■■

CHAPTER 3

Microsoft Office 2007 Overview for Developers

Microsoft Office 2007 is the latest edition of a long line of productivity applications that have become commonplace on the desktops of information workers. Though the years, the Office brand has extended to new applications like InfoPath, Communicator, and Groove. It has also gained enterprise servers in SharePoint. Yet its core continues to be Word, Excel, PowerPoint, and Outlook. Information workers use these four applications to generate numerous files that hold organizational information. With each new edition of this software suite, Microsoft not only focuses on the spreadsheets, documents, presentations, and email, but enhances the ability for these items to participate in the enterprise. These enhancements include collaboration, enterprise search, and interaction with business data and line-of-business systems. The 2007 release steps up the support for extension by developers. In this chapter we will provide an overview of some of these enhancements and point out which solutions in the book incorporate them.

History of Microsoft Office Development

When most people are asked to describe developing with Microsoft Office, their first response involves Microsoft Visual Basic for Applications (VBA). This scripting language is the development environment for Office macros. Anyone who has tried to automate an Office application is familiar with the technique of starting a macro recording, performing the action they wish to automate, and then looking at the resulting code script. It is important to understand that VBA code is tightly integrated with the application it operates against. In fact, the code itself is persisted with the document. In addition to VBA scripts, Office developers are familiar with COM add-ins. These are programs written in a COM language like Visual Basic and are loaded by the Office application; they extend the application to include new functionality or specialized features. A COM add-in runs within the application and is capable of interacting with the Office application's object model. Another development technique of Office developers is *automation*. This is when the developer creates an external application that instantiates the Office application. The external application then uses the application's object model to have it perform certain actions. In some cases, the Office application is never shown to the user, yet it does load fully. Some developers use automation for server-based applications. Since the Office application must load in an automation scenario, this solution does not scale and is not supported by Microsoft.

With Microsoft Office 2003, the Office development environment was extended to managed code and the .NET languages. This meant that the Office applications could now interact with Web services. Plus, Word and Excel gained XML support with their ability to be attached to custom schemas and to save XML data. The result of this convergence was Office applications evolving into a platform for smart-client solutions. These solutions extended Word and Excel, allowing users to interact with back-end data and systems while still in the context of their document or spreadsheet. Shortly after Office 2003 debuted, Microsoft released an enhancement to Visual Studio called Visual Studio Tools for Office (VSTO). It allowed Office developers to use the powerful Visual Studio development environment. This reduced the complexity of developing with Office and provided a rapid application-development experience. Developers could drag familiar Windows controls onto the surface of Excel spreadsheets or Word documents and design user controls that could be loaded as document actions panes. This aligned the Office development with the Web and Windows development experiences. This meant that the community of .NET developers could, with little ramp-up time, tackle Office development. Much like a web page or form had a code-behind file, documents and spreadsheets became the user interface with a .NET class file acting behind the scenes. The VSTO team also tried to appease developers' desire to automate the Office applications on the server by providing a ServerDocument object that allowed the insertion of a data island into documents. This did help, but was limiting in that developers could not manipulate the entire document's content. We will cover VSTO in detail in Chapter 4.

Why Developers Should Care About Office

Developers should care about Microsoft Office because it has a proven value that few other technologies can compare with. The tools of Word, Excel, Outlook, and PowerPoint have been on the corporate desktop for more than a decade and users are comfortable with them. This means that when a developer is presented with a challenge involving a document, spreadsheet, presentation, or email, she should avoid the temptation to create a completely custom solution. Instead, she should look to develop a solution that integrates seamlessly with the environment the user is familiar with. Presenting this solution as an enhancement to Office aids user adoption and likely reduces the amount of code since the developer can take advantage of the Office application's functionality.

Development Opportunities with Office 2007

Microsoft Office 2007 provides the developer with many options for solution development. The new Office Open XML file format (see the following section) opens up new possibilities for document generation on the server. Using this file format, developers will be able to create or modify documents on the server without having to load the Office application. In fact, the Office applications do not even need to be installed on the server. This allows document-generation solutions to be server-based and scale to meet the needs of an enterprise. Managed code solutions are also enhanced with the latest version of Visual Studio Tools for Office. Now developers will be able to create managed code add-ins and application task panes. Developers will be able to extend Office's new user interface—*the ribbon*. Outlook forms also enter the managed-code world, as they can be customized and extended with .NET code. This section is by no means a complete reference to Office development and therefore we will include links to external content that you can use to read more about a specific topic that interests you. We will also call out certain features that we will incorporate into the solutions in the remainder of the book.

The Open XML File Format

The most significant opportunity for developers with Microsoft Office 2007 is not something that an end user will ever see. The opportunity derives from Microsoft's change in the file formats that the Office applications use. In previous versions, Office files were stored in a proprietary binary format that captured serializations of in-memory data structures. This was largely done to conserve space within the file and increase the speed at which the Office application could parse its contents. With Office 2007, Microsoft has switched the default file format to an open, XML-based standard. This standard (called Office Open XML or just Open XML) was an output of Ecma International's Technical Committee 45 and was approved by the Ecma General Assembly on December 7, 2006.

■Note Ecma International was founded in 1961 as an industry association dedicated to the development of standards and technical reports that apply to information and communication technology as well as consumer electronics. Its members include many familiar companies such as Adobe, Microsoft, Intel, Sony, Yahoo!, IBM, Fujifilm, and Pioneer. This association has produced over 370 standards and 90 technical reports, of which more than two-thirds have gone on to become international standards or technical reports. Ecma is a major participant in "fast-tracking" standards through the process of other global standards bodies such as ISO. To read more about Ecma, visit its web site: http://www.ecma-international.org.

Within Ecma, Technical Committee 45 took on the responsibility to standardize Office Open XML so that it can be used by other productivity applications and platforms. This committee is responsible for the standard, its documentation, and the comprehensive set of schemas. The committee includes representatives from Apple, Barclays Capital, BP, The British Library, Essilor, Intel, Microsoft, NextPage, Novell, Statoil, Toshiba, and the United States Library of Congress. To read more about this committee, including updates on their activities, visit its web site: http://www.ecma-international.org/memento/TC45.htm. Since its adoption, many companies have announced support for the Open XML format. This includes Novell's OpenOffice and Corel's WordPerfect Office X3 suite.

So why the change? One of the most interesting trends over the past few decades is the pace at which we are generating electronic information. This trend becomes disturbing when you realize that with a binary file format, the information is strongly tied to the specific versions of applications that generated them. With long retention policies, it becomes more difficult to maintain these documents reliably. Imagine if a document as important as the Declaration of Independence were written using Microsoft Word 95. For this reason, organizations and governments have been demanding that the technology industry reduce dependencies of files being locked to a specific version of a specific application by switching to an open format.

Of course, the new file format has to do more than fix this trend moving forward; it also has to address the billions of documents that already exist. This was an important goal of the Open XML initiative. The schemas for the format were designed to reflect existing documents. Microsoft has several efforts that will help in terms of adoption and backward compatibility. The Office Migration Planning Manager (OMPM) contains a set of tools to help organizations scan their documents and identify migration issues. One of the important tools in this set is the Office File Converter, which will enable you to convert large quantities of files that use the binary format to the XML one. You can find more information about OMPM at `http://technet2.microsoft.com/Office/en-us/library/d8f318d4-84ea-4d3e-8918-ea8dacd14f7e1033.mspx?mfr=true`. Also, Microsoft is providing an extension to older versions of Microsoft Office that enables people to work with Open XML–formatted files. This extension is called the Microsoft Office Compatibility Pack. By installing the pack, users will be able to open, edit, and save files in the Open XML format using Microsoft Office 2000, Office XP, or Office 2003. This is important because organizations often take more time to update their standardized desktops than to deploy new application servers. This means that developers will still be able to use this format on the server and in custom development projects even if the end user does not have Microsoft Office 2007. This add-on can be obtained at `http://www.microsoft.com/downloads/details.aspx?FamilyId=941B3470-3AE9-4AEE-8F43-C6BB74CD1466&displaylang=en`.

What does the Office Open XML file format mean to developers? It opens the possibility of generating or modifying an Office file from code without having to automate the Office application. Previously, developers would have to code against the Office application's API. When this happened on a server, it was equivalent to a user launching the application and performing the necessary steps. These solutions did not scale well and Microsoft backed off of supporting them. However, with the Open XML format, these files can be manipulated by modifying their XML structures. The Office application does not even have to be installed on the server. Even in Ecma's Open XML white paper (referenced in the "Further Reading" section of this chapter), the committee was anticipating what developers would do with the format. Some of the new applications called out in the document were

- The ability for applications to generate documents automatically

- The extraction of data from documents to be consumed by line-of-business applications

- Enhancing accessibility options for users with special needs, such as the blind

- Using the documents on a variety of hardware, such as mobile devices

The best way to understand the Open XML file format is to make a copy of an existing file and explore how it is put together. Regardless whether the file is a spreadsheet, a presentation, or a document, it is really a package of parts and items. Parts are pieces of content for the file, whereas items are metadata describing how the parts should be assembled and rendered. Most of these pieces are XML files, making it possible for them to be manipulated through code. You can gain insight into the structure of an Open XML–based file by replacing its file extension with **.zip** since the file is really an ordinary Zip archive. We will use a PowerPoint presentation as an example to illustrate the structure of an Open XML file. Figure 3-1 shows the root of the archive for a PowerPoint presentation.

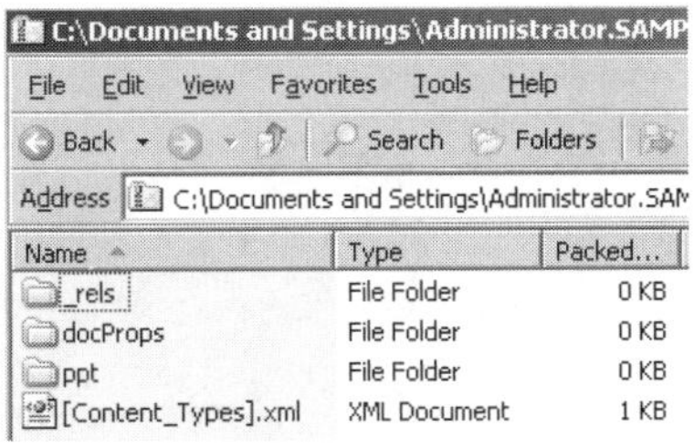

Figure 3-1. *Examing the archive of a PowerPoint presentation*

The XML file in the root is named [Content_Types].xml and it stores content-type directives for all the parts that appear in the archive. A content type contains metadata about a particular part or groups of parts and, more importantly, contains a directive as to how the application should render that part. For example, Listing 3-1 shows just a few lines from the file, but it clearly delineates how this file tells the rendering application which parts are slides, images, note pages, etc.

Listing 3-1. *A Presentation's Content Types*

```
<Override PartName="/ppt/slides/slide1.xml"
  ContentType="application/vnd.openxmlformats-
  officedocument.presentationml.slide+xml" />
<Default Extension="jpeg"
  ContentType="image/jpeg" />
<Override PartName="/ppt/notesSlides/notesSlide1.xml"
  ContentType="application/vnd.openxmlformats-
  officedocument.presentationml.notesSlide+xml" />
```

Of the parts in Listing 3-1, the slide parts are the most interesting to us. They store the presentation's content described using a markup language specific to presentations. This language is named PresentationML. It is XML-based and one of the easier Open XML file formats to understand because presentations have an obvious composition. A presentation is made up of the following:

- Masters for slides, notes, and handouts

- Slide layouts

- Slides and note pages

Open the presentation.xml file that is located in the ppt folder of the archive. Viewing this file in Internet Explorer will display XML similar to that in Figure 3-2.

```xml
<?xml version="1.0" encoding="UTF-8" standalone="yes" ?>
- <p:presentation xmlns:a="http://schemas.openxmlformats.org/drawingml/2006/main"
    xmlns:r="http://schemas.openxmlformats.org/officeDocument/2006/relationships"
    xmlns:p="http://schemas.openxmlformats.org/presentationml/2006/main" saveSubsetFonts="1">
  - <p:sldMasterIdLst>
      <p:sldMasterId id="2147483660" r:id="rId4" />
    </p:sldMasterIdLst>
  - <p:sldIdLst>
      <p:sldId id="256" r:id="rId5" />
      <p:sldId id="257" r:id="rId6" />
      <p:sldId id="258" r:id="rId7" />
      <p:sldId id="259" r:id="rId8" />
    </p:sldIdLst>
    <p:sldSz cx="9144000" cy="6858000" type="screen4x3" />
    <p:notesSz cx="6858000" cy="9144000" />
  + <p:defaultTextStyle>
  </p:presentation>
```

Figure 3-2. *The presentation.xml File*

The presentation.xml file contains the list of slides (<p:sldLst>), references to the slide and notes masters, and the sizes of the slides (<p:sldSz>) and notes pages (<p:notesSz>). The sequence of the slide nodes is important; the rendering application will display them in the order they are listed here. Notice that each slide node, as well as the master nodes, has a r:id attribute. This identifier is a key to a specific relationship that will tell the rendering application where the part for this item is located. The relationship information for this presentation is stored in presentation.xml.rels file located in the ppt_rels folder of the archive. Listing 3-2 is the XML node in this file that tells the application that the first slide's content is stored in slide1.xml.

Listing 3-2. *Example of a Presentation Relationship*

```
<Relationship
Id="rId5" Type="http://schemas.openxmlformats.org/officeDocument/~
    2006/relationships/slide" Target="slides/slide1.xml"
/>
```

Following the relationship links, you can see that the contents of the slides are stored in the ppt\slides folder of the archive. When building solutions that work with the Open XML file formats, it is often useful to employ this technique of exploring the archive to examine its contents before trying to manipulate it through code. In fact, you could extract these contents to a folder, modify them, and repackage them to a new Zip archive. Renaming this archive with a .pptx extension would in fact create a new presentation, allowing you to see the changes in PowerPoint.

Within a slide, there are shapes marked up as <p:sp> in the XML. A shape could be the slide's title, a bulleted list of text, or even a table. Shapes are grouped into trees that you will see as <p:spTree> elements in the XML. Figure 3-3 shows a sample slide that has a shape containing a bulleted list of three items.

```
- <p:sp>
  - <p:nvSpPr>
      <p:cNvPr id="2" name="Content Placeholder 1" />
    + <p:cNvSpPr>
    ⊞ <p:nvPr>
    </p:nvSpPr>
    <p:spPr />
  - <p:txBody>
      <a:bodyPr />
      <a:lstStyle />
    - <a:p>
      - <a:r>
          <a:rPr lang="en-US" dirty="0" smtClean="0" />
          <a:t>Item 1</a:t>
        </a:r>
      </a:p>
    - <a:p>
      - <a:r>
          <a:rPr lang="en-US" dirty="0" smtClean="0" />
          <a:t>Item 2</a:t>
        </a:r>
      </a:p>
    - <a:p>
      - <a:r>
          <a:rPr lang="en-US" dirty="0" smtClean="0" />
          <a:t>Item 3</a:t>
        </a:r>
        <a:endParaRPr lang="en-US" dirty="0" />
      </a:p>
    </p:txBody>
  </p:sp>
```

Figure 3-3. *A sample slide's XML*

WordprocessingML is the Open XML markup language for documents. It defines a document as a collection of stories. Stories within a document could refer to the main document contents, its glossary, a header, or its footer. By examining the main document, document.xml, you will find a body that contains paragraphs. Within a paragraph, there will be a collection of runs. A *run* is a continuous section of text that has the same properties. The text itself is stored within a text range. The text range is restricted to containing text only and cannot have additional formatting, line breaks, tables, or graphics. The text range gains its formatting from the run or paragraph it is contained within. Figure 3-4 contains a portion of a WordprocessingML file. Notice the paragraph delimiters, the runs, and the text ranges.

```
- <w:p w:rsidR="009A0BD8" w:rsidRDefault="009A0BD8" w:rsidP="009A0BD8">
  + <w:pPr>
    <w:proofErr w:type="gramStart" />
  - <w:r>
      <w:t>So why the change?</w:t>
    </w:r>
    <w:proofErr w:type="gramEnd" />
  - <w:r>
      <w:t xml:space="preserve">One of the more interesting trends over the past few decades is the pace at which we
      are generating electronic information. This trend becomes disturbing when you realize that with a binary file
      format, the information is strongly tied to the specific versions of applications that generated them. With long
      retention policies, it becomes more difficult to reliably maintain these documents. For this reason,
      organizations and governments have been demanding the technology industry to reduce these risks by
      switching to an open format.</w:t>
    </w:r>
  </w:p>
```

Figure 3-4. *Examining WordprocessingML*

SpreadsheetML files are defined by a workbook part. Like a PowerPoint file whose presentation is made up of slides, workbooks are made up of worksheets. The workbook part includes information such as the file version and its collection or worksheets. Within a worksheet part, you will find the sheet's data, containing rows of cells that have values. Figure 3-5 shows a simple spreadsheet we created to explore its Open XML structure.

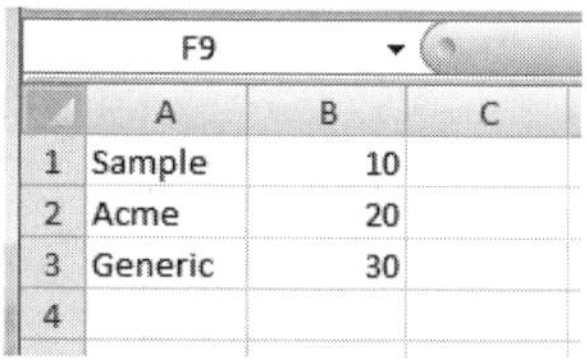

Figure 3-5. *A simple Excel 2007 spreadsheet*

Figure 3-6 shows you a portion of the markup. Notice how the sheetData element contains row elements. Within each row element, there are cells (<c>) that have values (<v>). The reason you do not see the strings of the company names is that they are stored separately in a sharedStrings.xml part. This separation allows for reuse since the file needs to store a string value only once, regardless of the number of cells that contain it.

```xml
<?xml version="1.0" encoding="UTF-8" standalone="yes" ?>
- <worksheet xmlns="http://schemas.openxmlformats.org/spreadsheetml/2006/main"
    xmlns:r="http://schemas.openxmlformats.org/officeDocument/2006/relationships">
    <dimension ref="A1:B3" />
+ <sheetViews>
    <sheetFormatPr defaultRowHeight="15" />
- <sheetData>
  - <row r="1" spans="1:2">
    - <c r="A1" t="s">
        <v>0</v>
      </c>
    - <c r="B1">
        <v>10</v>
      </c>
    </row>
  - <row r="2" spans="1:2">
    - <c r="A2" t="s">
        <v>1</v>
      </c>
    - <c r="B2">
        <v>20</v>
      </c>
    </row>
```

Figure 3-6. *Sample SpreadsheetML*

Working with these large XML files can be a burden. To make it easier, download the schemas for the Open XML file formats so that Visual Studio's IntelliSense can help you create valid structures while modifying the files. The schemas are available for download at http://www.microsoft.com/downloads/details.aspx?familyid=15805380-F2C0-4B80-9AD1-2CB0C300AEF9&displaylang=en.

To build .NET applications that operate on Open XML files, Microsoft has added a new namespace in the .NET 3.0 framework. The namespace is System.IO.Packaging and its classes are contained in the WindowsBase.dll assembly. You may have this assembly in your references dialog box in Visual Studio; if not, you can browse to it at `C:\Program Files\Reference Assemblies\Microsoft\Framework\v3.0\WindowsBase.dll`. Code that acts on Open XML files works in a similar manner to what someone would have to do if they were editing the file by hand. First the package must be opened and the file's main part located. In PowerPoint, the main part is the `presentation.xml` file you examined earlier. For spreadsheets the main part is `workbook.xml` and for documents it is `document.xml`. Once this is located, the relationship information helps the code locate the XML part with the content it wants to operate on. After this part is located, the XML part is loaded into an XML document. It can then be read, manipulated, and saved back. Since there are so many steps to working with these files, Microsoft has provided Visual Studio snippets that have common operations for you to use as a starting point. The snippets can be obtained at `http://www.microsoft.com/downloads/details.aspx?familyid=8D46C01F-E3F6-4069-869D-90B8B096B556&displaylang=en`.

To provide insight into how this code works, we will walk through the code snippet (called PowerPoint: Get a List of Slide Titles) for obtaining the list of slide titles in a PowerPoint presentation. As shown in Listing 3-3, the snippet is a function that receives the filename of the Open XML file to operate on. From this filename, the code instantiates a package and locates the main part of the file. The code locates the main part by examining the relationships within the file for the part that is the TargetUri of the file.

Listing 3-3. *Opening an Open XML Package with System.IO.Packaging*

```
Public Function PPTGetSlideTitles(ByVal fileName As String) As List(Of String)
Const documentRelationshipType As String = "http://schemas.openxmlformats.org~
        /officeDocument/2006/relationships/officeDocument"
Const presentationmlNamespace As String = "http://schemas.openxmlformats.org~
        /presentationml/2006/main"
Dim titles As New List(Of String)
Dim documentPart As PackagePart = Nothing
Dim documentUri As Uri = Nothing

Using pptPackage As Package = Package.Open(fileName, FileMode.Open, FileAccess.Read)
  ' Get the main document part (presentation.xml).
For Each relationship As PackageRelationship In~
        pptPackage.GetRelationshipsByType(documentRelationshipType)
   documentUri = PackUriHelper.ResolvePartUri(New Uri("/", UriKind.Relative), _
                        relationship.TargetUri)
   documentPart = pptPackage.GetPart(documentUri)
   'There's only one document part.
   Exit For
Next
```

With the main part located, the function continues by using the information in `presentation.xml` to get the list of identifiers for the presentation's slides. Listing 3-4 contains the related code.

Listing 3-4. *Obtaining the Identifiers of the Presentation's Slides*

```
' Manage namespaces to perform Xml XPath queries.
Dim nt As New NameTable()
Dim nsManager As New XmlNamespaceManager(nt)
nsManager.AddNamespace("p", presentationmlNamespace)
Dim xDoc As New XmlDocument(nt)
xDoc.Load(documentPart.GetStream())
Dim sheetNodes As XmlNodeList = xDoc.SelectNodes("//p:sldIdLst/p:sldId", nsManager)
```

Once the slides' identifiers have been found, the code uses the relationship information to locate the XML part that contains each slide. Listing 3-5 shows this portion of the function.

Listing 3-5. *Locating the Slide XML Parts*

```
If sheetNodes IsNot Nothing Then
    Dim relAttr As XmlAttribute = Nothing
    Dim sheetRelationship As PackageRelationship = Nothing
    Dim sheetPart As PackagePart = Nothing
    Dim sheetUri As Uri = Nothing
    Dim sheetDoc As XmlDocument = Nothing
    Dim titleNode As XmlNode = Nothing
    ' Look at each sheet node, retrieving the relationship id.
    For Each xNode As XmlNode In sheetNodes
        relAttr = xNode.Attributes("r:id")
        If relAttr IsNot Nothing Then
            ' Retrieve the PackageRelationship object for the sheet:
            sheetRelationship = documentPart.GetRelationship(relAttr.Value)
            If sheetRelationship IsNot Nothing Then
                sheetUri = PackUriHelper.ResolvePartUri(documentUri, _
                                sheetRelationship.TargetUri)
                sheetPart = pptPackage.GetPart(sheetUri)
```

At the end of Listing 3-5, the sheetPart variable has been associated with a specific slide in the presentation. Finally, this is where the slide's title is stored. To get access to this content, the snippet loads the part into a XML document and uses an XPath query to retrieve the necessary information. Listing 3-6 details this final step.

Listing 3-6. *Working with the Slide's XML Part*

```
If sheetPart IsNot Nothing Then
' find the title.
sheetDoc = New XmlDocument(nt)
sheetDoc.Load(sheetPart.GetStream())
titleNode = sheetDoc.~
    SelectSingleNode("//p:sp//p:ph[@type='title' or @type='ctrTitle']", nsManager)
If titleNode IsNot Nothing Then
    titles.Add(titleNode.ParentNode.ParentNode.ParentNode.InnerText)
End If
```

In addition to modifying or generating documents using the different markup languages, the Open XML standard supports having a custom XML folder that is capable of storing information. Within this folder, you or your applications can store your own XML data islands. Though all of the Office 2007 files can store custom XML, Microsoft Word 2007 has the unique added benefit of having a set of controls that can bind to the custom XML parts, displaying the data inline with the document. These controls are called *content controls* and they can be used to display data in the custom XML part, as well as serve as an input device for modifying the values there.

Several solutions in this book leverage the benefits of the Open XML file format. Chapter 7 works with Open XML Word documents and shows how to serialize SharePoint list content as a custom XML part. This solution is a different twist on the mail-merge concept. The solution details how to add content controls to the document to allow the user to interact with its contents. The solution in Chapter 8 facilitates multiple users working on different sections of a document by splitting it up into multiple files—one for each section. Once the work is complete, the team can merge the pieces back into a single document. Chapter 10 leverages PresentationML to dynamically build a PowerPoint presentation by merging SharePoint list content with a presentation template.

Using Managed Code

Even in the 2007 release, the Office applications are founded on a COM code base. This means that managed code solutions written in .NET languages must communicate with Office through its primary interop assemblies (PIAs). To provide a buffer layer of abstraction from the COM plumbing, Microsoft has released Visual Studio Tools for Office. VSTO provides classes that mask a lot of the COM interop, and it extends Visual Studio with Office development projects. Since Chapter 4 is dedicated to Visual Studio Tools for Office, we will only summarize the types of opportunities this provides for Office developers.

When users first see the Office 2007 applications, the feature that always gets the most attention is the ribbon— the new and improved user interface of the Microsoft Office 2007 system. One of the primary goals of the ribbon interface is to surface application functionality that users desired but simply didn't know was there because of how buried or obscure that menu item was. The ribbon also provides context sensitivity, showing different tabs and controls based on the type of object the user is focused on. The ribbon (Figure 3-7) occupies the top portion of most Office applications and provides a different experience then the layered menus and toolbars of previous Office releases.

Figure 3-7. *The ribbon in Microsoft Word*

This interface provides a simpler experience for the user by improving the organization of commands and providing a more graphical representation of options. In addition, the ribbon interface provides the developer with an improved programming model for manipulating it compared to the toolbars and menus of earlier versions of Office. This model is based on customizations that are defined in an XML file. With the file, a developer can manipulate the ribbon, controlling its tabs, groups, and controls. Customizations can include adding new elements as well as hiding default ones. The XML file is served up to the application by a custom class. Visual Studio Tools for Office provides Visual Studio project types for Office solutions, including an item called Ribbon Support. This Ribbon Support item includes sample XML and the necessary wrapper class. Throughout this book we will explore how to add custom graphics to the ribbon, programmatically control the state of controls we place there, and coordinate the ribbon with multiple windows of the application. Ribbon customizations are included in Chapter 9 (PowerPoint) and Chapter 11 (Outlook).

As mentioned earlier, Office add-ins let the developer extend the application with new functionality. Application-level add-ins are not tied to a specific file or document and are loaded when the application starts. An add-in can have custom code that responds to an application's events. As in Figure 3-8, add-ins often utilize task panes to present their user interface. Chapters 9, 11, and 12 all include solutions that incorporate add-ins and task panes.

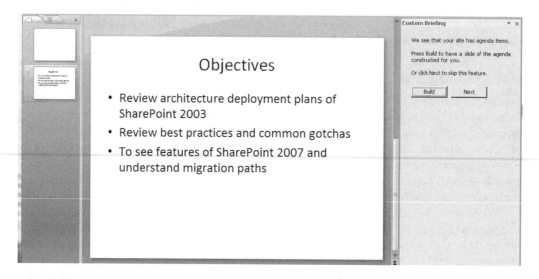

Figure 3-8. *A task pane presented from a PowerPoint add-in*

Whereas an add-in runs at the application level, a *smart document* is a solution that customizes a specific document or spreadsheet. .NET developers will recognize this technique as code-behind, but instead of a web page or a Windows form, a Word document or Excel spreadsheet is the design surface. With Microsoft Office 2003, VSTO supported smart document development with managed code, and these solutions continue to run in Office 2007. Chapter 5 incorporates this technique to provide offline editing of list content from multiple SharePoint sites in a spreadsheet.

Outlook users interact with several types of objects, including messages, contacts, tasks, and events. Each of these objects is presented in an Outlook form. It seems as if from the very beginning organizations have wanted to customize, extend, and inject code into these forms. This is largely due to the prominent placement of Outlook. Many users leave it open all day, checking messages and maintaining their calendar. Before Outlook 2007, developers who wanted to customize an Outlook form usually found themselves redesigning the entire form—even when all they wanted to do was add a few fields. Outlook 2007 introduces a new concept called *form regions*, which brings managed code to Outlook form development. Figure 3-9 shows a sample form region. We will use this feature and VSTO in Chapter 12 to enable the Outlook contact form to retrieve data from a line-of-business application.

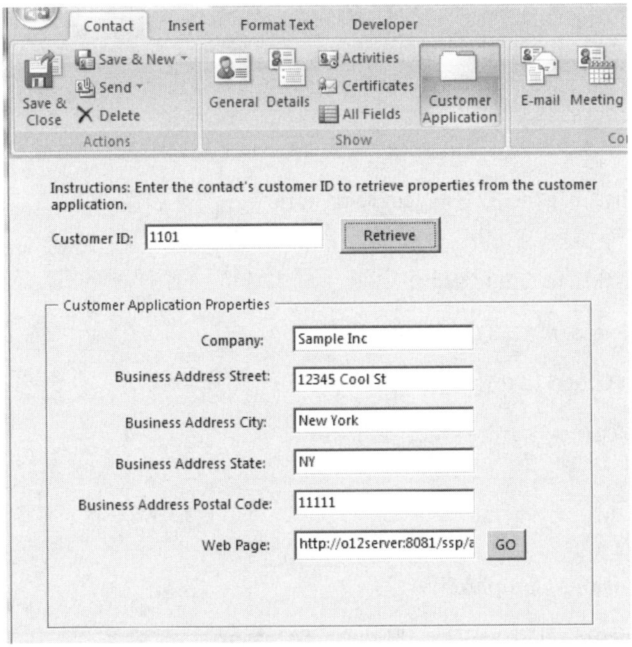

Figure 3-9. *An Outlook form region*

Chapter 6 includes a technique to register methods of a .NET class to be surfaced as functions in Microsoft Excel. These functions appear as native Excel functions, but since they are .NET code they can leverage all of the capability of the .NET Framework. These methods can communicate with databases, call web services, or use mathematic functions that are not normally available in Excel. Figure 3-10 shows a custom function named GetProductBasePrice (whose implementation includes calling a stored procedure) being incorporated into an Excel 2007 spreadsheet.

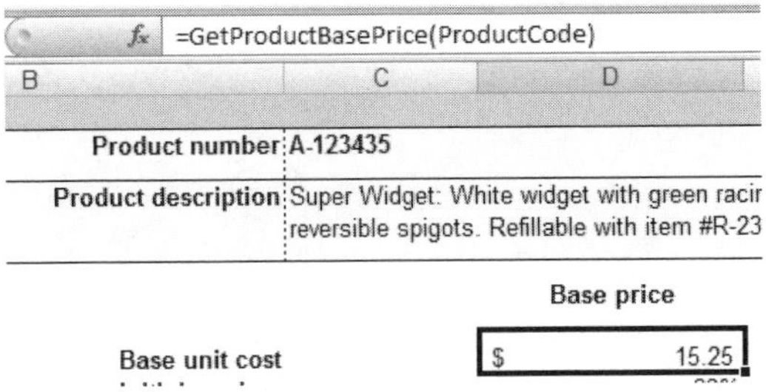

Figure 3-10. *Calling a .NET class' method from Excel*

We wouldn't want to forget the power of applying a custom schema to a document or spreadsheet. This technique enables developers to add their own markup into the Office file, permitting code to easily retrieve specific portions. We will use an XML schema in Chapter 8. There the schema will enable a user to specify separate sections of a Word document. These delimiters are then used to support split and merge operations.

Further Reading

- Office Open XML Overview:

  `http://www.ecma-international.org/news/TC45_current_work/`
  `OpenXML%20White%20Paper.pdf`

- Novell adds Microsoft's Open XML to OpenOffice:

  `http://www.linux-watch.com/news/NS5248375481.html`

- New WordPerfect will support Office 12 formats:

  `http://labs.pcw.co.uk/2006/01/new_wordperfect_1.html`

- OpenXMLDeveloper.org:

  `http://openxmldeveloper.org/`

- VBA and Managed Code Extensions Compared:

  `http://msdn2.microsoft.com/en-us/library/ss11825b(VS.80).aspx`

- Differences between the 2007 Office System and Office 2003:

  `http://technet2.microsoft.com/Office/en-us/library/`
  `a9189734-e303-4d7d-93eb-3584c358d1c91033.mspx?mfr=true`

- Common Tasks in Office Programming:

  `http://msdn2.microsoft.com/en-us/library/htx7t4k0(VS.80).aspx`

- What's New in Visual Studio Tools for Office:

  `http://msdn2.microsoft.com/en-us/library/86bkz018(VS.80).aspx`

- Brian Jones: Open XML Formats:

  `http://blogs.msdn.com/brian_jones/`

CHAPTER 4

Visual Studio Tools for Office Overview

Microsoft Office is one of the world's most used information-worker applications. This level of exposure and recognition has made these tools an enticing area for customization as developers wish to extend a tool that users are already comfortable with. Developing with Microsoft Office has traditionally meant developing in a COM-based world. This began to change with Office 2003 when Microsoft shipped primary interop assemblies (PIAs) as part of the advanced installation. These PIAs opened Office to the .NET developer community and their managed code projects. A primary interop assembly enabled a Visual Studio developer to write code against the Office applications by adding a reference in the project. This assembly took on the responsibility of translating between the COM and managed code environments. Even with the PIAs, this development was not for the faint of heart. .NET developers often struggled. Their code had to deal with the way Office maintained object lifetimes and they had to contend with lots of COM plumbing. In addition, the managed code solution was limited to running outside the process of the Office application. What was missing was a layer between the PIAs and the developer's custom application. Microsoft Visual Studio Tools for Office (VSTO) fills that gap. Visual Studio Tools for Office extends the Visual Studio environment to support the development of managed code solutions for Microsoft Office. With VSTO, the developer can create solutions that leverage Microsoft Office applications, including the construction of add-ins, custom task panes, ribbon customizations, and smart documents.

This chapter is by no means a complete reference to VSTO. It provides enough background information for you to understand the solutions that are presented in the remainder of the book. We will include links to sites where you can read more about specific topics that interest you. We will also point out which chapters in this book rely on the features discussed here.

History of Visual Studio Tools for Office

Even without VSTO, Microsoft Office 2003 was an important release for developers interested in customizing the Office tools to specific business needs. Microsoft Office 2003 allowed the developer to attach custom XML schemas to documents and spreadsheets, and to mark up their contents into a specific structure. Office 2003 could also store these files as XML, which allowed their data to be processed easily by other systems and applications. In Microsoft Word, this "save as XML" feature offered two options: storing just the data, discarding style information such as font color, size, etc., or encoding all of the information into the XML.

To store the style information in an XML file format, Word relied on its own markup schema, WordML. In addition to XML support, Microsoft Office 2003 introduced the concept of an *actions pane*. The actions pane often opened on the right-hand side of the document and allowed the user to interact with its interface. Microsoft Office applications used this pane to provide a research center for initiating searches and to show SharePoint site data without making the user go back to the web browser. Each of these features became launching points for developers.

The version of VSTO that was initially released was for Office 2003 and was called Visual Studio Tools for Office 2003. This version was an add-on to Visual Studio .NET 2003 and provided developers with project types that enabled their code to run in process with Microsoft Word 2003 and Microsoft Excel 2003. These project types focused on creating applications by building on top of documents. Developers would select their project type as an Excel workbook, Word document, or Word template. By writing their customizations in the managed-code world, developers were able to leverage the power of the .NET languages C# and VB.NET. These languages were more appealing than VBA and provided powerful access to manipulate XML and connect to data stores through ADO.NET, plus support for web services. By running within Office, the resulting assembly could interact with application- and document-level events, command bars, and the document itself. An important limitation of these solutions was that they were not compatible with Office Standard Edition 2003 because some of the necessary elements, such as XML and smart documents, were not supported. For more information on VSTO 2003 see `http://msdn.microsoft.com/office/tool/vsto/2003/default.aspx`.

With Visual Studio 2005 and the .NET Framework 2.0, VSTO took a major leap forward. Visual Studio 2005 Tools for Office literally brought Microsoft Word and Excel into Visual Studio and presented them as a designer surface. As shown in Figure 4-1, when a developer was working on an Excel-workbook solution, Microsoft Excel appeared just like a form surface would for a Windows developer.

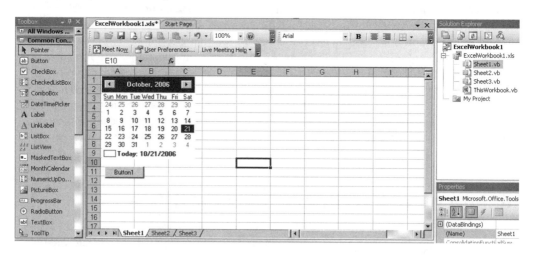

Figure 4-1. *Microsoft Excel as a visual design surface*

With the application as a design surface, the developer could drag Windows forms controls from the Visual Studio toolbox directly onto the spreadsheet or document. VSTO provided a host control wrapper to deal with the fact that this was a managed code control in a COM-based application. Double-clicking a button control would take the developer to an event handler in a code-behind file. This experience moved Office development in line with the experiences of working with Windows forms or ASP.NET. It provided Office developers with a rapid application-development environment. In addition to the dragging of controls onto the surface, data binding was supported. The custom actions panes that were difficult to build in VSTO 2003 became straightforward user controls. VSTO 2005 also widened the types of scenarios it would support. An Outlook add-in project type was added. ADO.NET datasets populated from databases or web services could be cached so their data would be available in offline scenarios. This data could even be manipulated by the VSTO runtime without the Office application being launched. This opened up server-side programming solutions in which the data cached in an XML island could be populated and then surfaced in the viewing of the document. However, VSTO projects were still limited to only the enterprise versions of the Office applications. The customizations were not supported in the Office Standard SKUs. The following URLs provide more information on Visual Studio 2005 Tools for Office:

- Getting Started (Visual Studio Tools for Office)

  `http://msdn2.microsoft.com/en-us/library/23cw517s.aspx`

- What's New in Visual Studio Tools for Office

  `http://msdn2.microsoft.com/en-us/library/86bkz018.aspx`

Visual Studio 2005 Tools for Office Second Edition (VSTO 2005 SE) is the latest edition to be released. This version was code-named Cypress during its development. VSTO 2005 SE is an interim release that still applies to the Visual Studio 2005 development environment. The main reason for this "second edition" is to address compatibility concerns with the release of Microsoft Office 2007. With VSTO 2005 SE, any solution constructed with Office 2003 and VSTO 2005 will run in Office 2007. In addition to supporting existing code, VSTO 2005 SE adds development support for key features of Office 2007, such as the ribbon, custom task panes, and Microsoft Outlook form regions. Managed code add-ins are now supported in Outlook, Excel, Word, PowerPoint, InfoPath, and Visio. Though this edition does provide design-time support for InfoPath 2007 form templates, missing is support for document-based projects with Word 2007 and Excel 2007. This means that if you wish to develop a document-level solution, such as a smart document, you must do so with Office 2003 on the development machine. Simply put, the visual design surface presented by Visual Studio is not compatible with Word 2007 and Excel 2007. There are a few important differences between the current and preceding versions of VSTO and Office. First, all versions of Office 2007 are able to support VSTO solutions. There is no exclusion of the standard SKU that existed in Office 2003. Also, VSTO 2005 SE supports Visual Studio 2005 Professional Edition in addition to the versions previously supported. VSTO 2005 SE is the version that we will use for any solution in this book that utilizes VSTO. The "Developing with VSTO" section of the chapter details the types of development you can accomplish with VSTO and which solutions in the book incorporate them. The following URLs provide more information on Visual Studio 2005 Tools for Office Second Edition:

- Visual Studio 2005 Tools for Office Second Edition

  `http://msdn.microsoft.com/office/tool/vsto/2005SE/default.aspx`

- Microsoft Visual Studio 2005 Tools for the 2007 Microsoft Office System Beta Tutorial

  `http://go.microsoft.com/?linkid=5467323`

Visual Studio 2007 Tools for Office will be the next major release of VSTO. It will be part of the Visual Studio 2007 development environment, which is code-named Orcas. Judging by features of the early Community Technology Previews (CTPs), it appears VSTO Orcas will provide the document-level project types and visual designer for Word 2007 and Excel 2007. Other possible features include support for Word 2007 content controls, ClickOnce deployment, and a designer for ribbon customizations. The following URL provides more information on Visual Studio 2007 and downloads of the latest CTPs:

- Visual Studio Code Name "Orcas" Related CTP Downloads

  `http://msdn2.microsoft.com/en-us/vstudio/aa700831.aspx`

Versions and Compatibility

From the previous section, it is quite obvious that Office development involves a lot of moving parts and version dependencies. Getting the right combination in a development environment is an important step since different permutations put limits on the types of projects you can create. Should you install Microsoft Office 2003 or 2007? Visual Studio 2005 Tools for Office exists in its original form as well as Second Edition flavor. And even the version of Visual Studio itself needs to be part of the equation since Visual Studio Team Edition included VSTO 2005, whereas Visual Studio Professional Edition did not. Table 4-1 presents the compatibility table from the VSTO 2005 SE documentation.

So if you want to create a smart document solution (document-level project) with its support for the visual designer, offline data caching, and hosting of Windows forms controls, then the development environment should be based on Office 2003 and VSTO 2005. These solutions will still run in Office 2007 with the VSTO 2005 SE runtime. Want to develop Outlook form regions or ribbon customizations? Place Office 2007 in your development environment. VSTO 2005 SE add-ins for Office 2007 will run in any edition of Office 2007, whereas add-ins for Office 2003 will work in any edition of Office 2003.

Just in case you were thinking about it, installing Office 2003 and Office 2007 on the same machine breaks the VSTO design-time environment. We highly recommend virtualizing your different development environments. If you build a VSTO 2005 solution and try to run it using Office 2007, make sure you place the solution in a trusted folder. This is a security feature in the Office 2007 applications and is configurable from the Trusted Locations tab of the Trust Center, as shown in Figure 4-2. You can access this dialog by clicking the pearl button (Office logo) in the top-left corner of Microsoft Word 2007 and clicking the Word Options button.

Table 4-1. *VSTO Compatibility*

Project Type	VSTO 2005 or Visual Studio Team Edition	VSTO 2005 SE installed with VSTO 2005 or Visual Studio Team Edition	VSTO 2005 SE installed with Visual Studio Professional Edition
Document-level projects	Word 2003 Excel 2003 InfoPath 2003	Word 2003 Excel 2003 InfoPath 2007	InfoPath 2007
Application-level add-ins	Outlook 2003	Excel 2003 Excel 2007 InfoPath 2007 Outlook 2003 Outlook 2007 PowerPoint 2003 PowerPoint 2007 Visio 2003 Visio 2007 Word 2003 Word 2007	Excel 2003 Excel 2007 InfoPath 2007 Outlook 2003 Outlook 2007 PowerPoint 2003 PowerPoint 2007 Visio 2003 Visio 2007 Word 2003 Word 2007
Actions pane (document-level)	Word 2003 Excel 2003	Word 2003 Excel 2003	Not supported
Custom task panes (application-level)	Not supported	Excel 2007 InfoPath 2007 Outlook 2007 PowerPoint 2007 Word 2007	Excel 2007 InfoPath 2007 Outlook 2007 PowerPoint 2007 Word 2007
Ribbon customizations	Not supported	Excel 2007 Outlook 2007 PowerPoint 2007 Word 2007	Excel 2007 Outlook 2007 PowerPoint 2007 Word 2007
Outlook form regions	Not supported	Outlook 2007	Outlook 2007
Host controls (Windows form controls)	Word 2003 Excel 2003	Word 2003 Excel 2003	Not supported
Data cache	Word 2003 Excel 2003	Word 2003 Excel 2003	Not supported
Visual designer	Word 2003 Excel 2003	Word 2003 Excel 2003 InfoPath 2007	InfoPath 2007

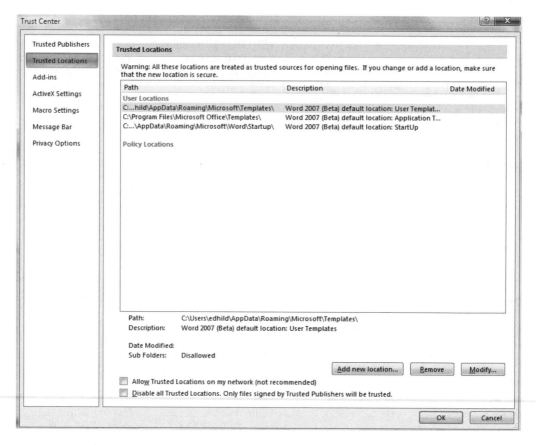

Figure 4-2. *Configuring trusted locations*

Developing with VSTO

The remainder of this chapter details the main types of development you can accomplish with Visual Studio Tools for Office. None of the descriptions here is of a complete project. Instead, this section establishes a baseline for the project types, basic vocabulary, and some of the key code fragments that you will find throughout our solutions in the remainder of the book. With each development effort, we reference which chapters contain solutions that incorporate that technique.

Add-Ins

Add-ins are defined by Microsoft Office Help as "supplemental programs that you can install to extend the capabilities of Microsoft Office by adding custom commands and specialized features." These programs run at the application level and are not tied to a specific document, spreadsheet, or presentation. In fact, the program can be loaded when the Office application starts before any of these files are opened. With VSTO 2005 SE, you can create add-ins for Word 2003 or 2007, Excel 2003 or 2007, Outlook 2003 or 2007, PowerPoint 2003 or 2007, Visio 2003 or

2007, and InfoPath 2007. Figure 4-3 shows the New Project dialog in Visual Studio with VSTO 2005 SE installed.

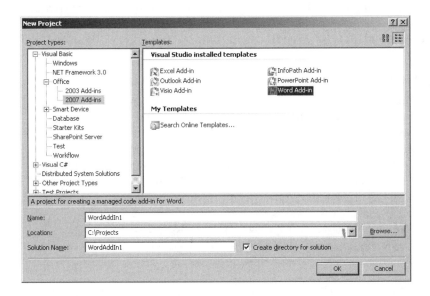

Figure 4-3. *Creating an Office add-in project*

Every add-in project includes a ThisAddin (.cs or .vb depending on the language) file. This file includes the ThisAddin class, which is the root of your application. Within this class you can respond to events such as startup and shutdown, where you can include initialization and clean-up commands. Listing 4-1 details a sample ThisAddin class that sets up a task pane. This task pane is a user control that loads within the Office application, allowing a developer to display a custom user interface.

Listing 4-1. *The ThisAddin Class*

```
Imports Microsoft.Office.Tools
public class ThisAddIn
    Public ctp As CustomTaskPane
    Private Sub ThisAddIn_Startup(ByVal sender As Object,~
            ByVal e As System.EventArgs) Handles Me.Startup
      ctp = Globals.ThisAddIn.CustomTaskPanes.Add( _
              New ucTaskPane(), "Custom Briefing")
      ctp.DockPosition = Office.MsoCTPDockPosition.msoCTPDockPositionRight
      ctp.Width = 250
    End Sub

    Private Sub ThisAddIn_Shutdown(ByVal sender As Object,~
            ByVal e As System.EventArgs) Handles Me.Shutdown

    End Sub
End class
```

With just a quick search on the Web, you can find a wide variety of Office add-ins for removing duplicate contacts in Outlook, creating surveys, redacting text in Word documents and more. In this book, the solution in Chapter 9 creates a PowerPoint 2007 add-in to create presentation slides from the content in a SharePoint Site. In Chapter 11, Outlook 2007 is extended to allow received emails to be saved to a SharePoint document library by an add-in.

Ribbon Customization

In earlier versions of Office, developers spent most of their efforts writing code utilizing the CommandBars object to create new buttons, extend menus, hide existing options, and make other user-interface customizations. Microsoft Office 2007 introduces a new user interface for organizing these commands, called the *ribbon*. The ribbon occupies the top portion of most Office applications and provides a different experience than the layered menus and toolbars of previous Office releases. Figure 4-4 shows Microsoft Word 2007's ribbon.

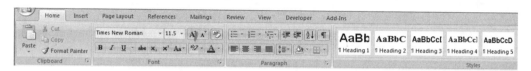

Figure 4-4. *The ribbon in Microsoft Word 2007*

This interface provides a simpler experience for the user by improving the organization of commands and providing a more graphical representation of options. One of the primary goals of the ribbon interface is to surface functionality of the applications that users desired but simply didn't know was there because of how buried or obscure that menu item was. The ribbon also provides context sensitivity. It will highlight certain tabs depending on the object you are focused on. For instance, the table tools are brought to your attention when you are in a table of a Word document. The controls on the ribbon are broken up into tabs (Home, Insert, Page Layout, etc.) and groups (Clipboard, Font, Paragraph, and so on). VSTO 2005 SE opens the ribbon interface to customization by the developer. In a VSTO project, you can select to add ribbon support from the Add New Item dialog of Visual Studio, as seen in Figure 4-5.

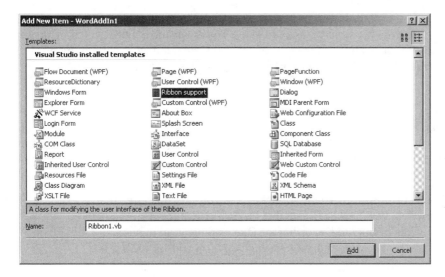

Figure 4-5. *Adding ribbon support*

When the new item process is complete, Visual Studio has actually added two files. These include the `Ribbon1.vb` code file (which includes the class that will contain any callback code as well as code to wire up your customizations). The other file is `Ribbon1.xml`, which is the markup of the ribbon-interface changes. Through this XML file, a developer can manipulate the ribbon interface, controlling its tabs, groups, and controls. This manipulation includes adding new elements as well as hiding default ones. Listing 4-2 details a sample XML file in which a new group named SharePoint is added to the Add-Ins tab with a single toggle button that uses a happy-face icon.

Listing 4-2. *Ribbon User Interface Markup*

```
<customUI xmlns="http://schemas.microsoft.com/office/2006/01/customui"~
        onLoad="OnLoad">
  <ribbon>
    <tabs>
      <tab idMso="TabAddIns">
        <group id="MOSSApps"
               label="SharePoint">
          <toggleButton id="toggleButton1"
                        size="large"
                        label="Briefing"
                        screentip="Import SharePoint items to create a briefing"
                        onAction="OnToggleButton1"
                        imageMso="HappyFace" />
        </group>
      </tab>
    </tabs>
  </ribbon>
</customUI>
```

The sample `Ribbon1.xml` file indicates that the new toggle button control is to call OnToggleButton1 when the button is pressed on or off. This is specified in the onAction attribute. Listing 4-3 contains an example of the type of code you will often write behind ribbon controls. This code toggles the display of a custom task pane defined by the add-in.

Listing 4-3. *OnToggleButton1 Callback*

```
Public Sub OnToggleButton1(ByVal control As Office.IRibbonControl,~
        ByVal isPressed As Boolean)
    Globals.ThisAddIn.ctp.Visible = isPressed
End Sub
```

For your ribbon customizations to be surfaced, your solution must include a RequestService function. VSTO 2005 SE adds this code for you at the top of the `Ribbon1.vb` file. It simply needs to be uncommented, allowing the Office application to hook into the ribbon customizations. To make it easy to find, we have included this code in Listing 4-4.

Listing 4-4. *The RequestService Method*

```
' This is an override of the RequestService method in the ThisAddIn class.
' To hook up your custom ribbon uncomment this code.
Partial Public Class ThisAddIn
    Private ribbon As Ribbon1
    Protected Overrides Function RequestService(~
        ByVal serviceGuid As Guid) As Object
        If serviceGuid = GetType(Office.IRibbonExtensibility).GUID Then
            If ribbon Is Nothing Then
                ribbon = New Ribbon1()
            End If
            Return ribbon
        End If
        Return MyBase.RequestService(serviceGuid)
    End Function
End Class
```

Several solutions in this book (Including those in Chapters 9 and 11) make use of ribbon customizations. The solution in Chapter 9 contains the same code described here, and details how to add your own graphics.

Task Panes

The concept of adding panes inside the Office applications was introduced in Office 2003. These panes display in the same window as the application, usually off to the right-hand side of the document, email, spreadsheet, or presentation. These panes can be scoped to the current open file or at an application level. When the pane is scoped to a file, we refer to it as an *actions pane*. When it is scoped to the application, we refer to is as a *task pane*. Actions panes are supported as part of the document code-behind model of VSTO 2005. Task panes are a feature of VSTO 2005 SE. Panes provide an interface for the user to interact with, where the result usually has some impact on the user's current document. Office uses the pane interface for many tasks, such as browsing for clip art, searching through the Research pane, or displaying SharePoint site data. As a developer, panes can be a method of extending the Office application with your own interface and process.

Office add-ins can include custom task panes by implementing the ICustomTaskPane-Consumer interface. Fortunately, VSTO already provides an implementation of this interface; therefore you need only to create the task panes as user controls and add them to the add-in's CustomTaskPanes collection. Figure 4-6 shows a sample user control that, with the code in Listing 4-5, is turned into a task pane in Excel 2007.

Figure 4-6. *Constructing a task-pane user control*

Listing 4-5. *Attaching a User Control as a Task Pane*

```
Imports Microsoft.Office.Tools
Imports Excel = Microsoft.Office.Interop.Excel

public class ThisAddIn
Dim pane1 As tsPane = New tsPane()

Private Sub ThisAddIn_Startup(ByVal sender As Object, _
    ByVal e As System.EventArgs) Handles Me.Startup
 ' Excluding some VSTO generated code
Dim customPane As CustomTaskPane = Me.CustomTaskPanes.Add(pane1, _
    "Custom Task Pane")
 customPane.DockPosition = Microsoft.Office.Core.MsoCTPDockPosition.~
    msoCTPDockPositionRight
 customPane.Visible = True
End Sub
End class
```

Once the user control is loaded as a task pane, it can interact with the host Office application through its Application object, obtained by Globals.ThisAddIn.Application. By placing code behind the user control, we can manipulate the application or its document. For example, the code in Listing 4-6 responds by placing the selected date in the A1 cell of the current worksheet when the user clicks the Insert button.

Listing 4-6. *Manipulating a Spreadsheet from a Task Pane*

```
Private Sub btnInsert_Click(ByVal sender As System.Object, _
    ByVal e As System.EventArgs) Handles btnInsert.Click
If (Globals.ThisAddIn.Application.ActiveSheet IsNot Nothing) Then
  Dim currentWorksheet As Excel.Worksheet =~
      CType(Globals.ThisAddIn.Application.ActiveSheet, Excel.Worksheet)
  currentWorksheet.Range("A1").Value =~
      MonthCalendar1.SelectionRange.Start.ToString("MM/dd/yyyy")
 End If
 End Sub
```

Figure 4-7 shows the user control as a custom task pane loaded to the right of the spreadsheet, and the result of the selected date being inserted into cell A1.

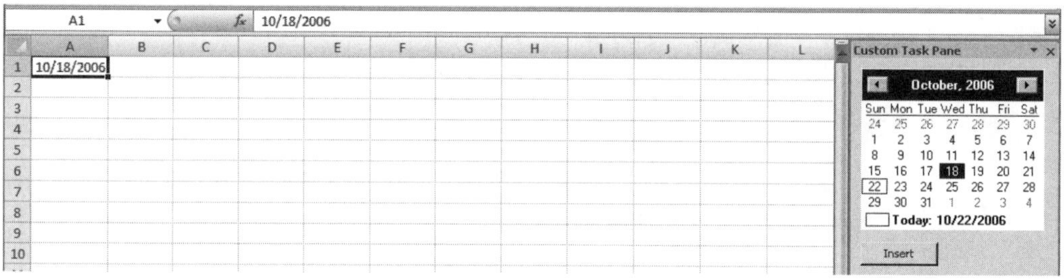

Figure 4-7. *The custom task pane in action*

Task panes allow developers to inject their own interface and code into the Office applications. The task pane becomes like its own helper application to completing the document. The solution in Chapter 5 includes an actions pane for pulling SharePoint site data into Excel for offline processing. PowerPoint is extended with a task pane in Chapter 9 so that slides can be built from SharePoint site content. Finally, the solution in Chapter 11 includes a task pane in Outlook for saving received emails to SharePoint sites.

Outlook Form Regions

In addition to add-ins, ribbons, and task panes, Outlook 2007 supports extensions through a new user interface element called *form regions*. Before Outlook 2007, developers who wanted to customize an Outlook form usually found themselves redesigning the entire form even when all they wanted to do was add a few fields. In older versions of Outlook, these custom forms were deployed centrally on the Exchange server and often took too long to open. Developers also had a difficult time injecting their own code or script for their form. Enter Outlook 2007's form regions, which will enable you to insert your own custom user interface into Outlook's inspectors. Do not confuse this approach with sending InfoPath forms through email. Form regions are used to extend the user interface of Outlook.

An Outlook 2007 form region is made up of three main elements. The first is an Outlook add-in that runs code in response to the user interacting with controls on the form region. The second is an Outlook Form Storage (OFS) file that contains the layout of the form and its controls. Lastly, a manifest XML file that Outlook finds through the Windows registry informs the application of the custom assembly to load and display names.

There are three ways to add a custom Outlook form region: You can append a region to an existing form, replace the first tab page of a built-in form, or completely replace an existing form. Regardless of the approach, Outlook 2007 provides the tools through its Developer ribbon to create the OFS file. Figure 4-8 shows Outlook in design mode, where a new form region is being added to the built-in contact form.

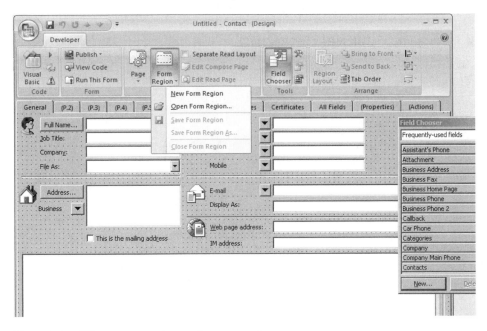

Figure 4-8. *Adding a new region to the contact form*

Once created, the new form region can be populated with fields and controls. When the layout is complete, the form region can be saved as an OFS file and embedded as a resource in an Outlook 2007 add-in project. This project overrides the RequestService function to inform Outlook of a helper class it can use to load the form region. Listing 4-7 includes this override and FormRegionHelper is a class that has been coded to comply with the FormRegionStartup interface.

Listing 4-7. *The Outlook Add-In's RequestService Function*

```
Private mFormRegionHelper As FormRegionHelper
Protected Overrides Function RequestService(~
    ByVal serviceGuid As System.Guid) As Object
    If serviceGuid = GetType(Outlook.FormRegionStartup).GUID Then
        If mFormRegionHelper Is Nothing Then
            mFormRegionHelper = New FormRegionHelper()
            Return mFormRegionHelper
        End If
    End If
Return MyBase.RequestService(serviceGuid)
End Function
```

The FormRegionHelper class is a COM-visible class that Outlook can interact with to render the form region. This class returns the OFS file as a byte array from the embedded resources. It also locates the controls that were placed on the form region and allows you to then write managed code for responding to user interactions. If the form region had the contact's FullName field and a command button, the BeforeFormRegionShow method in Listing 4-8 establishes these elements in the managed-code world.

Listing 4-8. *Locating the Controls on the Form Region*

```
Public Sub BeforeFormRegionShow(ByVal FormRegion As~
    Microsoft.Office.Interop.Outlook.FormRegion) Implements~
    Microsoft.Office.Interop.Outlook._FormRegionStartup.BeforeFormRegionShow
        Me.mFormRegion = FormRegion
        Me.mUserForm = FormRegion.Form
        OlkTextBox1 = mUserForm.Controls.Item("OlkTextBox1")
        CommandButton1 = mUserForm.Controls.Item("CommandButton1")
    End Sub
End result
```

With the controls now available from managed code, as a developer you can really do anything. An overly simply example would be to show the FullName value in a message box when the user clicks the Go command button. Since all of the controls are defined within our class, this is no more complicated than a Click event handler with a call to MessageBox.Show(). Figure 4-9 shows the end result.

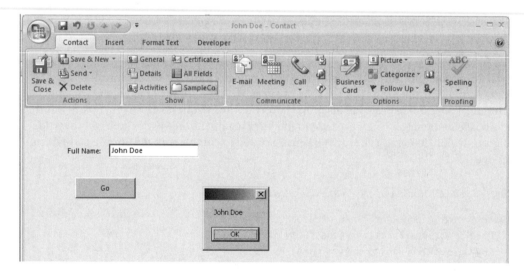

Figure 4-9. *.NET code responding to user interaction in the form region*

The solution in Chapter 12 includes a custom Outlook 2007 form region and goes into detail on the manifest XML file as well as dependencies on the Windows registry. You can also read more about Outlook form regions at the following URL:

- Building an Outlook 2007 Form Region with a Managed Add-In

  `http://msdn2.microsoft.com/en-us/library/ms788695.aspx`

Document-Level Projects

Document-level projects are solutions in which the application is a Word document or Excel spreadsheet. This technique is often referred to as a *code-behind* document or a *smart document*. The difference between this type of solution and the previous development efforts is that we are not just extending an Office application, but rather we're creating a tool out of a specific file. The document or spreadsheet starts out with all of the traditional Office functionality and then the developer can drag new controls onto its surface, add custom code, add user-interface elements to an actions pane, and even cache data for offline access. Usually this type of solution is implemented to build a tool that helps an information worker create a complex document. Sales proposals and contracts whose contents likely come from many corporate resources are typical candidates for smart documents.

As shown in Figure 4-1, Visual Studio Tools for Office provides a unique development environment for building document-level projects. When you start such a project, you have the option of creating a new file or importing an existing Word document or Excel spreadsheet. This is a useful feature for organizations that already have these assets and are looking to enhance them. Once in the designer, Windows form controls can be dragged onto the document's surface and event-handler code can be placed in the code-behind. These projects also support data-binding the controls and caching of datasets for offline access. The solution in Chapter 5 enables the user to edit list data from multiple sites in a single Excel spreadsheet, even in a disconnected environment. The following URL contains more information on smart documents:

- About Smart Documents

  `http://office.microsoft.com/en-us/word/HP030916741033.aspx?pid=CH010504591033`

Though VSTO provides support for document-level projects, it provides a development environment only on a machine with Office 2003 and VSTO 2005. The newer VSTO 2005 SE runtime enables projects built with Office 2003 to run in Office 2007. Therefore, Chapter 5's solution requires a different development environment than the others in the book. This uniqueness will be repeated many times just to make sure you catch it. Not until the Orcas release of VSTO will Office 2007 be supported in a development environment for document-level projects.

Further Reading

- Visual Studio 2005 Tools for Office Second Edition

    http://msdn.microsoft.com/office/tool/vsto/2005SE/default.aspx

- Creating Custom Task Panes using Visual Studio Tools for Office

    http://msdn2.microsoft.com/en-us/library/aa722570.aspx

- Trust Center and Office Development

    http://blogs.msdn.com/kevinboske/archive/2006/08/01/685546.aspx

- Deploying Office Solutions

    http://msdn2.microsoft.com/en-us/library/hesc2788.aspx

PART 2

■■■

Microsoft Excel Solutions

This section will focus on solutions built around Microsoft Excel. In Chapter 5 we will customize an Excel spreadsheet into a tool that an information worker can use to maintain content that is spread across multiple sites. By using the spreadsheet, we can consolidate this information into a single tool that also supports offline editing. In Chapter 6 the solution focuses on how Excel spreadsheets can be incorporated into the enterprise. This includes extending the spreadsheet to interact with line-of-business applications. Chapter 6 also shows you how to access the spreadsheet's calculation logic from a remote custom application.

CHAPTER 5

Maintaining Offline List Content from Multiple Sites

The collaboration sites of Windows SharePoint Services (WSS) provide a focused workspace for users to share information to achieve a goal or complete a process. Often these sites are customized by an organization so they meet the exact needs of the type of collaboration the group of users is trying to perform. Usually each site represents a specific instance of the process and has the appropriate lists and libraries to store the necessary information. Though the site adequately services the needs to the group for the specific instance of the process, it does very little for the user who may be involved in many of these sites. Even though each site has the same type of content, the user would be burdened with accessing each site during the day to make content changes. A better solution would be to consolidate the content from these similar sites into a single tool for the user. There the user could maintain the content for all of the sites and periodically save her changes back to the corresponding lists in SharePoint sites. Ideally the tool would also provide this information in a way that supports visualization techniques such as charting. In this chapter we will detail how, as a developer, you can extend Microsoft Excel to construct such a tool. In fact, we will make the list data available to the user even if she is offline and not able to reach the SharePoint sites.

Real-World Examples

Many organizations use SharePoint as a type of case-management system. *Case management*, in general terms, means that there is a documented process for which the organization manages many instances. For example, any time a military base gets notified of a distinguished visitor, there is a documented process of what types of actions need to be taken, documents completed, etc. Yet the base could easily have many instances of this process for different visitors at different times. The result is many SharePoint sites. The idea of case management can apply to many other scenarios: A software-consulting shop would provide a development life cycle with many specific project instances actively running. A marketing team would have a collaboration site for each of its campaigns. Lawyers would have sites for specific trials. It is not unusual to see Windows SharePoint Services sites used in a model where a site definition details the lists and libraries needed for the process and instances of that definition (sites) are created for each instance of the process. In the military example, each distinguished visit would have its own SharePoint site for the different groups on base to complete their tasks and documentation. This approach creates a problem for the user who is involved in many instances of the same type of site—or worse yet, oversees them all. Without any help, that worker spends more time navigating from site to site than working with the data those sites contain.

Solution Overview

Windows SharePoint Services sites often represent a unit of collaboration or an instance of a business process. Our solution sets out to address the scenario in which a user is faced with the challenge of maintaining the same type of content distributed across many sites. To provide some context for the chapter, we decided to use a list that contains information about projects. For each project we will store its title, project number, start date, and budget. Before building the tool for the user, we construct a list definition to enforce a specific list schema for sites that we want to maintain this type of information. To construct the list definition, we will build a list within a SharePoint site to contain the fields we are interested in. We will then use the SharePoint Solution Generator provided with the Visual Studio 2005 Extensions for Windows SharePoint Services to capture this list as a definition. This chapter details this process for you and shows you how any site administrator can then choose to make a Projects list type available to users.

With our scenario of multiple sites with Projects lists, we will develop an application that consolidates the information from these different sites into a single tool for our user. We'll develop the application by customizing a Microsoft Excel workbook using custom .NET code. When the user opens the spreadsheet, an action pane will open alongside the document, allowing the user to register the different SharePoint sites and lists she wishes to maintain in the tool. Each registration is termed a *connection*. Internally we store the connection name, the list's name, the URL of the site that contains the list, and a timestamp of the last time a modification was made to the site's list. This information will help us communicate with the site through web services and synchronize its data. The tool provides a synchronization interface that enables the user to retrieve all the list items for each of their connections. Internally, the solution will store this data in a DataSet while displaying it in a consolidated view for the user—a single Excel worksheet. The user will then be able to use the worksheet to modify any Projects list item, delete project items, or add new ones. By clicking a Sync Now button, all of the user's changes are committed to the original SharePoint sites' lists.

By creating the solution on top of a Microsoft Excel workbook, we gain some additional functionality that improves our tool for the user who is maintaining all of the content. First, by displaying the data in a worksheet, the user can sort and filter the data. Though the user could perform this action within the list's web part, the worksheet enables the user to do these actions across the entire set of data from all of the sites. The user can also create charts to better visualize the data. More importantly, our internal DataSet can be saved within the Excel workbook. This means that the list-item data the user retrieves can be stored with the workbook and made available even if the user cannot access the SharePoint sites. This provides the user the ability to edit the content while offline. Of course, the user will not be able to synchronize any changes, but this offline editing capability does provide a powerful alternative to navigating each site individually and making the changes online.

■**Note** You might wonder why we are relying on Microsoft Excel for this solution instead of Microsoft Access. With Windows SharePoint Services v3, a list can be taken offline into a Microsoft Access 2007 database. This feature has a limitation, however: each list that is taken offline is stored in its own table. This could create more confusion as the data will not be able to be worked on as a single set. In addition, Microsoft Access is not nearly as familiar as Microsoft Excel for most information workers, and Excel gives us a familiar interface for visualizing the data, including charts. Another benefit of our approach is that it will work with WSS v2 and v3 sites simultaneously.

Solution Walkthrough

This walkthrough will detail the major elements of the solution and the decisions that we made in coding it. We'll explain how we first provide a list definition to our SharePoint environment to make sure that sites we want to maintain project information do so uniformly. The walkthrough will then focus on the construction of a tool to allow a user to maintain project information from multiple sites, even offline. We will construct this tool by extending Microsoft Excel and the walkthrough will take you through the major pieces of development. Not every line of code is included in this text; therefore we recommend that you retrieve the solution available in the Source Code/Download section of http://apress.com. This way you can follow along with the text or fill in the extra lines while developing your own. The walkthrough will include the design of a DataSet to store the list information, the development of a strategy to detect network connectivity, and the construction of action panes to host our tool's custom interface. We will detail how the tool accomplishes the synchronization process between the DataSet and the collection of lists in SharePoint sites. We included a sample test case so you can see how to use the tool and explore its functionality. Lastly, the walkthrough details deployment options and how to get the solution to run in Excel 2007.

■**Caution** The solution in this chapter extends a Microsoft Excel spreadsheet, making it into a tool that maintains lists of project information from multiple SharePoint sites. Our solution is focused on customizing a specific spreadsheet—not the Excel application. This type of solution is called a *document-level project* or a *smart document*. Both Microsoft Word and Excel support these types of projects. They are characterized by having a .NET assembly as a code-behind to a document or spreadsheet. But be forewarned: Not until the next version of Visual Studio (code-named Orcas) will Visual Studio .NET support the development of document-level projects with Office 2007. Therefore, to develop this solution we will have to code in an environment running Excel 2003 Professional. However, the end result will still run on a machine with Excel 2007 installed—you just cannot use Excel 2007 to develop the solution.

In case you are considering it, your development environment cannot have both versions of Office. This is the only chapter that has an Office 2003–based development environment. The rest are all based on Office 2007. We felt that this solution is compelling enough to include and wanted to provide you with a solution that was deployable. At the time of this writing, Visual Studio "Orcas" is still a CTP (Community Technology Preview) and may change through its Beta and RTM (release to manufacturing) releases. If we had used Orcas the code in this book would very likely have been short-lived. Chapter 4 has more information on this compatibility issue as it is a constraint placed on us by Visual Studio Tools for Office.

■**Note** We are expecting that the Office 2003 development environment (mentioned in the Caution box) is on a different virtual machine than your MOSS server. To construct this solution, your development environment needs the following:

- .NET Framework 2.0

- Visual Studio .NET 2005 Team Edition or Visual Studio .NET 2005 Professional

- Visual Studio Tools for Office 2005 (included in VS.NET Team Edition)

- Visual Studio Tools for Office 2005 SE

- Office 2003 Professional (not Standard SKU) with primary interop assemblies

You might wonder why we are asking you to have both versions of VSTO installed if we are not using the Office 2007 support of the second edition. VSTO 2005 SE corrects some of the issues with the original runtime. In particular, databinding in Excel (which we will use) has been improved.

Creating the Projects List Definition

Before concentrating on the Excel spreadsheet, we want to tackle the issue of providing Share-Point sites with the capability to maintain information on projects. It is important that each site that stores project information do so with a uniform schema and that we can identify these lists among others that may be present in the site. There are two techniques that we could leverage: We could create a list template or a list definition. A list template is typically something an end user would create by using the web interface to set up the list and then use its Save as Template action in the list's settings. The result is a file with an STP extension that is stored in a site collection's List Template Gallery. Since it is in a gallery, this STP file ultimately is stored in a content database and it includes the customizations that the user made, as well as a reference to the original list definition type. When a user creates an instance of the template, the new list has the same customizations as the STP file but still references the original definition. This opens up some maintenance concerns and really doesn't solve the need of a new enterprise-wide type of list.

List definitions, on the other hand, are stored on the file system and contain a schema XML file that defines the fields in the list. View information, styles, and the forms the user interacts with are also a part of the list definition. By being deployed to the file system, the list definition can be made available to the enterprise easily and is more easily maintained. Creating list definitions is viewed as a developer task and yet even most developers hate making them because of the awkward syntax of XML and CAML (Collaborative Application Markup Language). In this solution we will show you how to get the benefits of having your list as a definition, with the ease of building a template.

The first step is to select a team site you use for development and to create a custom list named Projects. A custom list will by default have the Title, Created By, and Modified By columns. Add the new columns in Table 5-1 using the list's Settings administration screen.

Table 5-1. *Projects-List Columns*

Column Name	Data Type	Notes
ProjectNumber	Text	
StartDate	Date and time	Choose date only
Budget	Currency	Two decimal places

With the list created, we will use the SharePoint Solution Generator tool included in the Visual Studio 2005 Extensions for Windows SharePoint Services package. When we developed this solution, this package was still a CTP and had a few quirks, but it will be more than adequate for this task. It needs to be installed and run on the MOSS server since it accesses the object model directly. You can download these tools here:

- Windows SharePoint Services 3.0 Tools: Visual Studio 2005 Extensions

  `http://www.microsoft.com/downloads/details.aspx?~`
  `FamilyID=19f21e5e-b715-4f0c-b959-8c6dcbdc1057&DisplayLang=en`

Once you have installed them, the solution generator will be located at `C:\Program Files\` `Microsoft SharePoint Developer Tools\ssg\SPSolGen.exe` by default. If your MOSS environment does not have a web application accessible by a URL of the machine's name (`http://` `{LocalServerName}`), you will have to set the computername environment variable in a command prompt before launching the solution generator. This workaround is documented here:

- The Unwritten Work-Arounds for Using the SharePoint Solution Generator

  `http://blogs.msdn.com/edhild/archive/2007/01/25/~`
  `the-unwritten-work-arounds-for-using-the-sharepoint-solution-generator.aspx`

When successfully launched, the opening screen looks like Figure 5-1.

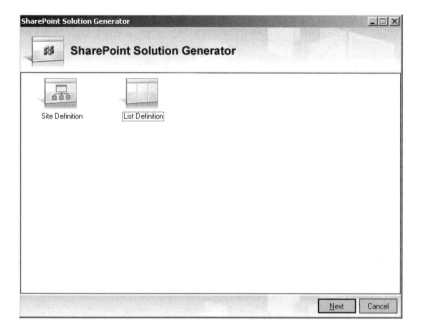

Figure 5-1. *Using the SharePoint Solution Generator*

The SharePoint Solution Generator will create a list definition from an existing SharePoint list. Follow these instructions through the wizard:

1. Select List Definition and click Next.

2. Select the SharePoint web that contains the Projects list you created earlier. Click Next.

3. You will see the set of lists contained within that site. Find your Projects list, check it, and click Next.

4. The Solution Generator creates a Visual Studio project that contains the definition. This screen asks you to name and select the location. Name the solution **ProjectsListDef**. The default location is in a SharePoint Definitions folder of your My Documents folder. Figure 5-2 shows these options.

5. Click Next.

6. On the last screen, click Start. The SharePoint Solution Generator will capture the list as a definition.

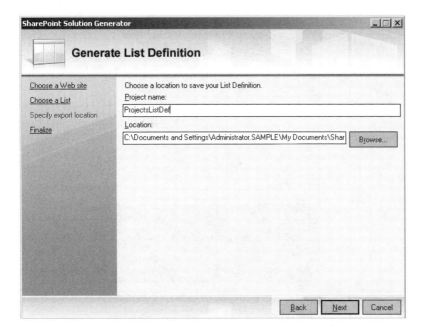

Figure 5-2. *Specifying the VS.NET project to contain the list definition*

Before you double-click and open the project that was created, you may need to deal with the computername environment variable problem. If you had to use a work-around earlier, launch Visual Studio from the same command prompt as you used to set the environment variable. This is because this project contains some additional dialogs that rely on this setting. While still working on your MOSS server, open the newly created project. There are two settings to be aware of. Both are accessible from the project's properties. The first is on the Debug tab. Make sure the start action is set to Start Browser with URL and its value is a valid Share-Point web application in your development environment. The second setting is within the new SharePoint Solution tab. This tab gives you visibility into the solution and feature that wrap this list definition, which will ease deployment. Expand the tree until you get to the Element Manifest section, which contains the attributes of the Projects list definition. Change the value of the Type attribute to **1001**. We want this to be a unique number so that we can tell Projects lists apart from other site lists. Figure 5-3 shows this change. Save these settings.

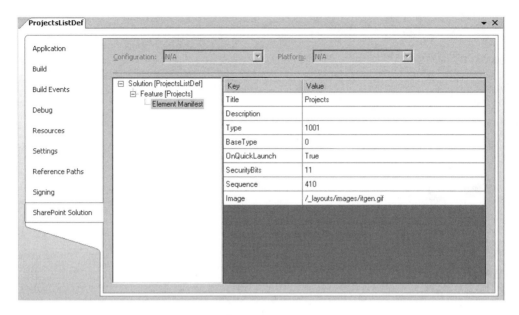

Figure 5-3. *Setting the Projects list definition type*

Take a moment to skim the schema.xml file in the project. This file contains the XML and CAML code that developers were left to write themselves without this tool. You can now right-click on the project and choose Deploy. Visual Studio will perform many actions, including defining your list definition as a SharePoint feature and then packaging it as a solution to be deployed into your environment. Most of the files this process generates are hidden in the project's bin folder but are left behind for you to examine. Features are not the focus of this solution, but other chapters in this book go into great detail on what is happening here. Specifically, Chapters 7 and 8 have you building SharePoint features from scratch.

Once the list definition is deployed, it can be activated in sites within that web application. You should delete the Projects list you created in your development site; it is not an instance of the definition you just deployed. Use the following steps to activate the Projects feature, which will make your list definition available.

1. Access the site's Admin area by selecting Settings from the Site Actions menu.

2. Click on the Site Features link in the Site Administration group.

3. Find the Projects feature and click the Activate button.

As Figure 5-4 shows, once the feature is activated you will see a new Projects list type in the Create dialog. Any site administrator in your environment can now selectively choose to maintain projects. We will be able to identify these lists by their type, and each list will use the same schema. Make sure you have at least two team sites that have the Projects feature enabled and have instances of the list definition.

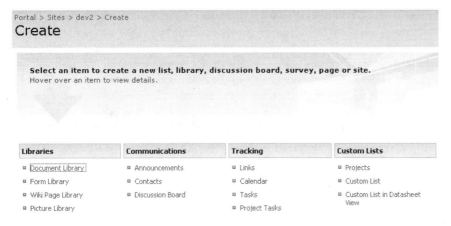

Figure 5-4. *Creating an instance of the Projects list definition*

Creating the Excel Smart Document Project

Creating an Excel smart document project in Visual Studio is made very straightforward by the project types VSTO adds. Simply start Visual Studio and select to create a new project. Under the Visual Basic language node, expand the Office node and locate the Excel Workbook project template. Name the project and solution **MaintainContentOffline**. Your New Project dialog should look like Figure 5-5.

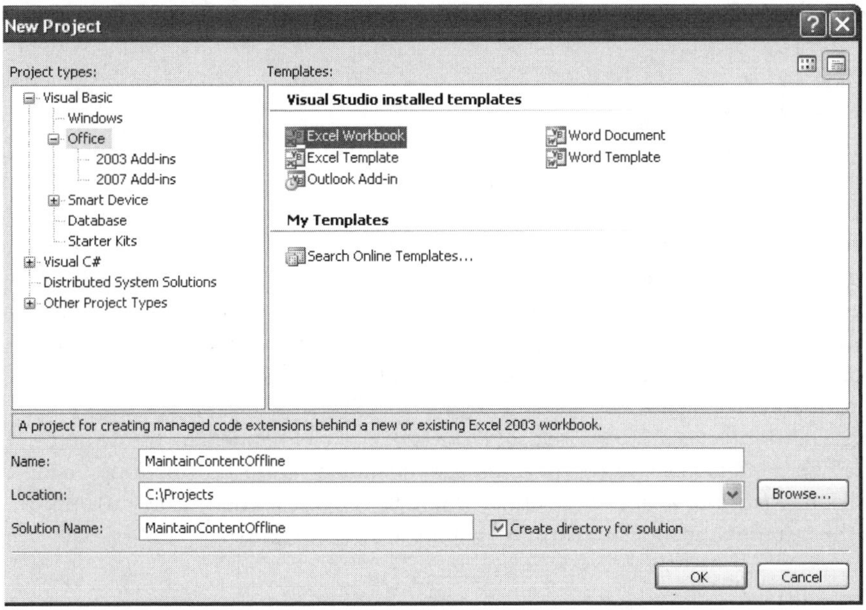

Figure 5-5. *Creating an Excel Workbook project*

Once you click OK, the VSTO Project Wizard will ask you if you want to create a new Excel workbook or import an existing one. Using an existing workbook would be useful if you want to add code to a spreadsheet that is already used by the enterprise. For this example, however, create a new document named Projects. Once the new project is created, your solution will already have a few files by default. These are visible in the Solution Explorer window of Visual Studio. There will be a `Projects.xls` node that, when expanded, will have files for each of the sheets in the Excel workbook. There are three by default. We will need only Sheet1, so in the Excel designer, right-click on a worksheet tab to get the delete option and remove the other worksheets. Notice how the corresponding code file is removed as well. Using the same technique, rename Sheet1 to **Projects Sheet**. The designer should reflect this change and you should see the name appear in parentheses in the Solution Explorer; however, the code file remains `Sheet1.vb`. The other file in the Solution Explorer is `ThisWorkbook.vb`. This file has no design interface since it is a class in which code can be written to respond to events at the document level. In this file's code, you will find event handlers such as Startup and Shutdown at the workbook scope level. Figure 5-6 shows what your project's structure should look like so far.

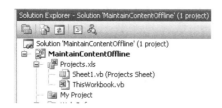

Figure 5-6. *Viewing the project in the Solution Explorer*

Designing the DataSet

This tool will allow the user to pull items in Projects lists from multiple sites and maintain them within the document. This data will be stored within the document and made available even if the user is offline. To facilitate this, we will leverage the smart document's capability to cache a DataSet in the document. We will use a single DataSet to store all of the necessary data for the solution, including the project information, the lists that contained that information, and some settings information. Add a new DataSet named **WorksheetData** to your solution. Figure 5-7 shows the structure of the DataSet, including a Settings DataTable to store settings information, a Lists DataTable to store the sources of the data, and a Projects DataTable to store the list information itself.

The Settings DataTable has only two fields: FieldName and FieldValue. The FieldName column is the table's primary key. Our solution will use the table to store information outside the maintained data. An example of such a setting would be the one named LastSyncTime, whose value is the last time the tool successfully synchronized with its lists.

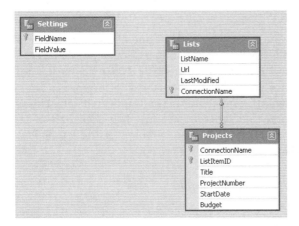

Figure 5-7. *The solution's DataSet*

The Lists DataTable stores the locations of the Projects lists that the user has requested to maintain within the tool. This DataTable stores the name of the list in the SharePoint site, a URL to the site, a timestamp of when the list was last modified, and a string representing the connection name. The connection name is a string value the user will specify when adding the list to the tool. We originally considered simply using the list's name, but that made it awkward for the user to maintain different lists from different sites that happened to have the same name. So this connection name becomes a unique identifier representing the data source of project information.

The Projects DataTable stores the project-information list items. This DataTable uses a combination of the connection name and the identifier of the list item as its primary key. The ListItemID field is an integer that SharePoint uses internally for list items. We then store the columns of data in the project list: Title (String), ProjectNumber (String), StartDate (System.DateTime), and Budget (System.Double). The Projects DataTable has a Relation defined with its parent Lists DataTable. The Relation is set up between the two Connection-Name fields. The Relation's properties are configured such that it creates the relation with a ForeignKeyConstraint. The ForeignKeyConstraint is configured to cascade on updates and deletes.

With the DataSet created, drag it from the Solution Explorer onto the surface of Sheet1 in the designer. This will add an instance of the DataSet to the spreadsheet. It will be shown in a panel directly below the spreadsheet because it is not a visible element. Name the instance **WorksheetData1**. To enable this DataSet to be cached in the document, you will have to set two of its properties. First change its Modifiers property to Public and then set the CacheIn-Document property to True. That is all you have to do to gain the feature of having the DataSet's data saved with the document. Notice the DataSet's DataHost property. It exposes an IsCacheInitialized Boolean value. Often it is necessary for you to know from code if the DataSet has been loaded from the document's cache. If IsCacheInitialized evaluates to True, there was a saved DataSet in the document that has been loaded. You will see this technique used in code later to determine if the tool has an empty DataSet or one loaded from cache.

Detecting Internet Connectivity

An important function of any tool that you want to work both online and offline is its ability to detect connectivity status. In this solution, this check is made within a ConnectionManager class. This class provides an IsOnline() method that simply returns True if the machine has a valid network connection or False if it does not. Within the method, the class leverages a PInvoke to a function defined within the Windows API named InternetGetConnectedState. This function is not part of the managed-code world; therefore the class must first declare the function, detailing its parameters and the library that contains it (wininet). Listing 5-1 details the code within the ConnectionManager class.

Listing 5-1. *Determining If the Machine Has a Network Connection*

```
Public Class ConnectionManager
    Private Declare Function InternetGetConnectedState Lib "wininet"~
        (ByRef dwflags As Int32, ByVal dwReserved As Int32) As Boolean

    Public Shared Function IsOnline() As Boolean
        Dim dwflags As Long
        Dim WebTest As Boolean
        WebTest = InternetGetConnectedState(dwflags, 0&)
        Return WebTest
    End Function
End Class
```

The ConnectionManager class is used several places within the tool—whenever it needs to determine if it should even attempt a web service call to SharePoint. For example, consider when a user opens the workbook. If the user has saved changes that have not been persisted back to the SharePoint sites and a connection is available, we would want the user to know she has pending changes and then be directed to the synchronization interface. Listing 5-2 contains this code from the InitData method of Sheet1.

Listing 5-2. *Using the ConnectionManager*

```
If (ConnectionManager.IsOnline) Then
    If (Me.WorksheetData1.HasChanges) Then
        MessageBox.Show("You are online and have changes that have not~
                                been saved. Please Sync.")
        Globals.ThisWorkbook.m_taskPaneHeader.DisplaySyncDialog()
    End If
End If
```

Constructing the Actions Pane

Microsoft Office 2003 introduced the concept of panes that would display within the Office application alongside the document. These panes would allow the user to research information, search, or see other data within a SharePoint site. With Visual Studio Tools for Office you can build two types of panes yourself: *Task panes* are scoped at the application level and can be viewed even if a document is not open. *Actions panes* are used within a specific document. Both can be developed via .NET user controls. Figure 5-8 shows the end result we are looking for.

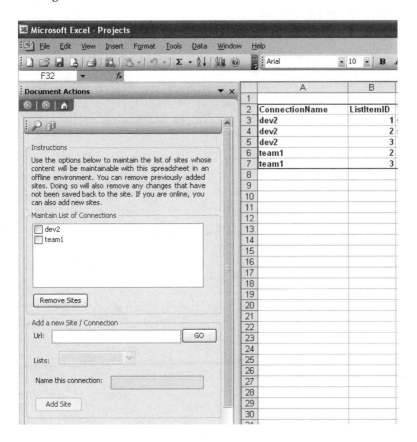

Figure 5-8. *A custom actions pane*

As we stated at the start of this chapter, we are not going to include every line of code in the text, so you will want to get the solution from the code download at http://apress.com and follow along. This will make it easier for us to focus on the important aspects of the solution and not get caught up in telling you the name and position of every text box, drop-down, or button. In this solution the actions pane is actually three user controls, not one. These controls are the header, body, and footer. We chose to create three so it would be easier to leave the header and footer as constant items and just swap other controls on and off of the body. In our example, the header contains the toolbar across the top of the pane and the footer contains a label in case we want to display any status information. The body is an empty user control that will selectively decide to hide or show other user controls depending on the interface we want to display.

Listing 5-3 contains code from the ThisWorkbook.vb class file. The three user controls are declared as fields of the workbook. A SetupTaskPane method is called within the workbook's startup event handler. This setup method establishes the size and position of the actions pane within the application. It then instantiates instances of the controls that will make up our pane's interface and adds them to the controls collection of the document's ActionsPane object. It also displays Sheet1 as the active worksheet.

Listing 5-3. *Setting Up the Document's Action Pane*

```
Friend WithEvents m_taskPaneHeader As TaskPaneHeader
Friend WithEvents m_taskPaneBody As TaskPaneBody
Friend WithEvents m_taskPaneFooter As TaskPaneFooter

Private Sub ThisWorkbook_Startup(ByVal sender As Object, ~
                    ByVal e As System.EventArgs) Handles Me.Startup
    SetupTaskPane()
End Sub

Private Sub SetupTaskPane()
    With Me.Application.CommandBars("Task Pane")
        .Width = 350
        .Position = Microsoft.Office.Core.MsoBarPosition.msoBarLeft
    End With
    Globals.Sheet1.Select()

    m_taskPaneHeader = New TaskPaneHeader()
    m_taskPaneBody = New TaskPaneBody()
    m_taskPaneFooter = New TaskPaneFooter()

    m_taskPaneHeader.Dock = DockStyle.Top
    m_taskPaneFooter.Dock = DockStyle.Bottom

    Me.ActionsPane.Controls.Add(m_taskPaneHeader)
    Me.ActionsPane.Controls.Add(m_taskPaneBody)
    Me.ActionsPane.Controls.Add(m_taskPaneFooter)
End Sub
```

Listing 5-3 establishes the pane's control structure, but places the toolbar and label on the pane only in terms of interface. The TaskPaneBody control will serve as host to most of the controls the user sees while using the tool. Instead of dragging text boxes and other controls onto the body directly, we chose to create other user controls that could be swapped on or off of the Body control. As Figure 5-9 shows, these controls are located in a Controls folder. We will go into greater detail on what they do in the next few sections of this chapter.

Figure 5-9. *The solution's actions-pane controls*

How do these controls get displayed to the user? If you look at the code of the TaskPane-Body control, which is shown in Listing 5-4, you will find that instances of these controls are declared, instantiated, and added to its controls collection. Notice that they are declared with a Public scope so that other code can easily set their visibility property. In fact, the TaskPane-Header control has a great example of what goes on when a user clicks a button in its toolbar.

Listing 5-4. *Loading Controls that Contain the User Interface for the Pane's Body*

```
Public WithEvents m_MaintainSites As MaintainSites
Public WithEvents m_SyncOptions As SyncOptions

Private Sub TaskPaneBody_Load(ByVal sender As Object, ~
             ByVal e As System.EventArgs) Handles Me.Load
   m_MaintainSites = New MaintainSites()
   Me.Controls.Add(m_MaintainSites)
   m_MaintainSites.Visible = True
   m_SyncOptions = New SyncOptions()
   Me.Controls.Add(m_SyncOptions)
   m_SyncOptions.Visible = False
End Sub
```

Maintaining the List of Site Connections

The interface that the user will see when opening the tool for the first time allows her to specify which Projects lists from which sites she wishes to manage in the spreadsheet. Each list that is maintained is stored with a connection name. This allows us to uniquely identify lists that may have the same name but were from different sites. Figure 5-10 shows the user control. The check-box list control at the top displays the set of established connections. A user can remove a connection, which in turn removes that list's items from the tool. The controls below the check box list enable new connections to be defined.

The two main actions the user can perform here are to add or delete a connection. To delete a connection, we are going to require that the DataSet has no pending changes. This is so that we can successfully remove the items for that connection and accept those changes to the DataSet without also accepting changes the user may have made. With this one restriction, the code to delete the connection and its items is very straightforward. Since we do allow the user to remove more than one connection in a single action (using the check boxes), the code in Listing 5-5 loops through the selected connections and deletes them from the DataSet's Lists DataTable. Since we set up the relation to cascade deletions to the child Projects Data-Table, this delete action also removes the associated list items. When the removal is complete, the changes to the DataSet are committed so that when we sync at some later time we don't accidentally delete these items from the site. They are simply no longer managed by the tool.

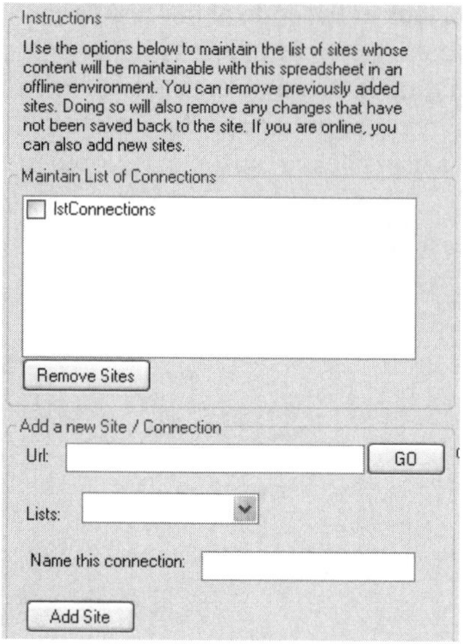

Figure 5-10. *Maintaining connections to Projects lists*

Listing 5-5. *Deleting Connections from the DataSet*

```
If (WorkSheetData1.Projects.GetChanges() Is Nothing) Then
    'we can make the deletion
    Dim items As ListBox.SelectedObjectCollection = lstConnections.SelectedItems
    Dim connectionName As String
    For Each connectionName In items
        Dim listRow as WorksheetData.ListsRow = ~
                    WorksheetData1.Lists.FindByConnectionName(connectionName)
        If (listRow IsNot Nothing) Then listRow.Delete()
    Next
    WorkSheetData1.AcceptChanges()
    PopulateCheckBoxList()
Else
    MessageBox.Show("You must be synced before removing a site connection.")
End If
```

Adding a new connection to the DataSet involves the user first entering the URL of the SharePoint site that contains the list she wants to maintain. The URL for the site should be in the format of http://portal.sample.com/SiteDirectory/dev2. Once the URL is entered and the user clicks the Go button, the solution examines the site to discover what lists it contains. In particular it is looking for lists that were created using the Projects list definition. Listing 5-6 shows the first half of this examination, where the application invokes SharePoint's Lists.asmx web service requesting information about the collection of lists in the site. This web-service call uses the URL of the site with the _vti_bin directory at the end of its URL. This technique of calling the web service through the site's URL informs the web service of the context of the call. This way the web service will return only list information for the site we are interested in. The call itself is asynchronous. The GetListCollectionCompleted method will be invoked when a response (or a timeout) is received.

Listing 5-6. *Asking a SharePoint Site for Information on Its Lists*

```
Private Sub btnExamine_Click(ByVal sender As System.Object, ~
            ByVal e As System.EventArgs) Handles btnExamine.Click
   'connect to the site and find lists that are instances of the project template
   If (Not ConnectionManager.IsOnline) Then
      MessageBox.Show("You need an internet connection add new lists.")
      Exit Sub
   End If
   Dim listService As WSLists.Lists = New WSLists.Lists
   listService.Credentials = System.Net.CredentialCache.DefaultCredentials
   listService.Url = Me.txtUrl.Text + "/_vti_bin/lists.asmx"
   AddHandler listService.GetListCollectionCompleted, _
                          AddressOf GetListCollectionCompleted
   listService.GetListCollectionAsync()
End Sub
```

When a response is received, the GetListCollectionCompleted method first checks to make sure there was not an error. If there wasn't, the result is an XmlNode that contains information on the lists in the site. Loading this into an XML document object enables us to query for the lists that were constructed using the Projects list definition. Remember that we set the Projects list definition type identifier to 1001. The code in Listing 5-7 shows how we can use an XPath query to select these lists from all of the others. Assuming some were found, the details of the lists are loaded into a DataTable that is bound to the drop-down in the interface.

Listing 5-7. *Selecting the Lists of Projects Type from the Response*

```
Dim projLibNode As XmlNodeList =~
      xmlDoc.SelectNodes("//sp:List[@ServerTemplate='1001']", namespaceMgr)
If (projLibNode Is Nothing Or projLibNode.Count = 0) Then
    'alert that none were found
    MessageBox.Show("No lists of type Projects were found in the site")
Else
   'store the name  and url of each proj list
   foundLists.Rows.Clear()
   Dim xmlNode As XmlNode
   For Each xmlNode In projLibNode
       Dim listRow As WorksheetData.ListsRow = foundLists.NewListsRow()
       listRow.ListName = xmlNode.Attributes("Title").InnerText
       listRow.ConnectionName = listRow.ListName
       …
```

The last step of adding a connection to the DataSet is for the user to select one of the project lists of the site and to name the connection. When the user clicks the Add Site button, the chosen connection is added to the DataSet. We inform the user that she will not see the items of this list in the tool until she performs synchronization. To help the synchronization process identify that that this list is a newly added one in the DataSet, we set its LastModified field to `DateTime.MinValue`. You will see this value used in the next section as part of Listing 5-8.

Constructing the Synchronization Interface

The synchronization interface can be brought to the forefront by the user clicking the Data button in actions pane's header. This interface persists changes the user has made to the project list items back to their respective SharePoint sites, as well as load changes from those lists back into the tool. When the interface is displayed, it informs the user of the last time the tool synchronized. This value is stored in the Settings DataTable of the DataSet. The interface also informs the user of the number of new lists the user added as new connections. These items need to be retrieved into the tool. Additionally, the interface displays the number of pending changes the user has made to items managed within the tool and that need to be saved back to the sites. These statistics are updated whenever the visibility of the synchronization interface is changed or if the user clicks the Refresh button. We have also included a Manage Collisions (Conflicts) area, which we will discuss in the "Extension Points" part of this chapter. Figure 5-11 shows this interface.

Figure 5-11. *The synchronization interface*

This control uses an UpdateSyncStats method to update the values of the number of new lists and the number of changes. Listing 5-8 shows the portion of this method that is responsible for determining the number of new connections. These connections were added by the user and at this point the tool has never retrieved any of the user's list items. Recall that we set the LastModified field to `DateTime.MinValue` for these new lists. The method leverages this, creating a view of the DataSet's List DataTable filtering for that value.

Listing 5-8. *Determining Number of New Lists to Capture*

```
Public Sub UpdateSyncStats()
    newListsView = New DataView(WorkSheetData1.Lists)
    newListsView.RowFilter = "LastModified='" + DateTime.MinValue.ToString() + "'"~
    Me.lblSyncNewLists.Text = String.Format(~
        "{0}: Number of new lists to capture",~
        newListsView.Count)
```

The UpdateSyncStats method determines the number of changes the user has made by calling the GetChanges method of the DataSet's Projects DataTable. As Listing 5-9 shows, if this method returns a DataTable object, then there are pending changes that need to be saved back to SharePoint sites.

Listing 5-9. *Determining the Number of Changes to Managed Items*

```
Dim changedItemsTable As DataTable =~
        WorkSheetData1.Projects.GetChanges()
If (changedItemsTable IsNot Nothing) Then
    Me.lblSyncChanges.Text = String.Format(~
    "{0}: Number of changes you made to data",~
    changedItemsTable.Rows.Count)
Else
    Me.lblSyncChanges.Text = String.Format(~
     "{0}: Number of changes you made to data",~
     0)
End If
End Sub
```

Architecting the Synchronization Process

The synchronization process is responsible for committing any changes that the user made to project information in the tool and making those same changes to the list items in the SharePoint sites. The process must also retrieve any list items that have been modified in the sites' lists from the last synchronization time. This includes retrieving items for any new connections. The tool's synchronization process accounts for most of the code in the solution. It is easiest to understand by viewing the entire process as a sequence of steps. These steps are shown in Figure 5-12, and detailed in the sections that follow.

■**Note** We deliberately simplified the synchronization process used in this solution to make the code easier to follow, focusing on how you can develop a solution that interacts with the SharePoint list content. In some solutions it would be necessary to include a lot more collision/conflict resolution to deal with scenarios related to changes in the site having occurred while the current user was offline. We detail how you should elaborate on the synchronization process in the "Extension Points" section of this chapter.

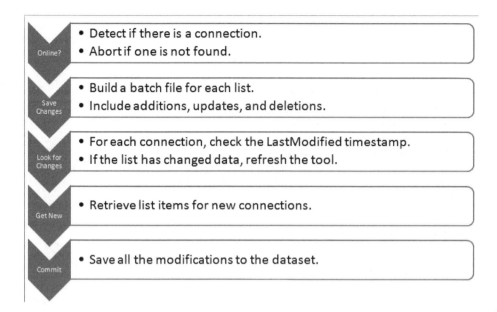

Figure 5-12. *The synchronization process*

Our synchronization process first makes sure the tool is not offline. If a connection is present, it begins to create a batch for each list to contain the changes the user made to its list items. This batch contains additions, updates, and deletions. Once the user-made changes are persisted back to the SharePoint sites, the tool looks for lists that have been modified since the last synchronization. If any are found, the items for that list are refreshed into the DataSet. When all of the changes have been retrieved, the tool grabs the content for the new connections. Finally, the changes made to the DataSet are committed so that we will be able to identify changes the user makes from this synchronization point. The remainder of this section details each of these steps and shows you key code fragments. If you have not done so already, please retrieve this project from the code download at http://apress.com so you can follow along.

Online?

For the synchronization process to be successful, the tool needs to be running on a machine with an enabled network connection. It shouldn't surprise you that we leverage the ConnectionManager class described earlier to make this check. This check only makes sure that there is a connection. It does not make sure that the SharePoint server is reachable. Therefore it is still possible to get a Not Found error when making the web-service calls. Listing 5-10 shows the use of the ConnectionManager class.

Listing 5-10. *Verifying that There Is a Network Connection*

```
If (Not ConnectionManager.IsOnline) Then
   MessageBox.Show("You need an internet connection to sync.")
   Exit Sub
End If
```

Save Changes

SharePoint's Lists.asmx web service has an UpdateListItems method that allows us to send a batch of actions to perform on items for a specific list. To build this batch, we need to first detect which rows in the DataSet's Projects DataTable have been modified by the user. A modification could mean a new row, an updated row, or a deleted row. Fortunately, the Projects DataTable provides us with a GetChanges method that returns all of the modified rows. Each row in turn has a RowStatus that tells us specifically if the modification was an addition, an update, or a deletion. The Save Changes process begins by looping through the different connections we have in the Lists DataTable and filtering the changed Projects rows to see if any of them were owned by that list. A DataManager class (which we will examine a bit later) starts a batch and records the actions made to items of that list. If changes are found, the DataManager class sends the batch to the SharePoint server for it to make the same changes to its list items. Listing 5-11 displays the code for this process.

Listing 5-11. *Finding Changes to the DataSet*

```
Dim list As WorksheetData.ListsRow
'Save changes made by user by connection (add, update, and delete)
Dim data As DataTable = WorkSheetData1.Projects.GetChanges()
If (data IsNot Nothing) Then
    For Each list In WorkSheetData1.Lists
        Dim dManager As DataManager = New DataManager()
        Dim batch As XmlDocument = dManager.CreateProjectBatch()
        'filter by each connection and build a batch
        Dim foundChanges = False
        'new and modified rows
        Dim dv As DataView = New DataView(data, "ConnectionName='" +~
            list.ConnectionName + "'", String.Empty, DataViewRowState.CurrentRows)
        If (dv.Count > 0) Then
           SaveChanges(dManager, batch, dv)
           foundChanges = True
        End If
        'deleted rows
        dv.RowStateFilter = DataViewRowState.Deleted
        If (dv.Count > 0) Then
           SaveChanges(dManager, batch, dv)
           foundChanges = True
        End If
        'save?
        If (foundChanges) Then dManager.CommitBatch(batch, list.ListName, list.Url)
    Next
End If
WorkSheetData1.Projects.AcceptChanges()
```

For each list that the tool identified as having changed items, the solution will make a single web-service call to persist those changes back to the SharePoint site. This is accomplished by recording the changes in a batch XML document that is passed to the UpdateListItems method of the Lists.asmx web service. The code in Listing 5-11 uses a SaveChanges method and a DataManager class to assist in building the batch XML. Before looking at this code, it is important to understand the end goal. Listing 5-12 contains a sample batch XML fragment that adds a new item, deletes an item, and updates an item. Notice how the add action does not provide an ID since the list will autogenerate one. The delete command needs only the list item's identifier to perform its operation. The update command needs to specify the ID of the item to apply the changes as well as values for the columns of the list. The "Further Reading" section of this chapter includes a link for more information on the UpdateListItems method.

Listing 5-12. *Batch XML Dxample for UpdateListItems*

```
<Batch OnError="Continue" >
    <Method ID="1" Cmd="New">
        <Field Name="Title">Sample Title</Field>
        <Field Name="ProjectNumber">12345</Field>
    </Method>
    <Method ID="2" Cmd="Delete">
        <Field Name="ID">4</Field>
    </Method>
    <Method ID="3" Cmd="Update">
        <Field Name="ID">5</Field>
        <Field Name="Title">Updated Title</Field>
        <Field Name="ProjectNumber">22222</Field>
    </Method>
</Batch>
```

To build the batch, the DataManager class first constructs an empty XML document with only the outer Batch element. Listing 5-13 provides this code.

Listing 5-13. *Creating the Batch*

```
Public Function CreateProjectBatch() As XmlDocument
    Dim batchXml As XmlDocument = New XmlDocument()
    Dim rootNode As XmlElement = batchXml.CreateElement("Batch")
    Dim attribute As XmlAttribute
    attribute = batchXml.CreateAttribute("OnError")
    attribute.InnerText = "Continue"
    rootNode.Attributes.Append(attribute)
    batchXml.AppendChild(rootNode)
    Return batchXml
End Function
```

Notice how the code in Listing 5-11 made calls to a SaveChanges method when it found changed items for a list. This method is displayed in Listing 5-14. In its implementation, it loops through the modified Projects rows, checking the RowState property of each. This property will tell us the type of modification that was made. Depending on the RowState value, different methods of the DataManager class are called to create the corresponding Method element in the batch.

Listing 5-14. *Detecting the Type of Modification Made to the Row*

```
Public Sub SaveChanges(ByVal dManager As DataManager, _
                ByVal batch As XmlDocument, ByVal dv As DataView)
    Dim drv As DataRowView
    For Each drv In dv
        Dim project As WorksheetData.ProjectsRow =~
                CType(drv.Row, WorksheetData.ProjectsRow)
        Select Case project.RowState
            Case DataRowState.Modified
                    dManager.BatchUpdateProject(drv, batch)
            Case DataRowState.Added
                    dManager.BatchAddProject(drv, batch)
            Case DataRowState.Deleted
                    dManager.BatchDeleteProject(drv, batch)
        End Select
    Next
End Sub
```

The DataManager class includes a subroutine for each type of method that needs to be added to the batch XML. Listing 5-15 shows the subroutine responsible for creating the updated version of the methods. Its implementation adds a new Method element with an ID that is simply a running total of the number of methods in the batch. The routine then continues to add the values for the different fields of the Projects list item.

Listing 5-15. *Adding an Update Method to the Batch*

```
Public Sub BatchUpdateProject(ByVal projectRow As DataRowView, _
            ByVal batchXml As XmlDocument)
    Dim methodNode As XmlElement = batchXml.CreateElement("Method")
    Dim attribute As XmlAttribute
    attribute = batchXml.CreateAttribute("ID")
    attribute.InnerText = batchXml.DocumentElement.ChildNodes.Count + 1
    methodNode.Attributes.Append(attribute)
    attribute = batchXml.CreateAttribute("Cmd")
    attribute.InnerText = "Update"
    methodNode.Attributes.Append(attribute)
    CreateFieldNode(methodNode, "ID", projectRow.Item("ListItemID").ToString())
    CreateFieldNode(methodNode, "Budget", projectRow.Item("Budget").ToString())
    CreateFieldNode(methodNode, "ProjectNumber",~
            projectRow.Item("ProjectNumber").ToString())
    CreateFieldNode(methodNode, "StartDate", CType(projectRow.Item("StartDate"),
            DateTime).ToString("yyyy-MM-dd HH:mm:ss"))
    CreateFieldNode(methodNode, "Title", projectRow.Item("Title").ToString())
    batchXml.DocumentElement.AppendChild(methodNode)
End Sub
```

When the synchronization process has completed building a batch for one of its managed lists, it needs to send the batch XML to the SharePoint site. This is accomplished using the

UpdateListItems method of SharePoint's Lists.asmx web service. Listing 5-16 shows the CommitBatch method of the DataManager that performs this action.

Listing 5-16. *Committing the Batch*

```
Public Sub CommitBatch(ByVal batchXml As XmlDocument, _
      ByVal listName As String, ByVal Url As String)
   Dim listService As WSLists.Lists = New WSLists.Lists
   listService.Credentials = System.Net.CredentialCache.DefaultCredentials
   listService.Url = Url + "/_vti_bin/lists.asmx"
   Dim returnInfo As XmlNode = listService.UpdateListItems(listName, ~
      batchXml.DocumentElement)
End Sub
```

■**Note** There is one more step that would be valuable; we cover it in the "Extension Points" section of this chapter. The call to UpdateListItems will return an XML result with details of the success or failure of each Method action. This would be important if we wanted to be sensitive to the user trying to update and item that another user had deleted from the site, or if a user were trying to delete something that is no longer there. Each of these cases could be detected in the UpdateListItems response, and you may want to ask the user what action should be taken instead of simply continuing.

Look for Changes

The next step in the synchronization process is for the tool to retrieve updates that have happened to each list since the last sync. These changes could be deletions, edits, or new items that other users have made while the application was offline. It may not be obvious, but these changes include the ones the tool just saved back to the sites. Since our changes may have added new items that were assigned their own ListItemID values, we want to make sure that our DataSet matches the values in the SharePoint sites. We can tell if a list has any changes we need by comparing its LastModified date with the timestamp we have in the DataSet. If the LastModified date is later, then there are changes in that list that we need to capture in our tool. We could do something fancy here like retrieve only the items that have a modified date later than the one in our DataSet and then perform a merge. Instead, we simply remove all the items for that list from the DataSet and recapture all of the list items. This capture also sets the list's LastModified date in the DataSet to reflect the current value in the SharePoint site. Listing 5-17 shows the code that contains this logic.

Listing 5-17. *Capturing Lists with Changed Items*

```
For Each list In WorkSheetData1.Lists
   Dim dManager As DataManager = New DataManager()
   Dim currentModifiedDate As DateTime =~
           dManager.GetListLastModified(list.ListName, list.Url)
   If (list.LastModified < currentModifiedDate) Then
      DeleteItems(list)
```

```
        GetAllItemsForList(list)
        WorkSheetData1.AcceptChanges()
    End If
Next
```

The application captures the items from a list by calling the GetListItems method of the Lists.asmx SharePoint web service. Again, this web service is called using the URL of the site to establish context. The parameters for this call include the name of the list, a query XML fragment, and an XML fragment with the list of fields we want returned. In this case we want all of the items of the list, so there is no need to specify any type of filter or where clause in the query. We request that the Title, ProjectNumber, StartDate, and Budget fields be included in the response. The "Further Reading" section of this chapter includes a link for more information on the GetListItems method. Listing 5-18 shows the method of the DataManager class that wraps this web-service call.

Listing 5-18. *Retrieving All Items of a List*

```
Public Function GetListItems(ByVal listName As String, ByVal url As String) ~
        As XmlNode
    Dim listService As WSLists.Lists = New WSLists.Lists
    listService.Credentials = System.Net.CredentialCache.DefaultCredentials
    listService.Url = url + "/_vti_bin/lists.asmx"
    Dim xmlDoc As XmlDocument = New XmlDocument()
    Dim ndQuery As XmlNode =~
        xmlDoc.CreateNode(XmlNodeType.Element, "Query", "")
    Dim ndViewFields As XmlNode =~
        xmlDoc.CreateNode(XmlNodeType.Element, "ViewFields", "")
    Dim ndQueryOptions As XmlNode =~
        xmlDoc.CreateNode(XmlNodeType.Element, "QueryOptions", "")
    ndQueryOptions.InnerXml =~
        "<IncludeMandatoryColumns>FALSE</IncludeMandatoryColumns>"
    ndViewFields.InnerXml =~
        "<FieldRef Name='Title'/><FieldRef Name='ProjectNumber'/>~
        <FieldRef Name='StartDate'/><FieldRef Name='Budget'/>"
    ndQuery.InnerXml = ""
    Dim ndItems As XmlNode
    ndItems = listService.GetListItems(listName, Nothing, ndQuery, ndViewFields, _
        Nothing, ndQueryOptions, Nothing)
    Return ndItems
End Function
```

The response of the GetListItems call in Listing 5-18 is an XML representation of all of the items in the list. If you examine the code download (in the Source Code/Download section of http://apress.com), you will see that this response is loaded into an XML document, allowing us to iterate through the set of items. For each item, a new row is added to the Projects Data-Table of the DataSet, which as a result stores the fields we are interested in.

Get New

After our user's changes have been saved back to the SharePoint sites and the changes in the sites have been refreshed in our DataSet, the next step is to capture the content for any newly added connections. This process is almost identical to the "Look for Changes" step except that there is no content in the DataSet that needs to be removed. In fact, we can leverage the same GetListItems method of the DataManager class since we want to retrieve all items for the new list. The code in Listing 5-19 shows that each new list's LastModified timestamp is recorded and then its items are added to the DataSet.

Listing 5-19. *Getting Items for Newly Added Lists*

```
Public Sub GetAllItemsForList(ByVal row As WorksheetData.ListsRow)
    Dim dManager As DataManager = New DataManager()
    'record the last modified time
    row.LastModified = dManager.GetListLastModified(row.ListName, row.Url)
    'Get items of this list
    Dim ndItems As XmlNode
    ndItems = dManager.GetListItems(row.ListName, row.Url)
    'add these items to the spreadsheet's dataset
    AddNewItems(ndItems, row.ConnectionName)
End Sub
```

Commit

The final step of the synchronization process is to commit all the changes we have made to the DataSet. As the code in Listing 5-20 shows, this is accomplished with the AcceptChanges method of the DataSet. We also record the current timestamp into the Settings DataTable so we can inform the user of the time of her last synchronization. Recording this information in the Settings DataTable is abstracted with a SettingsManager class.

Listing 5-20. *Committing the Synchronization*

```
'commit changes
SettingsManager.LastSyncTime = DateTime.Now.ToString()
WorkSheetData1.AcceptChanges()
Me.lblSyncStatus.Text = "Done"
lblLastSyncMessage.Text = SettingsManager. LastSyncTime
UpdateSyncStats()
```

Getting the Data on the Spreadsheet

Fortunately, displaying the DataSet's data on the spreadsheet requires much less code than the synchronization process. In fact, it requires no code at all. Open the designer of Sheet1. In Visual Studio's toolbox, locate the ListObject control in the Excel Controls group. This control will allow us to bind a range of cells to the Projects DataTable in the DataSet. Drag it onto the spreadsheet and specify it to occupy the **$A$2:$F$2** range. Then use the Properties window to specify a data source. Clicking on the down arrow of this property should display a dialog.

Select the WorksheetData1 DataSet in the Sheet1 List Instances category. Once that property has been set, select the Projects DataTable as the value for the DataMember property. The ListObject should refresh to display the column names for this DataTable. You have now bound the ListObject control so that it will display the items in the Projects DataTable of our DataSet. Your spreadsheet should look like Figure 5-13.

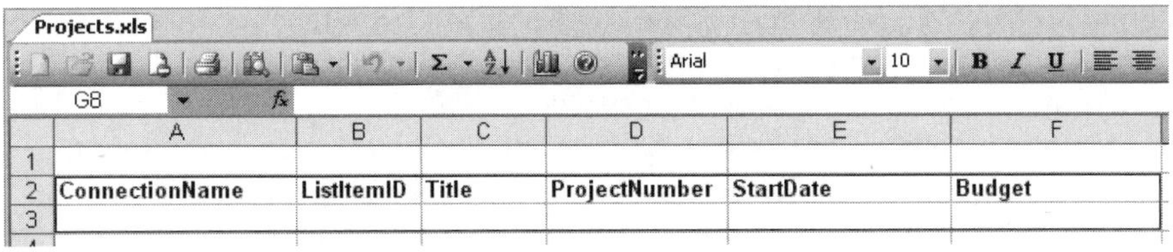

Figure 5-13. *Binding the ListObject to the Projects DataTable*

Using the Tool

Before running the solution, make sure you close the spreadsheet that's open in Visual Studio's designer. This is because running the program will launch Excel, which will open the workbook generated in the bin directory of your project. The same spreadsheet cannot be open in Visual Studio's designer and in Excel.

For a test, have at least two team sites with the Projects list definition available and a few list items already created. In our development environment, these sites were named dev2 and team1. We named both lists Projects just to illustrate the need for the connection-name value. Click the Start Debugging button in Visual Studio. Note that this action builds your solution and therefore the workbook. The solution will open more slowly in this scenario than normal and this action causes a new file to be created, which would wipe away the DataSet cache from a previous run. We will provide more detail on how to test the cache a bit later.

Add the two connections for your sites. Remember the URL should be in the format: `http://portal.sample.com/SiteDirectory/dev2`. In each case, we named the connection the name of the site. Use the actions pane's header to display the synchronization interface. This should tell you that there are two new lists for which you need to get content. Click the Sync Now button and watch the ListObject populate with your sites' content. The result should look like Figure 5-14.

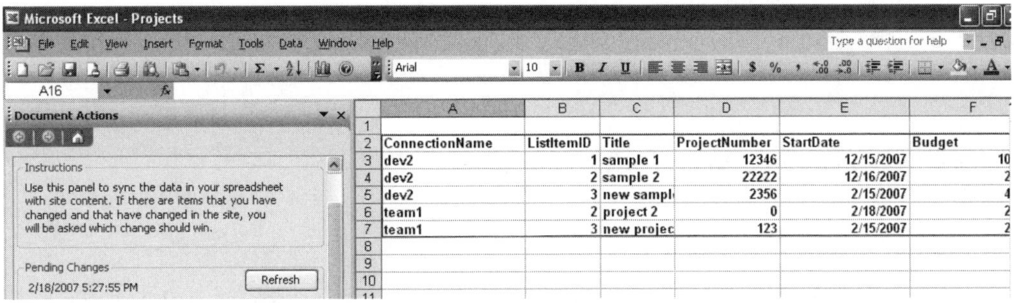

Figure 5-14. *Testing the tool*

Now make some changes. Change a title or a project number for one row. You can also highlight one whole row and right-click to delete it. If you place your cursor at the bottom of the ListObject where there is an asterisk (*), you can define a new row. When specifying a new item, you need to enter in a valid connection name and a unique list-item identifier. Remember that these two fields make up the primary key. (The list-item identifier doesn't really matter as long as it is an unused value, as we will pick up the actual value when we sync.) After you have made some changes, click Refresh in the synchronization interface; it will update to tell you the number of pending changes. Click the Sync Now button and revisit the lists in the SharePoint sites. Verify that your changes were persisted.

To see the caching capability, close Excel. When the application asks you if you want to save changes, select Yes. By saving the file, you are persisting the DataSet with the document. Closing the document should end your debug session in Visual Studio. Use Windows Explorer and navigate to your solution's bin directory. Double-click the `Projects.xls` file to open in Excel. Notice that the data is already there. (If you are using a virtual development environment, you can explore removing its network connection to confirm that the tool is able to detect it.)

Building Visualizations in Excel

One of the key benefits of this solution is that the data from multiple SharePoint lists is consolidated into a single Excel spreadsheet. This means that the user can leverage the visualization capabilities of Excel to compare, contrast, or understand her data. Take Figure 5-15 as an example. This chart shows the breakdown of money being spent on projects. Another interesting benefit of having the data in Excel is the fact that the column headings of the ListObject support filtering.

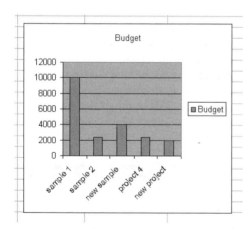

Figure 5-15. *Visualizing the SharePoint list data*

Running in Excel 2007

We are assuming that you are anxious to take this Excel 2003 smart document and copy it over to your development environment that has Excel 2007 to confirm that it runs there. It will; however, you will need to set up a code access security policy to allow Excel to access your code-behind assembly. Visual Studio was doing this for you when you ran the solution in your Office 2003/Visual Studio development environment. If you want to see this in action immediately as opposed to building a formal deployment strategy, follow these steps to set up a code-access security policy before opening `Project.xls` in Excel 2007:

1. Open the .NET Framework 2.0 Configuration tool from the administrative tools.

2. Expand My Computer.

3. Expand Runtime Security Policy.

4. Expand User.

5. Expand Code Groups.

6. Expand All_Code.

7. If you have a VSTOProjects node, expand it as well.

8. Right-click on either All_Code or VSTOProjects and select New.

9. Name the code group **MaintainContentOffline** and click Next.

10. Select URL as the condition for the code group. Specify the full path to the `MaintainContentOffline.dll` file. In our environment, this was `C:\Projects\MaintainContentOffline\MaintainContentOffline\bin\Debug\MaintainContentOffline.dll`.

11. Select Full Trust as the permission set to grant to the assembly.

12. Click Finish.

You should now be able to launch `Projects.xls` in Excel 2007. The spreadsheet will run in backward-compatibility mode, but all of the functionality for displaying the actions pane, caching the DataSet, and synchronizing will work as it did in Excel 2003.

Considering Deployment Options

For document-level projects (also called smart documents), an administrator needs to select a deployment model for distributing the customized document as well as the code-behind assembly. There are three main models characterized by the location of the files. Each has its benefits, and depending on your needs any one of them could be ideal.

The Local/Local deployment model is one where both the customized document and the assembly are deployed to the end user's desktop machine. This model is best suited when the solution needs to be available regardless of that machine's network state. This model can become quite cumbersome if there are frequent updates to either the document or the assembly, as the updates need to be distributed to user machines.

The Local/Network deployment model involves deploying the document to the user's computer but making the assembly available through the network. This could be accomplished using a network share or a web server. This is the most common deployment model, as it offers the widest range of benefits. It offers a single point of maintenance for the assembly for solutions where those changes are more likely than updates to the document. Also, the end-user machines will cache a copy of this assembly locally so the customized document can continue to work when the network is unavailable. However, any updates to the document still need to be distributed and now an administrator must properly secure the network resource.

The Network/Network deployment model places both the document and the assembly on a network share or web server. For solutions in which change is frequent this is ideal since the document and assembly are in a single location for all users. However, users must be connected to the network or the entire solution becomes unavailable.

Once you have decided on a deployment model, you can use the following references as a guide to walk you through the creation of the setup project that you'll use to deploy your solution. These walkthroughs include the creation of the installer, dealing with prerequisites, and configuring code-access security.

- Deploying Visual Studio 2005 Tools for Office Solutions Using Windows Installer (Part 1 of 2)

  `http://msdn2.microsoft.com/en-us/library/aa537173(office.11).aspx`

- Deploying Visual Studio 2005 Tools for Office Solutions Using Windows Installer (Part 2 of 2)

  `http://msdn2.microsoft.com/en-us/library/aa537179(office.11).aspx`

Important Lessons

The solution in this chapter incorporated several key techniques that are worth highlighting, as they could be reused easily in other projects.

VSTO document-level projects: The solution detailed how to customize an Excel workbook with .NET code to create a tool for an end user. This included adding an actions pane for additional user-interface elements and controls dragged onto the surface of the worksheet itself. To construct these solutions, the development environment must be Office 2003–based even though the end result will run in Office 2007.

Creating a list definition: We wanted to provide different SharePoint sites with a definition of a custom list that they could use uniformly to store project information. To create the list definition, we constructed an instance of it in a SharePoint site and used the SharePoint Solution Generator to capture it. The SharePoint Solution Generator created the list definition as a Visual Studio project, wrapping it in a feature definition that a site administrator could activate.

Discovering a site's lists and libraries: One of the interaction points this application had with SharePoint was to query the site to discover what lists and libraries it contained. This was accomplished through SharePoint's `Lists.asmx` web service. The GetListCollection method of this web service returned XML that detailed the lists and libraries that the site contained. With this XML, the solution used an XPath query to find all lists of a certain type, filtering on the ServerTemplate attribute.

Caching a DataSet in a document: Document-level projects in VSTO have the ability to persist a DataSet within the document. This is useful in offline scenarios in which you want your user to be able to continue to work with the data when its source is unavailable. To enable this functionality, the developer had to set the modifier of the DataSet instance to Public and set the CacheInDocument property to True. The DataSet is automatically cached when the document is saved.

Using a batch to update list items: The solution included a synchronization process that involved making changes to items in a SharePoint list. It was expected that there would be many changes to different items in the same list. The solution used the UpdateListItems method of SharePoint's `Lists.asmx` web service to make this possible. This method received an XML batch containing methods for each modification that should be made to items in the list.

Extension Points

While coding this example, we thought of several variations to the solution that we didn't incorporate because they distracted from the overall objective of the solution. We call them out now as extension points since they may be applicable to a specific project you are working on.

Extend collision detection: The synchronization process in the solution was quite simple and would likely need to be extended in other scenarios. Collisions and conflicts occur when the data in the SharePoint site has changed since the tool's last retrieval. What should happen when a user updates an item in the tool but the item has been deleted? What should happen if the user sends an update to an item that has already been updated? You may need to incorporate these scenarios in your solution. There are two points of opportunity for this collision detection in the code. You can detect an operation against an already deleted item by examining the response from the UpdateListItems method. Each action in the batch will have a node in the XML response. Included in this XML will be an error code that will tell you if the action could not be applied. This will solve most of the collisions, but not the one in which an update has happened in the site while the user was making her own changes. To account for this type of collision, you would want to retrieve all items in the list that were modified since the LastModified date in the DataSet. A method named GetListItemsChanges in the `Lists.asmx` service facilitates this. You could then check to see if a ListItemID is in this response as well as the batch you are about to send to the site. If such a ListItemID exists in both, then it has been modified in the site by another user, as well as locally by the user of the tool. If appropriate, ask the user to resolve which update she wants to keep.

Enhance the refresh process for changed items: In our example we refreshed a modified list by simply deleting all of the items in our DataSet and retrieving a fresh copy. This is adequate for lists that are not going to have a large number of items. There is a point, though, where this is a waste of time. An enhanced approach would be to ask for only the items that have been modified since the LastModified date in the DataSet and then merge those results into the DataSet. The GetListItemsChanges method of the `Lists.asmx` service facilitates this.

Further Reading

The following links are to resources a reader interested in this chapter's material will find useful:

- VSTO Deployment Models

  http://msdn2.microsoft.com/en-us/library/7b37fkst(vs.80).aspx

- UpdateListItems Method

  http://msdn2.microsoft.com/en-us/library/ms953758.aspx

- GetListItems Method

  http://msdn2.microsoft.com/en-us/library/ms953738.aspx

- DataSet.GetChanges Method

  http://msdn2.microsoft.com/en-gb/library/0f8054fy.aspx

- Smart Document Developer Portal

  http://msdn2.microsoft.com/en-us/office/aa905531.aspx

- Building an Excel 2003 Invoice Application Using Visual Studio 2005 Tools for Office

  http://msdn2.microsoft.com/en-us/library/aa537192(office.11).aspx

- Redesigning an Excel VBA Solution for .NET Using Visual Studio 2005 Tools for Office

  http://msdn2.microsoft.com/en-us/library/aa537191(office.11).aspx

CHAPTER 6

■ ■ ■

Integrating Spreadsheets into the Enterprise

Information workers have become accustomed to modeling business calculations with spreadsheets in Microsoft Excel. These spreadsheets may be updated on a time interval and distributed throughout the organization. This distribution is likely through email. There are many consequences to this strategy. Since there are so many copies of the spreadsheet, the organization loses its sense of what the authoritative version is. The spreadsheets themselves may be very large and laden with computations that make it unresponsive on an average desktop computer. In addition, the distributed spreadsheet contains the formulas and calculation logic that may be intellectual property that needs to be protected. Microsoft Office SharePoint Server 2007 provides a new application service called Excel Services that supports the publishing of such a spreadsheet so that users can view it using only their web browser. This means that there is one version of the truth, no large files to distribute, and the spreadsheet is processed on the server using its resources rather than the user's desktop.

Those advantages are usually enough to pique the interest of an organization, but developers will alert the business that such spreadsheets are usually stand-alone and don't play a major role in the enterprise's applications. Often users are copying values from legacy systems into the spreadsheets. There may be organizational systems that should impose their logic on the spreadsheet that are left out. And most importantly, the spreadsheet's calculation is not reusable. Developers often have to dissect the spreadsheet to incorporate the same logic into their applications.

For this chapter, we will detail how, as a developer, you can enhance Excel Services to incorporate methods of a .NET class. This way, the spreadsheet will be able to connect to external systems, databases, and even web services. Plus the methods can perform calculations that are not possible with Excel's native functions. We will also show you how the spreadsheet's calculation logic can be incorporated into a custom application without removing the possibility of the spreadsheet being modified by a business user.

Real-World Examples

We have encountered many customers whose users maintain and distribute large numbers of spreadsheets as part of the daily business process. Teams that coordinate floors of a hospital maintain spreadsheets of resources allocated to rooms. Housing companies maintain goals for production schedules. We have even worked with a military branch that uses Excel to record all the open positions and assignments of officers. In every instance, the maintenance of this data was a manual process and productivity was lost when users were unaware that they had an out-of-date version of the file. Even if the organization decides to centralize the spreadsheets in a file share or a document library, there is still the issue of download times for branch offices since the whole Excel file must be transported to the user before it will open. As a consultant, it is not unusual to walk into a requirements meeting where the customer has a pile of spreadsheet files that "show" what an application has to do. Of course, this logic is almost never complete and the calculations change over time. Unfortunately, developers often bake this calculation logic into their application, making it necessary to continually release updates to accommodate them. Decoupling this logic from the application would make it possible to decrease maintenance costs.

Solution Overview

For this solution, we will work with a spreadsheet that contains calculations for pricing a product. This begins with the base price it costs the company to manufacture the product. This price incorporates costs associated with raw materials, energy, etc. There is then a per-centage markup for a retail cost. Customers may get a volume discount based on the number of items they are placing in the order. Sales tax as well as shipping and handling costs must also be incorporated into the calculation.

The solution integrates this spreadsheet into the enterprise by registering methods of a .NET class so that Excel can call them as it would native functions. These methods will show how you can incorporate calls to external systems such as databases and web services. This connects the spreadsheet into other enterprise resources so that it is using accurate data as part of its calculations.

Once extended, the spreadsheet is published to Microsoft Office SharePoint Server's Excel Services so that users can view and interact with the spreadsheet through their web browser. This technique guarantees that there is a single, authoritative version of the spreadsheet. It also reduces the workload on the viewer's desktop since the spreadsheet's calculations are per-formed on the server. Additionally, it protects the logic in the spreadsheet by not exposing formulas or workbook elements that an end user doesn't need to see, and in fact we can lever-age SharePoint's item-level security to prevent direct access to the original spreadsheet file. Even after the spreadsheet has been published, we will be able to support a properly author-ized business user opening the spreadsheet and tweaking the calculations such as the markup percentage and the volume discount table.

Last, the solution will show you how developers can incorporate the spreadsheet's calcu-lation logic in their custom applications. This approach increases the flexibility of their solution since the calculation logic remains in the spreadsheet and is not hard-coded into the custom application. In fact, authorized business users can continue to edit the spreadsheet after the custom solution has been deployed. This integration is possible because of Excel Services' web-service API.

Solution Walkthrough

This section will detail the major elements of the solution and the decisions that were made in coding it. The walkthrough will introduce you to the product-pricing spreadsheet we will use as our example. We will construct two external sources for the spreadsheet to communicate with: a products database containing base price information, and a sample web service used to calculate shipping costs. We will go into detail about how to build a .NET class whose methods will be exposed as Excel functions. We will also show you the necessary COM plumbing that the class needs so it can be used in Excel 2007, as well as the configuration tasks needed for it to run in Excel Services. We will then walk you through publishing the spreadsheet to Excel Services. Finally, we will show how a custom application can interact with it through web services.

Introducing the Spreadsheet

For our example, we will be working with an instance of the Product Pricing Calculator spreadsheet template. This spreadsheet, shown in Figure 6-1, provides a way of capturing the rules and calculations involved in determining a discounted price for a product. These rules include the percentage markup from the company's base price and volume discounts, as well as calculations for shipping and sales tax.

			A1	▼	*f*x		
	B		C		D		E

Model Key

Numbers in white cells are entered by user.

Numbers in gray cells are calculated for you. These generally should not be altered.

	Base price	Discounted price
Product number:	A-123435	
Product description:	Super Widget: White widget with green racing stripes has two reversible spigots. Refillable with item #R-234. 1-year warranty.	
Base unit cost	$ 15.42	
Initial markup	23%	
Base unit price	$ 18.97	
Quantity in this order	144	144
Per unit discount		10%
Total savings per base unit		$ 1.90
Total line item price		$ 17.07
Lump sum total	$ 2,731.68	$ 2,458.51
Sales tax	7.50%	7.50%
Shipping and handling	$ 12.31	$ 12.31
Total	$ 2,948.87	$ 2,655.21
Total savings		$ 293.66

Figure 6-1. *The Product Pricing Calculator spreadsheet*

This template can be obtained from Microsoft Office Online. From the New Workbook dialog in Excel 2007, select More Categories and then Calculators to locate it. In case you have difficulty finding this template, we have included a copy in the Source Code/Download section of the Apress web site (http://apress.com). The file is named product pricing calculator.xlsx and is stored in a Starter Files directory for this chapter. If you download your own from Microsoft Office Online, make sure you save your spreadsheet in the Office 2007 file format with an .xlsx extension. You will also want to make sure that you are not run-ning Excel in the backward-compatibility mode. You can tell the mode you are in by looking at the title bar of Excel's window, as shown in Figure 6-2. You may need to close and reopen your spreadsheet in Excel after saving it in the 2007 file format to get out of this mode.

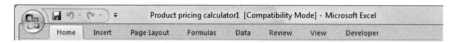

Figure 6-2. *Determining Excel's compatibility mode*

Our vision is that this spreadsheet will be integrated into the enterprise. This includes connectivity to back-end services as well as custom applications. For this reason we will be extending the rules in this spreadsheet to increase its touch points with other systems. Remember that we still want our business user to be able to tweak the rules within their con-trol; however, there are several places where the company likely already has other systems in place that should influence values on this spreadsheet.

For example, it is reasonable to assume that the company would have a products system that stores its current base-unit costs. These likely change as costs fluctuate for raw materials and energy. Instead of having the base price of the product as a static data element, as it is in cell D11, we will extend Excel to retrieve this value from a SQL Server database.

The shipping cost in cell D27 is also a static value. It isn't realistic to think that the cost of shipping would remain the same regardless of where the customer is located and the number of items in the order. For this reason, we will add a shipping worksheet that captures the zip codes of the customer and the company's warehouse as well as calculations for weight and handling fees. This shipping worksheet is shown in Figure 6-3.

	A	B
1	**Shipping Worksheet**	
2	Warehouse Zip Code	21227
3	Customer Zip Code	32803
4	Individual Weight	0.25
5	Total Weight	25
6	Total Shipping	17.56
7	Handling Fee	$5.00

Figure 6-3. *The shipping worksheet*

To calculate the shipping cost, we will rely on a web service call. There are many different providers of such services (UPS and the United States Postal Service, for instance), so this is a reasonable calculation method. We don't want you to have to set up accounts for these serv-ices and we don't anticipate that every development environment will have Internet access. For this reason, we will build a test shipping web service that takes the zip codes and weight as inputs and returns a cost. Of course, this service will not do any heavy lifting of trying to calcu-late distance; instead it will just return different costs for our different sets of test data.

The Per Unit Discount value of 10% is also a static value. Here we want to increase the flexibility of the rule and allow our business user to maintain a table that sets different discounts based on the number of items purchased. Later in this chapter we will show you how to incorporate a discount table that will be maintained on its own worksheet. Figure 6-4 shows a sample of this table, which specifies a different percentage discount based on the quantity of items in the order.

	A	B
1	**Discount Table**	
2	Min Num	% Discount
3	0	0.00%
4	10	0.50%
5	20	1.00%
6	50	5.00%
7	100	10.00%
8	200	15.00%

Figure 6-4. *The volume-discount table*

To round out our different techniques of leveraging managed code in the Excel spreadsheet, we will have the sales tax value in cell D25 be set based on the result of .NET class's method. Where the other examples include database or web service calls, this one will just be a single function of the class.

Despite taking over these elements of the spreadsheet by integrating them with back-end systems, the business user will still be able to have control over critical calculations. The initial markup value is a percentage that they can adjust. The business user can also change the end points of the volume-discount table. Our goal in this solution is to achieve a high level of integration while maintaining flexibility. In fact, our custom application that consumes this spreadsheet will be able to implement the business user's adjustments immediately.

Setting Up an External Source: Products Database

For our sample products system, we will use a SQL Server 2005 database named ProductsTest. This database stores details of the company's products and, in particular, the current base price. The code download at `http://apress.com` includes the database's data and log file, which you can attach to your development box using SQL Server Management Studio. Figure 6-5 is a diagram of the database showing the product table.

Figure 6-5. *Diagram of the ProductsTest database*

The database also includes a stored procedure. The GetProductBasePrice stored procedure is used to retrieve a particular row of data from the product table. For this reason, the stored procedure accepts a ProductCode as a parameter and returns the matching row. Listing 6-1 details this procedure.

Listing 6-1. *The GetProductBasePrice Stored Procedure*

```
CREATE PROCEDURE [dbo].[GetProductBasePrice]
        @ProductCode varchar(50)
AS
BEGIN
    SET NOCOUNT ON;
    SELECT BasePrice FROM Product
    WHERE ProductCode = @ProductCode
END
```

To set up the database in your environment, copy the MDF and LDF files of the Products-Test database to your SQL Server. If you did a default install, SQL Server 2005 is using the following path to store these database files: `C:\Program Files\Microsoft SQL Server\MSSQL.1\MSSQL\Data`. Once they are in place, right-click on the Databases node of Management Studio's Object Explorer and select Attach. In the dialog, click Add and locate the `ProductsTest.mdf` file. The default options are fine. Your dialog should look like Figure 6-6. Click OK; the Object Explorer will refresh to include the ProductsTest database.

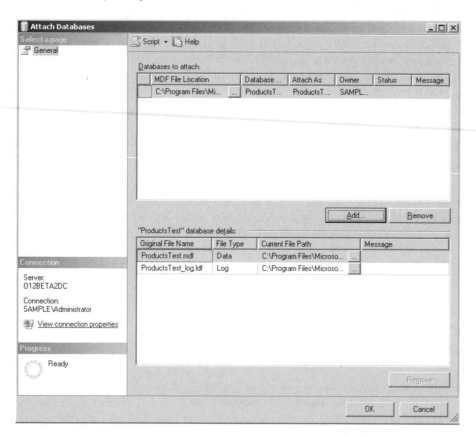

Figure 6-6. *Attaching the ProductsTest database*

If you need more help attaching databases in SQL Server 2005, use the steps outlined on MSDN: `http://msdn2.microsoft.com/en-us/library/ms190209.aspx`.

Setting Up an External Source: Shipping Web Service

In a real-world solution, the calculation of shipping cost would likely rely on a web service such as the ones provided by UPS and the United States Postal Service. Instead, for this chapter we will create our own service to simulate this calculation for the sets of test data we are interested in. Typically, shipping costs are a function of the zip codes of the beginning and end points as well as the weight of the shipment. For this reason we will create a TestShippingService ASP.NET web-service project.

This ASP.NET service can be created as its own Visual Studio solution or as an added project with the others in this chapter. If you want to match the way we set them up in the code download, you will first want to create a VB.NET class library project named ProductPricingCalc in a solution of the same name. The class library project will be used for our managed code functions for Excel and will be detailed in the next section of the chapter. With the ProductPricingCalc solution created, you can add the Visual Basic ASP.NET web service project by using the following steps:

1. From Visual Studio's File menu, select Add ➤ New Web Site.

2. Select the ASP.NET Web Service project template.

3. Make sure that the Location drop-down is set to File System and that Language is set to VB.NET.

4. Specify the path to be a folder within the ProductPricingCalc solution. We used `C:\Projects\ProductPricingCalc\TestShippingService` in our solution.

5. Click OK.

When the project is added, Visual Studio will add the default files `Service.asmx` and a `Service.vb` code file that is contained in the App_Code directory. Delete both of these and add a new ASP.NET web service item named `Shipping.asmx`. The corresponding code file in the App_Code folder will be added for you. The web service needs exactly one method that accepts two zip codes and the total weight as input parameters. The method will return a price. Again, we are just simulating the calculation here, so we will create a few paths through the method for a Boston zip code of 02108 and an Orlando zip code of 32803. We will also return different costs if the weight is over 70 pounds. Listing 6-2 details this method.

Listing 6-2. *The Web Service Method for Calculating Shipping*

```
<WebMethod()> _
Public Function CalcShipping(ByVal startZipCode As String, _
            ByVal endZipCode As String, ByVal totalWeight As Double) _
            As Double
    Dim retVal As Double = -1
    Select Case endZipCode
      Case "02108"
                If (totalWeight <= 70) Then
```

```
                retVal = 13.74
            Else
                retVal = 23.74
            End If
    Case "32803"
            If (totalWeight <= 70) Then
                retVal = 17.56
            Else
                retVal = 27.36
            End If
    Case Else
            Throw New ApplicationException("We do not ship to that location")
    End Select
    Return retVal
End Function
```

Once it's coded, you can test the web service by right-clicking on the Shipping.asmx file and selecting View in Browser. This will cause Visual Studio's local web server to run and a browser window will be opened to the web service. You can tell that the web server is running by the additional ASP.NET Development Server icon in the system tray. Notice that the URL is a specific port off of localhost. Remember this port—we will need to use this information to call the web service. We assume that you are developing with Visual Studio on your MOSS server and the localhost reference will be good enough for Excel Services to call. If not, you will want to use Visual Studio to publish this web service to a new IIS web site. Figure 6-7 shows what the test client will look like in the browser window. Be sure to leave the ASP.NET Development Server running, or your calls to this service will go unanswered.

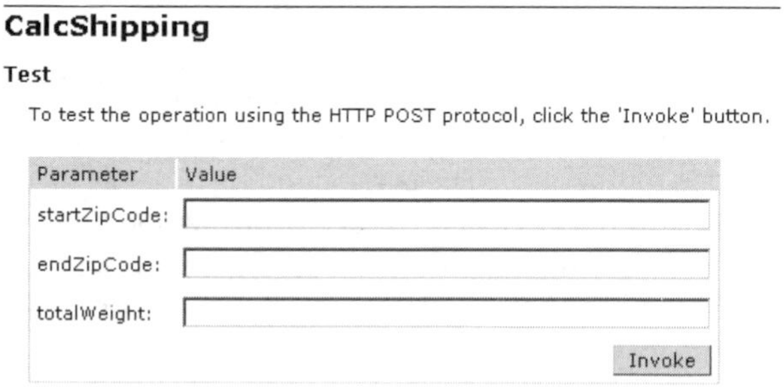

CalcShipping

Test

To test the operation using the HTTP POST protocol, click the 'Invoke' button.

Parameter	Value
startZipCode:	
endZipCode:	
totalWeight:	

Invoke

Figure 6-7. *Testing the shipping web service*

Constructing the UDF Class

User-defined functions (UDFs) provide a developer the opportunity to extend Microsoft Excel's calculation capabilities. To build a UDF, you construct a .NET class appropriately decorated with UDF attributes. Methods of this class that are marked with the UdfMethod attribute are then available to be invoked from cells in Excel, just like the native functions. A developer would look to construct a UDF when a spreadsheet needs a particular function that is not provided natively in Excel or when the spreadsheet must interact with external data provided by custom applications. This data could be retrieved from databases and even web services. Both Microsoft Excel 2007 and the Excel Services of Microsoft Office SharePoint Server 2007 support UDF classes. However, the deployment methods are dramatically different since the Excel client relies on COM plumbing and Excel Services relies on .NET assemblies. In this section, we will focus on the construction of the class, the UDF attributes, and the COM plumbing. Following this section we will detail the deployment steps for both Excel and Excel Services.

If you are following along, you have already created a ProductPricingCalc solution containing the web service we've discussed, as well as a ProductPricingCalc class library project that we have not touched on yet. This project will compile into the DLL assembly that will contain the UDF methods. Delete the default class file and add a new one named ProductPricingUdf.vb. To have access to the UDF attributes, you will need to add a reference to the Microsoft.Office.Excel.Server.Udf assembly. If you are developing a single MOSS server, this assembly should be on the .NET tab of Visual Studio's Add Reference dialog, but if it is not, the default location for this assembly is C:\Program Files\Common Files\Microsoft Shared\web server extensions\12\ISAPI. You will find this assembly only on a machine that has Excel Services. If you are developing remotely, you can copy this assembly to your development environment. With the reference set up, add the Imports statements in Listing 6-3 to the top of the class file; that'll give us easy access to the UDF attributes, SQL Server ADO.NET objects, and the namespaces containing the classes for the COM plumbing.

Listing 6-3. *Import Statements for Namespaces Used in the UDF Class*

```
Imports Microsoft.Office.Excel.Server.Udf
Imports System.Runtime.InteropServices
Imports Microsoft.Win32
Imports System.Data.Sql
Imports System.Data.SqlClient
```

Though it is not required, we will want our assembly to have a strong name. This opens up the deployment option of adding our assembly to the global assembly cache (GAC) and is also recommended for classes that are going to be COM-registered in the Windows registry. To give your assembly a strong name, do the following:

1. Right-click on the ProductPricingCalc project in Solution Explorer and select Properties.

2. Select Signing in the left-hand navigation.

3. Click the check box to sign the assembly. The drop-down directly below the check box will enable. Figure 6-8 depicts this choice.

4. Select New.

5. For the name of the file, type in **key**.

6. Deselect the check box for protecting the file with a password.

7. Click OK.

8. Click Visual Studio's Save toolbar button to commit this setting.

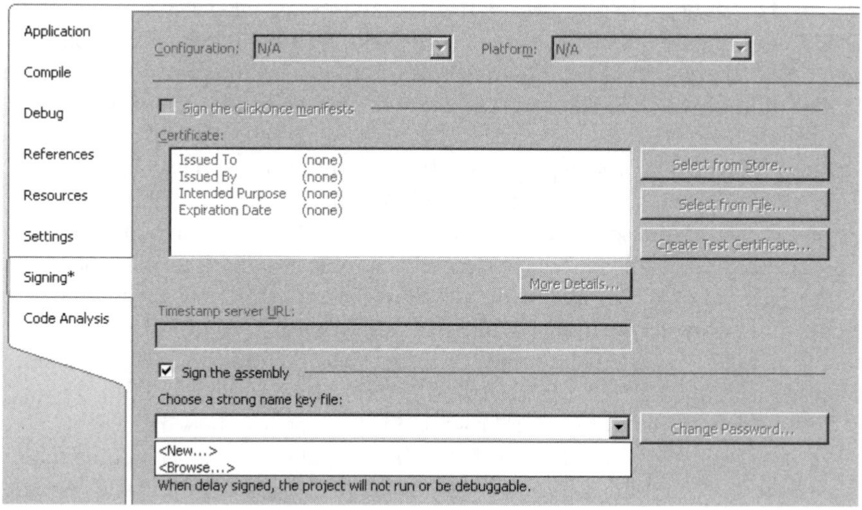

Figure 6-8. *Signing the assembly*

First we'll detail the class method that connects to the products database we added earlier. This method will be responsible for retrieving the base price of a product based on its product code (the table's primary key). Earlier you saw that the GetProductBasePrice stored procedure provided this capability. Before looking at the code of the method, we have to deal with where to store the connection string to the database. Ideally, we don't want to specify this in compiled code. Instead we will store this information as a setting that will be stored separately in a ProductPricingCalc.dll.config file. Use the following steps to add the connection-string setting:

1. Right-click on the ProductPricingCalc project in Solution Explorer and select Properties.

2. Select Settings in the left-hand navigation.

3. Add an item to the grid. Set the Name column to ConnectionString. Set the Type as String. Set the Scope as Application. For the Value, specify the connection string to your SQL Server and the ProductsTest database. Be sure to use values that match your environment. The connection string should be in this format: Integrated Security=SSPI;Persist Security Info=True;Initial Catalog=ProductsTest;Data Source=SQLServerName

4. Click Visual Studio's Save button to commit the setting.

The GetProductBasePrice method receives a string that contains the product's code as an input parameter and returns the product's base price stored in the external database. Notice the use of the UdfClass and UdfMethod attributes in Listing 6-4. These attributes make this class and this method available to Excel Services (the COM portion handles the Excel client). If you forget to add them, then the spreadsheet will not be able to call the method. The ADO.NET code is rather uneventful other than the retrieval of the connection string from the My.MySettings class. When the command object is executed, notice that an ExecuteScalar method is used. This is done since we are expecting only a single value ever to be returned. In a production system, you should incorporate your organization's technique for handling and logging exceptions. Here we just print it to the debug window and rethrow the exception.

Listing 6-4. *The GetProductBasePrice Method*

```
<UdfClass()> _
Public Class ProductPricingUdf

<UdfMethod()> _
Public Function GetProductBasePrice(ByVal productCode As String) As Double
    Dim retVal As Double
    Dim conn As SqlConnection = Nothing
    Try
        conn = New SqlConnection(My.MySettings.Default.ConnectionString)
        Dim cmd As SqlCommand = New SqlCommand()
        cmd.Connection = conn
        cmd.CommandType = CommandType.StoredProcedure
        cmd.CommandText = "GetProductBasePrice"
        Dim param As SqlParameter = New SqlParameter()
        param.DbType = SqlDbType.VarChar
        param.Direction = ParameterDirection.Input
        param.IsNullable = False
        param.ParameterName = "@ProductCode"
        param.Size = 50
        param.Value = productCode
        cmd.Parameters.Add(param)
        conn.Open()
        retVal = cmd.ExecuteScalar()
        conn.Close()
        Return retVal
    Catch ex As Exception
        Debug.Print(ex.Message)
        Throw (ex)
    Finally
        If (conn IsNot Nothing AndAlso~
            conn.State <> ConnectionState.Closed) Then
                conn.Close()
        End If
    End Try
End Function
```

Remember that we defined shipping costs as a function of the distance of the customer from the warehouse and the weight of the shipment. We also created a simulation web service for testing in a development environment. Make sure that the ASP.NET Development Server is still running. If it is not, you can start it by right-clicking on your Shipping.asmx file and selecting View in Browser. With the web service available, we will add a web reference to the ProductPricingCalc project:

1. In Visual Studio's Solution Explorer, right-click on the ProductPricingCalc project and select to Add Web Reference.

2. Type in the URL to your web service. You should be able to retrieve this from the browser window where you were testing the web service. The chosen port will be different in different environments. For our development machine it was `http://localhost:1180/TestShippingService/Shipping.asmx`.

3. Name the web reference **ShippingService** and click Add Reference.

Visual Studio will communicate with the web service, retrieve its WSDL, and generate a proxy class for you. Just like the database-connection string, we do not want the web service's URL to be hard-coded. If you examine the properties of the web reference, you should see that its URL Behavior is set to Dynamic. This means that the URL of the web service is stored in the same settings file we used for the connection string. Figure 6-9 shows the information that is automatically written there.

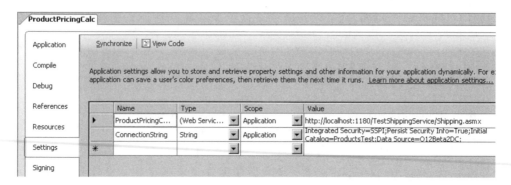

Figure 6-9. *Examining the project's configuration settings*

The GetShipping method in Listing 6-5 calls the web service. This method is decorated with the UdfMethod attribute so that it will be callable from Excel Services. The URL is retrieved from the configuration settings and assigned to the URL property of the proxy class.

Listing 6-5. *The GetShipping Method*

```
<UdfMethod()> _
Public Function GetShipping(ByVal warehouseZipCode As String, _
        ByVal customerZipCode As String, ByVal totalWeight As Double) _
        As Double
Dim retVal As Double = -1
Try
   Dim service As ShippingService.Shipping = New ShippingService.Shipping()
   service.Url = My.MySettings.Default.ProductPricingCalc_ShippingService_Shipping
   retVal = service.CalcShipping(warehouseZipCode, customerZipCode, totalWeight)
   Return retVal
Catch ex As Exception
   Debug.Print(ex.Message)
```

```
    Throw (ex)
End Try
End Function
```

You can obtain the GetSalesTax method from the code download at `http://apress.com`. It is not nearly as interesting as the other two UDF methods, as it tests only for our two different zip codes and returns 5% for Boston and 6% for Orlando. But remember that Excel is calling this method, and within it you have access to the whole .NET Framework. This means that you could perform complex operations and logic that are not available in Excel natively.

If you were going to use this spreadsheet only in Excel Services and you didn't mind not seeing any results as you build the spreadsheet in the Excel client, you would be done with this class. However, our vision is one where a business user can continue to use the Excel spreadsheet to tweak the calculations. Therefore these UDF methods need to be available in the client as well as in Excel Services. This means that we will have to COM-register this assembly. This will require a bit more code to be written in the class. First the class must be marked as COM-visible and decorated with other COM attributes (shown in Listing 6-6). Notice that the ClsId and ProgId values are new constants containing the full name of the class as well as a unique GUID. Specifying both of these values is a best practice and makes the registration process predictable and repeatable as opposed to some autogenerated values.

Listing 6-6. *Adding COM Attributes to the UDF Class*

```
<UdfClass()> _
<Guid(ProductPricingUdf.ClsId)> _
<ProgId(ProductPricingUdf.ProgId)> _
<ClassInterface(ClassInterfaceType.AutoDual)> _
<ComVisible(True)> _
Public Class ProductPricingUdf
Public Const ClsId As String = "C1C9EC29-16CB-4b13-9698-15810ACD3389"
Public Const ProgId As String = "ProductPricingCalc.ProductPricingUdf"
```

In addition to the class-level attributes, we will need to add two methods to control the registry information that is added or removed when this class is registered or unregistered. Listing 6-7 contains the Registration and Unregistration methods. You will see the impact of this code when we use regasm to register this class with the Windows registry (in the following section).

Listing 6-7. *Methods for COM Registration*

```
<ComRegisterFunction()> _
Public Shared Sub RegistrationMethod(ByVal t As Type)
   If (GetType(ProductPricingUdf) IsNot t) Then
      Exit Sub
   End If
   Dim key As RegistryKey = Registry.ClassesRoot.~
        CreateSubKey("CLSID\{" & ClsId & "}\Programmable")
   key.Close()
End Sub
```

```
<ComUnregisterFunction()> _
Public Shared Sub UnregistrationMethod(ByVal t As Type)
    If (GetType(ProductPricingUdf) IsNot t) Then
        Exit Sub
    End If
    Registry.ClassesRoot.DeleteSubKey("CLSID\{" & ClsId & "}\Programmable")
End Sub
```

Build the ProductPricingCalc project. This will create the `ProductPricingCalc.dll` assembly as well as the `ProductPricingCalc.dll.config` settings file. Take the time to navigate to where these files were built and open the configuration settings file in Notepad. Notice how these values could be changed without your having to recompile the solution.

Deploying the UDF Class and Registering It for Use in Excel

For this section we expect that you are using Visual Studio and Excel on the same machine (or virtual machine) as your MOSS server. Though this is not required, some of the steps here, like the use of a UDFs folder on the local drive of the machine, are done more for Excel Services' sake than Excel's. Regardless, this UDF class you constructed earlier must be COM-registered for it to work within the Excel client. Use the following steps to complete the configuration for use in Excel:

1. Create a folder named UDFs at the root of your local drive (`C:\UDFs`).

2. Copy the `ProductPricingCalc.dll` and `ProductPricingCalc.dll.config` files from your build directory to the UDFs folder. Remember that this location contains the assembly that the client will be executing just in case you want to make some changes and update it.

3. From a Visual Studio command prompt, navigate to the UDFs directory and type the following command: **regasm /codebase ProductPricingCalc.dll**

The register assembly command will write the Windows registry subkey information we specified in Listing 6-7. You can see the impact of this registration by opening the Windows registry and locating the subkey. To open the registry, type **regedit** in the Run dialog. Expand HKEY_CLASSES_ROOT and its CLSID folder. This location is organized by the GUIDs assigned via the CLSID attribute. Locate the GUID for the ProductPricingUdf class. If you used the same one provided here, it is {C1C9EC29-16CB-4b13-9698-15810ACD3389}. Figure 6-10 shows this registry information. Make sure the Programmable node is present in your environment. If not, Excel will not make your class available to be loaded.

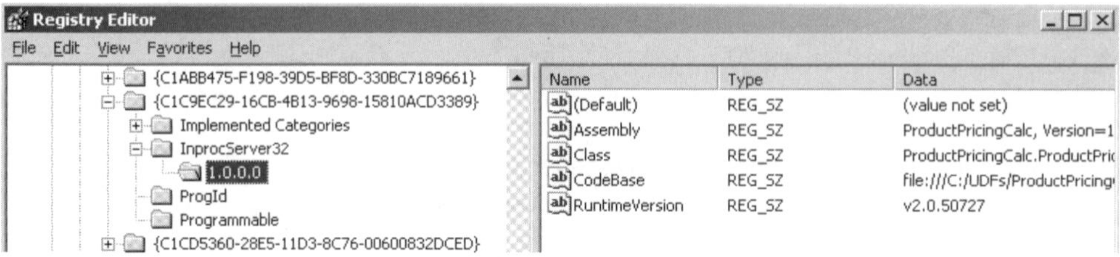

Figure 6-10. *Viewing the Windows registry information for the UDF Class*

In case you want to remove the registry information (to try again), you can use the following command to unregister the class: **regasm /unregister ProductPricingCalc.dll**.

Once the class is registered, you will need to load it in the Excel client. Open your spreadsheet in Excel 2007 and from the File menu, choose the Excel Options button. From the Add-Ins tab, make sure the Manage drop-down at the bottom is set to Excel Add-ins and click the Go button. In the new dialog, click the Automation… button, which will bring up a list of COM automation servers. Locate our class in this list. It will be named ProductPricingCalc. ProductPricingUdf. If it is not listed, then there was an error in the COM registration. Check the Windows registry and the COM RegistrationMethod in the class. Select our class in the list and click OK. You will get a warning about `mscoree.dll` that you can ignore. Click No in response to the warning since we do not want the file removed. Figure 6-11 shows the final result of this work in the Add-Ins dialog. You should also confirm that the class is loaded in the Add-Ins tab of the Excel Options dialog.

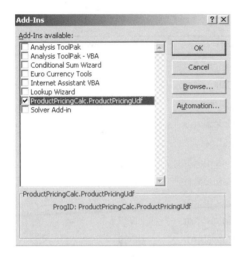

Figure 6-11. *Loading the UDF class in Excel 2007*

If you would like to avoid the dialog containing the `mscoree.dll` warning, you will need to create a shim for your managed code to run through COM Interop. You can find more information on techniques to create the shim at the following URLs:

Simple Shim: `http://msdn2.microsoft.com/en-us/library/aa164016(office.10).aspx`

Complex Shim: `http://msdn2.microsoft.com/en-us/library/aa163984(office.10).aspx`

Shim Wizard: `http://msdn2.microsoft.com/en-us/library/aa159894(office.11).aspx`

Enhancing the Spreadsheet

With the UDF class loaded in the Excel client, we can now begin to incorporate it into the spreadsheet and make the enhancements we detailed at the beginning of this walkthrough. (If you do not want to follow along and make these changes yourself, you can use the completed spreadsheet included in the code download.) Before going in and modifying formulas, we want to specify named ranges for certain cells that we will refer to often. To name a cell/range, do the following:

1. Click on the cell (or highlight the range) you wish to name.

2. Click on the Formulas tab in the ribbon.

3. Click the Define Name button in the Defined Names group.

4. Specify the name and the scope, and click Ok.

Table 6-1 details the named ranges that we want set up in the spreadsheet. You do not have all of these cells in your worksheet yet, but we wanted to present this as a single source for you to refer to. For all of our named ranges, use Workbook as the scope. We also specified the format we used for the cells.

Table 6-1. *Named Ranges Used in the Spreadsheet*

Name	Format	Worksheet	Cell Referred To
ProductCode	General	Pricing Calculator	C8
BaseUnitCost	Accounting	Pricing Calculator	D11
CustomerZipCode	Text	ShippingSheet	B3
DiscountedTotal	Accounting	Pricing Calculator	E29
HandlingFee	Currency	ShippingSheet	B7
OrderQuantity	General	Pricing Calculator	D15
PerUnitDiscount	Percentage	Pricing Calculator	E17
SalesTax	Percentage	Pricing Calculator	D25
ShippingAndHandling	Accounting	Pricing Calculator	D27
Total	Accounting	Pricing Calculator	D29
TotalShipping	General	ShippingSheet	B6
TotalWeight	General	ShippingSheet	B5
WarehouseZipCode	Text	ShippingSheet	B2

Begin to change the spreadsheet by deleting the worksheet that contains the chart. We will not use it as part of the example.

Add a worksheet named DiscountSheet. Build the discount table that was shown in Figure 6-4. Be very careful of formatting in Excel. The % Discount cells are formatted as a Percentage with two decimal places. You should not be typing in the % character yourself. You can access the format options by highlighting the cell, right-clicking, and selecting the Format Cell option from the context menu. Now go back to the Per Unit Discount cell (E17) on the Pricing Calculator worksheet and change it from a static value to a function. In this case, the function should be a vertical lookup on the discount table. The VLOOKUP function performs this action in Excel, looking for a match in the first column. If a match is not found, it matches against the greatest number that's less than the specified value. The function you need to enter is `=VLOOKUP(OrderQuantity,DiscountSheet!A3:B8,2)`. This formula specifies the order quantity as the input parameter, the range of the discount table, and that the value in the second column of the table should be returned. Test this method by changing the order quantity so that the discount should change.

To incorporate the UDF method that queries the products database, modify the BaseUnitCost cell on the Pricing Calculator spreadsheet (cell D11). Instead of the static value, enter the following formula: `=GetProductBasePrice(ProductCode)`. Notice how we can call the method of the UDF class just as if it were a native Excel function. There are two possible errors you could run into. If the cell displays a #NAME? value then it is having difficulty locating your UDF class and method. If the cell displays #VALUE! then an exception was encountered while calling your method. This could be because the input and return parameters of the method may not have matched what Excel expected or an exception within the execution of the method was encountered.

■**Note** At the end of this section we discuss debugging in the Excel client. The #NAME? and #VALUE! error values are also used by Excel Services. It is important to know that Excel and Excel Services rely on different types of casting for their parameters. Excel relies on casting in COM, whereas Excel Services relies on .NET casting. This means that it is possible to experience problems in only one of the environments. Make sure you test both fully.

Add a worksheet named ShippingSheet. Build the shipping worksheet that was shown in Figure 6-3. Be certain to format the zip codes as text. Excel should display a green corner in these cells warning you that you are formatting a number as text. Since zip codes are not used for arithmetic and we want leading zeros, this is fine. Be sure to use only the Boston (02108) and Orlando (32802) zip codes that we have incorporated into the test shipping web service. The formula for TotalWeight is `=OrderQuantity*ShippingSheet!B4`. To incorporate the call to the web service, set the TotalShipping cell's formula to `=GetShipping(WarehouseZipCode, CustomerZipCode,TotalWeight)`. Make sure your ASP.NET web service is running, or this will result in an exception.

To incorporate the sales-tax calculation of the UDF class, change the SalesTax cell's formula to `=GetSalesTax(CustomerZipCode)`. Finally, add the formula to total the shipping and handling fees. This is the ShippingAndHandling cell, whose formula should be set to `=TotalShipping+HandlingFee`.

Again remember that the #NAME? and #VALUE! results point to two separate issues. If you are getting the #VALUE! error, you may want to place Visual Studio in debug mode and step through your code. With your spreadsheet open in Excel 2007 and the UDF loaded, you can attach Visual Studio to the `Excel.EXE` process as shown in Figure 6-12. Once it's attached, set a breakpoint in a UDF method and simply modify a cell that causes one of the UDF class's methods to be invoked.

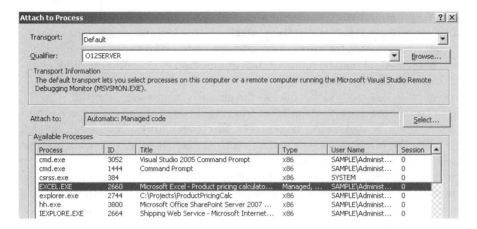

Figure 6-12. *Debugging the UDF class in Excel 2007*

Preparing Excel Services for the Spreadsheet

In this section we will be publishing the spreadsheet to Excel Services on the MOSS server. When published, the spreadsheet is placed in a document library, but for Excel Services to open the workbook, the library must be set up as a trusted location. Use the following steps to set up your target library as a trusted location:

1. From the Start Menu, launch SharePoint 3.0 Central Administration.

2. In the Quick Launch navigation on the left side, open your shared services administration. This is usually called something like SharedServices1. This must be the same shared service provider (SSP) that the site containing the document library leverages for services. If your environment contains more than one SSP, you can confirm which one your site uses in the Shared Services Administration screen.

3. In the Excel Services section, click Trusted File Locations.

4. Click Add Trusted File Location.

5. On the Add Trusted File Location page, enter the URL to your library in the Address text box. In our development environment, the library was named Excel in a team site named dev2. Therefore the Address URL was `http://portal.sample.com/SiteDirectory/dev2/Excel`.

6. Under the Location Type prompt, set the storage type to Windows SharePoint Services.

7. Leave the remaining items as their defaults except at the bottom of the page, where we want to enable User-Defined Functions. This check box should be checked so that Excel services will consider loading our assembly.

8. Click OK.

Setting up the trusted location allowed Excel Services to open our workbook, and we informed the system that we wish to allow UDF assemblies to be executed. However, we also need to register our UDF assembly so that Excel Services trusts it. Having these levels of trust enables administrators to control custom code that their environment is calling. Remember that we published our assembly and its configuration file to a local UDFs folder on the MOSS server. Therefore, use the following steps to register the UDF assembly:

1. From the SSP administration page, access the Excel Services User-Defined Functions page in the Excel Services section.

2. Click the Add User-Defined Function Assemblies button.

3. Enter the path to the assembly as `C:\UDFs\ProductPricingCalc.dll`.

4. Select File Path in the Assembly Location selection.

5. Make sure the Assembly enabled check box is selected.

6. Click OK.

As you may have noticed, there was an option to register the assembly if it were located in the global assembly cache. We did sign our assembly so this is an option for you to explore, but remember that you will have to account for the configuration file. If you were to have the assembly in the GAC, the assembly path would need to be `ProductPricingCalc,Version=1.0.0.0,Culture=neutral,PublicKeyToken=a7da6d4f64e40eec`. (Replace the public key token with the actual value for your solution, of course.)

It is possible to deploy UDFs using Windows SharePoint Services solution packages. If you are interested in this area, the following "How To" in the SDK is a good reference: `http://msdn2.microsoft.com/en-us/library/aa981325.aspx`. This would be appropriate for deploying in a production environment, as the solution would deploy your files to the appropriate servers of the farm and also support retraction. It is important to know that regardless of whether your UDF assembly is in the GAC or the local folder, it runs with a code-access security level of Full Trust. This is potentially a dangerous scenario—it means the code included in the assembly has full reign over the server and therefore must be reviewed carefully on each deployment. For this reason, it is a best practice to use code-access security to restrict the actions your UDF assembly can perform. The following reference details the steps for doing so: `http://msdn2.microsoft.com/en-us/library/aa981134.aspx`.

Publishing to Excel Services

We are now ready to publish the spreadsheet that we created earlier to the library that we configured as a trusted location. Make sure you have saved your changes to the spreadsheet locally, and then use the following steps to publish it:

1. With the spreadsheet open in Microsoft Excel 2007, select Publish ➤ Excel Services from the File menu. See Figure 6-13.

2. Enter the URL of the trusted location in the File Name prompt and press Enter. The dialog should communicate with the server and provide you with a view of the Share-Point library. Name the file `product pricing calculator.xlsx`.

Figure 6-13. *Publishing the spreadsheet to Excel Services*

3. Click the Excel Services Options button. This area allows us to configure how the spreadsheet will be run in Excel Services.

4. The first tab allows us to restrict which elements of the workbook will be available in the web-only view. This is an important choice, as it allows us to hide elements that were for our business user who was maintaining the calculations (and that were not necessarily interesting to the average viewer). Select Sheets in the drop-down and uncheck all of the sheets except the Pricing Calculator.

5. The parameters tab allows us to promote named ranges within the spreadsheet to be input parameters that Excel Services will ask for to open the workbook. Click the Add button to add a parameter.

6. Select CustomerZipCode, OrderQuantity, and ProductCode—these items need to be supplied by the end user for the spreadsheet to perform the calculation.

7. Click OK. The Parameters tab should look like Figure 6-14.

8. Click OK.

9. Click the Save button.

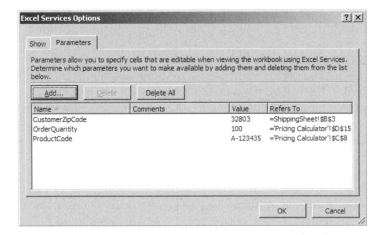

Figure 6-14. *Specifying input parameters for Excel Services*

When the save completes, a browser window will launch with the workbook open in Excel services. There will be a pane on the right side for you to enter the input parameters. Try both zip codes (01208 and 32803), the product code of A-123435, and quantities in the different discount ranges. Notice how the spreadsheet performs the calculations just like the full Excel client. Also notice how only the Pricing Calculator worksheet is viewable in the browser even though the calculations that rely on the other sheets still perform. The result should look like Figure 6-15.

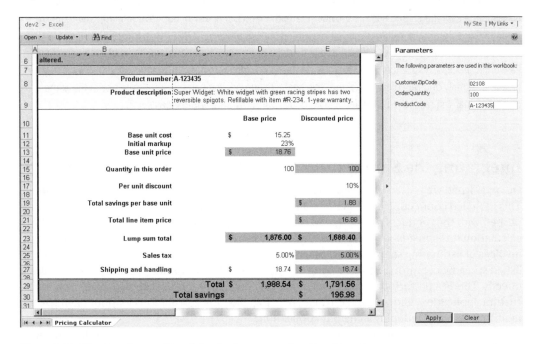

Figure 6-15. *Viewing the workbook in the browser using Excel Services*

Use the breadcrumb navigation just above the toolbar to return to the Excel document library. Once there, look at the Actions menu for your Excel file in the library. There are three options that relate to Excel.

The first, Edit in Microsoft Office Excel, would be employed by the business user who wishes to update some of the calculations like markup percentage or the volume-discount table. Provided such users have the UDF registered on their machines such that it works within the Excel client, they can edit the spreadsheet, make the adjustments, and save it back to the library. Don't forget that we are using a reference of localhost for the web service, and it would need to be altered if Excel were on a remote machine. Of course, the SharePoint library's security settings will control who is allowed access to update this file. After the save, there is no need to republish unless the parameters or viewable items need to change.

The second action, View in Web Browser, launches the workbook in the thin client Excel Services viewer. It is possible to have this view inside a web part so that the user does not have to come to the library first. The web part for this is called Excel Web Access Viewing and it is in the Business Data group of the Add Web Parts dialog.

Last, the Snapshot in Excel action would allow a user to have the spreadsheet loaded in Excel, but without any formulas or hidden items. This is useful for a viewing user who wishes to do additional filtering, sorting, or charting, but has no need to change the data in the spreadsheet. This option also protects the organization from distributing its intellectual property, such as Excel formulas.

■**Tip** When you are working with the spreadsheet in Excel Services, you may need to do further debugging of your UDF assembly. To attach Visual Studio to Excel Services, you first need to discover which process corresponds with the shared service provider (named SharedServices1 in our environment). The following command in a command window will return you the correct process ID **IISAPP /a SharedServices1**. With the process ID, you can then use Visual Studio's Attach to Process command and connect to the appropriate IIS worker process. Also, Excel Services loves to cache data to increase performance. If you make changes to your assembly and redeploy, make sure this cache is purged. You can accomplish this with the same command that will reset the SSP's application pool: **IISAPP /a SharedServices1 /r**.

Integrating the Spreadsheet into a Custom Application

Our goal when we presented this solution was to integrate the spreadsheet into the enterprise. This included connecting it to back-end line-of-business applications, which we accomplished with the products database and the web service call for shipping costs. However, the calculation this spreadsheet performs is likely useful for other applications (such as printing invoices or estimating sales). This is the power of Excel Services. We can interact with the published spreadsheet through code, asking it to perform calculations as if we were acting with it directly. This is a powerful technique since we are able to separate the spreadsheet from the custom application, allowing the business user to adjust the calculations without having to modify, retest, and redeploy a custom application.

In the code download on the Apress web site we have provided a simple Windows form project called PricingApp. This application shows you the steps necessary for interacting with a published spreadsheet through Excel Services' web service. The form is rather straightforward, allowing the parameters to be specified and the result to be displayed. Figure 6-16 shows the form in Visual Studio's designer.

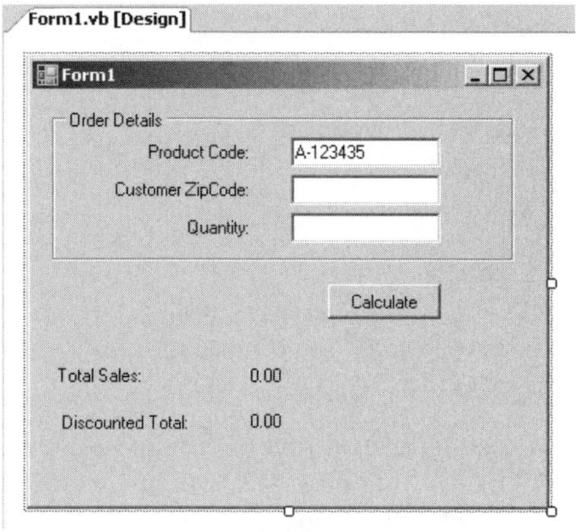

Figure 6-16. *The custom application that will interact with Excel Services*

To enable this application to communicate with Excel Services, you have to add a web reference. The web service can be found in the _vti_bin folder at the root of your SharePoint web application. The URL should be similar to `http://portal.sample.com/_vti_bin/excelservice.asmx`. In this custom application, the reference was named ExcelWebService. Just like with the UDF assembly, make sure that the web service URL is set to Dynamic so that it will be stored externally in a configuration file. The proxy for the web service class will pick up this URL automatically. We also added a WorkbookPath configuration setting to store the URL to our Excel spreadsheet. This setting is of type String, scoped to Application, and has a value of `http://portal.sample.com/SiteDirectory/dev2/Excel/product pricing calculator.xlsx`.

With these elements set up, the Calculate button's click event handler in Listing 6-8 sets up the proxy for the web reference. We will call Excel Services using the current user's logged-in Windows identity, assuming that this application is running within the same (or a trusted) security boundary as Excel Services. The very first call to the web service uses the OpenWorkbook method, which returns the session identifier that is used in subsequent calls.

Listing 6-8. *Establishing a Session with Excel Services*

```
Private Sub btnCalculate_Click(ByVal sender As System.Object,~
        ByVal e As System.EventArgs) Handles btnCalculate.Click
    Dim es As ExcelService = New ExcelService()
    Dim outStatus() As Status = Nothing
    Dim targetWorkbookPath As String = My.MySettings.Default.WorkbookPath
    Dim sessionId As String = String.Empty
    es.Credentials = System.Net.CredentialCache.DefaultCredentials
    Try
        sessionId = es.OpenWorkbook(targetWorkbookPath, "en-US", "en-US", _
                                            outStatus)
```

Once a session has been created, the event handler uses the SetCellA1 method to provide values for the cells that are the named ranges representing the input parameters. As shown in Listing 6-9, the SetCellA1 method accepts four parameters: the session ID, spreadsheet name, named range, and value. (You do not need to provide the spreadsheet name if you are using a named range.) It is important that the data types match, which is why the order quantity is parsed to be a double.

Listing 6-9. *Passing the Input Parameters to Excel Services*

```
es.SetCellA1(sessionId, String.Empty, "ProductCode", _
                    Me.txtProductCode.Text)
es.SetCellA1(sessionId, String.Empty, "CustomerZipCode", _
                    Me.txtCustomerZipCode.Text)
es.SetCellA1(sessionId, String.Empty, "OrderQuantity", _
                    Double.Parse(Me.txtQuantity.Text))
```

Now that we've set all of the input parameters, we can retrieve from the cells the values we want as output. For this application we are interested in retrieving the totals both before and after the discount has been applied. These values are stored in the named ranges Total and DiscountedTotal. As Listing 6-10 shows, the web service's GetCellA1 method returns these values. Since the cells were formatted as Accounting and we are requesting a formatted value, the data type returned is String. The Boolean value in the call designates whether we want the cell's formatted value (True) or the raw value (False).

Listing 6-10. *Retrieving Values of Cells through Excel Services*

```
Dim totalSales As String = es.GetCellA1(sessionId, String.Empty, _
                "Total", True, outStatus)
Dim discountedTotal As String = es.GetCellA1(sessionId, String.Empty, _
                "DiscountedTotal", True, outStatus)
Me.lblTotal.Text = totalSales
Me.lblDiscountedTotal.Text = discountedTotal
```

You may have noticed the use of an array of Status objects being used in some of the web service calls in this application. These status objects would return soft errors by Excel Services when it encountered something unexpected but was able to continue with the operation. These types of errors are called *Continue errors* since Excel Services can still perform the request. With Continue errors, no exception is raised. When Excel Services encounters an error that halts the execution of the request, it will raise an exception just like other .NET code will. Though we are not examining any Continue errors in this application, we do have some response to exceptions, as shown in Listing 6-11. If the exception occurred within Excel Services, it would be returned to our application as a SoapException and its SubCode would contain information about the error. If our application itself threw an exception, the subsequent catch clause would be invoked. For more information on Excel Services alerts, review the following portion of the SDK: http://msdn2.microsoft.com/en-us/library/ms564121.aspx. Of course, you should implement your organization's strategy for logging and reporting exceptions. We simply show them to make it easier to debug. We also use the Finally block to complete the event handler by closing the workbook asynchronously; not waiting for a response. This is a "fire and forget" technique.

Listing 6-11. *Handling Exceptions*

```
Catch ex As SoapException
    'would return InvalidSheetName or FileOpenNotFound
    MessageBox.Show(ex.SubCode.Code.Name)
Catch ex As Exception
    MessageBox.Show(ex.Message)
Finally
    If (sessionId <> String.Empty) Then es.CloseWorkbookAsync(sessionId)
End Try
End Sub
```

Important Lessons

The solution in this chapter incorporated several key techniques that are worth highlighting, as they could easily be reused in other projects.

User-defined functions: The solution utilized a .NET class to host methods that were surfaced in Excel as functions. This allows a developer to use the capabilities of the .NET Framework within Excel. You can call databases, perform complex calculations, and call web services.

Registering the UDF as a COM server for use in Excel: To allow our business user to see the results of the UDF methods, these methods needed to be available in the full Excel 2007 client. This required our class to comply with COM plumbing so that it could be loaded as an Excel add-in.

Preparing Excel Services: The solution needed to specify several configuration settings in the shared service provider admin pages for Excel Services to properly open the published spreadsheet. This involved registering the document library as a trusted source with UDF enabled. The UDF assembly also needs to be registered.

Publishing a spreadsheet to Excel Services: This feature allows the spreadsheet to use server resources for its calculations and presents the spreadsheet through a thin-client interface. Interestingly, not all elements of the spreadsheet need to be made available in the thin-client version. Parameters can be specified, and the interface automatically builds a pane for capturing them from the user.

Using Excel Services' web service: An added benefit of publishing a spreadsheet to Excel Services is that it can be invoked from a web service. This technique decouples the calculation logic from the consuming application. The separation means that the business user can continue to use Excel to tweak and update the calculations without needing to change the consuming application.

Extension Points

While coding this example, we thought of several variations to the solution that we didn't incorporate. Mostly, these were not included because they distracted from the overall objective of the solution. We call them out now as extension points since they may be applicable to a specific project you are working on.

Invoke real shipping cost and sales tax web services: In our example, we used test methods to calculate shipping costs and sales tax. Several organizations provide these as web services and your organization may have their own services. Provided your development environment has network or Internet access, determine the input parameters for these services and adjust accordingly.

Incorporate the business data catalog: In this solution we had the UDF method connect to the database directly using ADO.NET code. This could have been abstracted by having the solution use the Business Data Catalog to retrieve this value once the external application had been registered. To learn about the Business Data Catalog feature of MOSS and how to expose it as a web service, read the solution in Chapter 12.

Further Reading

The following links are to resources a reader interested in this chapter's material may find useful:

- Creating Custom Solutions with Excel Services (MOSS SDK)

  http://msdn2.microsoft.com/en-us/library/ms517343.aspx

- Excel Services User-Defined Functions

  http://msdn2.microsoft.com/en-us/library/ms493934.aspx

- How UDFs Work in Excel Services—A Primer

  http://blogs.msdn.com/cumgranosalis/archive/2006/04/04/UdfsPrimer.aspx

- Extending the Excel Services Programmability Framework

  http://msdn2.microsoft.com/en-us/library/bb267252.aspx

- Making Excel Service's UDFs Work in Excel 2007

  http://blogs.msdn.com/cumgranosalis/archive/2006/08/03/
  ServerClientUDFsCompat1.aspx

- Excel Services Blog by Luis Bitencourt-Emilio

  http://blogs.msdn.com/luisbeonservices/default.aspx

- Using Excel Web Services in a SharePoint Web Part

  http://msdn2.microsoft.com/en-us/library/aa973804.aspx

PART 3

■■■

Microsoft Word Solutions

This section will focus on solutions built around Microsoft Word. The next two chapters will explore enhanced ways to reuse data and enable collaboration. In Chapter 7, the solution illustrates how to merge SharePoint list data with Word document templates. In Chapter 8, the solution divides an uploaded document into individual files, one for each section. This enables different users to work on pieces simultaneously and merge them back together when they are all complete.

◼◼◼

Merging SharePoint List Data into Word Documents

Organizations often have sets of document templates that are used throughout their enterprise. It is often a challenge to make sure that information workers are uniformly using the latest template and capturing the appropriate metadata everywhere the document templates are used. It is not unusual for some templates to share common data elements such as customer information or product details. Often authors, who are responsible for working with these templates, are retyping, cutting and pasting, or otherwise repetitively importing data elements into the appropriate places in the document. Furthermore, they may have a completely separate application to locate and maintain the data set. In this chapter, we will detail how, as a developer, you can construct a solution on SharePoint site to enable users to merge list data into Microsoft Word documents.

Real-World Examples

Users have been looking for ways to automate data merges since the beginning of word processing. It is, in essence, a different take on a mail merge. In this case the data source will be a SharePoint list. More companies' workers are relying on SharePoint lists where they previously may have kept local spreadsheets or Access databases. The fact that a user can create a custom list with custom fields using just a browser makes it even easier to create these repositories without relying on a developer. The lure is enhanced once you add the benefits of the list being Web-based and supporting other users' ability to edit individual items. The situation is so generic that it could apply to almost any organization in any industry. If the list were customer contact information, the documents templates could be contracts, statements of work, and letters. If the list were task assignments, the document templates could be work orders, summary sheets, and status updates. If the list were product information, the document templates could include order forms.

Solution Overview

For this solution, we will develop a feature that, when enabled in a site, provides the functionality to merge list-item data into specific organizational document templates. To provide some context for our solution, we have focused our efforts on building a solution that deals with an organization's customers. Once the feature has been enabled in a site, the solution will create a Customer Contacts list along with a Customer Documents document library. The document library will reference the organization's document templates, which will be configured as SharePoint content types. The Customer Contacts list will be enhanced with an additional action so that for a specific contact, the user may select to build a customer document. After the selection, the user will be directed to a custom application page that enables him to select which specific type of customer document he would like to be constructed with the contact's data. In this sample, we will build a business fax template, a statement-of-work (or work-for-hire) template, and a template to thank new customers. Once the user has selected a document type, the application page will merge the contact's data with the document using the Open XML file format and send the resulting file to the user.

This solution should be flexible enough to allow any site administrator to simply turn on this functionality for the site. For this reason, we have developed the solution as a SharePoint feature. Features are a way of packaging a set of customizations as a single unit that can be activated or deactivated. Though features take a bit of effort to set up, they not only increase the reusability of the solution, but also ease deployment complexities. (See the section "Building the Customer Documents Feature Project" later in this chapter for more detail.)

Solution Walkthrough

This section details the major elements of the solution and the decisions that were made in coding it. The walkthrough will show you how to create content types for the organization's document templates. We will go into detail about how to package your solution as a feature that can be enabled by any site administrator that desires the functionality. This will include how to set up a feature project in Visual Studio, the XML files used to define the customizations of the feature, and how to deploy it. The walkthrough includes the construction of a custom SharePoint application page. Finally, the contact data and the document come together through the use of custom XML parts and Microsoft Word 2007 content controls.

Creating Content Types

In the scenario for this solution, an organization has a set of document templates that are often used to communicate with customers. These document templates and their required metadata should be used uniformly throughout the enterprise. We want to define the settings for each document type once and have any site or even any library in the site collection be able to reference them. For this reason, we will detail how to define each as a SharePoint content type.

SharePoint content types are new to Windows SharePoint Services v3; they allow organizations to reuse settings that apply to content of a particular category. These settings include metadata requirements, a template file, workflows, and policies. Once the content type is defined for the site collection, any library can be configured to support the content type. Enabling a content type for a library results in an additional selection being added to the library's New menu, as shown in Figure 7-1.

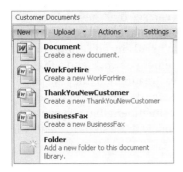

Figure 7-1. *Content types in a library's New menu*

Interestingly, the metadata columns associated with the library and the content type do not have to match. This allows for users to upload different files of different content types with different metadata to the same document library. This flexibility breaks down barriers that required administrators to create multiple libraries in WSS v2. It allows you to store different types of documents that should be grouped based on their user or security requirements. It also provides a single point of administration, as changes to the content type need to be made in only one place. Content types also support inheritance, where a derived type can reuse and extend its parent's settings.

To view the content types of a site collection, navigate to the Site Settings administration area from the top site in the collection. There you'll find the Site Content Types gallery. Figure 7-2 displays the gallery, including the Customer Metadata Model group and its content types, which you will create using the steps in the remainder of this section.

Portal > Site Settings > Site Content Type Gallery

Site Content Type Gallery

Use this page to create and manage content types declared on this site and all parent sites. Content types visible on this page are available for use on this site and its subsites.

📄 Create   Show Group: | All Groups   ▾ |

Site Content Type	Parent	Source
Business Intelligence		
Dashboard Page	Document	Portal
Indicator using data in Excel workbook	Common Indicator Columns	Portal
Indicator using data in SharePoint list	Common Indicator Columns	Portal
Indicator using data in SQL Server 2005 Analysis Services	Common Indicator Columns	Portal
Indicator using manually entered information	Common Indicator Columns	Portal
Report	Document	Portal
Customer Metadata Model		
BusinessFax	CustomerDocument	Portal
CustomerDocument	Document	Portal
ThankYouNewCustomer	CustomerDocument	Portal
WorkForHire	CustomerDocument	Portal
Document Content Types		
Basic Page	Document	Portal
Document	Item	Portal
Dublin Core Columns	Document	Portal
Form	Document	Portal

Figure 7-2. *Site Content Type Gallery page*

By browsing through some of the default content types, you can see that they include settings for columns, workflow, information panels, and information management policies. Each content type also has an associated template that can be set from its Advanced Settings page. The documents used in our example will be a business fax, a statement of work, and a thank-you letter for new customers. Though these documents templates are different, they are all related by a common/overlapping core of metadata requirements for the organization. So in defining them, we will first create a content type called CustomerDocument that will contain all of the common settings and serve as a parent for the others. Follow these steps to create the CustomerDocument content type:

1. Click the Create toolbar button on the Site Content Type Gallery page.

2. Enter **CustomerDocument** as the content type name.

3. Since all of our types are documents, select Document Content Types and then Document to identify the parent content type.

4. Use the radio button to create a new group named Customer Metadata Model.

Notice that this content type automatically inherits the Name and Title columns due to its child relationship with the Document content type. Both of these columns are SharePoint site columns. Like content types, site columns provide an element of reuse as they uniformly define a column for a site collection. For this reason, content types must use site columns. Follow these steps to extend the CustomerDocument content type to include a Company metadata column:

1. Since Company is a site column that already exists, select Add from Existing Site Columns.

2. Locate the Company site column in Core Contact and Calendar Columns.

3. Click the Add button.

4. Click OK.

5. Click on the Company column in the list and make it a required field.

6. Click OK.

Now repeat the content-type-creation steps (the first numbered list) for the BusinessFax, WorkForHire, and ThankYouNewCustomer types, except select the CustomerDocument content type as their parent. Notice that each gains the Company site column in its settings. Add a few different columns for each so you can explore how the library changes to accommodate the various schemas. Also, upload a Word 2007 document to serve as a template from the content type's Advanced Settings page. We will modify the templates later, but for now use the Business Fax Cover Sheet, Standard Work for Hire Contract, and Thank You to New Customer templates from Microsoft Office Online (available in the left-hand navigation of the New Document dialog in Microsoft Word 2007). Make sure that when you save them, you choose to use the new Office 2007 file format and a .docx file extension.

To test your content types, you will want to associate them with a document library. This library must be in the same site collection, but not necessarily the same site. Pick any test document library and follow these steps to enable the content types:

1. From the library's Settings menu, select Document Library Settings.

2. Select Advanced Settings from the General Settings group.

3. Use the radio buttons to enable the management of content types.

4. Click OK.

5. The library's Settings page should have a new section called Content Types. Use the Add from Existing Content Types link to associate our content types: BusinessFax, WorkForHire, and ThankYouNewCustomer. The result should look like Figure 7-3.

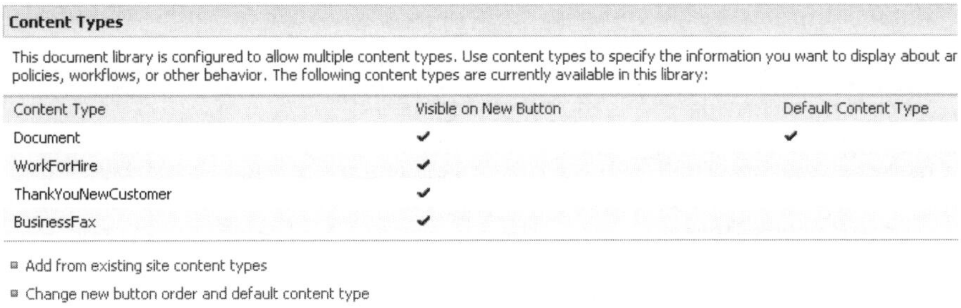

Content Types

This document library is configured to allow multiple content types. Use content types to specify the information you want to display about ar policies, workflows, or other behavior. The following content types are currently available in this library:

Content Type	Visible on New Button	Default Content Type
Document	✔	✔
WorkForHire	✔	
ThankYouNewCustomer	✔	
BusinessFax	✔	

▫ Add from existing site content types
▫ Change new button order and default content type

Figure 7-3. *A document library with content types listed*

Now create at least one instance of each document type and save them to the document library. Do not enter any new content into the files, but complete the metadata entry form. Later we will use these documents to explore their XML structures, modify them to hold custom data, and upload them as new templates for the content types.

Building the CustomerDocuments Feature Project

Our solution is going to provide the organization with a set of elements that together enable any site in the site collection to maintain a list of customer contacts, a customer documents library, and the ability to merge contact data into specific document templates. The important fact here is that we want to provide multiple instances of this capability throughout the site collection. Some sites may want to leverage it while others may not. For this reason, we will package our solution as a SharePoint feature.

A *SharePoint feature* is a deployable unit that packages site customizations and custom code into a single component that an administrator can activate or deactivate. Features have a defined scope that dictates the breadth of their influence. A feature can be scoped to the entire server farm, a single web application, a site collection, or just a site. This scope determines the level of administrator needed to turn it on or off and the level at which its customizations are applied. Features can include customizations such as list templates, list instances, or custom menu items, and can be used to provision new files such as master-page templates, web-part definitions, and web-content-management page layouts. Features can even run custom code in response to their activation or deactivation. Figure 7-4 displays the Site Features administration page from the Site Settings menu of a team site we will use in this chapter.

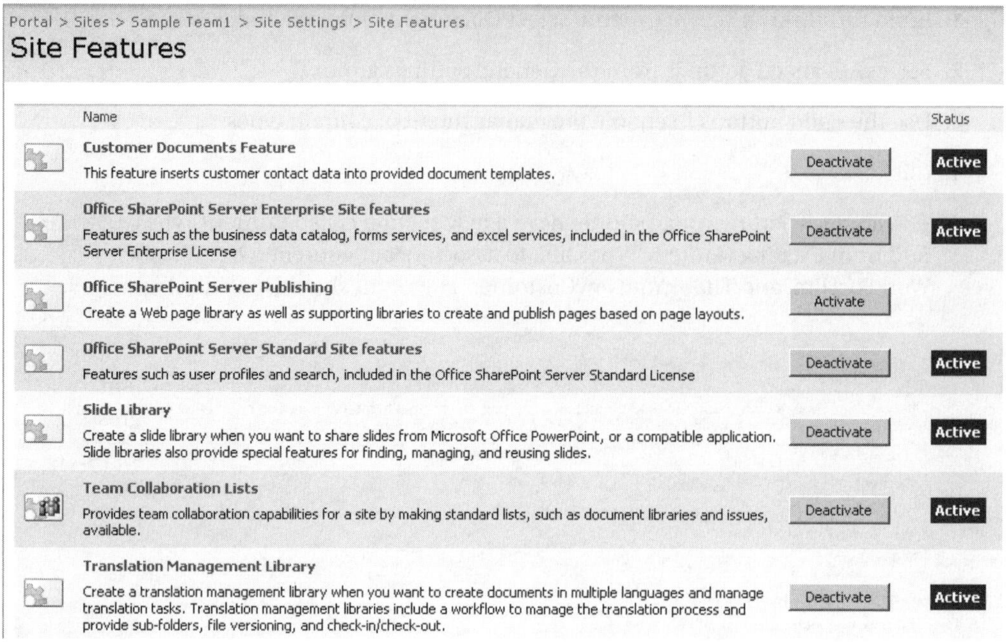

Figure 7-4. *Site features of a team site*

To understand the impact of a feature, explore what happens when you deactivate the Slide Library feature. You will receive a warning; deactivate it. Turning off this feature removes your ability to create instances of the slide library template in your site. In fact, this option will not even show up in any creation dialog. If you reactivate the feature, the options return. In case you are wondering, deactivating the Slide Library feature does not delete any slide libraries that have already been created. But that was a choice by the developers who created this feature. You will have to decide what you want to happen when your feature is activated and deactivated on a site.

To create the feature, we will use a Visual Studio VB.NET class library project. Name the project and solution **CustomerDocumentsFeature**. Delete the default class file and add one named CustomerDocumentsReceiver.vb. This class can be used as receiver containing custom code that runs in response to the feature being activated or deactivated. Be sure to add a reference to the Windows SharePoint Services assembly. This assembly should be listed in Visual Studio's Add Reference dialog; if it's not, you can find it in C:\Program Files\Common Files\ Microsoft Shared\web server extensions\12\ISAPI\Microsoft.SharePoint.dll. The project needs to be signed since the receiver will be deployed to the Global Assembly Cache. Follow these steps to sign the assembly:

1. Right-click on the project in Solution Explorer and select Properties.

2. Select Signing in the left-hand navigation bar.

3. Click the check box to sign the assembly.

4. Select New.

5. For the name of the file, type in **key**.

6. Deselect the check box for protecting the file with a password.

7. Click OK.

8. Click Visual Studio's Save toolbar button to commit this setting.

We will be adding several files to this project beyond the feature receiver. These additional files will need to be deployed to the server's TEMPLATE directory at `C:\Program Files\ Common Files\Microsoft Shared\web server extensions\12\TEMPLATE` by default. To make deployment easier, we will mirror the directory structure of the server so that our new files are placed in the appropriate location. Figure 7-5 illustrates the structure, beginning with a TEMPLATE directory and including directories named Features, CustomerDocuments, and Layouts. The files in these directories are ones that we will add as this chapter progresses.

Figure 7-5. *Feature project's TEMPLATE directory structure*

Defining the Feature

The CustomerDocuments folder defines the feature. It contains several XML files, including `feature.xml`. That file is the primary manifest file containing information about the feature, references to element files that detail the customizations the feature contains, and activation dependencies for other features that this one relies on. Listing 7-1 contains the feature-information section of this file.

Listing 7-1. *Definition of the Feature*

```
<?xml version="1.0" encoding="utf-8" ?>
<Feature Id="E619C929-77D0-47f2-95EF-CE2721B79350"
    Title="Customer Documents Feature"
    Description="This feature inserts customer contact data into provided~
                    document templates."
    Version="1.0.0.0"
    Scope="Web"
    ReceiverAssembly="CustomerDocumentsFeature, Version=1.0.0.0,~
```

```
                    Culture=neutral, PublicKeyToken=45a2811e9ad438d2"
ReceiverClass="CustomerDocumentsFeature.CustomerDocumentsReceiver"
Hidden="FALSE"
xmlns="http://schemas.microsoft.com/sharepoint/">
```

Throughout this section we will be creating several XML files like this one. To get more support, you should associate each file with the WSS schema. By doing so, you'll make Visual Studio's IntelliSense feature available while you are working with these files. Simply set the Schemas property in Visual Studio's Properties Explorer while editing the file. The WSS schema is located at: `C:\Program Files\Common Files\Microsoft Shared\web server extensions\12\TEMPLATE\XML\wss.xsd`. This definition of the feature includes a new GUID as its Id. You can use the Create Guid option from the Tools menu of Visual Studio to create a unique GUID. The ReceiverAssembly attribute is the strong name of the assembly. The public key token used here depends on the key you used to sign the assembly. To retrieve this you must first compile your project to create the DLL and then use Visual Studio's command-line `SN.exe` tool.

The next portion of `feature.xml` defines the element manifests. An element manifest contains the settings of the customizations that the feature will contain. You can have any number of manifests, but it makes sense to group them based on the type of customization. For this solution we will include one manifest for customizations that act on lists, and one manifest for custom actions that our feature places in the site. Listing 7-2 contains this section of the XML document, including references to an element manifest of custom actions and an element manifest of list customizations.

Listing 7-2. *A Feature's Element Manifests*

```
<ElementManifests>
  <ElementManifest Location="actionElements.xml"/>
  <ElementManifest Location="listElements.xml"/>
</ElementManifests>
```

The last section of `feature.xml` details this feature's activation dependencies. An *activation dependency* is a feature's way of enforcing that other features that include functionality it relies on are also activated. A feature's activation dependencies cannot reference a feature of a more restrictive scope. Since the CustomerDocuments feature is going to create a contacts list and a document library, it makes sense for each of these to be listed as a dependency. You can find these dependencies' feature IDs by browsing the `Template\Features` directory on the server. Both the DocumentLibrary and ContactsList features have their own folders and a `feature.xml` file that contains their GUIDs. Since these features are part of the core product, they will be the same on your system. Listing 7-3 shows how to construct the activation dependencies.

Listing 7-3. *A Feature's Activation Dependencies*

```
<ActivationDependencies>
   <!-- ContactsList Feature -->
   <ActivationDependency FeatureId="00BFEA71-7E6D-4186-9BA8-C047AC750105"/>
   <!-- DocumentLibrary Feature -->
   <ActivationDependency FeatureId="00BFEA71-E717-4E80-AA17-D0C71B360101"/>
</ActivationDependencies>
</Feature>
```

The listElements.xml file contains information about the customizations related to creating and configuring the necessary lists and libraries for the solution. In this case, the feature will create a contacts list named Customer Contacts and a document library named Customer Documents. Listing 7-4 details the portion of this file responsible for creating the Customer Contacts list.

Listing 7-4. *Creating the Customer Contacts List*

```
<?xml version="1.0" encoding="utf-8" ?>
<Elements xmlns="http://schemas.microsoft.com/sharepoint/">
  <ListInstance
   Id="30001"
   FeatureId="00BFEA71-7E6D-4186-9BA8-C047AC750105"
   Description="Customer Contacts"
   TemplateType="105"
   Title="Customer Contacts"
   OnQuickLaunch="TRUE"
   QuickLaunchUrl="Customer Contacts/AllItems.aspx"
   Url="Customer Contacts">
    <Data/>
  </ListInstance>
```

The ListInstance element instructs the site to create a Customer Contacts list upon activation. The Id attribute is a unique integer within this feature definition. The FeatureId attribute used here is the GUID of the feature containing the template for the list. Since Customer Contacts is to be a normal instance of the out-of-the-box contacts list, the identifier of the ContactsList feature is used in our ListInstance declaration. Also note the attributes related to the Quick Launch bar, which make sure this new list is included in the navigation of the site. The empty Data element of the instance is the area that could be used to preload data into the list; however, we will not use it here.

It is also possible to define your own list templates in an elements file instead of relying on a built-in list type. Listing 7-5 details the other ListInstance element responsible for creating the Customer Documents document library. In this case, the FeatureId is the GUID of the DocumentLibrary feature.

Listing 7-5. *Creating the Customer Documents Library*

```
<ListInstance
   Id="30002"
   FeatureId="00BFEA71-E717-4E80-AA17-D0C71B360101"
   Description="Customer Documents"
   TemplateType="101"
   Title="Customer Documents"
   OnQuickLaunch="TRUE"
   QuickLaunchUrl="Customer Documents/Forms/AllItems.aspx"
   Url="Customer Documents">
    <Data/>
  </ListInstance>
```

The last portion of this file is shown in Listing 7-6. It contains three ContentTypeBinding elements that are responsible for linking the content types we created earlier with the Customer Documents document library. Now the ContentTypeIds in Listing 7-6 will be specific to your environment since you created them in the earlier step. In the next section, we will show you how to find the IDs that the system generated for each of your content types.

Listing 7-6. *Binding Content Types to the Document Library*

```
<ContentTypeBinding
  ContentTypeId="0x01010062D1E4330D68444195C9641FCAFCB2FB01"
  ListUrl="Customer Documents"
/>
<ContentTypeBinding
  ContentTypeId="0x01010062D1E4330D68444195C9641FCAFCB2FB03"
  ListUrl="Customer Documents"
/>
<ContentTypeBinding
  ContentTypeId="0x01010062D1E4330D68444195C9641FCAFCB2FB02"
  ListUrl="Customer Documents"
/>
</Elements>
```

Each of these bindings maps to one of the CustomerDocument content types we created earlier: BusinessFax, WorkForHire, and ThankYouNewCustomer. Looking at the ContentType-Ids in Listing 7-6, it is easily to tell that they all share a common parent. The telling sign is that the ID is exactly the same up to the last digit. In SharePoint, when a content type is derived from another type, it simply extends the ID by a few characters. In addition, the fact that each of these types begins with 0x0101 tells us that an ancestor of this type is the base Document content type. As Figure 7-6 shows, you can obtain the content type IDs in your environment by copying the ctype query string parameter on the Site Content Type administration page. Use this technique to retrieve each of your ContentTypeIds and update the code in Listing 7-6 to match your environment.

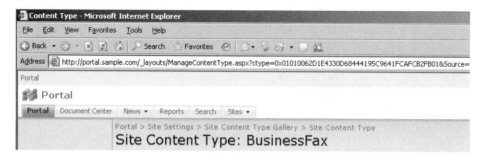

Figure 7-6. *Obtaining the content type ID*

The next element manifest file you need to create is `actionElements.xml`. This file contains information about the customizations related to adding links to menus for the solution. In this case, the feature will create a new link in the menu that displays when hovering over any contact item in the site. This menu is called the Edit Control Block menu. The custom action will be a link that directs the user to a custom application page that we will develop in the section "Building a Custom Application Page" later in this chapter. This page will allow the user to select which document template to merge with the chosen contact. Listing 7-7 contains the XML needed to add this custom action.

Listing 7-7. *Adding a Custom Action to the Edit Control Block Menu for Contacts*

```
<?xml version="1.0" encoding="utf-8" ?>
<Elements xmlns="http://schemas.microsoft.com/sharepoint/">
<!-- Per Item Dropdown (ECB)-->
<CustomAction Id="ECBItemToolbar"
              RegistrationType="List"
              RegistrationId="105"
              ImageUrl="/_layouts/images/ICDOC.GIF"
              Location="EditControlBlock"
              Sequence="225"
              Title="Build Customer Document">
<UrlAction~
 Url="~site/_layouts/BuildCustomerDoc.aspx?ItemId={ItemId}&amp;ListId={ListId}"/>
</CustomAction>
</Elements>
```

The most important attributes of the CustomAction element are RegistrationType, RegistrationId, and Location. The RegistrationType attribute details an attachment type. In this case, the action is associated with a list. Other possible attachment types include ContentType, FileType, or ProgId. The RegistrationId attribute further clarifies the attachment by specifying the identifier of the list, item, or content type that the attachment is associated with. In this case, the value of 105 represents the list template ID matching this action with contact lists. The Location attribute dictates where this action should be displayed for the list. In this case, we want the action to display when the user hovers over any specific content item, so we want it in the Edit Control Block. Figure 7-7 displays the combined effect of the RegistrationType, RegistrationId, and Location attributes.

Figure 7-7. *An Edit Control Block custom action*

When the user clicks on our action, we want to direct them to the custom application page (BuildCustomerDoc.aspx), which we will develop later in this chapter. Notice how the

URL specified in Listing 7-7 includes tokens that represent the current site (~site), the item selected ({ItemId}), and the list that contains it ({ListId}). Passing these values will allow the custom page to retrieve the selected contact item so it can merge it with a document template. As a developer, you can use custom actions within features to add links to just about everywhere within SharePoint. The following URL contains more information about other possible locations and URL tokens that you can use in actions: http://msdn2.microsoft.com/en-us/library/ms473643.aspx.

Deploying the Feature

At this point, there is enough functionality in this feature that it makes sense to deploy it to SharePoint to test that it successfully activates and deactivates. Deploying the feature involves first compiling the solution. Once it has been compiled, we will install the assembly that contains the feature receiver into the Global Assembly Cache (GAC), copy the project's XML files to their correct location in the server's TEMPLATE directory, and use STSADM.exe to install and activate the feature. To orchestrate these steps, we will rely on Visual Studio's support of post-build events and a custom installation batch file. Use the following steps to access the Build Events dialog for your project:

1. Right-click on your project and select Properties.

2. Select Compile in the left-hand navigation bar.

3. Click the Build Events button.

Figure 7-8 shows the Build Events dialog, where we will enter commands to add the assembly to the GAC and start the batch file.

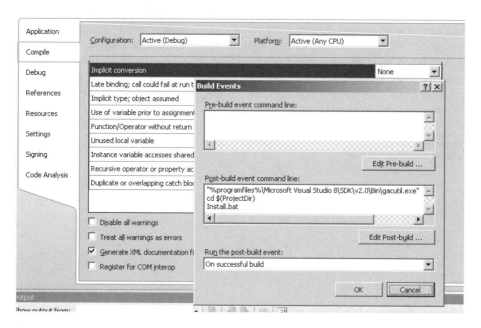

Figure 7-8. *Entering post-build events*

Three commands make up the post-build command script. The syntax of these commands is detailed in Listing 7-8. The first installs the built assembly into the GAC. The $(TargetPath) wildcard used here will be replaced with the path and name of the constructed assembly. The second command changes the current directory to the root level of the project using the $(ProjectDir) wildcard. The third command executes the installation batch file.

Listing 7-8. *Post-Build events*

```
"%programfiles%\Microsoft Visual Studio 8\SDK\v2.0\Bin\~
     gacutil.exe" -if $(TargetPath)
cd $(ProjectDir)
Install.bat
```

Add a batch file named install.bat to the root of your project directory. This installation batch file will do all the heavy lifting of interacting with SharePoint to properly deploy the feature. The batch file will first attempt to deactivate and uninstall the feature in the development site. This is to enable multiple iterations of a developer building, deploying, and testing the same feature in the same site. (You should expect to get errors from these two commands the first time you deploy a new feature since there is not a previous installation to deactivate or uninstall.) The batch file then copies the contents of the project's Template directory to the server's TEMPLATE directory. This is why we took so much care earlier to organize the project's directory structure to mirror that of the server. With the files deployed, the only remaining steps are to install the feature and activate it on our development site. Notice the batch file does include an IISRESET since the server could cache the definition of the feature in memory. Listing 7-9 includes the contents of the installation batch file. Be sure to customize the URLs here for the development site you are working with.

Listing 7-9. *Installation Batch File*

```
@SET TEMPLATEDIR="c:\program files\common files\microsoft shared\~
    web server extensions\12\Template"
@SET STSADM="c:\program files\common files\microsoft shared\~
    web server extensions\12\bin\stsadm"

Echo Deactivating feature
%STSADM% -o deactivatefeature -filename CustomerDocuments\~
    feature.xml -url http://portal.sample.com/SiteDirectory/team1/

Echo Uninstalling feature
%STSADM% -o uninstallfeature -filename CustomerDocuments\feature.xml

Echo Copying files
rd /s /q %TEMPLATEDIR%\Features\CustomerDocuments
xcopy /e /y TEMPLATE\* %TEMPLATEDIR%

Echo Installing feature
%STSADM% -o installfeature -filename  CustomerDocuments\feature.xml -force
```

```
IISRESET

Echo Activating features
%STSADM% -o activatefeature -filename CustomerDocuments\~
    feature.xml -url http://portal.sample.com/SiteDirectory/team1/ -force
```

Before compiling the project and deploying the feature to the server, you must address one more item for the test to be successful. Even though we have not used it yet, the feature receiver must be coded to derive from SPFeatureReceiver and stubbed out, or the activation will fail since the receiver will have the opportunity to run. Listing 7-10 is the code for the CustomerDocumentsReceiver class.

Listing 7-10. *Coding a Feature Receiver*

```
Imports Microsoft.SharePoint
Public Class CustomerDocumentsReceiver
    Inherits SPFeatureReceiver

    Public Overrides Sub FeatureInstalled(ByVal properties As~
            Microsoft.SharePoint.SPFeatureReceiverProperties)
    End Sub
    Public Overrides Sub FeatureUninstalling(ByVal properties As~
            Microsoft.SharePoint.SPFeatureReceiverProperties)
    End Sub
    Public Overrides Sub FeatureActivated(ByVal properties As~
            Microsoft.SharePoint.SPFeatureReceiverProperties)
    End Sub
    Public Overrides Sub FeatureDeactivating(ByVal properties As~
            Microsoft.SharePoint.SPFeatureReceiverProperties)
    End Sub
End Class
```

Now build the project. Assuming the build is successful, the post-build events will execute, as will the installation batch file. When complete, the feature should be activated on the site. Because of the IISRESET, occasionally the activation will time out and you may have to activate it from the Site Features administration page. Look for the newly created Customer Contacts list and Customer Documents library. Add a new item to the contacts list and test to make sure the custom action Build Customer Document displays. We have not built the destination page for the link, so clicking on the action will direct you to an error page. Visit the Customer Documents library and click on the New menu to confirm that the content types have been associated. Last, deactivate the feature. You will notice that the list and document library remain. Remember that the decision of how much to clean up is yours. By default, the lists and libraries will not be removed since they could contain content that you may not want your users to lose. If deletion were desired, the feature receiver would have code to perform the removal of the list and library in its FeatureDeactivating event. Even without including any deletion code, you will be able to see the impact of deactivating. After you've deactivated the CustomerDocuments feature, visit your contact item in Customer Contacts. Notice that the custom action has been removed from the Edit Control Block menu. Reactivating the feature does not create duplicate lists or libraries.

Building a Custom Application Page

When a user selects the Build Customer Document custom action from a contact item in the site, the solution will redirect the user to an application page that will show the document templates that are available from the Customer Documents document library. After the user makes a selection, the page will serialize the contact list item and place it into the Word 2007 document template as a custom XML part. The next section of this chapter goes into further detail about Microsoft Word 2007's support for custom XML parts. We will focus on creating the page, laying out its controls, and initial processing. Figure 7-9 depicts the end goal for BuildCustomerDoc.aspx (the Build Customer Documents page).

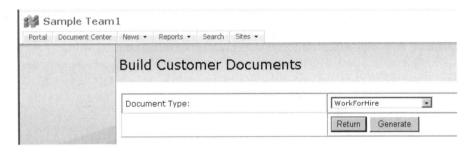

Figure 7-9. *The Build Customer Documents custom application page*

The Build Customer Documents page is termed an *application page* because it is not part of a site definition, but rather lives in SharePoint's Layouts directory. This means that the ASPX page can be accessed off of the path of any site through the _layouts virtual folder. Application pages are ASP.NET pages that derive from a SharePoint class LayoutsPageBase and rely on the application.master master page for their layout, look, and feel. These pages do not use the code-behind model and instead include their code within script blocks of the ASPX page. Listing 7-11 details the initial page directives, including referenced assemblies, imported namespaces, and page directives.

Listing 7-11. *Custom Application Page Directives*

```
<%@ Assembly Name="Microsoft.SharePoint, Version=12.0.0.0, Culture=neutral,~
      PublicKeyToken=71e9bce111e9429c"%>
<%@ Import Namespace="System.Collections.Generic" %>
<%@ Import Namespace="System.Xml" %>
<%@ Import Namespace="System.IO" %>
<%@ Assembly Name="WindowsBase, Version=3.0.0.0, Culture=neutral,~
      PublicKeyToken=31bf3856ad364e35"%>
<%@ Page Language="VB" MasterPageFile="~/_layouts/application.master"~
      Inherits="Microsoft.SharePoint.WebControls.LayoutsPageBase"~
      EnableViewState="true" EnableViewStateMac="false"    %>
<%@ Import Namespace="Microsoft.SharePoint" %>
<%@ Import Namespace="Microsoft.SharePoint.ApplicationPages" %>
<%@ Import Namespace="Microsoft.SharePoint.Administration" %>
<%@ Import Namespace="System.IO.Packaging" %>
```

```
<%@ Register Tagprefix="SharePoint" Namespace="Microsoft.SharePoint.WebControls"~
       Assembly="Microsoft.SharePoint, Version=12.0.0.0, Culture=neutral,~
       PublicKeyToken=71e9bce111e9429c" %>
<%@ Register Tagprefix="Utilities" Namespace="Microsoft.SharePoint.Utilities"~
       Assembly="Microsoft.SharePoint, Version=12.0.0.0, Culture=neutral,~
       PublicKeyToken=71e9bce111e9429c" %>
```

In Listing 7-11, the Assembly directive is responsible for linking an assembly to the page. Notice that there is an Assembly directive for the WindowsBase assembly. This assembly contains the System.IO.Packaging namespace, which contains classes for manipulating files based on the Office Open XML file format. In addition, you will need to add a reference to your project for the WindowsBase assembly. The Import directives associate particular namespaces so that referring to classes or controls within them does not require a fully qualified name. The Register directives identify tag prefixes that we can use to refer to server controls within the page's HTML. Finally, the Page directive details the page attributes, including the language we will use for coding and the fact that we want this page to maintain ViewState through postbacks. By maintaining ViewState, the controls on the page will maintain their values through round-trips to the server that result from the user clicking one of the buttons.

The application master page identifies three placeholders where the page can place content. The most important is PlaceHolderMain, which holds the server controls and layout for the body of the page. On the Build Customer Documents page, the main content area is an HTML table containing a drop-down list and two button controls. The other two placeholders just contain titles for the application page. Listing 7-12 details the content of the Build Customer Documents application page.

Listing 7-12. *Content of the Build Customer Documents Application Page*

```
<asp:Content ID="Main" contentplaceholderid="PlaceHolderMain" runat="server">
 <table border="1" cellpadding="5" cellspacing="0"~
        style="width:100%; font-size: 9pt" >
 <tr>
    <td>Document Type:</td>
    <td><asp:DropDownList ID="lstContentTypes"  runat="server"~
            EnableViewState="true"/></td>
 </tr>
 <tr>
    <td></td>
    <td><asp:Button ID="btnCancel"  Text="Return" runat="server" /> 
           <asp:Button ID="btnOK" Text="Generate" runat="server"~
           OnClick="btnOK_Click" />
    </td>
 </tr>
 </table>
</asp:Content>
<asp:Content ID="PageTitle" contentplaceholderid="PlaceHolderPageTitle"~
     runat="server">
```

```
Build Customer Documents
</asp:Content>
<asp:Content ID="PageTitleInTitleArea"~
    contentplaceholderid="PlaceHolderPageTitleInTitleArea" runat="server">
Build Customer Documents
</asp:Content>
```

This application page would be shown in response to a user clicking on the Build Customer Document action from any site that has the feature activated. For this reason, the page must first establish its context and get references to the site collection and the site from which it is being invoked. With these pieces of information, the application page can use the query string parameters that were passed by the custom action to identify the contacts list the user was in when he selected the action, as well as the individual item he selected. Listing 7-13 includes the code for these initial operations.

Listing 7-13. *Intializations of the Application Page*

```
Dim siteCollection As SPSite = Nothing
Dim webObj As SPWeb = Nothing
Dim listId As Guid = Nothing
Dim itemId As Integer = 0
Dim customerDocLib As SPFolder = Nothing

Protected Overrides Sub OnLoad(ByVal e As EventArgs)
Try
    siteCollection = SPContext.Current.Site
    webObj = SPContext.Current.Web
    listId = New Guid(Server.UrlDecode(Request.QueryString("ListId")))
    itemId = Integer.Parse(Request.QueryString("ItemId"))
    customerDocLib = webObj.GetFolder("Customer Documents")
```

During the page-load event, several of the server controls on the page are initialized. The Cancel button is set up to return the user to the previous page, where the custom action was selected. The drop-down list is populated with the content types that are bound to the site's Customer Documents document library. We exclude the Document content type since it is not a custom one that will support the contact's data as a custom XML part. Listing 7-14 includes the code necessary to set up the server controls.

Listing 7-14. *Setting Up the Server Controls*

```
If (Not Me.IsPostBack) Then
    Me.btnCancel.OnClientClick = "javascript:history.go(-1);return false;"
    Dim contentTypes As Generic.IList(Of SPContentType) =~
        customerDocLib.ContentTypeOrder
      'populate drop-down
    Dim contType As SPContentType = Nothing
    Dim i As Integer = 0
```

```
    For Each contType In contentTypes
        If (contType.Name <> "Document") Then
            Dim item = New ListItem(contType.Name, i)
            lstContentTypes.Items.Add(item)
        End If
        i += 1
    Next
End If
```

Using a Custom XML Part in a Document Template

The custom application page will merge the selected contact item with the chosen document template. To facilitate this operation, we will leverage the fact that the document templates are Microsoft Word 2007 files saved using the new Open XML file format. As explained in Chapter 3, the Microsoft Office 2007 desktop tools have switched from their proprietary binary-formatted files to formats based on Open XML specifications. Now each file—whether it be a spreadsheet, a presentation, or a document—is really a package of parts and items. *Parts* are pieces of content for the file, whereas *items* are metadata describing how the parts should be assembled and rendered. Most of these pieces are XML files, making it possible for them to be manipulated through code. You can gain insight into the structure of an Open XML–based file by replacing its file extension with **.zip** since the file is really an ordinary Zip archive. We will use an instance of the business-fax template we created earlier. Make sure that you are modifying a BusinessFax document that has been saved to the site's Customer Documents document library once before. This will help you understand how SharePoint uses the Open XML file formats, as well. Figure 7-10 shows the root of the archive for the Business Fax document.

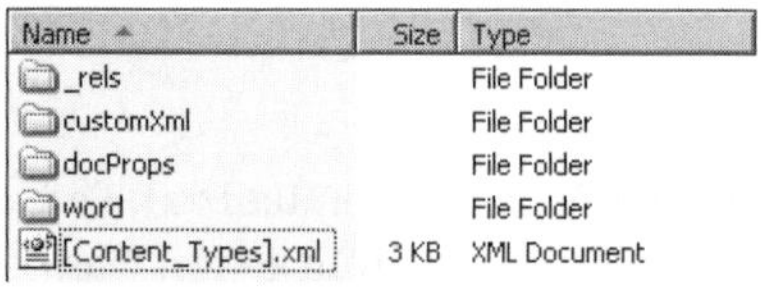

Name ▲	Size	Type
_rels		File Folder
customXml		File Folder
docProps		File Folder
word		File Folder
[Content_Types].xml	3 KB	XML Document

Figure 7-10. *Examining the archive of a Word document*

The XML file in the root is named [Content_Types].xml and it stores content-type directives for all the parts that appear in the archive. A content type contains metadata about a particular part or groups of parts and, more importantly, contains a directive as to how the application should render that part. For example, Listing 7-15 shows just a few lines from the XML file, but clearly delineates how this file tells the rendering application which parts are images, styles, relationships, custom properties, and even the main document.

Listing 7-15. *The Document's Content Types*

```
<Override PartName="/customXml/itemProps1.xml"
  ContentType="application/vnd.openxmlformats-officedocument.~
         customXmlProperties+xml"/>
<Default Extension="wmf" ContentType="image/x-wmf"/>
<Default Extension="rels"
  ContentType="application/vnd.openxmlformats-package.relationships+xml"/>
<Default Extension="xml" ContentType="application/xml"/>
<Override PartName="/word/document.xml"
   ContentType="application/vnd.openxmlformats-officedocument.~
         wordprocessingml.document.main+xml"/>
<Override PartName="/word/styles.xml"
   ContentType="application/vnd.openxmlformats-officedocument.~
         wordprocessingml.styles+xml"/>
```

Pay particular attention to the first line of Listing 7-15. The Override element is describing the itemProps1.xml file as being something more than just any XML file inside the document package. In fact, itemProps1.xml is a file that contains the properties of a custom XML part. It describes item1.xml, which stores the actual custom XML data. All of the Office document types support having a custom XML folder that is capable of storing information. In fact, SharePoint itself creates three custom XML parts in Office 2007 files when they are uploaded into site libraries. These XML parts are for storing metadata values, the schema of the document information panel, and workflow information. Though all of the Office 2007 files can store custom XML, Microsoft Word 2007 offers the unique added benefit of having a set of content controls that can bind to the custom XML parts, displaying the data inline with the document. So open the BusinessFax document you created earlier and follow these steps to add content controls that we will bind to contact data:

1. Delete the text following the Fax Number: prompt.

2. Click on the Developer tab in the Microsoft Word ribbon. This tab may be hidden on your machine, but it can be enabled through the Popular settings of the Word Options dialog. The Word Options dialog is accessible by clicking on the new pearl (Office logo) button in the top-left corner of Microsoft Word 2007.

3. Place your cursor after the colon (:) and click the plain-text button Aa in the Controls group.

4. Click the Properties button in the ribbon on the right-hand side of the Controls group.

5. Set the Title and Tag values to **FaxNumber**.

6. Click the check box to keep the content control from being deleted accidentally.

7. Click the check box to disable editing of the control's content. The end result should look like Figure 7-11.

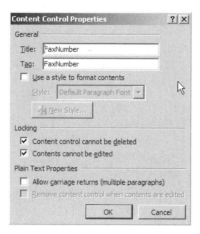

Figure 7-11. *Adding content controls to a document*

Repeat the same steps to add a plain-text content control for the To field. Name the content control **FullName**. The document could have many more content controls, but these two will be enough to illustrate the solution. In this example, we are relying on just the plain-text content control, but Microsoft Word does support others, such as picture, rich text, drop-down list, and a calendar control for dates. Save the file, change it to a Zip archive, and extract its contents to a folder. With all of the package's parts available to use as individual files, we can take the necessary steps to create a new custom XML part named item4.xml and bind these controls to its data. We will be making many of our edits directly to the XML parts. For this reason, we recommend downloading and using the schemas for the Open XML file format that Microsoft makes available (http://www.microsoft.com/downloads/details. aspx?FamilyId=15805380-F2C0-4B80-9AD1-2CB0C300AEF9&displaylang=en). Once the schemas are installed, you can edit these parts inside Visual Studio and, with the schemas referenced, receive IntelliSense support.

Start by creating the custom XML part item4.xml. This file should be inside the customXml folder. Eventually the application page will replace this file with data of its own, so we need to put in only enough data to confirm the bindings are set up appropriately. Listing 7-16 contains sample XML for this part. Notice that we use our own XML namespace to differentiate the data here from the rest of the parts, and that the element names are encoded. This encoding is done deliberately since the names of the list columns will need this same treatment when the custom application page serializes the contact data.

Listing 7-16. *The item4.xml Custom XML Part*

```xml
<?xml version="1.0"?>
<sc:Contact xmlns:sc="http://www.sample.com/2006/schemas/contact/">
  <sc:ID>1</sc:ID>
  <sc:Last_x0020_Name>hild</sc:Last_x0020_Name>
  <sc:First_x0020_Name>ed</sc:First_x0020_Name>
  <sc:Full_x0020_Name>ed hild</sc:Full_x0020_Name>
  <sc:E-mail_x0020_Address/>
```

```
  <sc:Company>sample inc</sc:Company>
  <sc:Fax_x0020_Number>333-333-333</sc:Fax_x0020_Number>
  <sc:Address/>
  <sc:City/>
  <sc:State_x002F_Province/>
  <sc:ZIP_x002F_Postal_x0020_Code/>
</sc:Contact>
```

Each custom XML part has a paired properties file. So in the same customXML folder create an `itemProps4.xml`. This properties file contains a key piece of information: the data-storeItem identifier. This identifier is a unique GUID. Be sure to keep this ID handy; we will have to reference it in the bindings as well as the merging code in the custom application page. Listing 7-17 shows the XML in `itemProps4.xml`.

Listing 7-17. *itemProps4.xml*

```
<?xml version="1.0" encoding="UTF-8" standalone="no"?>
<ds:datastoreItem ds:itemID="{9CBB321F-B9AE-4BDE-84BC-641A5A11251C}"~
      xmlns:ds="http://schemas.openxmlformats.org/officeDocument/2006/customXml">
  <ds:schemaRefs>
    <ds:schemaRef ds:uri="http://www.sample.com/2006/schemas/contact/"/>
  </ds:schemaRefs>
</ds:datastoreItem>
```

The package's customXml folder contains a subfolder named _rels. This folder contains relationship files that pair the custom XML part with its properties. Create a new file named `item4.xml.rels` with the contents of Listing 7-18.

Listing 7-18. *Relating the Custom XML Part to Its Properties*

```
<?xml version="1.0" encoding="UTF-8" standalone="yes"?>
<Relationships
   xmlns="http://schemas.openxmlformats.org/package/2006/relationships">
<Relationship Id="rId1"
   Type="http://schemas.openxmlformats.org/officeDocument/~
                 2006/relationships/customXmlProps"
   Target="itemProps4.xml"/>
</Relationships>
```

The next step is to make sure the package understands that we have added a custom XML part. To inform Microsoft Word, the part needs to be registered in the `[Content_Types].xml` file from Listing 7-15. Add another Override element to this file, which is identical to the other itemProps#.xml files. There is one other relationship file that must be modified. The file is located in the Word folder of the package and is named `document.xml.rels`. This file contains information about the relationships between the package and the actual document. Add another relationship to this file with a unique relationship number. The added line should be similar to the one in Listing 7-19.

Listing 7-19. *Relating the Custom XMLPpart to the Document*

```
<Relationship Id="rId11"
    Type="http://schemas.openxmlformats.org/officeDocument/2006/~
                    relationships/customXml"
    Target="../customXml/item4.xml"/>
```

The last set of modifications binds the content controls to specific data contained in the custom XML part. To create these bindings, we must edit the document.xml file contained in the package's Word folder. This file contains the BusinessFax document itself. Locate the FaxNumber content control; it's displayed in Listing 7-20 along with a new dataBinding element and default text.

Listing 7-20. *The FaxNumber Content Control in document.xml*

```
<w:sdt>
    <w:sdtPr>
    <w:alias w:val="FaxNumber"/>
    <w:tag w:val="FaxNumber"/>
    <w:id w:val="204026034"/>
    <w:lock w:val="sdtContentLocked"/>
    <w:placeholder>
        <w:docPart w:val="DefaultPlaceholder_22675703"/>
    </w:placeholder>
    <w:showingPlcHdr/>
    <w:dataBinding
        w:prefixMappings="xmlns:sc='http://www.sample.com/2006~
         /schemas/contact/'"~
        w:xpath="/sc:Contact/sc:Fax_x0020_Number"~
        w:storeItemID="{9CBB321F-B9AE-4BDE-84BC-641A5A11251C}"/>
    <w:text/>
    </w:sdtPr>
    <w:sdtContent>
        <w:r w:rsidR="00C947A8" w:rsidRPr="001362A5">
            <w:rPr>
                <w:rStyle w:val="PlaceholderText"/>
            </w:rPr>
            <w:t>Insert fax number</w:t>
        </w:r>
    </w:sdtContent>
</w:sdt>
```

The dataBinding element in Listing 7-20 uses the same namespace as the custom XML part and includes an attribute to the data-store identifier, which was the GUID used in item4Props.xml. The XPath query must resolve to a single node, as Microsoft Word's content controls will not automatically repeat for node collections. Notice the string *Insert fax number*. This is default text that will be used if the data binding is unable to locate a value in the custom XML part. Make the same type of edit for the FullName content control.

Now that the modifications are complete, zip the package contents such that [Content_Types].xml is at the root of the archive. Rename the Zip file to have a **.docx** file extension and open it in Microsoft Word 2007. If the modifications were made correctly, the data placed in item4.xml should display in the document. If they do, use this document to replace the template that we uploaded for the content type. We have included a BusinessFax. docx with these modifications in the Source Code/Download section of the Apress web site (http://apress.com) in case you are having problems. You can also use these steps to make similar edits to the other content-type templates.

Performing the Merge

The BuildCustomerDoc.aspx application page has the responsibility of serializing the contact list item and placing it in the custom XML part we created in the preceding section. All of this work happens when the user clicks the Generate button on the custom application page shown in Figure 7-9 to generate the document. The code in the button's OnClick event handler locates the document template for the selected content type and copies it to a memory stream. This way the copy can be modified without changing the content type's template. Listing 7-21 includes this code.

Listing 7-21. *Copying the Content Type's Cocument Template*

```
Dim docStream As Stream = New MemoryStream
Dim contentType As SPContentType =~
    customerDocLib.ContentTypeOrder.~
    Item(lstContentTypes.SelectedValue)
Dim templateFile As SPFile =~
    contentType.ResourceFolder.Files~
    (contentType.DocumentTemplate)
Dim templateStream = templateFile.OpenBinaryStream()
Dim reader As BinaryReader = New BinaryReader(templateStream)
Dim writer As BinaryWriter = New BinaryWriter(docStream)
writer.Write(reader.ReadBytes(CInt(templateStream.Length)))
writer.Flush()
reader.Close()
templateStream.Dispose()
```

The next step is to locate the custom XML part where the application page needs to place the content data. Unfortunately, this is not as easy as it may seem. We cannot be guaranteed that the custom XML part we created earlier is still named item4.xml—SharePoint may have reordered the parts when we uploaded the document to the system. Therefore, the code in Listing 7-22 opens the stream as a package and iterates through the custom XML parts, looking for the namespace used to represent the contact data.

Listing 7-22. *Finding the Contact Data Custom XML Part*

```
'open .docx file in memory stream as package file
docStream.Position = 0
Dim pkgFile As Package = Package.Open(docStream, FileMode.Open, _
                                      FileAccess.ReadWrite)
```

```
'retrieve package part with XML data
Dim partNameTemplate As String = "/customXml/item{0}.xml"
Dim partName As String = Nothing
Dim pkgprtData As PackagePart = Nothing
Dim xDoc As XmlDocument = Nothing
Dim i As Integer = 1
While True
     partName = String.Format(partNameTemplate, i)
     If pkgFile.PartExists(New Uri(partName, UriKind.Relative)) Then
          pkgprtData = pkgFile.GetPart(New Uri(partName, UriKind.Relative))
          xDoc = New XmlDocument()
          xDoc.Load(pkgprtData.GetStream())
          If (xDoc.DocumentElement.NamespaceURI =~
                  "http://www.sample.com/2006/schemas/contact/") Then
               'this is the one we are looking for
               Exit While
          End If
     End If
     ' Pick an arbitrary number of part names to try.
     If i = 1000 Then
       Throw New InvalidOperationException("Unable to find XML part.")
     End If
     i += 1
End While
```

With the custom XML part located, the code continues. The next step is to serialize the selected contact into an XML representation and store the result in the custom XML part. Listing 7-23 includes the code that performs this operation. Notice the use of the XmlConvert class to make sure that the column names are properly escaped for XML.

Listing 7-23. *Serializing the Contact to the Custom XML Part*

```
Dim contactItem As SPListItem = Nothing
contactItem = webObj.Lists(Me.listId).GetItemById(Me.itemId)
'serialize the contact item into this customXml part
Dim rootNode As XmlNode = xDoc.DocumentElement
rootNode.RemoveAll()
Dim field As SPField
For Each field In contactItem.Fields
    Dim fieldNode As XmlNode = xDoc.CreateElement("sc", _
        XmlConvert.EncodeName(field.Title), _
        "http://www.sample.com/2006/schemas/contact/")
    If (contactItem(field.Id) IsNot Nothing) Then
      Dim fieldVal As XmlNode = xDoc.CreateTextNode~
            (contactItem(field.Id).ToString())
      fieldNode.AppendChild(fieldVal)
    End If
```

```
        rootNode.AppendChild(fieldNode)
Next
xDoc.Save(pkgprtData.GetStream(FileMode.Create, FileAccess.Write))
```

In modifying the contents of the custom XML part, we need to make sure that the data-store identifier remained unchanged. This is because the GUID is used in the data bindings of the content controls in document.xml. The code in Listing 7-24 finds the file that corresponds with the found custom XML part and makes sure the GUID is the one defined earlier.

Listing 7-24. *Setting the Data Store Identifier*

```
Dim dataStoreID As String = "{9CBB321F-B9AE-4BDE-84BC-641A5A11251C}"
'check the itemsProps to sync dataStoreID
partNameTemplate = "/customXml/itemProps{0}.xml"
partName = String.Format(partNameTemplate, i)
pkgprtData = pkgFile.GetPart(New Uri(partName, UriKind.Relative))
xDoc = New XmlDocument()
xDoc.Load(pkgprtData.GetStream())
xDoc.DocumentElement.Attributes(0).InnerText = dataStoreID
xDoc.Save(pkgprtData.GetStream(FileMode.Create, FileAccess.Write))
```

At this point, the memory stream contains the properly constructed document with the selected content data injected into the custom XML part. The only remaining task is to send this constructed document to the user via the code in Listing 7-25, which copies the contents of the memory stream into that of the HTTP response.

Listing 7-25. *Sending the Document to the User*

```
  'deliver stream to client
Response.ClearContent()
Response.ClearHeaders()
Response.AddHeader("content-disposition", "attachment; filename=" &~
        templateFile.Name)
Me.Response.ContentType = "application/vnd.ms-word.document.12"
Response.ContentEncoding = System.Text.Encoding.UTF8
docStream.Position = 0
Const size As Integer = 4096
Dim bytes(4096) As Byte
Dim numBytes As Integer
numBytes = docStream.Read(bytes, 0, size)
While numBytes > 0
    Response.OutputStream.Write(bytes, 0, numBytes)
    numBytes = docStream.Read(bytes, 0, size)
End While
Response.Flush()
docStream.Close()
docStream.Dispose()
Response.Close()
```

With the custom application page complete and the document templates updated with their content controls and custom XML parts, redeploy the feature. Place a contact in the Customer Contacts list and run the merge by selecting the Build Customer Document action. Choose the BusinessFax content type and generate the merged document.

Important Lessons

This chapter incorporated several key techniques that are worth highlighting, as they could easily be reused in other projects.

Defining content types: The solution detailed how to define the settings associated with a type of content for an organization. By creating a SharePoint content type, administrators have a single definition that can be reused uniformly throughout the site collection.

Developing a feature: The solution was packaged as a SharePoint feature. This enables any administrator in the site collection to activate or deactivate the functionality included in it. This technique increases the flexibility of the solution as well as centralizes the steps needed to deploy it.

Custom application page: The feature included a custom application page that was deployed to the server's Layouts directory. The page was created using the `application.master` master page and was integrated seamlessly to extend the site's functionality.

Open XML file format: The manipulation of the Microsoft Word documents on the server was made possible by the fact that the templates were stored using the Open XML file format. The format's support for custom XML parts enabled us to insert data into the file without requiring Word to be installed on the server.

Microsoft Word 2007 content controls: Inserting the data into a custom XML part would have done little if it were not for Microsoft Word 2007's content controls. These controls can be placed into a document and bound to the custom XML part through an XPath query. Though we used them in a read-only manner in this chapter, if a user were able to change the value in the control, the control would have updated the custom XML part.

Extension Points

While coding this example, we thought of several variations to the solution that we didn't include because they distracted from the solution's overall objective. We call them out now as extension points since they may be applicable to a specific project you are working on.

Delete a list and a library on feature deactivation: The solution detailed how to create the feature receiver, but didn't leverage it. You could use the FeatureDeactivating event to find the CustomerDocuments library and CustomerContacts list and delete them. We do not see this as an automatic action every feature should take, since the user could very well lose some important data. Every feature is unique and you'll want to consider the cleanup activities carefully.

Set company property in the customXml part: In our example the contact data was serialized into the custom XML part. However, all of the content types used in the example expected a Company value to be specified as a metadata property since the Company site column was added to the parent content type. We also mentioned that SharePoint uses the custom XML parts for data, including the file's metadata. Use the same technique to set the Company property before it is streamed to the user.

Configure the content types as a feature: In the solution the content types are created by interacting with the site, but they could have been made a feature. They could not, however, be in the same feature as the rest of the solution since content types cannot be declared inside a feature of web-level scope (usually site collection). You would need a completely separate feature. Of course, you would then want to set an activation dependency between them.

Further Reading

The following links are to resources a reader interested in this chapter's material will find useful:

- How To: Add Actions to the User Interface

  http://msdn2.microsoft.com/en-us/library/ms473643.aspx

- Working with Features

  http://msdn2.microsoft.com/en-us/library/ms460318.aspx

- Brian Jones: Open XML Formats Blog

  http://blogs.msdn.com/brian_jones/

- Open XML Developer.org

  http://openxmldeveloper.org/

- Word 2007 Content Controls and XML

  http://blogs.gotdotnet.com/modonovan/archive/2006/05/23/604704.aspx

- Creating ContentTypes in SharePoint 2007 by Using a Feature

  http://www.sharepointblogs.com/tonstegeman/archive/2006/07/18/9314.aspx

- HOW TO: Creating a Custom Document Library Feature in MOSS 2007

  http://www.sharepointblogs.com/tbaginski/archive/2006/06/02/8062.aspx

- How to: Supply a Doc Template for a Content Type in a Feature

  http://blogs.msdn.com/edhild/archive/2007/02/05/how-to-supply-a-doc-template-for-a-content-type-in-a-feature.aspx

- Introducing the Office (2007) Open XML File Formats

  http://msdn2.microsoft.com/en-us/library/ms406049.aspx

■ ■ ■

CHAPTER 8

Working Collaboratively with Document Fragments

Windows SharePoint Services provides an enhanced storage system that facilitates collaboration. This system improves upon old collaboration techniques of simply emailing documents back and forth or dropping them in a file share. Relying on email is an awkward system, as team members are never sure they have the most up-to-date version of the document and consolidating the changes becomes a laborious task. File shares are also limited in that files dumped there are often difficult to find, users have no idea if the file is currently being edited by another team member, and versioning is reduced to a Save As operation. SharePoint's system of Web-enabled content databases provides a rich experience for the team working on the document. The environment provides check-in/check-out functionality, versioning, metadata, search, and an entire web site for storing lists of data related to the creation of the document.

However, even this system becomes strained in scenarios in which the team's document is really a collection of separate sections. Frequently, these sections are independent and different team members are responsible for different pieces. Under these circumstances, the team members ideally would begin to work simultaneously. Yet this work often takes place serially because the file in a SharePoint library can be checked out by only one user at a time. In this chapter, we will detail how, as a developer, you can enhance this experience by enabling a Word 2007 document to be split into separate files, one for each of its sections. This will allow different team members to work on their sections simultaneously. When complete, your solution will support merging the individual sections back into a single document.

Real-World Examples

The key identifier that makes this solution applicable to an organization is any process in which different team members work on specific sections of a document. Consulting firms often have a sales resource, a project manager, and a development lead working on distinct portions of a proposal. The sales resource is focusing on background information on the company, case studies, and pricing. The project manager is responsible for documenting the project lifecycle, creating a high-level project plan, and detailing the change/review mechanisms. Meanwhile, the developer is taking the customer's functional requirements and outlining a proposed solution. All of these pieces have to be put together to complete the proposal. This problem is rather generic and can be found across many different customer types. In the construction industry, different team members are often responsible for certain sections of a contract. Even in the military, different organizations or levels of an organization are tasked with completing specific sections of a deliverable, such as in a policy review from different functional areas of the military branch. By allowing the team to divide and conquer the work, the solution in this chapter provides an efficient process that reduces the amount of time it takes to complete an entire document.

Solution Overview

Our scenario starts with a user who has a document with some boilerplate content. As described earlier, this document is made up of several sections that different users are responsible for completing. The sections' begin and end points are not easily deduced. Some sections include multiple headings while others may be just a paragraph. For this reason, we will allow the user to highlight each section, recording the selections within an XML structure. When the user has completed marking up the document and saved it to a SharePoint library, we will display a custom action named Split into Sections in that document's drop-down. After choosing this action, the user will be directed to a custom application page that we will construct, where the user will be given the option to create a new document library to hold the section files, or to use an existing one. We prefer the scenario of a new document library since it represents a container for the process of working on these files. We will store enough information about the source document in the properties of this document library (its property bag) to support a merge operation later. The solution will use the previous XML markup to create a document for each section. The team will be able to work with the separate files simultaneously, setting security and maintaining versions. When the sections are complete, we will allow the user to select a merge action (called Merge Sections) from the document library's toolbar. This will take the user to another custom application page where he can choose to write the merged document over the one that was split, or to save it to a new location.

Both the split and merge operations are operating on Microsoft Word 2007 documents. The modification of these files is made possible by the new Open XML file format. In both cases, we are able to perform these operations on the server interacting with streams and XML documents. At no time are we automating Microsoft Word on the server. In fact, it doesn't even need to be installed on the server for this solution to work.

This solution should be flexible enough to allow any site administrator to simply turn on this functionality for a site. For this reason, we have developed the solution as a SharePoint *feature*. Features are a way of packaging a set of customizations as a single unit that can be activated or deactivated. Though it takes a bit of effort to set up, it not only increases the reusability of the solution, but also eases deployment complexities.

Solution Walkthrough

The following section will detail the major elements of the solution and the decisions that were made in coding it. The walkthrough will show you how to create an XML schema and apply it to a Microsoft Word document. We will go into detail about how to package your solution as a feature that can be enabled by any site administrator who desires the functionality. This will include how to set up a feature project in Visual Studio, the XML files used to define the customizations of the feature, and how to deploy it. We will also show you how to create a custom document library template that we will use to distinguish the libraries of section files from the other document libraries on the site. The walkthrough includes the construction of the custom application pages for both splitting and merging. Finally, we will detail the manipulation of the XML in the documents, which facilitates the split and merge operations.

Creating the XML Schema

An XML schema is a file that defines a specific type of XML document. It provides information that describes the structures that will be present in any XML document constructed to comply with the schema. With this file, we can define the set of valid elements and attributes, the relationships between them, and the type of data that can be stored. Schemas are often used to validate that XML document instances are well-formed.

In this solution we will use an XML schema to describe the structure of the Microsoft Word documents that we want to split. The schema will be a rather simple one. It will dictate that the object we are operating on is a document and that the document is made up of a sequence of sections. You might think that we could obtain this information from Microsoft Word by itself. After all, the application is already saving its files in XML. We could, but such a solution would require us to infer the begin and end points of a section. This could lead us to use headings to mark the beginning and end of sections. Our goal is to be much more flexible, and allow the user to designate which document content belongs to which section. By providing our own schema, we will allow the author to highlight any range of the document and tag it as a section.

Creating an XML schema file could be accomplished using Notepad. Visual Studio also provides XML schemas as an item type that can be added to a project. The Visual Studio environment provides enhancements such as IntelliSense to make sure you are closing elements appropriately. It also provides a designer tool. Different developers have different comfort levels with the various techniques. In our solution, we did use Visual Studio, but we worked in the code window, where we could just type the schema instead of using the designer. If you are using Visual Studio, the solution or project type will not matter as the schema is not a part of the SharePoint feature we will be coding later. Listing 8-1 includes the contents of our `SectionedDocument.xsd` file, which is the schema we will apply to the documents we want to split.

Listing 8-1. *The Sectioned Document XML Schema*

```
<?xml version="1.0" encoding="utf-8"?>
<xs:schema id="SectionedDocument"~
    targetNamespace="http://tempuri.org/SectionedDocument.xsd"~
    elementFormDefault="qualified"~
    xmlns="http://tempuri.org/SectionedDocument.xsd"~
    xmlns:mstns="http://tempuri.org/SectionedDocument.xsd"~
    xmlns:xs="http://www.w3.org/2001/XMLSchema">
<xs:element name="Document" type="DocumentType">
</xs:element>
<xs:complexType name="DocumentType" mixed="true">
    <xs:sequence>
        <xs:element name="Section" minOccurs="1" maxOccurs="unbounded">
        </xs:element>
```

```
    </xs:sequence>
  </xs:complexType>
</xs:schema>
```

In the schema in Listing 8-1, notice that we have specified a namespace that the schema targets: `http://tempuri.org/SectionedDocument.xsd`. This namespace will be important because it will be the clue as to which XML markup of the Word document is ours versus that used by the application.

The first element defined is the Document element. It will represent the entire contents of the Microsoft Word document. It is the outer container of the rest of our markup. Notice the type of the Document element is DocumentType. This is a custom complex type. The definition of this type in the remainder of the schema specifies that a document contains a sequence of sections. This sequence must include at least one section (minOccurs) and can contain any number greater than that (maxOccurs).

Applying the Schema to a Document

Since Microsoft Word 2003, we have been able to attach custom schemas to Microsoft Word documents. For the developer, this feature provides a way of injecting custom XML markup into the file. This makes it easier to grab specific portions out of the document from custom code. For the user, Word provides an easy tool for selecting which portions of the document match the different elements of the schema.

Our first step will be to create a Microsoft Word 2007 document that we want to split. For this solution, we are limiting ourselves to documents that are text-only (they do not contain pictures or other embedded objects). In the "Extension Points" section of this chapter, we will point out how the solution would need to evolve to remove this restriction. For our sample document, we grabbed a few paragraphs of "Greeking" text in a variety of languages. The following URL is for a web site that hosts a Greeking application that you can use to generate this text: `http://www.duckisland.com/GreekMachine.asp`. To make the sections of the document obvious, we used some text in the Classical Latin, Marketing, and Techno Babble languages, separated with headings. Figure 8-1 shows our sample document, `TestDocument.docx`.

Use the following steps to attach the schema to the test document:

1. Click the Developer tab in the ribbon. This may be hidden. If it is, you can enable it through the Word Options interface. In the Popular section, there is a check box to Show Developer Tab in the Ribbon.

2. Click the Schema button in the XML group of controls.

3. Click the Add Schema button on the XML Schema tab.

4. Browse to where you saved the `SectionedDocument.xsd` schema file. In a production environment, this schema would be in a central location such as a SharePoint library.

5. Give the schema an alias of **SectionedDoc** and uncheck the option to have these changes affect the current user only.

6. Make sure the SectionedDoc schema is selected when you click OK to close the Templates and Add-ins dialog. This is shown in Figure 8-2.

Figure 8-1. *The sample document*

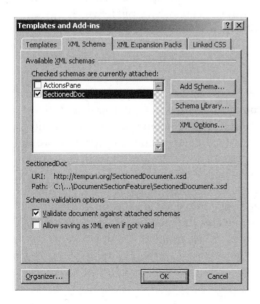

Figure 8-2. *Attaching the schema to the document*

When you close the Templates and Add-ins dialog, the XML Structure task pane will open alongside the document. This interface will enable you to select portions of the document and associate them with elements defined in the XML schema. Follow these steps to tag the test document appropriately:

1. Use Ctrl+A to select the entire document.

2. Click on the Document element in the Choose an Element to Apply to Your Current Selection area.

3. Click the Apply to Entire Document button in the dialog prompt. Once that's done, you should notice that the outer element node is displayed at the top of the XML Structure task pane and that markup tags have been inserted in the beginning and end of the document.

4. Now highlight from the Classical Latin heading (including the heading) through the paragraphs of text that are in Latin.

5. With the Classical Latin section highlighted, click the Section element in the Choose an Element to Apply to Your Current Selection area.

6. Repeat steps 4 and 5 for the Marketing and Techno Babble sections.

7. Save the document.

By following these steps, you have inserted custom markup into the Microsoft Word document. These custom tags detail the beginning and end of the document, as well as each section within it. The code we will develop later in the chapter will use these tags to locate, split, and merge the content. With all the tags in place, your document should look like Figure 8-3.

We will use this document as the source file that our code will operate on in the remainder of this chapter. We will upload it to a SharePoint site and choose to split it, which will create new files for each section in a new library. When the split is completed, there will be separate files for each of the Classical Latin, Marketing, and Techno Babble sections. The next few sections of this chapter explore this document's XML structures to show how we will be able to perform the necessary manipulations, as well as the development of a SharePoint feature that will contain our code. In a production environment, if this document were one that might be used repeatedly, it should be made a template for a content type. This would allow the organization to specify the boilerplate content, attached the schema, and designate the sections, freeing a user from having to perform these steps. Establishing a content type would give each new instance of the template these characteristics. In addition, the XML tags would likely be hidden from the user. To hide the tags in production documents, you would uncheck the Show XML Tags in Document check box in the XML Structure task pane. Do not do that for this sample—seeing these tags will provide greater insight into what is going on. If the topic of content types is new to you and you are interested in how they can be used in a solution, review Chapter 7.

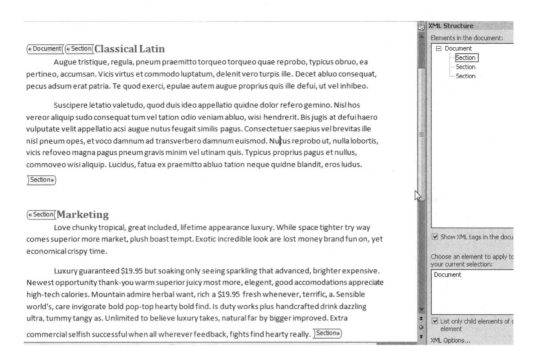

Figure 8-3. *Inserting custom XML tags into the document*

Examining the Document's XML

The split and merge operations are going to manipulate the content of the source document. The fact that we have saved this document as a Microsoft Word 2007 document allows us to take advantage of the new Open XML file format. As explained in Chapter 3, the Microsoft Office 2007 desktop tools have switched from their proprietary binary-formatted files to formats based on Open XML specifications. Now each file—whether it be a spreadsheet, presentation, or document—is really a package of parts and items. *Parts* are pieces of content for the file, whereas *items* are metadata describing how the parts should be assembled and rendered. Most of these pieces are XML files, making it possible for them to be manipulated through code. You can gain insight into the structure of an Open XML–based file by replacing its file extension with **.zip** since the file is really an ordinary Zip archive. Figure 8-4 shows the root of the archive for our test document.

Name ▲	Size	Type
_rels	0 KB	File Folder
docProps	0 KB	File Folder
word	0 KB	File Folder
[Content_Types]...	2 KB	XML Document

Figure 8-4. *Examining the archive of a Word document*

The XML file in the root is named [Content_Types].xml and it stores content-type directives for all the parts that appear in the archive. A content type contains metadata about a
particular part or groups of parts and more importantly, contains a directive about how the
application should render that part. For example, Listing 8-2 shows just a few lines from the
file, but clearly delineates how the file tells the rendering application which parts are styles,
relationships, settings, and even the main document.

Listing 8-2. *The Document's Content Types*

```
<Override PartName="/word/settings.xml"
  ContentType="application/vnd.openxmlformats-officedocument.~
        wordprocessingml.settings+xml"/>
<Default Extension="rels"
  ContentType="application/vnd.openxmlformats-package.relationships+xml"/>
<Default Extension="xml" ContentType="application/xml"/>
<Override PartName="/word/document.xml"
    ContentType="application/vnd.openxmlformats-officedocument.~
        wordprocessingml.document.main+xml"/>
<Override PartName="/word/styles.xml"
    ContentType="application/vnd.openxmlformats-officedocument.~
        wordprocessingml.styles+xml"/>
```

Pay particular attention to the Override element for the part named /word/document.xml.
This file contains the document's contents, and by inspecting it we can see the impact of tag-
ging the document with the custom schema elements. Figure 8-5 shows the document.xml file
in Internet Explorer. We have collapsed a few of the XML nodes to make it easier to see what is
going on.

```
- <w:body>
  - <w:customXml w:uri="http://tempuri.org/SectionedDocument.xsd" w:element="Document">
    - <w:customXml w:uri="http://tempuri.org/SectionedDocument.xsd" w:element="Section">
      - <w:p w:rsidR="0090501B" w:rsidRDefault="0090501B" w:rsidP="0090501B">
        - <w:pPr>
            <w:pStyle w:val="Heading1" />
          </w:pPr>
        - <w:r>
            <w:t>Classical Latin</w:t>
          </w:r>
        </w:p>
      + <w:p w:rsidR="0090501B" w:rsidRDefault="0090501B" w:rsidP="0090501B">
      + <w:p w:rsidR="0090501B" w:rsidRDefault="0090501B" w:rsidP="0090501B">
      </w:customXml>
    + <w:customXml w:uri="http://tempuri.org/SectionedDocument.xsd" w:element="Section">
    + <w:customXml w:uri="http://tempuri.org/SectionedDocument.xsd" w:element="Section">
    </w:customXml>
  + <w:sectPr w:rsidR="00AF2387" w:rsidSect="00AF2387">
  </w:body>
</w:document>
```

Figure 8-5. *The document.xml file with an attached schema*

Notice how this document includes several customXml elements whose Uri attribute has
the value of the custom schema's target namespace. This is Microsoft Word's way of including
our schema in its own. These customXml nodes were placed in the document to match the

selections made by the person using the XML Structure task pane. The element attribute of these nodes describes which element from our custom schema was applied to the selection. Looking at Figure 8-5, it is easy to see the outer document element with a sequence of three sections. We have expanded the first section so you can see the heading of Classical Latin is contained within it. To perform the split and merge operations our code will query this file, looking for these customXml nodes.

Building the Document Section Feature Project

Our solution is going to provide the organization with a set of customizations that together enable any site in the site collection to take advantage of this split and merge functionality. The important fact here is that we want to provide multiple instances of this capability throughout the site collection. Some sites may want to leverage it while others may not. For this reason, we will package our solution as a SharePoint feature.

A SharePoint *feature* is a deployable unit that packages site customizations and custom code into a single component that can be activated or deactivated by an administrator. Features can have a defined scope that dictates the breadth of their influence. A feature can be scoped to the entire server farm, a single web application, a site collection, or just a site. This scope determines the level of administrator needed to turn it on or off and the level at which its customizations are applied. Features can include customizations such as list templates, list instances, or custom menu items, and can be used to provision new files such as master-page templates, web-part definitions, and page layouts for web-content management. Features can even run custom code in response to their activation or deactivation. Figure 8-6 displays the Site Features administration page from the Site Settings of a team site we will use in this chapter. (Your site will not have the Document Section Feature item until you deploy this solution, and the Customer Documents Feature is covered in Chapter 7.)

Portal > Sites > dev2 > Site Settings > Site Features

Site Features

	Name		Status
	Customer Documents Feature This feature inserts customer contact data into provided document templates.	Activate	
	Document Section Feature This feature supports splitting a document into its sections and merging them back together.	Deactivate	Active
	Office SharePoint Server Enterprise Site features Features such as the business data catalog, forms services, and excel services, included in the Office SharePoint Server Enterprise License	Deactivate	Active
	Office SharePoint Server Publishing Create a Web page library as well as supporting libraries to create and publish pages based on page layouts.	Activate	
	Office SharePoint Server Standard Site features Features such as user profiles and search, included in the Office SharePoint Server Standard License	Deactivate	Active
	Slide Library Create a slide library when you want to share slides from Microsoft Office PowerPoint, or a compatible application. Slide libraries also provide special features for finding, managing, and reusing slides.	Deactivate	Active
	Team Collaboration Lists Provides team collaboration capabilities for a site by making standard lists, such as document libraries and issues, available.	Deactivate	Active

Figure 8-6. *Site features of a team site*

To understand the impact of a feature, explore what happens when you deactivate the Slide Library feature. You will receive a warning, but go ahead and deactivate it. Turning off this feature removes your ability to create instances of the Slide Library template on your site. In fact, this option will now not even show up in any creation dialog. When you reactivate the feature the options return. In case you are wondering, deactivating the Slide Library feature does not delete any slide libraries that have already been created. But that was a choice by the developers who created this feature. You will have the same decisions to make as to what you want to happen when your feature is activated and deactivated.

To create the Document Section feature, we will use a Visual Studio VB.NET class library project. Name the project and solution **DocumentSectionFeature**. Delete the default class file and add one named DocumentSectionReceiver.vb. This class can be used if you want to execute custom code in response to the feature being activated or deactivated. Be sure to add a reference to the Windows SharePoint Services assembly. This assembly should be listed in Visual Studio's Add Reference dialog, but if it's not, you can find it in C:\Program Files\Common Files\Microsoft Shared\web server extensions\12\ISAPI\Microsoft.SharePoint.dll. The project needs to be signed since the assembly will be deployed to the global assembly cache. Follow these steps to sign the assembly:

1. Right-click on the project in Solution Explorer and select Properties.

2. Select Signing in the left-hand navigation.

3. Click the check box to sign the assembly.

4. Select New.

5. For the name of the file, type in **key**.

6. Deselect the check box for protecting the file with a password.

7. Click OK.

8. Click Visual Studio's save toolbar button to commit this setting.

We will be adding several files to this project beyond the feature receiver that will need to be deployed to the server's Template directory (at C:\Program Files\Common Files\Microsoft Shared\web server extensions\12\TEMPLATE by default). To make deployment easier, we will mirror the directory structure of the server so that our new files are put in the appropriate place. Figure 8-7 illustrates the structure beginning with a TEMPLATE directory, including directories named Features, DocumentSectionFeature, ListTemplates, SectionsLibrary, and Layouts. The files in these directories are ones that we will add as the solution is constructed, but go ahead and create the directory structure.

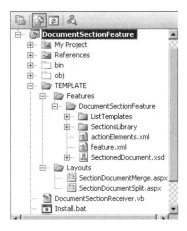

Figure 8-7. *The feature project's TEMPLATE directory structure*

Defining the Feature

The DocumentSectionFeature folder represents the definition of the feature. It contains several XML files. Feature.xml is the primary manifest file containing information about the feature, references to element files that detail the customizations the feature contains, and activation dependencies for other features that this one relies on. Listing 8-3 contains the feature-information section of this file.

Listing 8-3. *Definition of the Feature*

```
<?xml version="1.0" encoding="utf-8" ?>
<Feature Id="5FC9A8B0-5EF4-46b6-9B82-4DAB2E4B8448"
    Title="Document Section Feature"
    Description="This feature supports splitting a document into its sections~
                 and merging them back together."
    Version="1.0.0.0"
    Scope="Web"
    ReceiverAssembly="DocumentSectionFeature, Version=1.0.0.0,~
                 Culture=neutral, PublicKeyToken=45a2811e9ad438d2"
    ReceiverClass="DocumentSectionFeature.DocumentSectionReceiver"
    Hidden="FALSE"
    xmlns="http://schemas.microsoft.com/sharepoint/">
```

Throughout this section we will be creating several XML files like this one. To get more support, you should associate each file with the WSS schema to receive IntelliSense support while working with these files. This can be set up by setting the Schemas property in Visual Studio's Properties Explorer while editing the file. The WSS schema is located at C:\Program Files\Common Files\Microsoft Shared\web server extensions\12\TEMPLATE\XML\wss.xsd.

The definition of the feature includes a new GUID as its ID. You can use the Create GUID option from the Tools menu of Visual Studio to create a unique GUID. The ReceiverAssembly attribute is the strong name of the assembly. The public key token used here depends upon your key used to sign the assembly. To retrieve this you must first compile your project to create the DLL and then use Visual Studio's command-line SN.exe tool.

The next portion of feature.xml defines the element manifests. An element manifest contains the settings of the customizations that the feature will contain. You can have any number of manifests, but it makes sense to group them based on customization type. For this solution we will include one manifest for customizations that involve lists and one manifest for custom actions that our feature places in the site. Listing 8-4 contains this section of the XML document that includes references to an element manifest of custom actions and an element manifest of list customizations. We will create the files referenced here later in this chapter.

Listing 8-4. *A Feature's Element Manifests*

```
<ElementManifests>
    <ElementManifest Location="actionElements.xml"/>
    <ElementManifest Location="ListTemplates/sectionLibrary.xml"/>
</ElementManifests>
```

The last section of feature.xml details this feature's activation dependencies. An activation dependency is a feature's way enforcing that other features that include functionality it relies on are also activated. A feature's activation dependencies cannot reference a feature of a more restrictive scope. Since the Document Section Feature is going to include customizations for document libraries, it makes sense to specify the Document Library feature as a dependency. The FeatureIds of these dependencies can be found by browsing the Template\ Features directory on the server. The DocumentLibrary feature has its own folder, which includes a feature.xml file that will contain its GUID. Since this feature is part of the core product, the identifier will be the same on your system. Listing 8-5 shows how to construct the activation dependencies.

Listing 8-5. *A Feature's Activation Dependencies*

```
<ActivationDependencies>
    <!-- DocumentLibrary Feature -->
    <ActivationDependency FeatureId="00BFEA71-E717-4E80-AA17-D0C71B360101"/>
  </ActivationDependencies>
</Feature>
```

actionElements.xml is an element manifest file that contains information about the customizations this feature will make to the site. In this file, we will specify the customizations related to adding links to menus. The feature will create a new link in the menu (Edit Control Block) that displays when hovering over any Microsoft Word 2007 document contained within a document library of the site. The custom action will be a link that directs the user to a custom application page that we will develop in a later section of this chapter. This page will be responsible for collecting the user's preferences and performing the document split. Listing 8-6 contains the XML needed to add this custom action.

Listing 8-6. *Adding a Custom Action to Microsoft Word 2007 Documents*

```xml
<?xml version="1.0" encoding="utf-8" ?>
<Elements xmlns="http://schemas.microsoft.com/sharepoint/">
  <!-- Per Item Dropdown (ECB)-->
  <CustomAction Id="DocumentSection.SplitAction"
        RegistrationType="FileType"
        RegistrationId="docx"
        ImageUrl="/_layouts/images/ICDOC.GIF"
        Location="EditControlBlock"
        Sequence="225"
        Title="Split Into Sections">
    <UrlAction
        Url="~site/_layouts/SectionDocumentSplit.aspx?ItemId={ItemId}~
            &amp;ListId={ListId}"/>
  </CustomAction>
```

The most important attributes of this CustomAction element are RegistrationType, RegistrationId, and Location. The RegistrationType attribute details the type of attachment for the custom action. In this case, the action is associated with a particular type of file. Other possible values include ContentType, List, and ProgId. The RegistrationId attribute further clarifies the attachment by specifying the identifier of the list, item, or content type that the attachment is associated with. In this case, the value docx represents the file extension of Microsoft Word 2007 documents. The Location attribute dictates where this action should be displayed. In this case, we want the action to display when the user hovers over any specific document. This location is the Edit Control Block. The combined effect of these attributes is displayed in Figure 8-8.

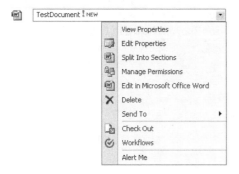

Figure 8-8. *An Edit Control Block custom action*

When the user clicks on our action, we want to direct him to the custom application page (SectionDocumentSplit.aspx) that we will develop in the "Building a Custom Application Page for Splitting" section of this chapter. Notice how the URL specified in the XML includes tokens that represent the current site (~site), the item selected ({ItemId}), and the list it is contained within ({ListId}). Passing these values will allow the custom page to retrieve the selected document and the library that contains it.

In addition to an action to split the document, the feature needs an action to allow the user to merge the section files back together. Since this is an action on a set of files, it is not appropriate to add the action to the Edit Control Block. In this case, the action will be located in the library's toolbar under the Actions menu. Now before looking at the XML for this action, we need to take a step back and realize that we don't want to put this merge menu option on every document library. We only really need it in libraries that were constructed to contain the section files. For this reason, our solution is going to include a custom document library template to hold the section files. By having a different library template with a different identifier, we will be able to tell apart the site's normal document libraries from the ones containing section files. We will build this template a bit later, but for now just understand that these libraries will have a unique ID of 10001. This identifier is used to appropriately locate the merge custom-action XML. The remainder of the `actionElements.xml` file contains this custom action, as shown in Listing 8-7.

Listing 8-7. *The Merge Custom-Action XML*

```
<CustomAction Id="DocumentSection.Merge"
    RegistrationType="List"
    RegistrationId="10001"
    ImageUrl="/_layouts/images/ICDOC.GIF"
    Location="Microsoft.SharePoint.StandardMenu"
    GroupId="ActionsMenu"
    Sequence="225"
    Title="Merge Sections">
<UrlAction Url="~site/_layouts/SectionDocumentMerge.aspx?ListId={ListId}"/>
</CustomAction>
```

In this custom action, the scope is limited to libraries of type 10001, which we will define as a library that stores section files. The Location and GroupId attributes place the Merge Sections action in the appropriate place in the library's toolbar, as shown in Figure 8-9.

Figure 8-9. *The merge action in a library of section files*

As a developer, you can use custom actions within features to add links to just about anywhere within SharePoint. The following URL contains more information about other possible locations and URL tokens that you can use in actions:

- How to: Add Actions to the User Interface

  `http://msdn2.microsoft.com/en-us/library/ms473643.aspx`

Now we will shift our attention to the `sectionLibrary.xml` element manifest file in the List-Templates directory of the feature. This file contains a definition of a new list template. This template will be a copy of the document library template with a unique type identifier of 10001. In the XML shown in Listing 8-8, the key attributes are the name of the template, its type identifier, the BaseType (which classifies it as a library), and DocumentTemplate (which specifies that a blank Word document—101—should be returned to a user who clicks the New button).

Listing 8-8. *The SectionsLibrary Template*

```
<?xml version="1.0" encoding="utf-8" ?>
<Elements xmlns="http://schemas.microsoft.com/sharepoint/">
  <ListTemplate Name="SectionsLibrary" Type="10001"
      BaseType="1" SecurityBits="11"
      DisplayName="Document Sections Library"
      OnQuickLaunch="TRUE" Unique="FALSE"
      Image="/_layouts/images/itdl.gif"
      Description="Stores sections of a document as individual files"
      DocumentTemplate="101" />
</Elements>
```

The ListTemplate declaration in Listing 8-8 simply calls out to the feature that there is a custom list template named SectionsLibrary. The schema of this list and forms for interacting with it will be added later in this chapter. This is the purpose of the SectionsLibrary folder in the feature. Since our custom SectionsLibrary template is almost identical to a document library, we can start by populating the SectionsLibrary folder with the items in the Document-Library feature's folder. The default location for these files is `C:\Program Files\Common Files\ Microsoft Shared\web server extensions\12\TEMPLATE\FEATURES\DocumentLibrary\DocLib`. We then want to modify the SectionsLibrary `schema.xml` file to update the List element shown in Listing 8-9.

Listing 8-9. *The SectionLibrary's schema.xml File*

```
<?xml version="1.0" encoding="utf-8"?>
<List xmlns:ows="Microsoft SharePoint" Title="SectionsLibrary"
    Direction="$Resources:Direction;" Url="Sections Library"
    BaseType="1">
```

Though it may seem like all we are doing is copying the out-of-the-box document library template, we are actually setting ourselves up for having a distinction between libraries that contain section files, and other site document libraries. This is an important step because it also provides an extension point we will discuss in the "Extension Points" section of this chapter: customizing this library's schema.

Deploying the Feature

At this point, there is enough functionality in this feature that it makes sense to deploy it to SharePoint to test that it successfully activates and deactivates. Deploying the feature involves first compiling the solution. Once it has been compiled, we will install the assembly that contains the feature receiver into the GAC, copy the project's XML files to their correct location in the server's Template directory, and use STSADM.exe to install and activate the feature. To orchestrate these steps, we will rely on Visual Studio's support of post-build events and a custom installation batch file. Use the following steps to access the Build Events dialog for your project:

1. Right-click on your project and select Properties.

2. Select Compile in the left-hand navigation.

3. Click the Build Events button.

Figure 8-10 shows the Build Events dialog where we will enter commands to add the assembly to the GAC and start the batch file.

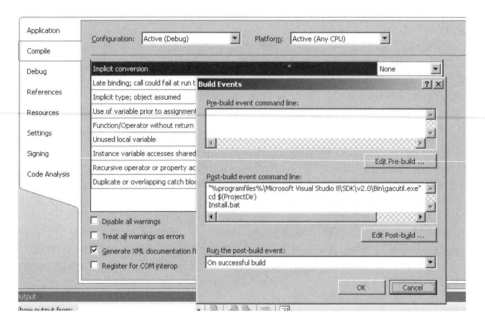

Figure 8-10. *Entering post-build events*

Three commands make up the post-build command script. The first installs the built assembly into the GAC. The $(TargetPath) wildcard used in the first command will be replaced with the path and name of the constructed assembly. The second command changes the current directory to the root level of the project using the $(ProjectDir) wildcard. The third command executes the installation batch file. Listing 8-10 details the syntax of these commands.

Listing 8-10. *Post-Build Events*

```
"%programfiles%\Microsoft Visual Studio 8\SDK\v2.0\Bin\~
      gacutil.exe" -if $(TargetPath)
cd $(ProjectDir)
Install.bat
```

Add a batch file named `install.bat` to the root of your project directory. This installation batch file will do all the heavy lifting of interacting with SharePoint to properly deploy the feature. Since we will be using the `STSADM.exe` SharePoint administration command-line tool, we're assuming that this batch file will be run locally on the MOSS server. The batch file will first attempt to deactivate the feature in the development site. This is to enable multiple interactions of a developer building, deploying, and testing the same feature in the same site. The installation file will then uninstall the feature. (You should expect to get errors from these two commands the first time you deploy a new feature since it is not there to deactivate or uninstall.) The batch file then copies the contents of the project's Template directory to the server's Template directory. This is why we took so much care earlier to organize the project's directory structure to mirror that of the server. With the files deployed, the only remaining steps are to install the feature and activate it on our development site. Notice the batch file does include an IISRESET since the server could cache the definition of the feature in memory. Listing 8-11 includes the contents of the installation batch file. Be sure to customize the URLs here for the development site you are working with.

Listing 8-11. *Installation Batch File*

```
@SET TEMPLATEDIR="c:\program files\common files\microsoft shared\~
    web server extensions\12\Template"
@SET STSADM="c:\program files\common files\microsoft shared\~
    web server extensions\12\bin\stsadm"

Echo Deactivating feature
%STSADM% -o deactivatefeature -filename DocumentSectionFeature\~
    feature.xml -url http://portal.sample.com/SiteDirectory/dev2/

Echo Uninstalling feature
%STSADM% -o uninstallfeature -filename DocumentSectionFeature\feature.xml

Echo Copying files
rd /s /q %TEMPLATEDIR%\Features\DocumentSectionFeature
xcopy /e /y TEMPLATE\* %TEMPLATEDIR%

Echo Installing feature
%STSADM% -o installfeature –filename DocumentSectionFeature\feature.xml -force

IISRESET

Echo Activating features
%STSADM% -o activatefeature -filename DocumentSectionFeature\~
    feature.xml -url http://portal.sample.com/SiteDirectory/dev2/ -force
```

Before compiling the project and deploying the feature to the server, we need to address one more item for the test to be successful. Even though we have not used it yet, the feature receiver must be coded to derive from SPFeatureReceiver and stubbed out, or the activation will fail since this class will have the opportunity to run. We want your solution to have the DocumentSectionReceiver class so you know how to add a receiver (though not every feature has to have one). Make sure you added a reference to the Windows SharePoint Services assembly (Microsoft.SharePoint namespace). Listing 8-12 is the code for the DocumentSectionReceiver class.

Listing 8-12. *Coding a Feature Receiver*

```
Imports Microsoft.SharePoint
Public Class DocumentSectionReceiver
    Inherits SPFeatureReceiver

    Public Overrides Sub FeatureInstalled(ByVal properties As~
            Microsoft.SharePoint.SPFeatureReceiverProperties)
    End Sub
    Public Overrides Sub FeatureUninstalling(ByVal properties As~
            Microsoft.SharePoint.SPFeatureReceiverProperties)
    End Sub
    Public Overrides Sub FeatureActivated(ByVal properties As~
            Microsoft.SharePoint.SPFeatureReceiverProperties)
    End Sub
    Public Overrides Sub FeatureDeactivating(ByVal properties As~
            Microsoft.SharePoint.SPFeatureReceiverProperties)
    End Sub
End Class
```

Now build the project. Assuming the build is successful, the post-build events will execute, as will the installation batch file. When complete, the feature should be activated on the site. Because of the IISRESET, occasionally the activation times out and you may have to activate it from the Site Features administration page. Upload the test document you created earlier to a document library in the site and see if the Split custom action displays. From the View All Site Content page, use the Create button to create your own Document Section library. This library is our custom template, so make sure the Merge action has been added to the toolbar.

Building a Custom Application Page for Splitting

When a user selects the Split into Sections custom action from a Word 2007 document in the site, the solution will redirect the user to an application page. This page will allow the user to select where the individual section files are to be stored. The target location is specified using one of two options. The first is to create a new instance of our SectionLibrary document template; the other is to select an existing one in the site. Of course, if the user is opting to create a new library, he must have permission to do so in the site. If not, the application page will return an Access Denied message. This may not be desirable, and we discuss a way to work around it in the "Extension Points" section of this chapter.

After the user selection, the page will create the new library (if necessary), place a file for each section into the library, and save properties about the source document in the library to support the merge operation. There is a good bit of code in the next few sections of this chapter. We will focus on the important fragments, but please refer to the code download (at the Source Code/Download section of the Apress web site) to get every line. Figure 8-11 depicts the end goal for SectionDocumentSplit.aspx.

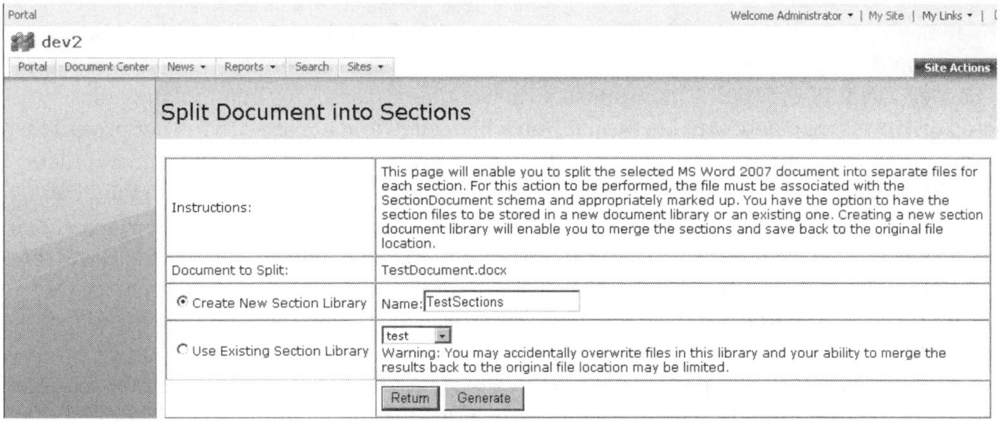

Figure 8-11. *The SectionDocumentSplit custom application page*

The SectionDocumentSplit page contains our custom code. This page will be the same regardless of the site or document the user came from. For this reason, we will construct it as an application page. This type of page is termed an *application page* because it is not a page that is part of a site definition, but rather one that lives in SharePoint's Layouts directory. This means that the ASPX page can be accessed off of the path of any site through the _layouts virtual folder. Application pages are ASP.NET pages that derive from a SharePoint class called LayoutsPageBase and rely on the application.master master page for their layout, look, and feel. These pages typically do not use the code-behind model and instead include their code within script blocks of the ASPX page. Listing 8-13 details some of the initial page directives, including referenced assemblies and imported namespaces. For a complete list, please refer to the code download on the Apress web site.

Listing 8-13. *Custom Application Page Directives*

```
<%@ Assembly Name="Microsoft.SharePoint, Version=12.0.0.0, Culture=neutral,~
        PublicKeyToken=71e9bce111e9429c"%>
<%@ Import Namespace="System.Collections.Generic" %>
<%@ Import Namespace="System.Xml" %>
<%@ Assembly Name="WindowsBase, Version=3.0.0.0, Culture=neutral,~
        PublicKeyToken=31bf3856ad364e35"%>
<%@ Assembly Name="DocumentSectionFeature, Version=1.0.0.0, Culture=neutral,~
        PublicKeyToken=45a2811e9ad438d2"%>
<%@ Page Language="VB" MasterPageFile="~/_layouts/application.master"~
        Inherits="Microsoft.SharePoint.WebControls.LayoutsPageBase"~
```

```
                    EnableViewState="true" EnableViewStateMac="false"     %>
<%@ Import Namespace="Microsoft.SharePoint" %>
<%@ Import Namespace="System.IO.Packaging" %>
<%@ Import Namespace="DocumentSectionFeature" %>
<%@ Register Tagprefix="SharePoint" Namespace="Microsoft.SharePoint.WebControls"~
            Assembly="Microsoft.SharePoint, Version=12.0.0.0, Culture=neutral,~
            PublicKeyToken=71e9bce111e9429c" %>
```

In Listing 8-13, the Assembly directive is responsible for linking an assembly to the page. Notice that there is an Assembly directive for the WindowsBase assembly. This assembly contains the System.IO.Packaging namespace, which contains classes for manipulating files based on the Office Open XML file format. You will need to add a reference to your project for this assembly in addition to the Assembly directive, as we will be writing code to manipulate Open XML documents. The Import directives associate particular namespaces so that referring to classes or controls within them does not require a fully qualified name. The Register directive identifies tag prefixes that we can use to refer to server controls within the HTML of the page. Lastly, the Page directive details attributes of the page, including the language we will use for coding as well as the fact that we want this page to maintain ViewState through post-backs.

The application master page identifies three placeholders where this page can place content. The most important is PlaceHolderMain—it holds the server controls and layout for the body of the page. In this example, the main content area is an HTML table that contains instructions and controls for the user to enter preferences. The other two placeholders just hold titles for the application page. Please refer to the downloadable code to get the exact HTML and names of the controls.

As an application page, the code running here would be in response to a user clicking on the action from any site that has the feature activated. For this reason, the page must establish its context and get references to the site collection and site from which it is being invoked. With these pieces of information, the application page can then use the query-string parameters that the custom action passed to identify the document library the user was in when he selected the action, as well as the specific document that was operated on. Listing 8-14 includes the code for these initial operations.

Listing 8-14. *Intializations of the Application Page*

```
Dim siteCollection As SPSite = Nothing
Dim webObj As SPWeb = Nothing
Dim listId As Guid = Nothing
Dim itemId As Integer = 0
Protected Overrides Sub OnLoad(ByVal e As EventArgs)
Try
    siteCollection = SPContext.Current.Site
    webObj = SPContext.Current.Web
    listId = New Guid(Server.UrlDecode(Request.QueryString("ListId")))
    itemId = Integer.Parse(Request.QueryString("ItemId"))
```

During the page-load event, several of the server controls on the page are initialized. The Cancel button is set up to return the user to the previous page where the custom action was selected. The drop-down list is populated with the set of existing document libraries that are instances of our SectionLibrary template. For each library, we want to examine its properties to retrieve its name and URL. Listing 8-15 includes this portion of the code.

Listing 8-15. *Setting Up the Server Controls*

```
If (Not Me.IsPostBack) Then
   Dim libs As SPListCollection = webObj.GetListsOfType~
         (SPBaseType.DocumentLibrary)
   Dim library As SPList
   For Each library In libs
   Dim doc As XmlDocument = New XmlDocument()
   doc.LoadXml(library.PropertiesXml)
   If (doc.DocumentElement.GetAttribute("ServerTemplate").~
         ToString() = "10001") Then
      Dim libraryUrl As String = doc.DocumentElement.~
            GetAttribute("DefaultViewUrl").ToString()
      Dim webUrl As String = doc.DocumentElement.~
            GetAttribute("WebFullUrl").ToString()
      libraryUrl = libraryUrl.Replace(webUrl, String.Empty)
      libraryUrl = libraryUrl.Substring(1, libraryUrl.IndexOfAny("/", 1) - 1)
      Dim item = New ListItem(library.Title, libraryUrl)
      lstLibs.Items.Add(item)
   End If
Next
```

When the user clicks the Generate button, the event handler has to first determine the target location for section files that will be created as a result of the split. This target could be an existing instance of our SectionLibrary template, or the page may have to create a new one if the user requests that. Either way, after the code in listing 8-16 has run, the targetLibrary variable has a reference to the library that will contain the section files.

Listing 8-16. *Identifiying or Creating the Target Library*

```
Dim targetLibrary As SPFolder = Nothing
If (Me.rdExistingLib.Checked) Then
   targetLibrary = webObj.Folders(Me.lstLibs.SelectedValue)
Else
   'create new library with name in textbox
   Dim template As SPListTemplate = webObj.~
         ListTemplates("Document Sections Library")
   Dim newListId As Guid = webObj.Lists.Add(Me.txtLibName.Text, _
         "Sections of " + Me.lblDocumentName.Text, template)
   webObj.Update()
   Dim newLib As SPFolder = webObj.Folders.Add(Me.txtLibName.Text)
   targetLibrary = webObj.Folders(Me.txtLibName.Text)
End If
```

With the target library determined, the SectionDocumentSplitPage gets a reference to the source Word 2007 document. It then creates an instance of a Splitter class we will code in the next section of the chapter and passes in enough information for the section files to be generated. Finally, the page uses the property bag of the target document library to store the listId of the source document, as well as its URL and filename. These pieces of information will be retrieved by the merge operation to give the user the option of saving back to the original location. Listing 8-17 includes the code that performs these operations.

Listing 8-17. *Performing the Split*

```
Dim sourceItem As SPListItem = webObj.Lists(listId).GetItemById(itemId)
Dim sourceFile As SPFile = sourceItem.File
If (sourceFile IsNot Nothing) Then
    Dim sourceStream As Stream = sourceFile.OpenBinaryStream()
    Dim splitObj As Splitter = New Splitter()
    splitObj.SplitDocument(sourceStream, targetLibrary, _
            Me.lblDocumentName.Text)
    'store the source file info in the property bag of target library
    If (Me.rdCreateNewLib.Checked) Then
        targetLibrary.Properties.Add("SourceListId", listId.ToString())
        targetLibrary.Properties.Add("SourceFileUrl", sourceFile.Url)
        targetLibrary.Properties.Add("SourceFileName", _
            Me.lblDocumentName.Text)
        targetLibrary.Update()
    End If
End If
```

Examining the Splitter Class

Add a class file named Splitter.vb to the root of the feature project. We will use this splitter class to work with the source file to generate the individual section files. As shown in the previous section of this chapter, the splitter class receives a binary stream of the source file, a reference to the library where the section files are to be stored, and a string of the source filename. Again, refer to the code download for the complete contents of this class. The first key section of the SplitDocument method is where this class determines the number of sections in the source file. This class obtains this information by querying for the customXml nodes we saw in the document.xml part earlier. Listing 8-18 includes this code.

Listing 8-18. *Determining the Number of Sections in the Document*

```
Dim nodes As XmlNodeList = xdoc.SelectNodes("//w:customXml[@w:uri=~
        'http://tempuri.org/SectionedDocument.xsd' and~
        @w:element='Section']", nsManager)
Dim numSections As Integer = nodes.Count
documentPart.Package.Close()
Me.GenDocs(numSections, docStream, library, fileName)
```

The last line of the code in Listing 8-18 is a call to the GenDocs method, which creates the section files and saves them to the library. The algorithm used by this method creates a section file by first creating a copy of the entire source document—which, of course, includes all the sections. This stream-copy operation is detailed in Listing 8-19.

Listing 8-19. *Copying the Source-File Stream*

```
Dim i As Integer
Dim reader As BinaryReader = New BinaryReader(docStream)
For i = 0 To numSections - 1
    'make copies
    Dim instanceStream As Stream = New MemoryStream
    docStream.Position = 0
    Dim writer As BinaryWriter = New BinaryWriter(instanceStream)
    writer.Write(reader.ReadBytes(CInt(docStream.Length)))
    writer.Flush()
```

With a copy of the entire source document, the algorithm continues by deleting all of the sections that are not needed for this specific section file. This sequence of removals occurs through a nested loop that skips the deletion only when its index matches that of the outer loop. So with the first copy of the source document, all sections but the first are removed. For the second copy, all sections but the second are removed. The end result of each iteration is a file with exactly one section. Once the stream has been reduced to a single section, it is saved and added to the target document library. Listing 8-20 completes the operation of generating the section files.

Listing 8-20. *Generating the Section Files*

```
Dim nodes As XmlNodeList = xdoc.SelectNodes("//w:customXml[@w:uri=~
    'http://tempuri.org/SectionedDocument.xsd' and~
    @w:element='Section']", nsManager)
Dim j As Integer = 0
Dim sectionNode As XmlNode = Nothing
For Each sectionNode In nodes
    If (i <> j) Then
        sectionNode.ParentNode.RemoveChild(sectionNode)
    End If
    j += 1
Next
'save changes to XML
xdoc.Save(documentPart.GetStream(FileMode.Create, FileAccess.Write))
'save this as a document
instanceStream.Position = 0
library.Files.Add(GenerateNum(i) + fileName, instanceStream, True)
```

When completed, the result is a document library containing individual files for each of the sections of the source document. This means that each of these sections can now be worked on simultaneously. In addition, they can be secured and versioned separately. Figure 8-12 shows the Classical Latin section document along with the list of files in the library.

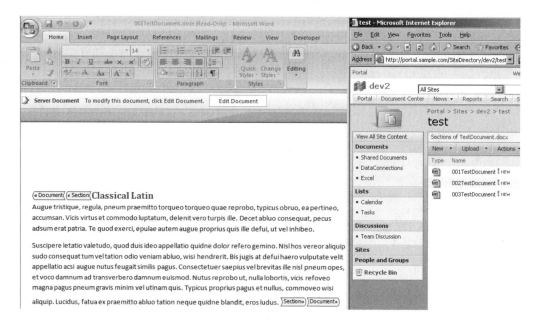

Figure 8-12. *Results of the split operations*

Building a Custom Application Page for Merging

The custom application page for merging is very similar to its split counterpart. In this page, the user is specifying preferences for where the merged result should be placed. There are two options: The page can place the resulting file in the same location as its original source (which would overwrite the source file if it is still present) or the user can choose any other document library in the site and specify a filename for the resulting document. Figure 8-13 shows the SectionDocumentMerge.aspx application page.

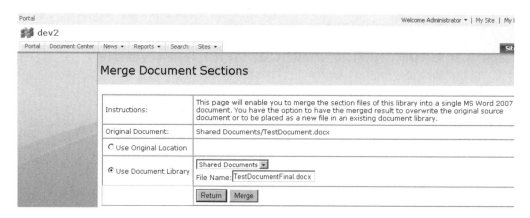

Figure 8-13. *The SectionDocumentMerge application page*

Like the split application page, this one includes code to discover what objects it is operating on as well as initializing its controls. The major difference is that this page can use the property bag of the document library that contains the section files to retrieve information that the split operation stored there. This information includes the identifier of the document library that contained the source file as well as its URL and filename. Listing 8-21 shows how the page retrieves these values from the property bag.

Listing 8-21. *Retrieving Values from the Property Bag*

```
targetListId = New Guid(currentLibrary.Properties.Item("SourceListId").ToString())
targetFileUrl = currentLibrary.Properties.Item("SourceFileUrl").ToString()
targetFileName = currentLibrary.Properties.Item("SourceFileName").ToString()
```

When the user clicks the Merge button, the event handler gets a reference to the target library where the merged file should be stored. This library is either the original one that contained the source document, or a library in the site that the user selected with the drop-down. From there, the merge operation is performed using a SectionMerge class we will review in the next section. This class includes a method called Merge, which receives a reference to the section library, the destination library, the filename for the merged file, and its URL as parameters. Listing 8-22 shows the merge operation being called as well as the confirmation message being displayed.

Listing 8-22. *Performing the Merge*

```
Dim mergeObj As SectionMerge = New SectionMerge()
mergeObj.Merge(sourceLibrary, targetLibrary, targetFileName, targetFileUrl)
lblMessage.Text = "The sections of your document have been merged in the~
        requested library. Use the link below to navigate there"
lblMessage.Visible = True
lnkResult.NavigateUrl = targetLibrary.ServerRelativeUrl
lnkResult.Text = targetLibrary.Name
lnkResult.Visible = True
```

Examining the SectionMerge class

To the root of the feature project, add a class-file named SectionMerge.vb. We will use this SectionMerge class to merge the individual section files into a single document. As shown in the previous section of this chapter, the SectionMerge class receives a reference to the library of section files, a reference to the library where the merged document is to be stored, a filename, and a URL for the result. (Refer to the code download in the Source Code/Download section of the Apress web site for the complete contents of this class.) The Merge method begins by creating a MemoryStream copy of the first section file. It then calls AddSection for every other section file in sequence. The AddSection method is passed the current section number, a reference to the document element defined in our schema, a reference to the library of sections, and the filename. Listing 8-23 is the code fragment where AddSection is being called for every section after the first.

Listing 8-23. *Adding Sections to the Document*

```
Dim documentNode As XmlNode = xdoc.SelectSingleNode(~
    "//w:customXml[@w:uri='http://tempuri.org/SectionedDocument.xsd'~
    and @w:element='Document']", nsManager)
'loop through others and append
Dim i As Integer = 0
For i = 2 To numberSections
    AddSection(i, documentNode, sectionLibrary, fileName)
Next
```

Within the AddSection method, the section node of the appropriate section file is located and copied into the MemoryStream that started out as a copy of the first section file. To perform the copy, we must use the ImportNode method of the XML document since we are copying nodes from one context to another. The value of True in this method call tells the import to perform a deep copy, which is necessary to make sure we get all of the contents of the document's XML within this node. Since we are appending the sections in order, the InsertAfter method places the imported section node last within the document. Listing 8-24 shows the code for copying a node from a section file into our merged document.

Listing 8-24. *Copying a Section Node into the Merged Document*

```
Dim sectionNode As XmlNode = xdoc.SelectSingleNode(~
    "//w:customXml[@w:uri='http://tempuri.org/SectionedDocument.xsd' and~
    @w:element='Section']", nsManager)
If (sectionNode IsNot Nothing) Then
    Dim newNode As XmlNode = documentNode.OwnerDocument.~
            ImportNode(sectionNode, True)
    documentNode.InsertAfter(newNode, documentNode.LastChild)
End If
```

Important Lessons

The solution in this chapter incorporated several key techniques that are worth highlighting, as they could easily be reused in other projects.

Applying custom schema to a Word document: The solution utilized a custom schema that was attached to a Microsoft Word document. This association allowed us to mark up the document, selecting which portions matched our schema's elements. By injecting this XML markup into the document, our code was able to find these markers, making it easy to split and merge the document contents.

Developing a feature: The solution was packaged as a SharePoint feature. This enables any administrator in the site collection to activate or deactivate the functionality included in it. This technique increases the flexibility of the solution as well as centralizes the steps needed to deploy it.

Custom application page: The feature included two custom application pages that were deployed to the server's Layouts folder. These pages were created using the `application.master` master page and were integrated seamlessly to extend the site's functionality.

Open XML file format: The manipulation of the Microsoft Word documents on the server was possible because the documents were stored using the Open XML file format.

Using property bags: In this solution the split operation placed several values in the property bag of the target document library. This allowed later code in the merge operation to retrieve where the sections had come from. Libraries, lists, and even webs in the SharePoint object model support this property bag. It can be a useful container to place information for the object to "remember" later.

Custom document library template: The ability to distinguish libraries that contain sections of a document from other site libraries was important for the solution. This enabled us to appropriately place the merge action on the toolbar only for libraries that contained section files. It also allowed us to anticipate that the library's property bag would contain the necessary information about the source file.

Extension Points

While coding this example, we thought of several variations to the solution that we didn't incorporate. Mostly, these were not included because they distracted from the overall objective of the solution. We call them out now as extension points since they may be applicable to a specific project you are working on.

Use content types: In our example, we uploaded the test document that we marked up to a SharePoint library. To fulfill the vision of the solution, this would likely be published as a content type. Likewise, the solution would gain value by having a content type representing a blank section. This could be the default template of our SectionLibrary template and would give users the ability to add a section after the split had occurred.

Add support for pictures: Currently, the solution supports only document with text. No graphics or embedded objects are supported. Removing this restriction for images is a bit more work; you would have to examine the contents of each section, looking for references to embedded graphics. If an image were found, your code would need to use the XML relationships to find the corresponding image file inside the package. The split operation would then become a bit more complicated, making sure that each section file has the right image files. And the merge operation would have to be wary of image files that may have the same name.

Add support for a section title element: In our example, the generated section files were named with a 00# string and the name of the original file. You could make this a bit more user-friendly by adding a title element to the schema and using its value as the title for the section files. Of course, you would then need to address retrieving the files in order. This is one reason why we made the SectionLibrary document library template. You can modify its `schema.xml` file to include a SectionNumber column. You could also use the Solution Generator included in the Visual Studio Extensions for Windows SharePoint Services to create the document library template. This technique is detailed in Chapter 5.

Only merge selected sections: In our merge operation we always merged all of the sections. An interesting option would be to display the list of sections as check boxes, letting the user decide which ones should be included in the merged document. This change would be implemented in the merge custom-application page.

Run with elevated privileges: In this solution the user who is splitting the document would receive an Access Denied message if he chose to create a new library and didn't have enough permission to do so. There is a way to work around this to elevate the security level of the running code above that of the current user's for just enough time to complete the desired operation. The key to this technique is the SPSecurity.RunWithElevatedPrivileges method. We have included a link to an article about this technique in the "Further Reading" section.

Remove section libraries on deactivation: The solution included a feature receiver for running code in response to the activation and deactivation of the feature. If desired, you could use this class to delete the section libraries when the feature is deactivated. We are not sure this is always desirable, as your users may expect otherwise and they may lose content if they have not published the merged file.

Further Reading

The following links are to resources a reader interested in this chapter's material may find useful:

- How To: Add Actions to the User Interface

  http://msdn2.microsoft.com/en-us/library/ms473643.aspx

- Working with Features

  http://msdn2.microsoft.com/en-us/library/ms460318.aspx

- Brian Jones: Open Xml Formats Blog

  http://blogs.msdn.com/brian_jones/

- OpenXMLDeveloper.org

  http://openxmldeveloper.org/

- What's New for Developers in Word 2007

  http://msdn2.microsoft.com/en-us/library/ms406055.aspx

- Creating Content Types by Using a Feature

  http://www.sharepointblogs.com/tonstegeman/archive/2006/07/18/9314.aspx

- Creating a Custom Document Library Feature in MOSS 2007

  http://www.sharepointblogs.com/tbaginski/archive/2006/06/02/8062.aspx

- Elevation of Privilege

  `http://msdn2.microsoft.com/en-us/library/aa543467.aspx`

- Introducing the Office (2007) Open XML File Formats

  `http://msdn2.microsoft.com/en-us/library/ms406049.aspx`

PART 4

■■■

Microsoft PowerPoint Solutions

This section will focus on solutions built around Microsoft PowerPoint. Very often users spend too much time retrieving data from other systems or other users to construct presentations. Windows SharePoint Services team sites provide the enterprise with a collaborative space to collect information about an event, process, or project. For this reason, the next two chapters will present different approaches to automating the construction of presentations based on SharePoint site content.

■ ■ ■

CHAPTER 9

Extending PowerPoint to Build a Presentation Based on Site Content

Windows SharePoint Services provides the enterprise with easily creatable workspaces where information can be collected to support the sharing of information among users working toward a common goal. This goal could be many different things, including preparation for an event, execution of a business process, or even materials for a project. Often, organizations build presentations as an output of this collaboration or for routinely reporting on the status of the team. Microsoft PowerPoint provides users with a powerful canvas to construct presentations. However, information workers expend too much effort and time to locate, duplicate, and organize this information into the presentation. Not only are we looking to reduce this effort; we also want to increase its accuracy. The presentation's authors are likely retyping, cutting, and pasting, or otherwise manually importing content. So in this chapter we will detail how, as a developer, you can extend PowerPoint to provide a tool that is capable of building out slides populated with content stored in a SharePoint site.

Real-World Examples

This problem is one that we have seen from many customers. Almost any time you have a chain of command in an organization, people farther down are always summarizing and reporting up. Not surprisingly, this type of solution is very popular in the military. Each of our branches spends considerable resources aggregating information from outside content repositories and applications to construct briefings for higher officers. It is not unheard of for a team to get an extremely early start on the day to gather the information required for a commander's briefing. These efforts are too manual today, resulting in authors digging through old emails in organizational mailboxes, searching file shares, and copying data from the user interfaces of other applications. The commercial world is also full of examples. Just look at any company that has projects and managers responsible for them. Not only could these presentations be used to present the status of a project internally, but the audience could be the customer as well.

Solution Overview

For this solution, we will extend Microsoft PowerPoint to provide a tool for the author to import data from a SharePoint site. To provide some context for our solution, we have focused our efforts to building a briefing presentation made of imported items that reside in a typical meeting workspace. Once the custom import tool has been launched, it will examine a user-supplied site to see if it contains an objectives list, a list of agenda items, or any slide libraries. The objectives and agenda lists are a part of the default template for meeting workspaces in SharePoint. In this sample, we added a slide library because it is not too far-fetched to think that users who are a part of this collaboration may have built slides of their own that should be included in our briefing output. Once the site has been examined, the custom import tool will walk the user through a wizard process that offers to build slides for the content it finds in the site.

This application should be flexible enough to support the construction of slides in any presentation the author may be working on. To meet these requirements, the solution will be an application-level add-in. As an add-in, this tool will always be available to the authoring user from within PowerPoint. To provide a launching point, the tool will add controls to the Microsoft Office ribbon interface. From the ribbon, the author will be able to start the tool, which presents itself as a custom task pane. This pane presents the user with the wizard experience of steps and prompts, building slides as instructed in the current presentation.

As the wizard executes, it prompts the user about whether he wishes to have a presentation slide built for the content it finds it the site. If the user chooses to build a slide for the objectives, the add-in will query the SharePoint site for the objective list items and place them in a new slide as a bulleted list. If the user chooses to build a slide with the agenda, the add-in will query the SharePoint site for the agenda list items and place them in a new slide displayed within a table. In addition, the add-in will populate the notes page of this slide with details such as owner of the agenda item and notes that are contained in the SharePoint site. Lastly, the add-in will display a list of links to slide libraries it finds on the site. Each link will open the library in the browser so that the user can select slides to import into the presentation he is working on.

Solution Walkthrough

The following section will detail the major elements of the solution and the decisions that were made in coding it. The walkthrough will show you how to get started with Visual Studio to create the briefing PowerPoint add-in. We will detail how you can use VSTO to extend the Office ribbon interface. The wizard process will also be examined so you can see how we simplified coding an experience where the user would move through a series of steps, each representing a specific function with its own user interface and actions. The walkthrough will then explain the work that goes into building each of the PowerPoint slides for our briefing. This work includes creating new slides, placing content as a bulleted list, inserting and populating a table, placing content on a slide's notes page, and linking in the SharePoint slide libraries.

Creating the Project

Using Visual Studio to build a PowerPoint add-in project is made very straightforward by the VSTO's project types. Simply start Visual Studio and select to create a new project. Under the Visual Basic language node, expand the Office node and select the 2007 Add-ins category. This will display the Office 2007 VSTO project templates.

From the listing of Visual Studio installed templates, select PowerPoint Add-in. Name the project and solution **BriefingVB**. Your New Project dialog should look like Figure 9-1.

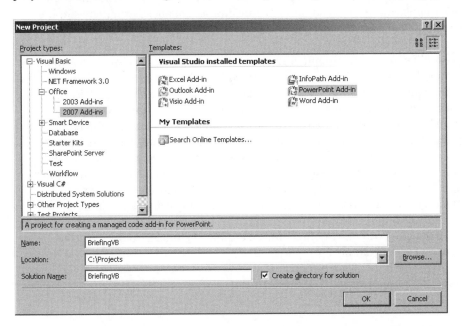

Figure 9-1. *Creating a PowerPoint add-in project*

Once the new project is created, your solution will already have a few files by default. These are visible in the Solution Explorer window of Visual Studio. You'll see a PowerPoint node that, when expanded, will have a code file named `ThisAddin.vb`. This file is the main entry point for add-ins. It is where developers can write code for events at the add-in scope. These events include common items like Startup and Shutdown. There are also PowerPoint application-level events such as SlideShowBegin and SlideShowEnd. These are accessible by selecting the Application object in the left-hand drop-down above your code window. The solution will also include a setup project that you can use to deploy your add-in.

Ribbon Customization

First, we are going to need a way for the user to launch our briefing application from within PowerPoint. To provide this starting point, we will focus our attention on the new-and-improved user interface of the Microsoft Office 2007 system—the ribbon. The ribbon interface occupies the top portion of most of the Office applications and provides a different experience then the layered menus and toolbars of previous Office releases. This interface provides a simpler experience for the user by improving the organization of commands and providing a more graphical representation of options. One of the primary goals of the ribbon interface is to surface application functionality that users desired but simply didn't know was there because of how buried or obscure that menu item was previously.

In earlier versions of Office, developers spent most of their efforts writing code utilizing the CommandBars object to create new buttons, extend menus, hide existing options, and make other user-interface customizations. By using compiled code to make these changes, developers found themselves writing lengthy code for a relatively simple result. Also, the code was typically not portable from project to project and couldn't be reused across different Microsoft Office applications. So, in addition to providing an enhanced experience for the end user, the ribbon interface provides the developer with an improved programming model for manipulating it.

The biggest difference in the ribbon programming model is that customizations to the user interface are defined using XML, not compiled code. Through a custom XML file, a developer can manipulate the ribbon interface, controlling its tabs, groups, and controls. This manipulation includes adding new elements as well as hiding default ones. Since the customizations are XML-based, they are easier to reuse in different projects and different Office applications. In addition to the XML declarations that alter the ribbon's user interface, a typical implementation will include a class that serves the XML to the application and includes event handlers for running code in response to user interaction. You might think that you are in for writing a ton of code to get your add-in, XML file, and class to align properly. Fortunately, VSTO does most of this plumbing automatically, allowing you to focus just on the customizations needed.

Before we get started with the briefing project, examine Figure 9-2 to see the desired end state of our ribbon customizations.

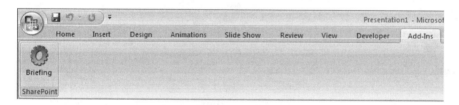

Figure 9-2. *The customized ribbon interface*

Figure 9-2 shows that the briefing add-in has customized the Office ribbon interface to include new items on the Add-Ins tab. On this tab there is a SharePoint group with a toggle button control that displays Briefing with a custom graphic. When the user presses this toggle button, the application will display a custom task pane to walk the user through the wizard process.

To implement this in your briefing project, first add a new item. From the Add New Item dialog, select the Ribbon support template and name the file Ribbon1.vb. When the process is complete, Visual Studio will have actually added two files. These include the Ribbon1.vb code file that includes the class that has plumbing and callback code. The other file is Ribbon1.xml, which is the markup of the ribbon interface changes. It is in this file that the additional tab, group, and toggle button are defined. Listing 9-1 details the XML needed to make the desired customizations.

Listing 9-1. *Ribbon User-Interface Markup*

```
<customUI xmlns="http://schemas.microsoft.com/office/2006/01/customui"~
        onLoad="OnLoad">
  <ribbon>
    <tabs>
      <tab idMso="TabAddIns">
        <group id="MOSSApps"
               label="SharePoint">
          <toggleButton id="toggleButton1"
                        size="large"
                        label="Briefing"
                        screentip="Import SharePoint items to create a briefing"
                        onAction="OnToggleButton1"
                        getImage="GetImage" />
        </group>
      </tab>
    </tabs>
  </ribbon>
</customUI>
```

The VSTO template for the new file provided almost the entire markup in Listing 9-1. To get the customizations we needed for this project, we added some literal strings for labels and a screen tip. Of particular importance is the onAction attribute of the toggle button element. It is this attribute that designates the callback. Searching through the Ribbon1.vb code file (downloadable from the Source Code/Download section of the Apress web site), you will find an OnToggleButton1() subroutine that will be wired up to our new toggle button automatically. The sample code in this class needs to be modified to that of Listing 9-2.

Listing 9-2. *OnToggleButton1 Callback*

```
Public Sub OnToggleButton1(ByVal control As Office.IRibbonControl,~
      ByVal isPressed As Boolean)
   Globals.ThisAddIn.ctp.Visible = isPressed
End Sub
```

This code will take on the responsibility of hiding and showing a custom task pane for our application. Of course, we need the task pane, which is nothing but a user control called ucTaskPane. You will need to add this control to the project as well if you want to test at this point. Listing 9-3 shows how the add-in creates an instance of the custom task pane. Also add an Imports statement for the Microsoft.Office.Tools namespace in the ThisAddIn.vb class file.

Listing 9-3. *Creating the Task Pane*

```
Public ctp As CustomTaskPane

Private Sub ThisAddIn_Startup(ByVal sender As Object,~
      ByVal e As System.EventArgs) Handles Me.Startup
   ctp = Globals.ThisAddIn.CustomTaskPanes.Add( _
```

```
                    New ucTaskPane(), "Custom Briefing")
     ctp.DockPosition = Office.MsoCTPDockPosition.msoCTPDockPositionRight
     ctp.Width = 250
End Sub
```

A class at the top of the `Ribbon1.vb` file needs to be uncommented; it allows the application to hook into our ribbon customizations. Lastly, the XML in Listing 9-1 contained a getImage attribute for the toggle button. This attribute allows us to specify a callback where our code can return a picture to be placed on the button. .NET managed code and the Office COM applications prefer to work with graphics differently. Specifically, the COM world of Office relies on IPictureDisp objects, whereas in managed code we are provided Image or Bitmap objects. Listing 9-4 is a class that you can add to the end of the `Ribbon1.vb` file to help with the translations. It relies on the AxHost class, which wraps ActiveX controls for the managed Windows Forms environment.

Listing 9-4. *Translating Graphics*

```
Friend Class PictureDispMaker
    Inherits System.Windows.Forms.AxHost
Sub New()
    MyBase.New(Nothing)
 End Sub


 Public Shared Function ConvertImage(ByVal image As~
       System.Drawing.Image) As stdole.IPictureDisp
    Return AxHost.GetIPictureDispFromPicture(image)
End Function


Public Shared Function ConvertIcon(ByVal icon As~
       System.Drawing.Icon) As stdole.IPictureDisp
   Return ConvertImage(icon.ToBitmap())
End Function
End Class
```

The GetImage callback method then uses the PictureDispMaker class to convert the image and return it to the application. For this project, we selected the icon graphic `otheroptions.ico` from the VS 2005 Image Library and embedded it into the project as a resource. Listing 9-5 details the GetImage callback's retrieval of the resource image and the image's conversion before the picture is returned to the Office application. You can read more details about adding project resources here:

- How to: Add or Remove Resources

  `http://msdn2.microsoft.com/en-us/library/3bka19x4.aspx.`

Listing 9-5. *GetImage Callback*

```
Public Function GetImage(ByVal control As Office.IRibbonControl) As~
        stdole.IPictureDisp
    Dim pic As stdole.IPictureDisp = Nothing
    Select Case control.Id
        Case "toggleButton1"
                pic = PictureDispMaker.ConvertIcon(My.Resources.otheroptions)
    End Select
    Return pic
End Function
```

By our adding ribbon support to the project, the user now has a way to launch the briefing application, which will present the user with a series of steps for building PowerPoint slides from SharePoint site content.

Architecture of the Task Pane and Wizard Step User Controls

The briefing add-in presents its user interface through a custom task pane that loads to the right-hand side of PowerPoint's application window. The wizard experience for the user is a series of steps. The necessary logic and actions for each of these steps is wrapped into a single user control. The following list summarizes the primary goal of each step.

1. Receiving the URL of the SharePoint site and examining its contents

2. Building a presentation slide for the items in the objectives list

3. Building a presentation slide for the items in the agenda list

4. Displaying a list of slide libraries so the user can import presentation slides from the site

5. Conclusion message

The user may not actually need to do each of these five steps. Based on the examination of the site entered in step 1, it may be appropriate for the wizard to skip certain subsequent steps. For example, if the site does not contain any slide libraries, the user should not even be exposed to step 4. For this reason, our architecture compartmentalizes each of the steps into its own user control. A step user control is responsible for displaying an interface, gathering input from the user, doing its work, and reporting back. The task-pane control serves as a controller, taking on the responsibility of orchestrating the step controls and collecting the information they report back that may be necessary later in the process.

To provide uniformity to the step user controls, we defined an object interface with some common elements that each control must implement. This makes it easier for our task-pane controller to interact with them since it can be guaranteed that the elements of the interface are a part of the step control. Listing 9-6 details the contents of the interface.

Listing 9-6. *The IStep Interface*

```
Public Interface IStep
    ReadOnly Property ParentPane() As ucTaskPane
    Event Completed(ByVal sender As Object, ByVal e As EventArgs)
    Sub WorkComplete()
    Sub Start()
End Interface
```

The IStep interface requires that each step user control have the following:

- A read only property that provides a reference to the task pane

- An event named Completed that will be used to inform the task pane that a particular step has done its work and the task pane should move on

- A WorkComplete() procedure used to support multithreading so that the step control can execute its work on a separate thread than the user interface

- A Start() method that will be called by the task pane, telling the step control that it is its turn in the process

The task-pane controller is a user control but has no user interface of its own. It is simply a container that will orchestrate the step controls that present themselves to the user. For this reason, an instance of each of the Step*n* controls named wizard*n* (where *n* represents the sequence number) is loaded into its controls collection. Since these are loaded from code, each has a default visibility property of false. In the task pane's load event, the instance wizard1 is told to start.

Most of the remaining code in the task pane is dedicated either to orchestrating the hiding or showing of step controls, or to collecting information from the work that they do. Listing 9-7 details the critical elements of the step-orchestration process.

Listing 9-7. *Task Pane's Orchestration of Steps*

```
Private currentStep As Integer = 1

Private Sub wizard_Completed(ByVal sender As Object, ByVal e As EventArgs) _
        Handles wizard1.Completed, wizard2.Completed, wizard3.Completed, _
        wizard4.Completed
    If currentStep < 5 Then Me.MoveToNextStep()
End Sub

Private Sub MoveToNextStep()
    Me.Controls(currentStep - 1).Visible = False
    currentStep += 1
    CType(Me.Controls(currentStep - 1), IStep).Start()
End Sub
```

The currentStep variable from Listing 9-7 is the task pane's internal cursor, which keeps track of which step is being shown to the user. The wizard_Completed event handler is a code block that runs when any of the first four steps are finished with their work. Notice that the

Handles portion of its declaration includes a list of step-control instances wizard1 through wizard4. Since the code we are going to run in response is the same for each step, there is no reason to have an event-handler code block for each of them individually. The MoveToNext-Step() procedure performs the orchestration. It first hides the control that is currently being displayed. currentStep - 1 is used here since the Controls collection is zero-based and we started our count with 1. The MoveToNextStep() routine then finds the next control; by converting it to the interface that the task pane knows it must implement, it is able to call its Start method. You may be wondering how we account for a step needing to be skipped. The answer is that the Start() method of each of the step controls determines whether it has work to do before showing itself. Listing 9-8 is a representative Start() method from step 2 of the wizard.

Listing 9-8. *A Sample Step Control Start() Method*

```
Public Sub Start() Implements IStep.Start
    If (ParentPane.HasObjectivesList) Then
        'show this step
        Me.Visible = True
    Else
        'skip over this step
        Me.WorkComplete()
    End If
End Sub
```

The task-pane control also maintains some information obtained from a step control that will be used later in the process. This includes the URL of the SharePoint site the user entered, information about whether it had any of the lists it could build content from, as well as a collection of information about the slide libraries contained in the site.

The step1 User Control: Examining the Site

The first step control is responsible for examining the SharePoint site specified by the URL the user entered. For our example, we simply created a meeting workspace to act as a test environment and populated it with content. Specifically, the control is looking to see if the site contains a list named Objectives, a list named Agenda, and information on any slide libraries. The Objectives and Agenda lists are there by default, but you will have to create at least one slide library if you want to see that piece in action. Take the following steps to add a slide library to your site:

1. Navigate to your meeting workspace site.

2. From the Site Actions menu, choose Site Settings.

3. In the Site Administration column, click the hyperlink titled Site Libraries and Lists.

4. Click the Create New Content link.

5. In the Libraries column, click the Slide Library link.

6. Enter a name for the slide library. For example, enter **Meeting Slides**.

7. Leave both of the radio buttons on their default value of No and click Create.

8. You will be redirected to a page that displays the library's items.

9. You need a sample PowerPoint 2007 presentation to upload here. Just a presentation with a few slides will do. From within PowerPoint, select Publish from the File menu and choose Publish Slides. Click the button to select all the slides. Note that since this sample relies on a meeting workspace, you will have to publish to the 1 folder in the library. A sample URL: `http://portal.sample.com/SiteDirectory/meeting1/Meeting Slides/1/`.

10. After choosing the location for the publication, a wizard will launch to walk you through uploading your PowerPoint presentation to the SharePoint site. When finished, the library should contain an item for every slide in your presentation. The slide library breaks apart your presentation into individual slides, which would allow different users to work on different slides at the same time.

The step control is designed to first ask the user for the URL of the meeting workspace. When the user clicks the Next button, the step control goes to work. To discover information about the lists and libraries contained in the site, the briefing application will rely on the GetListCollection method of SharePoint's `lists.asmx` web service. The GetListCollection method returns information about all the lists and libraries in the site. To call this method, you will need to add a web reference in the briefing add-in project. The following steps let you create the web reference:

1. In Visual Studio's Solution Explorer window, right-click the References node of the BriefingVB project and select Add Web Reference.

2. Type in the URL of the meeting workspace with a `_vti_bin/lists.asmx` ending. SharePoint's web services are called by adding the `_vti_bin` folder on to the end of any site URL. This enables the web service call to discover its context and return answers specifically to the site referred to by the rest of the URL. So continuing with our example, the URL would be `http://portal.sample.com/SiteDirectory/meeting1/_vti_bin/lists.asmx`.

3. Click Go. The window below the URL should display a listing of all of the methods in the Lists web service.

4. In the Web reference name text box, change the text to **WSLists**.

5. Click Add Reference.

With the web reference in place, the Next button's click event handler can be coded. This code is displayed in Listing 9-9.

Listing 9-9. *Retrieving the Site's Lists and Libraries*

```
Private Sub btnNext_Click(ByVal sender As System.Object,~
    ByVal e As System.EventArgs) Handles btnNext.Click
  Me.UseWaitCursor = True
  'check to see if there are lists for agenda and objectives
  Dim listService As WSLists.Lists = New WSLists.Lists
  listService.Credentials = System.Net.CredentialCache.DefaultCredentials
```

```
listService.Url = Me.txtSiteUrl.Text + "/_vti_bin/lists.asmx"
AddHandler listService.GetListCollectionCompleted,~
    AddressOf GetListCollectionCompleted
listService.GetListCollectionAsync()
End Sub
```

When the user clicks next, we want to make sure that all the hard work of examining the site does not interfere with the PowerPoint application's user interface. Therefore, this work will be set up to run on a different thread. To support this background processing, the Next button's event hander first changes the user's cursor to the WaitCursor (typically an hourglass). The web-service proxy is then configured to make the call under the user's security context and to access the service through the site URL entered by the user. When the GetListCollection method is called, we actually call its Async implementation so that the current thread will not wait for a response. Instead, the proxy class will call the GetListCollectionCompleted method of this step user control when it receives its response. This is controlled by the AddHandler line just before the call.

Once the web service has returned a response to the briefing add-in application, our code will execute the GetListCollectionCompleted subroutine. This method first informs the task pane of the URL the user entered and then examines the response, looking for the Objectives and Agenda lists as well as any slide libraries. The response from the web-service call is a string of XML that includes references to many different namespaces. Therefore this method loads that XML into an XmlDocument object and sets up an XmlNamespaceNavigator so that it can easily search for the information it is looking for. All of the SharePoint list-based information will reside in the XML namespace sp. Listing 9-10 details the XPath query technique for discovering if there is a specific list in the site. The solution assumes such a list exists and informs the task pane only if it cannot find one.

Listing 9-10. *Looking for the List Named Agenda*

```
Dim namespaceMgr As XmlNamespaceManager =~ _
    New XmlNamespaceManager(xmlDoc.NameTable)
namespaceMgr.AddNamespace(~
    ucTaskPane.SharePointNamespacePrefix,~
    ucTaskPane.SharePointNamespaceUri)
'is there a list named agenda
Dim agendaListNode As XmlNodeList = _
    xmlDoc.SelectNodes("//sp:List[@Title='Agenda']", namespaceMgr)
If (agendaListNode Is Nothing Or agendaListNode.Count = 0) Then
    ParentPane.HasAgendaList = False
End If
```

After looking for the Objectives and Agenda lists, the add-in needs to record any slide libraries it finds in the site. This information can be obtained by looking for lists that have a ServerTemplate attribute with a value of 2100. This value is a constant representing a slide library. The step control informs the task pane if it cannot find any slide libraries. When it does find some, it records the title and URL of each library. For the URL, we are interested in storing only the portion after the site's URL. Listing 9-11 shows the XPath query technique for finding the collection of slide libraries, as well as the population of a list of structs containing data about each library it finds.

Listing 9-11. *Looking for Slide Libraries*

```
'are there any slide libraries
Dim slideLibNode As XmlNodeList = _
xmlDoc.SelectNodes("//sp:List[@ServerTemplate='2100']", namespaceMgr)
If (slideLibNode Is Nothing Or slideLibNode.Count = 0) Then
    ParentPane.HasSlideLibrary = False
Else
    'store the name  and URL of each slide library
    Dim xmlNode As XmlNode
    For Each xmlNode In slideLibNode
        Dim item As LibraryItem = New LibraryItem
        item.Name = xmlNode.Attributes("Title").InnerText
        item.Url = xmlNode.Attributes("DefaultViewUrl").InnerText
        'remove portion of Url we don't need
        item.Url = item.Url.Replace(xmlNode.Attributes("WebFullUrl").InnerText,~
            String.Empty)
        ParentPane.SlideLibraries.Add(item)
    Next
End If
```

Now the control has completed its examination of the site and informed the task pane of the information that it found there. As you can see in the code download, this control then wraps up its work in the same manner as the others. At the end of this method, the WaitCursor is turned off and the task pane invokes a delegate referring to the WorkComplete method. By using the Me.Parent.Invoke() technique, we are returning control back to the original thread, leaving the one that performed the background processing. Once in the WorkComplete() method, the step control raises its Completed event so the task pane can take control and move the processes along to the next step.

The step2 User Control: Building Objectives

The step2 user control is responsible for building a presentation slide containing the content in the SharePoint site's Objectives list. The task pane will shift control to this step by calling its Start method. In this method, the control checks to see if the briefing add-in previously found an Objectives list in the user's site. If it did, the step makes itself visible, exposing its user interface to the user. If it didn't, this control simply calls WorkComplete to raise its Completed event, skipping itself and moving on to the next step in the process. Assuming the user interface is displayed, the user is presented with two options. The first is for the application to build a presentation slide that contains a bulleted list of the objective items from the site. The other option is to simply skip this feature and move on to the next step.

If the user chooses to have an objectives slide built, the add-in again uses SharePoint's lists.asmx web service. This time, the GetListItems method is used to retrieve the set of objective list items in the list. Like the previous step, this control uses the Async implementation of this method to place the bulk of the processing on a separate thread. Listing 9-12 shows the construction of the parameters passed to the GetListItems call.

Listing 9-12. *Requesting Items in the Objectives List*

```
Private Sub btnBuild_Click(ByVal sender As System.Object,~
        ByVal e As System.EventArgs) Handles btnBuild.Click
    Me.UseWaitCursor = True
    'retrieve objectives
    Dim listService As WSLists.Lists = New WSLists.Lists
    listService.Credentials = System.Net.CredentialCache.DefaultCredentials
    listService.Url = ParentPane.SiteUrl + "/_vti_bin/lists.asmx"

    'build query parameters for list items
    Dim xmlDoc As XmlDocument = New XmlDocument()
    Dim ndQuery As XmlNode = xmlDoc.CreateNode(XmlNodeType.Element, "Query", "")
    Dim ndViewFields As XmlNode = xmlDoc.CreateNode(XmlNodeType.Element, _
                "ViewFields", "")
    Dim ndQueryOptions As XmlNode = xmlDoc.CreateNode(XmlNodeType.Element, _
                "QueryOptions", "")
    ndQueryOptions.InnerXml = _
                "<IncludeMandatoryColumns>FALSE</IncludeMandatoryColumns>"
    ndViewFields.InnerXml = "<FieldRef Name='Objective'/>"
    ndQuery.InnerXml = ""
    AddHandler listService.GetListItemsCompleted, AddressOf GetListItemsCompleted
    listService.GetListItemsAsync("Objectives", Nothing, ndQuery,~
            ndViewFields, Nothing, ndQueryOptions, Nothing)
End Sub
```

In Listing 9-12, the GetListItemsAsync method is called with some key parameters. The first parameter is a literal string with the value Objectives. This parameter specifies the name of the list we wish to work with. The ndQuery parameter is an XML node that would normally specify something similar to a SQL Where clause that would determine which records are returned and in what order. In this example, the XML node is empty since we want all the Objective items to be returned. The ndViewFields parameter is also an XML node that specifies which fields are to be returned by the query and in what order. In this example, the code asks for the Objective field to be returned. The ndQueryOptions parameter is another XML node that specifies various properties of the query. In this example, the code is asking for the query to exclude mandatory columns as part of the result set.

Once the GetListItemsAsync code has received its results, it transfers control to the GetListItemsCompleted method. The query results are actually stored as an XML node that is accessible through e.Result. To parse through the result set, the code in Listing 9-13 loads the returned XML into an XML Document object. The document allows us to use an XPath query to cycle through each result item. The result set is organized into row elements. Again, this code needs to be namespace-aware, as the rows are defined in the z namespace.

Listing 9-13. *Loading the Query Results*

```
Public Sub GetListItemsCompleted(ByVal sender As Object,~
     ByVal e As WSLists.GetListItemsCompletedEventArgs)
If (e.Error is Nothing) Then
   Dim ndItems As XmlNode
   ndItems = e.Result
   Dim xmlDoc As XmlDocument = New XmlDocument()
   xmlDoc.LoadXml(ndItems.OuterXml)
   Dim namespaceMgr As XmlNamespaceManager =~
          New XmlNamespaceManager(xmlDoc.NameTable)
   namespaceMgr.AddNamespace(ucTaskPane.ListItemsNamespacePrefix,~
          ucTaskPane.ListItemsNamespaceUri)
   Dim objectiveNodeList As XmlNodeList =~
           xmlDoc.SelectNodes("//z:row", namespaceMgr)
```

At this point, objectiveNodeList contains each individual objective from the result set and we are ready to build our PowerPoint slide in the user's presentation. Listing 9-14 details how the new slide is added and how the objectives are populated as a bulleted list.

Listing 9-14. *Building the Objectives Slide*

```
Dim slide As PowerPoint.Slide
Dim presentation As PowerPoint.Presentation
presentation = Globals.ThisAddIn.Application.ActivePresentation
slide = presentation.Slides.Add(presentation.Slides.Count + 1,~
      PowerPoint.PpSlideLayout.ppLayoutText)
slide.Shapes.Item(1).TextFrame.TextRange.Text = "Objectives"

Dim sBuilder As StringBuilder = New StringBuilder()
Dim objNode As XmlNode
For Each objNode In objectiveNodeList
    sBuilder.Append(objNode.Attributes("ows_Objective").InnerText)
    sBuilder.Append(vbCr)
Next
slide.Shapes.Item(2).TextFrame.TextRange.Text = sBuilder.ToString()
Globals.ThisAddIn.Application.ActiveWindow.View.GotoSlide(slide.SlideIndex)
```

To construct the slide, the code obtains a reference to the user's active presentation and uses its slide collection's Add method. The Add method takes two parameters: the index where the new slide should be placed and the layout the slide should use. In this case we want the slide to be at the end of the presentation and the layout should be the one that has only a title and a text box. With the slide created, the content is placed on it by accessing its various shapes. Because of our layout selection, two shapes need our attention. The first is at index one and it represents the title of the slide. This is set to the literal string "Objectives". The second shape, at index two, is populated using a StringBuilder. The text of the StringBuilder is the text of each objective separated by a carriage return (vbCr). Placing the carriage-return character is what gives us each objective as a bullet item. Lastly, PowerPoint is directed to make our new slide the current one. Figure 9-3 shows the end result.

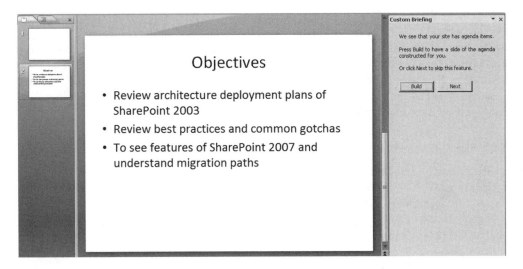

Figure 9-3. *The contructed Objectives slide*

The step3 User Control: Building Agenda Items

The step3 user control is not very different from step2. In its Start method, it also decides whether it should show itself. Assuming the site had an Agenda list and that the user selected to build a presentation slide, step3's Next button-click event handler uses the GetListItems-Async method. This time the control is querying for all of the items in the Agenda list. The call specifically asks for the Title, Owner, Time, and Notes fields to be a part of the result set.

Instead of simply building another bulleted list, this slide ambitiously presents the agenda items in a PowerPoint table while providing more-detailed content in the Notes portion of the slide. To get the slide set up for a table, the layout used in the Add method is ppLayoutTable. After we set the title of the presentation slide, the table is added by accessing the slide's Shapes collection and calling its AddTable method. This method expects two parameters: the number of rows (which in this case in the number of agenda list items) and the number of columns. In this example, we will populate the table with two columns of information: the time and title of the agenda item. Finally, the width of each column is set appropriately and the FirstRow property is set to false since our table will not have any column headings. Listing 9-15 details this code segment.

Listing 9-15. *Adding a Table to the Slide Presentation*

```
slide = presentation.Slides.Add(presentation.Slides.Count + 1,~
    PowerPoint.PpSlideLayout.ppLayoutTable)
slide.Shapes.Item(1).TextFrame.TextRange.Text = "Agenda"
Dim tblAgenda As PowerPoint.Shape =~
    slide.Shapes.AddTable(agendaNodeList.Count, 2)
tblAgenda.Table.Columns(1).Width = 200
tblAgenda.Table.Columns(2).Width = 400
tblAgenda.Table.FirstRow = False
```

With the table on the slide, our attention focuses on the processing of agenda items. Like objectives, we will cycle through a collection built using each row of the result set. This time we will retrieve all four attributes of the agenda item: Time, Title, Owner, and Notes. With this information we will not only place content into the table, but also keep a running StringBuilder that will be used to write text to the Notes portion of the slide. Listing 9-16 details this processing, where content is placed in the table and the ConstructNotesItem subroutine is called to format the content into the StringBuilder.

Listing 9-16. *Processing the Agenda Items*

```
Dim notesText As StringBuilder = New StringBuilder()
Dim i As Integer
For i = 1 To agendaNodeList.Count
    Dim time As String = agendaNodeList(i - 1).Attributes("ows_Time").InnerText
    Dim title As String = agendaNodeList(i - 1).Attributes("ows_Title").InnerText
    Dim owner As String = agendaNodeList(i - 1).Attributes("ows_Owner").InnerText
    Dim notes As String = String.Empty
    If (agendaNodeList(i - 1).Attributes("ows_Notes") IsNot Nothing) Then
        notes = agendaNodeList(i - 1).Attributes("ows_Notes").InnerText
    End If
    tblAgenda.Table.Cell(i, 1).Shape.TextFrame2.TextRange.Text = time
    tblAgenda.Table.Cell(i, 2).Shape.TextFrame2.TextRange.Text = title
    ConstructNotesItem(notesText, time, title, owner, notes)
Next
BuildNotesPage(slide, notesText)
```

Inside the ConstructNotesItem method, the StringBuilder is populated with the agenda list item along with some formatting characters such as parentheses, tabs, and carriage returns. One thing of interest is the treatment of the Notes field content before it is added to the StringBuilder. In SharePoint, the Notes field of an agenda item is a rich text box supporting style formatting. This formatting is stored as HTML, meaning that even simple carriage returns result in <div> tags being added to the content. HTML has little value for formatting in the Notes portion of the presentation slide. For this reason, this example uses a replace operation of a regular expression—Regex.Replace(HTML, "<[^>]*>", String.Empty)—to remove all HTML tags.

When the loop is complete, the table is completely populated with content and the StringBuilder is populated with text as well. The only remaining item is to place the StringBuilder text on the Notes portion of the slide. This is accomplished by locating the first shape on the Notes page that is capable of supporting text and then placing our StringBuilder content there. Listing 9-17 shows the code that completes this task.

Listing 9-17. *Putting Content on the Notes Page of the Slide*

```
Private Sub BuildNotesPage(ByVal slide As PowerPoint.Slide, _
                                        ByVal notesText As StringBuilder)
    'Find the first shape that has a textframe where we can put the notes
    Dim oShape As PowerPoint.Shape
    For Each oShape In slide.NotesPage.Shapes
```

```
    If (oShape.Type = Microsoft.Office.Core.MsoShapeType.msoPlaceholder) Then
        If (oShape.HasTextFrame) Then
            oShape.TextFrame2.TextRange.Text = notesText.ToString()
            Exit For
        End If
    End If
Next
End Sub
```

The result of our efforts is a slide that presents the time and title of each agenda item in a nicely formatted table. In addition, more-detailed content is added to the Notes portion of the slide to help the presenter deliver the material. Figure 9-4 shows a sample result.

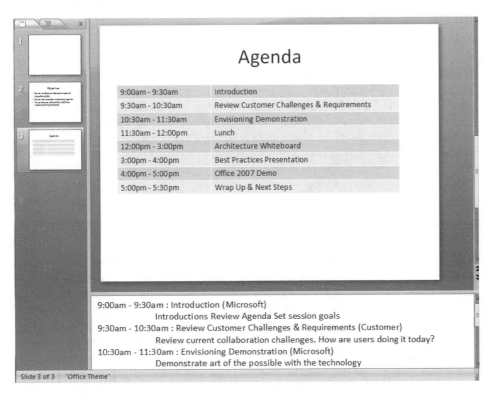

Figure 9-4. *Complete Agenda presenation slide*

The step4 User Control: Integration with Slide Libraries

The step4 user control is responsible for informing the user of the slide libraries that exist in the SharePoint site. A slide library is a new SharePoint library type that allows users to work on individual slides. This granularity allows for a great collaboration experience as users are able to work on just their portion while others edit their own portions simultaneously. The slide library also promotes slide reuse because these slides can be imported into other decks. Our assumption with this example is that the meeting workspace has at least one slide library and that there are existing slides there that should be imported into this presentation.

Like the other steps, step4 does check to see if at least one slide library was discovered previously and shows itself only if that is the case. In addition, this control's Start method includes a call to the ListSlideLibraryLinks method. This method is going to populate a panel with LinkLabel controls for each of the slide libraries discovered on the site. The experience we are going for is that the briefing application's task pane will provide links that open the user's browser directly to the chosen slide library. From there, the user will be able to select the desired slides and import them into this presentation. Listing 9-18 details the construction of the LinkLabel controls.

Listing 9-18. *Building LinkLabel Controls for Slide Libraries*

```
Private Sub ListSlideLibraryLinks()
    pnlLinks.Controls.Clear()
    Dim i As Integer
    Dim linkControls(ParentPane.SlideLibraries.Count) As LinkLabel
    For i = 0 To ParentPane.SlideLibraries.Count - 1
        linkControls(i) = New LinkLabel()
        linkControls(i).Location = New Point(5, 25 * i)
        AddHandler linkControls(i).LinkClicked, AddressOf LinkLabel_Click
        linkControls(i).LinkBehavior = LinkBehavior.AlwaysUnderline
        linkControls(i).Text = ParentPane.SlideLibraries(i).Name
        Dim link As LinkLabel.Link = linkControls(i).Links.Add(0, _
                        ParentPane.SlideLibraries(i).Name.Length)
        link.LinkData = ParentPane.SiteUrl & ParentPane.SlideLibraries(i).Url
    Next
    pnlLinks.Controls.AddRange(linkControls)
End Sub
```

In Listing 9-18, linkControls is an array of LinkLabels containing enough controls for the number of slide libraries that was discovered previously. Within the loop, a new LinkLabel control is created for each slide library. The LinkLabel's Location property specifies the horizontal and vertical placement of the control. Since we will be creating a number of controls, the vertical position is a calculation based on the iteration of the loop. The next line of code sets up an event handler for the LinkLabel so that we can run code in response to the user clicking on it. The LinkLabel's LinkBehavior is set to always present its text as underlined, and the actual text value is set to be the name of the slide library. In addition to these properties, the LinkLabel control needs to have a link created within it that specifies which portion of its text should be the active link. In this case, we want the link to be the entire length of the slide library's name. We also place the URL that the browser should open to as LinkData that will be retrieved in our event handler. Figure 9-5 shows what this step looks like in the task pane, where there are two slide libraries in the meeting workspace.

When the user clicks on one of the LinkLabels, our event handler responds by opening the browser and directing the user to the URL of the slide library. This event handler launches the browser automatically by using the System.Diagnostics namespace and starting a process with the URL as a parameter. This opens the browser to the location we specify. The event handler obtains the URL of the slide library by accessing the LinkData of the event argument. Listing 9-19 shows this event handler's code.

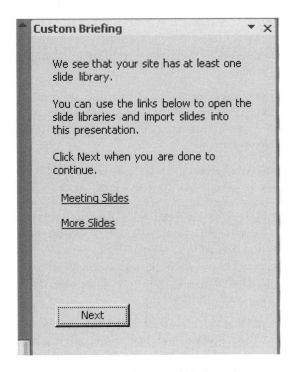

Figure 9-5. *Displaying links to slide libraries*

Listing 9-19. *Launching the Browser to a Selected Slide Library*

```
Private Sub LinkLabel_Click(ByVal sender As Object,~
    ByVal e As LinkLabelLinkClickedEventArgs)
  System.Diagnostics.Process.Start(e.Link.LinkData)
End Sub
```

Once in a browser, the user will be able to use the out-of-the-box functionality of selecting slides and importing them into the current presentation. To perform this operation, the
user must select the check boxes next to the slides he wants to import and click the Copy Slide
to Presentation button. The user is then asked if he wants to send the selected slides to a new
or open presentation. Select the Open Presentation option to have the slides imported into
the presentation we have been constructing. Notice there is also an option to receive notifications if the slide in the site were to change after this import has occurred. This is the Tell Me
When this Slide Changes option. If that's selected, the slide will be imported/copied into the
current presentation, but with a pointer back to the site. Each time the user opens the presentation, PowerPoint will check to see if the source slide has been modified since the import. If
so, the user will be alerted and asked if he wishes to update the presentation. This is a powerful feature that enhances the reuse of content within the organization.

Though there is a step5 user control, this is the last step in which presentation slides are
constructed. The last step user control simply informs the user that he has completed the
briefing application and that he can close the task pane by clicking the button in the ribbon
user interface.

Important Lessons

The PowerPoint briefing application incorporated several key techniques that are worth highlighting, as they could easily be reused in other projects.

Launching the task pane from the ribbon user interface: The briefing add-in utilized VSTO's ribbon support to add a custom applications tab to the ribbon and provide a toggle button to launch and close the briefing add-in's task pane. This integrated the custom application into the common Office experience.

Creating a wizardlike experience in the task pane: To complete the process of building slides based on site content, the briefing add-in led the user through a series of steps. This application designated the task pane as a controller of the process and gave it the responsibility of orchestrating the step controls. Other projects you construct with a wizardlike experience can benefit from the architecture used in this solution. Specifically, the briefing add-in streamlined the amount of code that needed to be written by defining a common interface for all step controls and encapsulated each step's functionality into its respective control. The task pane then became trivial to code, only moving the user from step to step and storing any necessary data during the process.

Discovering a site's lists and libraries: One of the main interaction points this application had with SharePoint was to query the site to discover what lists and libraries it contained. This was accomplished through SharePoint's Lists.asmx web service. The GetListCollection method of this web service returned XML that detailed the lists and libraries that the site contained. With this XML, the briefing add-in used XPath queries to find lists by name and by type. To find all lists of a certain type, the XPath query filtered on the ServerTemplate attribute.

Retrieving a particular list's items: The other interaction point with SharePoint was when the briefing add-in requested all the items of a specific list. This was used to obtain the content of the Objectives and Agenda lists. The application accomplished this through SharePoint's Lists.asmx web service. By calling this web service's GetListItems method, the application was able to obtain the XML detailing the items of the list. This method call supported a where clause, a list of fields to be included in the results, and other query options.

Extension Points

While coding this example, we thought of several variations to the solution that we didn't incorporate. Mostly, these were not included because they distracted from the overall objective of the solution. We call them out now as extension points since they may be applicable to a specific project you are working on.

Include check boxes to allow a user to select which items to import: In our example, the user was presented with only the option to build the slide with all of the objectives or to skip them entirely. There is a rather elegant third option in which the briefing add-in could query to get the items and display them in the task pane with check boxes. The user could then select which of the objective or agenda items should be placed into the new slide. Coding this option would be very similar to the technique used to build the collection of LinkLabels in step 4.

Add an update operation: Currently, the briefing add-in simply creates new slides in the open presentation. Other than the built-in notifications for slide libraries, it does not have an update operation. An update may allow for the application to check if the lists have changed and incorporate those changes into existing slides. For this to be successful, the application would first need to store the URL that was initially used to construct the slides. This URL could be stored in a custom property of the PowerPoint application or simply in a Notes page of one of the slides. Assuming that the titles of the slides have not changed, the add-in could iterate through to find the right slide, use the stored URL to get the new items, and repopulate the necessary shapes.

Further Reading

The following links are to resources a reader interested in this chapter's material will find useful:

- 13 Productivity Tips for Generating PowerPoint Presentations:

    `http://www.code-magazine.com/Article.aspx?quickid=0607151`

- Talk to SharePoint through Its Web Services:

    `http://www.developerland.com/DotNet/Enterprise/253.aspx`

- Video—Customizing the Ribbon with Microsoft's VSTO "v3" June CTP:

    `http://channel9.msdn.com/ShowPost.aspx?PostID=199934`

- Customizing the Office (2007) Ribbon User Interface for Developers:

    `http://msdn2.microsoft.com/en-us/library/ms406046.aspx`

- SPQuery Members:

    `http://msdn2.microsoft.com/en-us/library/microsoft.sharepoint.`
    `spquery_members.aspx`

- SPQuery.IncludeMandatoryColumns Property:

    `http://msdn2.microsoft.com/en-us/library/microsoft.sharepoint.spquery.`
    `includemandatorycolumns.aspx`

- The PowerPoint FAQ:

    `http://pptfaq.com`

■ ■ ■

CHAPTER 10

Building a Presentation Server-Side within a Web Part

Windows SharePoint Services provides the enterprise with easily creatable workspaces where information can be collected to support the sharing of information among users working toward a common goal. This goal could be many different things, including preparation for an event, execution of a business process, or even creation of materials for a project. Often organizations build presentations as an output of this collaboration or for routinely reporting on the team's status. Microsoft PowerPoint provides users with a powerful canvas to construct their presentations. Like in the previous chapter, we will look to reduce the amount of work placed on information workers to put the presentation together. In this chapter we will assume that the organization has a preconstructed template for presentations of a particular type and that building the presentation is a repeatable process of putting site content on slides. So for this chapter, we will completely automate the construction of a presentation by combining site content with the provided presentation template. This construction occurs server-side by a custom web part that leverages the new Microsoft Office Open XML file formats.

Real-World Examples

This problem is very similar to the one presented in Chapter 9. It therefore applies to the same types of customers. Any time someone is responsible for reporting on the status or state of a project or process you find users constructing briefings. We see this all the time, with military and commercial customers alike. Each type of a process has a specific PowerPoint template and each briefing involves a user or team of users gathering the necessary information to populate the template with content. This requires the team to dig through old emails in organizational mailboxes, search file shares, or even copy data from the user interfaces of other applications. The result is a waste of productivity and an increase in the chance of an error when transferring the information into the PowerPoint presentation.

Solution Overview

The biggest difference between this solution and the one in the previous chapter is the level of automation. In Chapter 9 we built a Microsoft PowerPoint add-in that was capable of pulling SharePoint site content and building corresponding slides in the user's presentation. That approach facilitates the presentation creation by providing the user with a tool. For this solution, we add an additional assumption that the organization has a PowerPoint file serving as a template. This template is then used over and over, with the only difference being the site content that is placed in it. To provide some context for our solution, we have focused our efforts on building a presentation whose slides contain items from a SharePoint site's Issues list. The Issues list in our site is an instance of the Issue Tracking list type. An Issue Tracking list is useful when users want to manage a set of tasks or problems. Each issue can be categorized, assigned, and prioritized. The resulting presentation should contain a title slide along with a slide for each of the issue categories. In our sample site, all of our issues are things that might be action items when a team is setting up a software application in a datacenter. They include items like the following:

- Install a backup device

- Optimize IIS

- Install service packs

Each of the items in the site's Issues list is categorized as Hardware, Software, or Other. These categories will be the titles of the main slides in the presentation we're creating.

In this chapter's solution we shift the work from a tool on the user's desktop to the Share-Point server. Since no human interaction is necessary, the work of merging the issues into the slides will be accomplished entirely server-side. The user will simply invoke the process by clicking a button in a custom web part. This web part will execute the merger by opening up the PowerPoint presentation that serves as the template, placing content on the slides and saving the new presentation back to a site document library. In the past, this type of solution would involve installing Microsoft PowerPoint on the server and automating it through its primary interop assemblies. This type of solution is neither scalable nor supported by Microsoft. Thankfully, Microsoft Office 2007 presents developers with a new option. This alternative derives from the fact that the Office applications now rely on the Open XML file format. So our web part will be able to modify the presentation template simply by adding new XML nodes at key places.

As the web part executes, it will retrieve its settings information to discover the filename of the presentation template and the name of the document library it is stored in. With the template, the web part will then iterate through the deck, using each slide's title to determine the work necessary to populate the slide with content. For the title slide, the web part will place the name of the team site, the account name of the user who clicked the button, and a timestamp. The second slide will be a bulleted list of the titles of the hardware issues. The software issues will be placed on the next slide, in a table displaying the title of the issue, who it is assigned to, and its priority. The last slide will be a bulleted list of the Other category's issues. When the construction is complete, the web part will store the presentation as a new file in the same document library as the template. This file will be named according to a web-part setting.

Solution Walkthrough

The following section will detail the major elements of the solution and the decisions that we made in coding it. The walkthrough will show you how to get started with Visual Studio to create the web part as well as to deploy and debug it. We will detail how you can use the System.IO.Packaging objects to examine the contents of an Office document that is saved in the new Open XML file format. This walkthrough will then show you how to manipulate the presentation slides, placing content in specific shapes, as bullet lists, and even as a table.

Setting Up the Team Site and Content

Our example relies on an Issue Tracking list named Issues in a WSS team site. So from either a new or existing team site, use the following steps to create the list:

1. Click View All Site Content in the left navigation control of the team site.

2. Click the Create button in the toolbar.

3. In the tracking category, select the Issue Tracking list type.

4. Name the list **Issues** and select to show it in the quick navigation.

With the list created, there is an additional step to configure the categories to use our desired vocabulary of Hardware, Software, and Other. The Issues list should now be in the left-hand navigation of the team site. Use the following steps to modify the list's categories:

1. Click on its link to display the list.

2. From the Settings drop-down in the toolbar, select List Settings.

3. In the Columns section, click on Category.

4. The choices are defined halfway down the page in a list box. Change the items to be **Hardware**, **Software**, and **Other**. Place each string on a separate line.

5. Click OK.

For this example, it is useful to add the Category column to the default view so you can easily check that the items are being placed on the correct slide. From the List Settings page, perform the following steps:

1. Locate the Views section and click on the All Issues view.

2. Click the check box next to the Category column and set its position to 3.

3. Click OK.

You are now ready to enter some content for this solution. Be sure to choose a variety of items for each category. Changing up the Assigned To and Priority values for the Software issues will be reflected in that slide's table. When complete, your list's contents should look something like Figure 10-1.

☑	Issue ID	Category	Title	● Assigned To	Issue Status	Priority	Due Date
	1	Software	DNS Name resolution error on Server A	Administrator	Active	(2) Normal	9/28/2006 12:00 AM
	2	Hardware	Memory Read Error on Dim on Server 2	Administrator	Active	(1) High	9/6/2006 12:00 AM
	3	Other	Customer feedback changing scope	Administrator	Active	(2) Normal	9/15/2006 12:00 AM
	4	Hardware	Install backup device	Administrator	Resolved	(2) Normal	9/5/2006 12:00 AM
	5	Software	Optimize IIS	Administrator	Closed	(3) Low	9/1/2006 12:00 AM
	6	Hardware	Setup external storage array	Administrator	Active	(1) High	9/8/2006 12:00 AM
	7	Software	Install service packs	Administrator	Active	(2) Normal	9/14/2006 12:00 AM

Figure 10-1. *The contents of the Issues list*

Creating the Presentation Template

In addition to the Issues content, this solution will also need a Microsoft PowerPoint 2007 file to use as a template. This is a presentation made up of the slides and design that we desire, but no content. So create a new PowerPoint presentation, apply your favorite visual design, and use the remaining details of this section to build the template slides.

■**Note** These instructions include literal text strings in boldface that you should be placing on slides. Place the words that appear in boldface italics into the presentation.

For this solution there will be four slides in the template:

Slide 1 uses the default Title Slide layout. Place the text **Site Title** in the text box designated to contain the presentation's title. Our web part will replace this text with the name of the WSS team site during its processing. In the Sub-Title textbox place two lines of text. For the first one, simply write **Author** and for the second, place the word **Timestamp**. Be sure you are pressing the Enter key from one line of text to the other, creating two paragraphs. We will use this information during the merge process when we insert the account name of the user, as well as a timestamp instead of these placeholders.

Slide 2 uses the Title and Content layout. Place the text **Hardware Issues** in the text box designated to contain the presentation's title. Simply leave the content area as is.

Slide 3 also uses the Title and Content layout. Place the text **Software Issues** in the text box designated to contain the presentation's title. Click the icon that represents a table to insert one into the content area. For the dimensions of the table, specify one row and three columns. Basically, all we want to do is enter the column headings; the web part will take care of putting the rows into the table for each of the issues in the Software category. For the column headings, use **Title**, **Assigned To**, and **Priority**. The resulting slide should look something like Figure 10-2, depending on what design you applied to the presentation.

Slide 4 uses the Title and Content layout. Place the text **Other** in the text box designated to contain the presentation's title. Simply leave the content area as is.

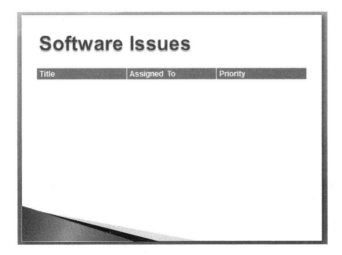

Figure 10-2. *The presentation template's Software Issues slide*

Now save this presentation as `template.pptx` in the Shared Documents library of the site where you created the Issues list. Be sure the "save as" type you are using is PowerPoint Presentation (that's where the pptx file extension comes from). This is important, as this file format type is using the Open XML format, enabling us to open and modify the file without using the PowerPoint application.

Creating the Web-Part Project

Microsoft Office SharePoint Server 2007 and Windows SharePoint Services v3 are built upon ASP.NET 2.0. As described in Chapter 2, one of the changes this means for developers is a switch from a SharePoint-specific web-part base class to the class provided by ASP.NET 2.0 (System.Web.UI.WebControls.WebParts.WebPart). The change increases the possibility of reusing these controls as part of both a SharePoint solution and a custom ASP.NET web site. Therefore, v3 web parts do not require a reference to the Microsoft.SharePoint assemblies— unless they want to access the SharePoint object model to interact with the application's specific features, such as lists, libraries, search, etc.

■**Note** There is still a SharePoint web-part base class (Microsoft.SharePoint.WebPartPages.WebPart) in the v3 versions of these products. This class is present mainly for backward compatibility. It now derives from the ASP.NET 2.0 web-part class. Developers may still have to rely on this class should they find themselves using some v2-specific features, such as web parts that use connections with other web parts that are not in web-part zones, or web parts that rely on WSS v2 data-caching features.

For this example, we will start as bare-bones as we can get and layer on functionality for the web part. Begin by opening Visual Studio and creating a VB.NET Class Library project.

Name the project and the solution **BookWebParts**. Delete the automatically added class `Class1.vb`, add a `DynamicPowerPoint.vb` class, and then add the following references:

Windows SharePoint Services (`Microsoft.SharePoint.dll`): This assembly will allow us to read the Issue list items as well as interact with the Shared Documents library.

System.Security: This assembly will allow us to specify some security attributes of our assembly.

System.Web: This assembly contains the web-part base class that we want to inherit from.

WindowsBase: This assembly allows us access to the System.IO.Packaging namespace, which supports reading a file saved in the Office XML file format.

Before we start coding, we will set up some assembly attributes that are required for our web part to run in a SharePoint web application. First, this assembly must allow partially trusted applications to invoke it. This is necessary since the web part assembly will be an assembly with a strong name, which we will deploy to the web application's bin directory for debugging in a development environment. The result is that the web part may be accessed by a not-fully-trusted caller. Ultimately, this setting impacts how .NET code access security is enforced. To add this setting, you must first select to Show All Files for your BookWebParts project in Solution Explorer. This reveals many additional files and folders. Figure 10-3 shows where you can find the `AssemblyInfo.vb` file, which needs to be modified.

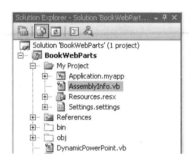

Figure 10-3. *Locating AssemblyInfo.vb in Solution Explorer*

With the `AssemblyInfo.vb` file open in the editor add an Imports line for System.Security at the top of the file and place the assembly attribute detailed in Listing 10-1 at the bottom of the file.

Listing 10-1. *Specifying AllowParticallyTrustedCallers*

```
<Assembly: AllowPartiallyTrustedCallers()>
```

In a production environment, this assembly usually would be added to the global assembly cache (GAC). For it to be deployed there, we will sign it. To give your assembly a strong name, do the following:

1. Right-click on the project in Solution Explorer and select Properties.

2. Select Signing in the left-hand navigation.

3. Click the check box to sign the assembly. The drop-down directly below the check box will enable. Figure 10-4 depicts this choice.

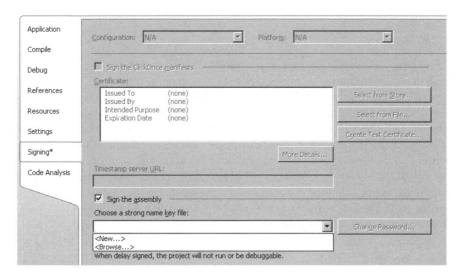

Figure 10-4. *Signing the assembly*

4. Select New.

5. For the name of the file, type in **key**.

6. Deselect the check box for protecting the file with a password.

7. Click OK.

8. Click Visual Studio's save toolbar button to commit this setting.

Basics of the DynamicPowerPoint Web Part

In Chapter 2 you were introduced to some of the new syntax involved with building Share-Point web parts derived from the ASP.NET 2.0 web-part base class. This section will go one step further, putting some of the basic elements in place for our web part that will merge the site content into the PowerPoint presentation. This includes adding some ASP.NET web controls that we will render to make up the web part's user interface. First make sure that your DynamicPowerPoint class derives from System.Web.UI.WebControls.WebParts.WebPart. Then add the Imports statements in Listing 10-2 to the top of your class file. These statements are the key namespaces that we will use in the code and keep us from having to fully qualify their class names.

Listing 10-2. *Imports Statements*

```
Imports System.Web.UI.WebControls.WebParts
Imports System.Web.UI.WebControls
Imports Microsoft.SharePoint
Imports Microsoft.SharePoint.WebControls
Imports System.IO
Imports System.IO.Packaging
Imports System.Xml
```

When a user places this web part on a SharePoint page, she is creating a specific instance. She could, in fact, place many instances of the same web part on the same page. A fundamental feature of web parts is for each instance to maintain its specific configuration or settings data. There are some common settings, such as width, height, visibility, border, etc. that our web part will get for free, but our code must account for any specific configuration information that we want during execution. For this solution we have identified three different pieces of information that we want an author to be able to input into a specific instance of our web part (but the values will be shared among all site visitors). These three settings are the name of the library that's storing our files, the name of the presentation template file, and the name that should be used when saving the generated file. Listing 10-3 shows how a web-part property can be coded to hold a setting value.

Listing 10-3. *A Web-Part Property*

```
Private m_libraryName As String = String.Empty
<WebBrowsable(), Personalizable(PersonalizationScope.Shared)> _
    Public Property LibraryName() As String
        Get
            Return m_libraryName
        End Get
        Set(ByVal value As String)
            m_libraryName = value
        End Set
    End Property
```

In Listing 10-3 a private variable m_libraryName is declared; it will hold the value of the setting. The property LibraryName() allows the value stored in the variable to be assigned and retrieved. The important items here that are different from any other VB.NET class are the attributes preceding the property: WebBrowsable and Personalizable. The WebBrowsable attribute describes this property as one that should be displayed in an administrative-settings interface that is shown when the web part is configured. This interface is shown in Figure 10-5.

The Personalizable attribute has a parameter of PersonalizationScope.Shared. The other possible value here is PersonalizationScope.User. This scope dictates whether the value stored applied to all users (Shared) or can be set differently for different users (User). The User setting is handy when you want to allow each site visitor to customize the setting in his own version of the page.

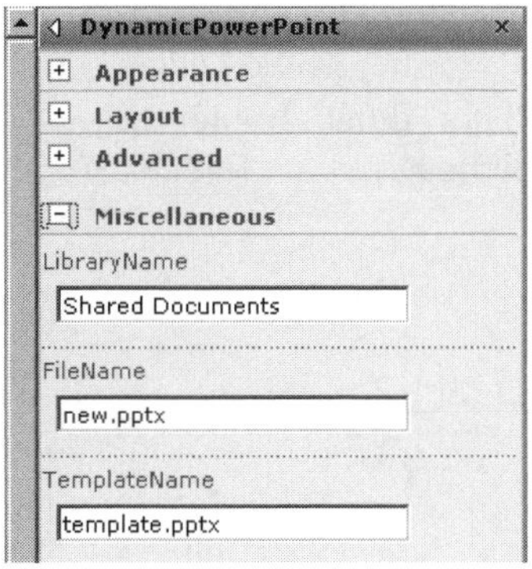

Figure 10-5. *Entering a web part's configuration settings*

Most examples of web parts that you will find in SDKs or on how-to web sites simply rely on what are effectively print statements in the web part's RenderContents() method to generate the user interface. It is not unusual to see web-part code with dozens of output.write() statements that are outputting raw HTML into the response. This approach results in developers writing an awful lot of code since they are printing every HTML tag, and it doesn't easily take into account alternate renderings for different browsers or different devices. Fortunately there is a set of controls that is already sensitive and outputs HTML accordingly. These controls are the ASP.NET web controls and since a web part is nothing but a server control, it can use them as well. The code in Listing 10-4 shows how to declare and instantiate the label and button controls we will use in this web part.

Listing 10-4. *Working with Web Controls*

```
Private WithEvents btn_Generate As Button
Private lbl_Message As Label

Protected Overrides Sub CreateChildControls()
    Me.btn_Generate = New Button()
    btn_Generate.Text = "Build Briefing"
    btn_Generate.Visible = True
    Me.Controls.Add(btn_Generate)
    Me.lbl_Message = New Label()
    lbl_Message.Text = String.Format( _
                "The presentation has been created as {0} in the {1} library", _
                m_fileName, m_libraryName)
    lbl_Message.Visible = False
    Me.Controls.Add(lbl_Message)
    MyBase.CreateChildControls()
End Sub
```

The first two lines of Listing 10-4 declare the two ASP.NET web controls. The button uses the additional keyword WithEvents since we will want to write code that responds to its Click event. Notice how each control is instantiated in the CreateChildControls() override. The base class uses this method to create controls that are contained within the web part. In addition to creating the instance of each web control class, we also added each instance to this web part's controls collection. This is an important step, as the web part will automatically render each control that is referenced in this collection. Notice in Listing 10-5 how much simpler the RenderContents method has become as compared to printing all the necessary HTML tags.

Listing 10-5. *Rendering the Web Part*

```
Protected Overrides Sub RenderContents(ByVal writer As~
      System.Web.UI.HtmlTextWriter)
  Me.EnsureChildControls()
   If m_errorMessage <> String.Empty Then
      writer.Write(m_errorMessage)
   Else
      MyBase.RenderContents(writer)
   End If
End Sub
```

The last piece of functionality we want to implement at this point is the Click event of the button. As shown in Listing 10-6, this event handler will hide the button and show the label.

Listing 10-6. *The Button-Click Event Handler*

```
Private Sub btn_Generate_Click(ByVal sender As Object, _
      ByVal e As System.EventArgs) Handles btn_Generate.Click
   Me.btn_Generate.Visible = False
   Me.lbl_Message.Visible = True
End Sub
```

This will give us enough functionality to deploy and test. These steps are explained in the following section. We will come back to this event handler in the "Iterating through the Template" section of this chapter and add the code to open the template presentation, merge the Issue list content, and save the new file.

Deploying the Web Part

Before adding more code to the web part, you will want to make sure it compiles and runs on a SharePoint page. This section will detail the steps required to deploy the DynamicPower-Point web part to SharePoint. First we need an additional piece of information to properly set up SharePoint to run our web part. That piece of information is the public key token of the assembly. This exists because we signed the assembly earlier. An easy way to retrieve the key is through the sn.exe .NET Framework command-line tool. Use the following steps to retrieve the public key token:

1. Open a Visual Studio command prompt. You can select it from your Program Files menu, in the Visual Studio Tools folder.

2. Navigate to your project's Debug folder in its bin directory. When you list the files, you should see BookWebParts.dll. This is your assembly.

3. Type **sn.exe –T BookWebParts.dll**. The T is here is case-sensitive—and make sure you use the uppercase.

4. Highlight and copy the response into Notepad. You may need to switch your command prompt into QuickEdit mode (by accessing the properties of the command-prompt window by right-clicking on the window's title bar).

Now that we have the web part assembly's public key token, we can inform SharePoint that we have reviewed this code and that we approve the controls within it to be run. This step is simply telling SharePoint it is OK to try to run this code. The web application's trust level, which we will discuss later, still places restrictions on what actions this code can perform. We can inform SharePoint by registering the assembly and its controls as safe in the `web.config` file. To access your web application's `web.config` file, navigate to its folder, which is typically located in `c:\Inetpub\wwwroot\wss\VirtualDirectories`. If you are using more than one web application, make sure you are modifying the `web.config` in the application you plan to test. Make sure you create a backup your configuration file before making any change. Open the `web.config` file and add the single line shown in Listing 10-7 in the SafeControls section. (The line is wrapped here for display only.) Be sure to use the public key token you retrieved earlier in this section.

Listing 10-7. *Registering a Safe Control*

```
<safeControl Assembly="BookWebParts, Version=1.0.0.0, Culture=neutral,~
    PublicKeyToken=9e4c7a60c0679071" Namespace="BookWebParts"~
    TypeName="*" Safe="True" />
```

In the same `web.config` file, you will also want to check the trust level assigned to the web application. The trust level is important here since we will be deploying the assembly to the local bin directory on the development machine. Code run from this location is not as trusted as code in the GAC. Placing your assembly in the GAC is typically done on production machines, not developer boxes. Locate the trust element, which is by default WSS_Minimal. Since you're working on the development machine, you can set this to Full and just move on. However, a preferred practice is to have a custom code-access security policy. For more information on defining these policies, visit the following URL:

• Microsoft Windows SharePoint Services and Code Access

  `http://msdn2.microsoft.com/en-us/library/ms916855.aspx`

Now copy your `BookWebParts.dll` assembly into the web application's bin directory. Also copy over the .pdb file since we will want debugging information to be available. (You can also deploy web parts to the global assembly cache, but that is more appropriate for finished assemblies than for a solution still in development.) Additionally, you will want to reset IIS to make sure your changes are implemented. This approach is a bit manual and can be automated by creating a solution package and using the `stsadm.exe` SharePoint command-line tool. The WSS SDK has a complete section on wrapping web parts and other elements into a package:

• Solutions and Web Part Packages

  `http://msdn2.microsoft.com/en-us/library/ms413687.aspx`

After the IISReset, we will add the web part to the web-part gallery so it is available to be added to the SharePoint site. The following steps walk you through this process:

1. Open your site in the browser, and from the Site Actions menu select Site Settings.

2. If your team site is not a top-level site, click the Go to Top Level Site Settings link.

3. Once at the top level site settings admin page, click the link for web parts in the Galleries column.

4. Click New in the toolbar.

5. Check the check box next to the BookWebParts.DynamicPowerPoint web part.

6. Click Populate Gallery.

Once the web part has been placed into the gallery, it will display in the Add Web Parts interface. To gain access to this interface, place the site in edit mode by selecting Edit Page from the Site Actions menu. Click the Add a Web Part button in the zone where you want to add the part. The resulting Add Web Parts interface is shown in Figure 10-6. Click the check box next to the DynamicPowerPoint web part and click Add to place it on the page.

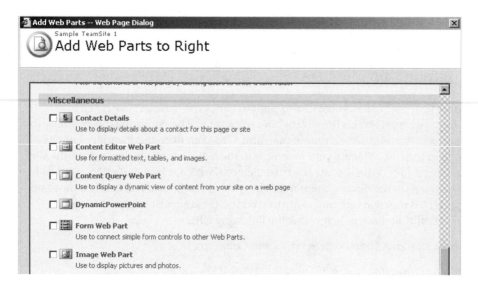

Figure 10-6. *Adding the DynamicPowerPoint web part*

Debugging the Web Part

At some point, you are going to want to debug a web part. The easiest way to do that is to make sure at least one page of SharePoint's web application has been loaded and then to attach Visual Studio. Loading a page ensures that there is a corresponding worker process for that web site. From your web-part project in Visual Studio, do the following:

1. Select Debug in the top menu.

2. Select Attach to Process.

3. Locate the `w3wp.exe` worker process.

You may have more than one worker process. This is especially true if you have deployed SharePoint's shared service provider to a dedicated web application or you simply have other IIS web sites on the machine. To aid in the selection of the right worker process, run the following command from a command prompt:

```
c:\windows\system32\iisapp.vbs
```

This script will list the PIDs and AppPoolIds for the IIS worker processes. The AppPoolId should help you determine which w3wp process is MOSS; the corresponding PID is displayed in the Visual Studio's Attach to Process dialog. Once Visual Studio is attached, set breakpoints accordingly in your code and navigate to a SharePoint page containing your web part. Visual Studio will enter debug mode once one of your breakpoints is hit.

Overview of Office XML Formats and PresentationML

The web part is going to merge the contents of the Issues list into the slides, leveraging the fact that our presentation template was saved using the new Open XML file format. As explained in Chapter 3, the Microsoft Office 2007 desktop tools have switched from their proprietary binary-formatted files to formats based on Open XML specifications. Now each file—whether it be a spreadsheet, presentation, or document—is really a package of parts and items. *Parts* are pieces of content for the file whereas *items* are metadata describing how the parts should be assembled and rendered. Most of these pieces are XML files, making it possible for them to be manipulated through code. You can gain insight into the structure of an Open XML–based file by replacing its file extension with **.zip** since the file is really an ordinary Zip archive. Figure 10-7 shows the root of the archive for the PowerPoint presentation we built earlier.

Figure 10-7. *Examining the archive of a PowerPoint presentation*

The XML file in the root is named `[Content_Types].xml` and it stores content-type directives for all the parts that appear in the archive. A content type contains metadata about a particular part or groups of parts and, more importantly, contains a directive for how the application should render that part. For example, Listing 10-8 shows just a few lines from the file, but clearly delineates how this file tells the rendering application which parts are slides, images, note pages, etc.

Listing 10-8. *A Presentation's Content Types*

```
<Override PartName="/ppt/slides/slide1.xml"
  ContentType="application/vnd.openxmlformats-
    officedocument.presentationml.slide+xml" />
<Default Extension="jpeg"
  ContentType="image/jpeg" />
<Override PartName="/ppt/notesSlides/notesSlide1.xml"
  ContentType="application/vnd.openxmlformats-
    officedocument.presentationml.notesSlide+xml" />
```

PresentationML is one of the easier Open XML file formats to understand, as presentations have an obvious composition. A presentation is made up of slides. Each slide has a collection of shapes, which in turn hold content. Picture a PowerPoint slide that contains a title at the top and a bulleted list below. Such a slide contains two rectangle shapes. The first rectangle contains the user-entered title and the second one contains paragraphs of text formatted to be displayed as a bulleted list. Exploring the files located in the presentation's archive will help you understand how PowerPoint assembles these elements.

Begin with `presentation.xml` which is located in the ppt folder of the archive. Opening this file in Internet Explorer will display XML similar to that in Figure 10-8.

```
<?xml version="1.0" encoding="UTF-8" standalone="yes" ?>
- <p:presentation xmlns:a="http://schemas.openxmlformats.org/drawingml/2006/main"
    xmlns:r="http://schemas.openxmlformats.org/officeDocument/2006/relationships"
    xmlns:p="http://schemas.openxmlformats.org/presentationml/2006/main" saveSubsetFonts="1">
  - <p:sldMasterIdLst>
      <p:sldMasterId id="2147483660" r:id="rId4" />
    </p:sldMasterIdLst>
  - <p:sldIdLst>
      <p:sldId id="256" r:id="rId5" />
      <p:sldId id="257" r:id="rId6" />
      <p:sldId id="258" r:id="rId7" />
      <p:sldId id="259" r:id="rId8" />
    </p:sldIdLst>
    <p:sldSz cx="9144000" cy="6858000" type="screen4x3" />
    <p:notesSz cx="6858000" cy="9144000" />
  + <p:defaultTextStyle>
  </p:presentation>
```

Figure 10-8. *The presentation.xml file*

The `presentation.xml` file contains the list of slides (<p:sldLst>), references to the slide and notes masters, as well as the sizes of the slides (<p:sldSz>) and notes pages (<p:notesSz>). The sequence of the slide nodes is important, as the rendering application will display them in the order they are listed here. Notice that each slide node, as well as the master nodes, has a r:id attribute. This identifier is a key to a specific relationship that will tell the rendering application where the part for this item is located. The relationship information for this presentation is stored in `presentation.xml.rels` file in the ppt_rels folder of the archive. Listing 10-9 is the XML node in this file that tells the application that the first slide's content is stored in `slide1.xml`.

Listing 10-9. *Example of a Presentation Relationship*

```
<Relationship
Id="rId5" Type="http://schemas.openxmlformats.org/officeDocument/~
    2006/relationships/slide" Target="slides/slide1.xml"
/>
```

Following the relationship links, you can see that the contents of the slides are stored in the ppt\slides folder of the archive. In our example, this directory contains four XML files; one for each of our slides in the presentation we created to act as the template. When building solutions that work with the Open XML file formats, it is often useful to employ this technique of exploring the archive to examine its contents before trying to manipulate it through code. In fact, you could extract these contents to a folder, modify them, and repackage them to a new Zip archive. Renaming this archive with a .pptx extension would, in fact, create a new presentation, allowing you to see the changes in PowerPoint.

■Tip Editing large XML files can be a burden. To make it easier, download the schemas for the Open XML file formats so that Visual Studio can provide you with IntelliSense support. You can download the schemas from this site: http://www.microsoft.com/downloads/details.aspx?familyid=15805380-F2C0-4B80-9AD1-2CB0C300AEF9&displaylang=en.

Iterating through the Template

To get the web part to place content into the template, we will revisit the button's click event handler, adding code to open the presentation template and iterate through its slides. We will be placing a lot more code into this web part in this section. If you get overwhelmed, please download the code for this chapter from the Source Code/Download section of http://apress.com. Each slide's title will control what content gets placed there. When this process is complete, the web part will save the modified file back to the site's document library. Listing 10-10 details the modified button-click event handler.

Listing 10-10. *Opening the Presentation Template and Saving the New File*

```
Private Sub btn_Generate_Click(ByVal sender As Object, _
        ByVal e As System.EventArgs) Handles btn_Generate.Click
Dim templateStream As Stream = Nothing
Try
   m_web = SPControl.GetContextWeb(Me.Context)
   Dim sharedDocs As SPFolder = m_web.GetFolder(m_libraryName)
   Dim templateFile As SPFile = sharedDocs.Files.Item(m_templateName)
   templateStream = templateFile.OpenBinaryStream()
   Me.ProcessSlides(templateStream)
   'save the modified(File)
   sharedDocs.Files.Add(m_fileName, templateStream, True)
   Me.btn_Generate.Visible = False
```

```
    Me.lbl_Message.Visible = True
Catch ex As Exception
    m_errorMessage = ex.Message
Finally
    If (templateStream IsNot Nothing) Then templateStream.Close()
End Try
End Sub
```

The first line of the Try block enables the web part to get a reference to the particular SharePoint web that it is being invoked from. Since this web part could be reused on many different sites in a deployment, the web part must identify its container so that it can find the list, library, and files it needs to complete its task. Notice the use of the variables for retrieving the library and the presentation template file. These local variables have the values that were specified in the settings interface for the web part. This layer of abstraction adds flexibility to the solution instead of our having to hard-code these values. Once the template file has been located, it is opened as a stream and passed to a processing routine. This processing will include iterating over the collection of slides and placing content on them. When this is complete, the modified stream is saved back to the document library as a new file with the provided filename.

The outermost layer of the presentation template's processing involves iterating through the collection of slides and examining their titles. Instead of our having to write this entire block of code ourselves, we can use Microsoft-provided code snippets that include common tasks when working with Open XML–formatted files. You can obtain these snippets at http://www.microsoft.com/downloads/details.aspx?familyid=8D46C01F-E3F6-4069-869D-90B8B096B556&displaylang=en. These snippets include declarations of the XML namespaces that are used within the Open XML–formatted file. For this solution, there are three namespaces in particular that we will rely on with our code. They are declared as constants in Listing 10-11.

Listing 10-11. *Declaring the XML Namespaces*

```
Const documentRelationshipType As String =~
    "http://schemas.openxmlformats.org/officeDocument/2006~
    /relationships/officeDocument"
Const presentationmlNamespace As String =~
    "http://schemas.openxmlformats.org/presentationml/2006/main"
Const drawingmlNamespace As String =~
    "http://schemas.openxmlformats.org/drawingml/2006/main"
```

One of the snippets contains code for obtaining a list of a PowerPoint presentation's slide titles. Figure 10-9 shows this code snippet being placed in the class by using Visual Studio.

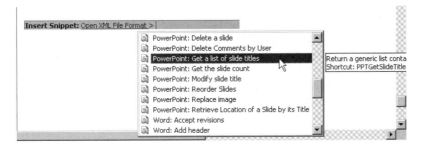

Figure 10-9. *Inserting a code snippet*

After the code snippet has been placed in the file, we have to make a few changes. First the function needs to be renamed from PPTGetSlideTitles to **ProcessSlides**, which is how it is called in Listing 10-10. Also, the parameter from the snippet is a string representing the physical path and the name of the file. Since the web part has already retrieved its file as a stream, rename the parameter to **fileStream** and change its type to Stream. You will have to make corresponding changes wherever the fileName parameter is used in this function. A final change is necessary because this code snippet constructs a list of strings containing only the slide titles. It accomplished this by iterating over the collection of slides and looking for shapes that contain slide titles. When it finds the titleNode of a given slide, we want to do more than simply record it in a list. Listing 10-12 includes the code that will call our different build methods based on the slide's title.

Listing 10-12. *Constructing Content Selectively Based on Slide Title*

```
titleNode = sheetDoc.SelectSingleNode( _
                "//p:sp//p:ph[@type='title' or @type='ctrTitle']", _
                nsManager)
If titleNode IsNot Nothing Then
  Dim title As String = _
  titleNode.ParentNode.SelectSingleNode("../../p:txBody/a:p/a:r/a:t", _
  nsManager).InnerText
  Select Case title
      Case "Site Title"
          BuildTitleSlide(sheetDoc, titleNode)
      Case "Hardware Issues"
          BuildHardwareSlide(sheetDoc)
      Case "Software Issues"
          BuildSoftwareSlide(sheetDoc)
      Case "Other"
          BuildOtherSlide(sheetDoc)
      End Select
  sheetDoc.Save(sheetPart.GetStream(FileMode.Create, _
                        FileAccess.Write))
End If
```

Building the Title Slide

The first slide of the presentation is the title slide. For content, we will place the name of the team site in the title shape, as well as the current user name and date in the subtitle shape. Merging the content into this presentation slide is rather easy since the template has place-holder content that the web part simply needs to replace. Figure 10-10 shows the slide1.xml file in the package focusing on the subtitle shape.

```
 - <p:sp>
   - <p:nvSpPr>
       <p:cNvPr id="3" name="Subtitle 2" />
       <p:cNvSpPr>
     - <p:nvPr>
         <p:ph type="subTitle" idx="1" />
       </p:nvPr>
     </p:nvSpPr>
     <p:spPr />
   - <p:txBody>
       <a:bodyPr />
       <a:lstStyle />
     - <a:p>
       - <a:r>
           <a:rPr lang="en-US" dirty="0" smtClean="0" />
           <a:t>Author</a:t>
         </a:r>
       </a:p>
     - <a:p>
       - <a:r>
           <a:rPr lang="en-US" dirty="0" smtClean="0" />
           <a:t>Timestamp</a:t>
         </a:r>
         <a:endParaRPr lang="en-US" dirty="0" />
       </a:p>
     </p:txBody>
   </p:sp>
```

Figure 10-10. *PresentationML of the Title Slide*

Notice that the PresentationML relies heavily on the use of XML namespaces. The p namespace corresponds with PresentationML, whereas the a namespace is DrawingML. The BuildTitleSlide method uses XPath queries to navigate to the XML nodes to locate the placeholder content. Each of these queries includes a namespace manager to resolve the namespace prefixes. Once the nodes are found, their InnerText property is set, replacing the placeholder value with the desired text. Listing 10-13 details the BuildTitleSlide method.

Listing 10-13. *Building the Title Slide*

```
Private Sub BuildTitleSlide(ByVal doc As XmlDocument, _
                                        ByVal titleNode As XmlNode)
'the title is the first text node
titleNode.ParentNode.SelectSingleNode("//a:t", _
                            nsManager).InnerText = m_web.Title
'locate the subtitle
Dim subTitleNode As XmlNode
subTitleNode = doc.SelectSingleNode("//p:sp//p:ph[@type='subTitle']", _
                            nsManager)
```

```
If (subTitleNode IsNot Nothing) Then
    'there are two text elements in this part:
    'user name and date/time
    Dim textNodes As XmlNodeList = _
                    subTitleNode.SelectNodes("../../../p:txBody/a:p/a:r/a:t", _
                                                        nsManager)
    If (textNodes IsNot Nothing) Then
        textNodes(0).InnerText = Me.Context.User.Identity.Name
        textNodes(1).InnerText = DateTime.Today.ToShortDateString()
    End If
End If
End Sub
```

The result of this work is a presentation whose title slide has the name of the team site, the user name of the user who generated the presentation, and the date the presentation was created. Figure 10-11 shows this slide in the resulting PowerPoint presentation file.

Figure 10-11. *The completed title slide*

Building the Slide for Hardware Issues

The second slide is to contain a listing of the hardware-issue items. In the presentation template, this slide contains only two shapes. The first is for the title of the slide. This is already populated and will not have to be modified. The second shape is an empty rectangle where the titles of the hardware issues are to be placed as bulleted items. The BuildHardwareSlide method first queries the site's Issues list to retrieve the list items that have been categorized as hardware. As Listing 10-14 shows, this is achieved through an SPQuery object with a where clause filtering on the Category field. (The "Further Reading" section of this chapter has a link to a reference on the SPQuery object in case this is the first time you have tried to use it.)

Listing 10-14. *Query to Retrieve Issues Categorized as Hardware*

```
Private Sub BuildHardwareSlide(ByVal doc As XmlDocument)
Dim list As SPList = m_web.Lists("Issues")
Dim query As SPQuery = New SPQuery()
query.Query = "<Where><Eq><FieldRef Name='Category'/><Value
                       Type='CHOICE'>Hardware</Value></Eq></Where>"
Dim items As SPListItemCollection = list.GetItems(query)
```

With the content retrieved, the web part needs to find the location in the slide where it is to be placed. Figure 10-12 shows the target Content Placeholder 1 shape with some sample bulleted paragraphs of text (Item 1, Item 2, and Item 3).

```
– <p:sp>
  – <p:nvSpPr>
      <p:cNvPr id="2" name="Content Placeholder 1" />
    + <p:cNvSpPr>
    ⊞ <p:nvPr>
    </p:nvSpPr>
    <p:spPr />
  – <p:txBody>
      <a:bodyPr />
      <a:lstStyle />
    – <a:p>
      – <a:r>
          <a:rPr lang="en-US" dirty="0" smtClean="0" />
          <a:t>Item 1</a:t>
        </a:r>
      </a:p>
    – <a:p>
      – <a:r>
          <a:rPr lang="en-US" dirty="0" smtClean="0" />
          <a:t>Item 2</a:t>
        </a:r>
      </a:p>
    – <a:p>
      – <a:r>
          <a:rPr lang="en-US" dirty="0" smtClean="0" />
          <a:t>Item 3</a:t>
        </a:r>
        <a:endParaRPr lang="en-US" dirty="0" />
      </a:p>
    </p:txBody>
  </p:sp>
```

Figure 10-12. *PresentationML of a bulleted list*

The web part uses an XPath query to retrieve the shape's txBody XML node. This node will be the parent of the paragraphs we will construct for each of the hardware-issue items returned from the earlier query. When inserting a new paragraph, the web part places it just before the last child of this node. This is because our template presentation has an empty paragraph that we will leave as last in the list. Listing 10-15 contains the rest (continuing from Listing 10-14) of the BuildHardwareSlide method, showing how each list item gets added into the slide.

Listing 10-15. *Adding the Hardware List Items into the Slide*

```
'Find the part containing rectangle two
Dim rectangleNode As XmlNode
rectangleNode = doc.SelectSingleNode~
     ("//p:sp//p:cNvPr[@name='Content Placeholder 1']", _
                              nsManager)
If (rectangleNode IsNot Nothing) Then
    'Locate that part's txt area to add the bullet items to
    Dim textNode As XmlNode = rectangleNode.SelectSingleNode("../../p:txBody", _
                              nsManager)
    If (textNode IsNot Nothing) Then
        Dim item As SPListItem
        For Each item In items
            'append the item to the slide as a bullet
            Dim paraNode As XmlNode = BuildTextPar(item("Title"), textNode)
             textNode.InsertBefore(paraNode, textNode.LastChild)
        Next
    End If
End If
End Sub
```

The only remaining detail is the construction of the XML for each new paragraph. The BuildTextPar function contains this logic. You can obtain this function from the code download at http://apress.com. It tediously constructs a paragraph XML node structure. This construction includes placing its string parameter as the text content of the paragraph. The returned XML structure is identical to the paragraphs containing the items in Figure 10-12. This routine is coded as a function because it will be reused any time we need to build a paragraph of text to place on a slide. Figure 10-13 shows the Hardware Issues slide in the resulting PowerPoint presentation file.

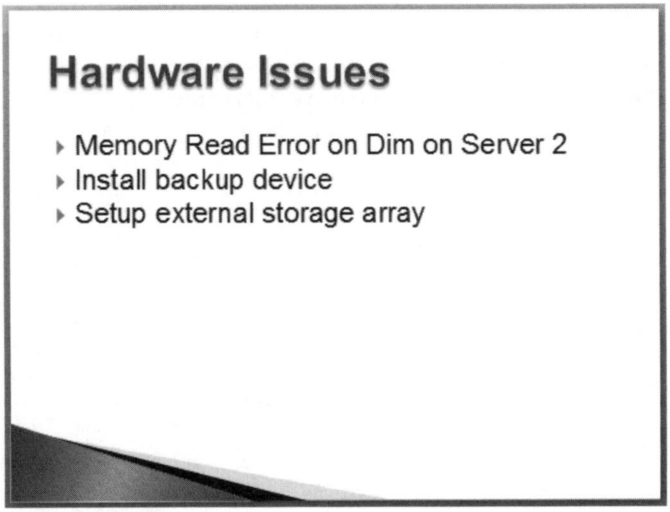

Figure 10-13. *The completed Hardware Issues slide*

■**Note** The techniques used in building the Hardware Issues slide are also used to build the presentation's fourth slide, containing the Other category's issues.

Building the Slide for Software Issues

The third slide is to contain a table of the software issues. In the presentation template, we placed the slide's title as well as a three-column table containing only column headings. The first column will contain the title of the issue items. The second column will contain the name of the user who the item is assigned to, and the last column will contain the item's priority. The BuildSoftwareSlide method first queries the site's Issues list to retrieve the list items that have been categorized as software. This is identical to the technique we used to retrieve the hardware items earlier. With the content retrieved, the web part needs to find the location in the slide where the content is to be placed. Listing 10-16 details the web part's code for finding the table in the slide as well as adding a new table row for each item.

Listing 10-16. *Finding the Slide's Table and Adding Table Rows*

```
'Find the part containing rectangle two
Dim tableNode As XmlNode
tableNode = doc.SelectSingleNode("//p:graphicFrame//a:tbl", nsManager)
If (tableNode IsNot Nothing) Then
    Dim item As SPListItem
    For Each item In items
        'append the item to the slide as a bullet
        Dim rowNode As XmlNode = BuildTableRow(item, tableNode)
        tableNode.InsertAfter(rowNode, tableNode.LastChild)
    Next
End If
```

Table rows in PresentationML are not very different from those in HTML. Each table row contains table cells, which in turn contain paragraphs of text. Figure 10-14 shows a sample table row of three columns, with the first cell expanded so you can see its contents.

```
- <a:tr h="0">
  - <a:tc>
    - <a:txBody>
        <a:bodyPr />
        <a:lstStyle />
      - <a:p>
        - <a:r>
            <a:rPr lang="en-US" dirty="0" smtClean="0" />
            <a:t>Item1</a:t>
          </a:r>
          <a:endParaRPr lang="en-US" dirty="0" />
        </a:p>
      </a:txBody>
      <a:tcPr />
    </a:tc>
  + <a:tc>
  + <a:tc>
  </a:tr>
```

Figure 10-14. *PresentationML of a table row*

The BuildTableRow function begins building the XML structure that represents one row of the table. It creates the table row element (<a:tr>) and then calls the BuildTableCell function for each of the three columns. The BuildTableCell function will take care of building out the table cell with the contents specified by the passed parameter. Listing 10-17 details the Build-TableRow function, including each of its calls to BuildTableCell with the issue's title, assigned user's name, and priority as arguments.

Listing 10-17. *Constructing a Row for the Slide's Table*

```
Private Function BuildTableRow(ByVal item As SPListItem, _
                        ByVal tableNode As XmlNode) As XmlNode
 'Create a new table row node
 Dim rowNode As XmlNode = _
        tableNode.OwnerDocument.CreateElement( _
        "a", "tr", drawingmlNamespace)
Dim rowAttr As XmlAttribute = _
        tableNode.OwnerDocument.CreateAttribute("h")
rowAttr.Value = "0"
rowNode.Attributes.Append(rowAttr)
'add row cells based on item
rowNode.AppendChild(BuildTableCell(item("Title"), rowNode))
'the assigned to column has a # between ID and name
Dim name As String = item("Assigned To")
If (name IsNot Nothing) Then
   Dim parts() As String = name.Split("#")
   name = parts(1)
End If
rowNode.AppendChild(BuildTableCell(name, rowNode))
rowNode.AppendChild(BuildTableCell(item("Priority"), rowNode))
Return rowNode
End Function
```

Building any single table cell is the job of the BuildTableCell function. The table cell is contained within the <a:tc> element, which contains a txBody node. Like the bulleted list we constructed for the hardware issues, this node is the parent of the paragraph of text whose contents will display in the table cell. Listing 10-18 contains the BuildTableCell function, which relies on our BuildTextPar function for building paragraphs.

Listing 10-18. *Adding a Cell to the Slide's Table*

```
Private Function BuildTableCell(ByVal text As String, _
                      ByVal tableRow As XmlNode) As XmlNode
'Create a new table cell node
Dim cellNode As XmlNode = _
        tableRow.OwnerDocument.CreateElement( _
        "a", "tc", drawingmlNamespace)
Dim txBodyNode As XmlNode = _
        tableRow.OwnerDocument.CreateElement( _
```

```
        "a", "txBody", drawingmlNamespace)
Dim bodyPrNode As XmlNode = _
        tableRow.OwnerDocument.CreateElement(_
        "a", "bodyPr", drawingmlNamespace)
Dim lstStyleNode As XmlNode = _
        tableRow.OwnerDocument.CreateElement( _
        "a", "lstStyle", drawingmlNamespace)
Dim tcPrNode As XmlNode = _
        tableRow.OwnerDocument.CreateElement( _
        "a", "tcPr", drawingmlNamespace)
txBodyNode.AppendChild(bodyPrNode)
txBodyNode.AppendChild(lstStyleNode)
txBodyNode.AppendChild(Me.BuildTextPar(text, tableRow))
cellNode.AppendChild(txBodyNode)
cellNode.AppendChild(tcPrNode)
Return cellNode
End Function
```

Figure 10-15 shows the Software Issues slide in the resulting PowerPoint presentation file.

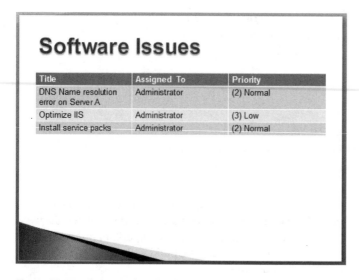

Figure 10-15. *The completed Software Issues slide*

Important Lessons

The DynamicPowerPoint web part incorporated several key techniques that are worth highlighting, as they could easily be reused in other projects.

Web-part construction including configuration settings. This solution detailed the steps necessary to build, deploy, and debug your own SharePoint web part. The web part contained other ASP.NET web controls, which it orchestrated to render the user interface. Many of the values that this web part needed for processing—such as the template filename, document library, and filename for the created file—were implemented as configuration settings as opposed to being hard-coded. This increases the flexibility of the web part, as these values could change from site to site.

The Open XML format schemas and code snippets. The Open XML file format opens the door for developers to create or modify Microsoft Office files without having to automate an application installed on the server. This solution explored the structure of an Open XML–formatted file, including an explanation of the package, its parts, and items. This chapter also included a link to the schemas that are useful for editing the parts in Visual Studio, as well as a link to code snippets for common tasks when working with these types of files.

Placing new content in an Open XML–formatted file. This solution involved a lot of manipulation of PresentationML to insert new content into the slides. The techniques of finding locations and constructing XML content will be useful regardless of the file type.

Extension Point

While coding this example, we thought of a variation to the solution that we didn't incorporate because it distracted from the overall objective of the solution. We call it out now as extension points since it may be applicable to a specific project you are working on.

Place content on the notes pages. Explore how PresentationML records the notes pages for slides. Start by generating a sample Open XML–formatted presentation with some slide content and notes. Rename the file so that you can explore the package and its parts. Use the relationship items to navigate to the notes page parts. Practice placing notes programmatically for a presentation slide.

Further Reading

The following links are to resources a reader interested in this chapter's material may find useful:

- Brian Jones: Open Xml Formats Blog

    http://blogs.msdn.com/brian_jones/

- Introduction to PresentationML

    http://blogs.msdn.com/brian_jones/archive/2006/04/11/573529.aspx

- OpenXMLDeveloper.org

    http://openxmldeveloper.org/

- Introducing the Office (2007) Open XML File Formats

  `http://msdn2.microsoft.com/en-us/library/aa338205.aspx`

- SPQuery Class

  `http://msdn2.microsoft.com/en-us/library/ms978519.aspx`

- Write Custom WebParts for SharePoint 2007

  `http://www.codeguru.com/csharp/.net/net_asp/webforms/article.php/c12293/`

- Writing Custom Webparts for SharePoint 2007

  `http://blah.winsmarts.com/2006/05/14/writing-custom-webparts-for-sharepoint-2007.aspx`

PART 5

■ ■ ■

Microsoft Outlook Solutions

This section will focus on solutions built around Microsoft Outlook. Chapters 11 and 12 will explore ways to combine Outlook and SharePoint to enhance the information worker's productivity. Chapter 11's solution illustrates how you can extend the Outlook application interface to provide a tool that interacts with a message and a SharePoint site. The solution in Chapter 12 extends the Outlook form for contacts to include data from a line-of-business application that has been registered with the Business Data Catalog.

■ ■ ■

Working with Email Messages and SharePoint

Too often organizations have important knowledge locked inside the email accounts of their information workers. Email messages contain information like project updates, status details, or even the latest version of an attachment. Although the contents of an important message could cause the organization to initiate a business process that requires a team to act based on that content, email is often just forwarded to team members, lost by some of them, and eventually filed away in some folder of a personal mail archive. It is not captured as an asset of the organization or of the business process. In this chapter we will detail how, as a developer, you can extend Microsoft Outlook to enable users to easily persist these messages to SharePoint repositories.

Real-World Examples

Any organization that receives emails from partners or customers struggles with this issue. It is one of the main drivers behind most CRM systems. Without any help, some organizations' workers spend more time filing, sorting, and searching through email than acting upon it. Even if they sort and file perfectly, users start creating personal mail archives due to storage quotas on the mail server. Over time, these archives become a huge burden for the organization as they are passed on from person to person as personnel change. Eventually the current worker in a specific role has a set of various email archives with different filing schemes and no idea of what the messages pertain to. So not only is there a concern about the loss or visibility of the data, but there is simply a need to provide context by including these messages in the same storage system as the rest of the business process. Request-for-information processes, helpdesk/support systems, and opportunity-generation systems are just a few examples of scenarios that suffer this loss of information in mailboxes.

Solution Overview

Windows SharePoint Services (WSS) sites often represent a unit of collaboration or an instance of a business process. For this solution, we will develop an Outlook add-in that extends the user interface when users are reading email messages. When activated, the add-in will provide a tool for persisting the message and its attachments to a SharePoint site. This tool will provide several enhancements over a simple Save As action from Outlook. It will present the user with a list of the site's document libraries, give the user options for creating a folder to contain the items, and (optionally) persist the message text with the attachments. These are the same options that a site administrator would have if that administrator were email-enabling a document library. Of course, an organization would not want to take on the burden of email-enabling every library. This would mean that a new email address would be created specifically for each library and all messages sent to the address would be stored. The add-in approach provides a more granular solution, allowing the user to decide which emails should be stored in the site. Of course, this solution could go much farther once you have a custom user interface alongside the email message. For example, you could allow the user to automatically create a new WSS site of a specific template and store the message. In this chapter we will focus on the work it takes to make a custom interface available to a user while she is reading a message, as well as the interaction of this interface with the email and the Share-Point site.

This application should be flexible enough to present its custom interface in any email the user may be reading. To meet these requirements, the solution will be an application-level add-in that is capable of presenting custom task panes for its user interface. As an add-in, this tool will always be available to the Outlook application; however, we will need to selectively provide a launching point to the user only when she is reading emails. To provide this launching point, the tool will add controls to the Microsoft Office ribbon interface. When reading an email, the user will be able to initiate a Save to SharePoint action that opens the custom task pane. Since a user could have more than one email open at a time, the solution will take great care to keep track of which task pane is for which email. It is important to understand that there is only ever one instance of the add-in running in Outlook even though there could be many task panes. Each task pane will provide an interactive interface for the user to persist the message to the SharePoint site.

The task-pane interface begins by asking the user for the URL of the team site she wishes to use for storage. Once entered, the application queries the site to provide the user with a list of that site's document libraries. The user selects the desired library, states a preference as to whether the message text should also be stored, and selects a folder-creation option. The folder options include storing the items in a folder whose name is based on the email sender's name or the email's subject. Simply selecting the root of the document library is also an option. With the preferences entered, the application creates the folder if necessary and uploads the message items to the site.

Solution Walkthrough

This section will detail the major elements of the solution and the decisions that we made in coding it. The walkthrough will show you how to create an Outlook add-in project in Visual Studio. We will detail the construction of the custom task pane and how to connect it selectively to the ribbon interface when the user is reading an email. The walkthrough also details how the solution manages the complexities of multiple Outlook windows, each of which could be an email message the user wants to save to a SharePoint site. We will explain the work behind the task pane—discovering the set of document libraries in the site, creating folders, and uploading files from the user's machine to the SharePoint site.

Creating the Outlook Add-in Project

The project types in VSTO make using Visual Studio to build an Outlook add-in very straightforward. Simply start Visual Studio and select to create a new project. Under the Visual Basic
language node, expand the Office node and select the 2007 Add-ins category. This will display
the Office 2007 VSTO project templates.

From the listing of Visual Studio installed templates, select Outlook Add-in. Name the
project and solution **SaveMsgAddin**. Your New Project dialog should look like Figure 11-1.

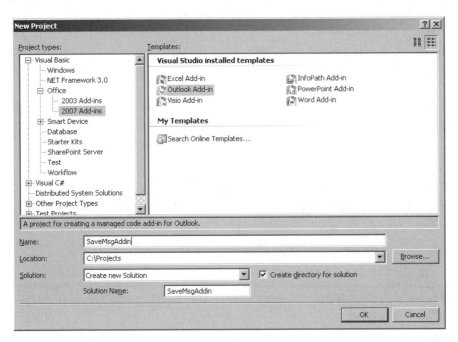

Figure 11-1. *Creating an Outlook add-in project*

Once you've created the new project, your solution will already have a few files by default.
These are visible in the Solution Explorer window of Visual Studio. Expanding an Outlook
node will reveal a code file named ThisAddin.vb. This file is the main entry point for add-ins.
It is where developers can write code for events at the add-in scope. These events include
common items like Startup and Shutdown. There are also Outlook application-level events
such as Quit, NewMail, and ItemSend. These are accessible by selecting the Application object
in the left-hand drop-down above your code window. The solution will also include a setup
project that you can use to deploy your add-in.

Building the Custom Task Pane

With the add-in project created, the first item we will focus on is the design of the task pane
that will provide the custom user interface. Add a Windows Form user control named
ucTaskPane to the project. This control will serve as the task pane. The remainder of this section will detail the controls that need to be placed on the task pane. Figure 11-2 shows the
result we are looking for.

Figure 11-2. *The task-pane interface for saving a message*

You can lay out these controls with the details in the following list or simply add this component from the code download available in the Source Code/Download section at http://apress.com. Here are the detailed controls from top to bottom on the task pane:

- The task pane control itself has a height of 383 and a width of 243.

- The Enter the URL instruction is just a label control.

- The text box is named txtURL. This control will capture the URL of the site to which the user wants to save the message.

- The GO button is named btnGO and its BackColor property is set to LightSteelBlue. When clicked, the task pane will query the site to discover information about its document libraries. This list of available libraries will be displayed in the drop-down.

- Notice the dotted line border around the controls in the midsection of the task pane. It shows that these controls are contained within a panel. This panel (named pnlDetail and set to AutoScroll) is used so that we can easily enable or disable this section of the task pane. The final action of the GO button's event handler is to enable the controls contained within the panel.

- The Library prompt is a label control.

- The selection control is a combo box named lstLibrary. Its DropDownStyle property is set to DropDownList so that the user will have to select one of the provided values rather than typing in a new one. The values of this selection will be populated dynamically when the task pane examines the site.

- The Save Original Email control is a check box named chkSaveEmail.

- The Attachment Option border is a group box connecting a set of radio buttons.

- The attachment preferences are radio-button controls named optRoot, optEmailSubject, and optEmailSender from top to bottom.

- The Save button is a button control named btnSave and its BackColor property is set to LightSteelBlue. When clicked, the event handler will create the folder in the library if necessary and upload the message items to the proper location.

- The Complete Message instruction is a label control named lblMessage whose Visible property is set to false. The task pane will use this control to display a confirmation when the save is complete. This would also be a useful place to display information about any errors that the task pane encountered during its processing.

This task pane may be displayed within multiple Outlook windows simultaneously if the user is interacting with more than one received email. Therefore, the add-in will take responsibility for creating instances of the task pane and correlating them with Outlook windows that the Outlook object model calls *inspectors*. The details of this are included in the next section of this chapter; right now we'll simply declare a variable for working with task panes and an array list for the active inspectors. The code in Listing 11-1 begins the ThisAddIn class.

Listing 11-1. *Beginning of the ThisAddIn Class*

```
Imports Outlook = Microsoft.Office.Interop.Outlook
Imports Microsoft.Office.Tools
Imports System.Collections

Public Class ThisAddIn
    Dim ctp As CustomTaskPane
    Private mInspectors As ArrayList = New ArrayList()
```

Customizing the Ribbon Interface

We need a way for the user to launch the task pane from within Outlook. To provide this starting point, we will focus our attention on the new and improved user interface of the Microsoft Office 2007 system—the ribbon. The ribbon interface occupies the top portion of most of the Office applications and provides a different experience than the layered menus and toolbars of previous Office releases. It provides a simpler experience for the user by improving the organization of commands and providing a more graphical representation of options. One of the primary goals of the ribbon interface is to surface functionality of the applications that users desired but simply didn't know was there because of how buried or obscure that menu item was previously.

Unlike Word, Excel, and PowerPoint, Microsoft Outlook 2007 has a set of ribbons that open in different types of inspectors. Each inspector type is specific to the type of Outlook item the user is interacting with and the action the user is performing. For example, a user who is working with an email message could see the Microsoft.Outlook.Mail.Read or Microsoft.Outlook.Mail.Compose ribbon, depending on whether the user is reading or writing the message. In fact, Outlook delays loading any ribbon customizations until they are needed for a specific inspector. Table 11-1 contains the list of Outlook RibbonIDs and their corresponding Outlook message class.

Table 11-1. *Outlook 2007's Ribbons*

Ribbon ID	Message Class
Microsoft.Outlook.Mail.Read	IPM.Note.*
Microsoft.Outlook.Mail.Compose	IPM.Note.*
Microsoft.Outlook.MeetingRequest.Read	IPM.Schedule.Meeting.Request or IPM.Schedule.Meeting.Canceled
Microsoft.Outlook.MeetingRequest.Send	IPM.Schedule.Meeting.Request
Microsoft.Outlook.Appointment	IPM.Appointment.*
Microsoft.Outlook.Contact	IPM.Contact.*
Microsoft.Outlook.Journal	IPM.Activity.*
Microsoft.Outlook.Task	IPM.Task.* and IPM.TaskRequest.*
Microsoft.Outlook.DistributionList	IPM.DistList.*
Microsoft.Outlook.Report	IPM.Report.*
Microsoft.Outlook.Resend	IPM.Resend.*
Microsoft.Outlook.Response.Read	IPM.Schedule.Meeting.Resp.*
Microsoft.Outlook.Response.Compose	IPM.Schedule.Meeting.Resp.*
Microsoft.Outlook.Response.CounterPropose	IPM.Schedule.Meeting.Resp.*
Microsoft.Outlook.RSS	IPM.Post.Rss
Microsoft.Outlook.Post.Read	IPM.Post.*
Microsoft.Outlook.Post.Compose	IPM.Post.*
Microsoft.Outlook.Sharing.Read	IPM.Sharing.*
Microsoft.Outlook.Sharing.Compose	IPM.Sharing.*

The biggest difference in the ribbon programming model is that customizations to the user interface are defined using XML, not compiled code. Through a custom XML file, a developer can manipulate the ribbon, controlling its tabs, groups, and controls. This manipulation includes adding new elements as well as hiding default ones. In addition to the XML declarations that alter the ribbon's user interface, a typical implementation will include a class that serves the XML to the application and includes event handlers for running code in response to user interaction. You might think that you are in for writing a ton of code to get your add-in, XML file, and class to align properly. Fortunately, VSTO does most of this plumbing automatically, allowing you to focus just on the customizations needed.

Figure 11-3 shows that the SaveMessage add-in has customized the Outlook ribbon interface specifically for when the user is reading email messages. This customization includes a new SharePoint group with a toggle button control displaying Save with a custom graphic. When this toggle button is pressed, the application will display the custom task pane we designed earlier.

Figure 11-3. *Customizing the Microsoft.Outlook.Mail.Read ribbon interface*

To implement this in your SaveMessage add-in project, first add a new item. From the Add New Item dialog, select the Ribbon support template and name the file **Ribbon1.vb**. When the add-item process is complete, Visual Studio will have added two files: the Ribbon1.vb code file, which includes the class that has plumbing and callback code, and the Ribbon1.xml file, which is the markup of the ribbon-interface changes. It is in this file that the additional tab, group, and toggle button are defined. Listing 11-2 details the XML needed to make the desired customizations.

Listing 11-2. *Ribbon User-Interface Markup*

```
<customUI xmlns="http://schemas.microsoft.com/office/2006/01/customui"~
    onLoad="OnLoad">
 <ribbon>
   <tabs>
       <tab idMso="TabReadMessage">
           <group id="SharePoint"
                   label="SharePoint">
               <toggleButton id="toggleButton1"
                   size="large"
                   label="Save"
                   screentip="Save email or attachments to a SharePoint~
                               library"
                   onAction="OnToggleButton1"
                   getImage="GetImage"
                   getPressed="GetPressed" />
           </group>
       </tab>
   </tabs>
 </ribbon>
</customUI>
```

The template for the new file provided almost the entire markup in Listing 11-2. To get the customizations we need for this project, we specified the internal ID of the Message tab. This is the idMso attribute that has the value of TabReadMessage. The Office internal control names are not always obvious. Fortunately, Microsoft provides a reference in the form of a set of Excel spreadsheets that document control names, types, etc. This reference is called the 2007 Office System Document: Lists of Control IDs (http://www.microsoft.com/downloads/details.aspx?familyid=4329d9e9-4d11-46a5-898d-23e4f331e9ae&displaylang=en). Figure 11-4 shows a portion of the OutlookMailReadItemRibbonControls.xls file; it highlights the fact that you can filter by the Control Type column.

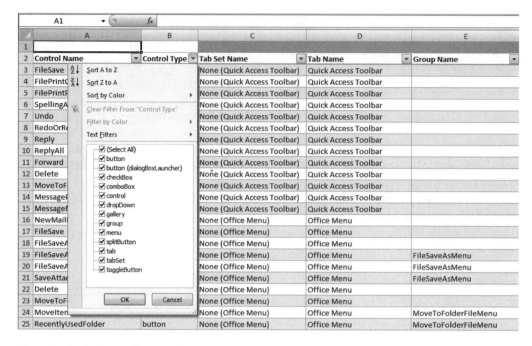

Figure 11-4. *Finding Office-application control IDs*

With the ribbon XML file complete, we will embed it into the assembly as a resource and adjust the code that serves it to Outlook. To include the file as a resource, add it through the Resources tab of the project's properties dialog. You can read more details about adding project resources here:

- How to: Add or Remove Resources

  http://msdn2.microsoft.com/en-us/library/3bka19x4.aspx

Now the GetCustomUI function of the Ribbon1 class in the Ribbon1.vb file needs to be adjusted to read from the assembly's resources. While making this edit, we will also add code to examine the identifier of the ribbon that is requesting the customizations. This will allow us to return the custom ribbon XML only when the user is reading an email. Listing 11-3 contains this code.

Listing 11-3. *Altered GetCustomUI Function*

```
Public Function GetCustomUI(ByVal ribbonID As String) As String~
     Implements Office.IRibbonExtensibility.GetCustomUI
Dim xmlMarkup As String = String.Empty
Select Case (ribbonID)
    Case "Microsoft.Outlook.Mail.Read"
            xmlMarkup = My.Resources.Ribbon1
End Select
Return xmlMarkup
End Function
```

The ribbon customization XML (Listing 11-2) file also included some literal strings for labels and a screen tip. Of particular importance is the onAction attribute of the toggle button element. This attribute designates the callback. Searching through the `Ribbon1.vb` code file, you will find an OnToggleButton1() subroutine that will be automatically wired up to our new toggle button. This code will invoke methods in the add-in class that will both hide and show the custom task pane in the active Outlook inspector. The sample code in this class needs to be modified to that of Listing 11-4. Since the solution is going to have to do some extra work to match task panes with inspectors, we will detail the ShowTaskPane and RemoveTaskPane methods in the next section of this chapter ("Managing the Task-Pane Instances"). The result of these methods will be to show the task pane when the toggle button is pressed and to hide the task pane when the toggle button is off.

Listing 11-4. *OnToggleButton1 Callback*

```
Public Sub OnToggleButton1(ByVal control As Office.IRibbonControl,~
    ByVal isPressed As Boolean)
If isPressed Then
    Globals.ThisAddIn.ShowTaskPane()
Else
    Globals.ThisAddIn.RemoveTaskPane()
End If
End Sub
```

There will be scenarios other than the user pressing the toggle button in which our add-in needs to alter that button's pressed state. An example is when the user shows the task pane and then simply closes the inspector window without hiding the task pane. In the ribbon XML, the getPressed attribute enables us to add a callback to dynamically control the pressed state of the toggle button. To control this properly, we will add two functions to the Ribbon1 class. The first is the GetPressed callback, in which we will call a method of the add-in to initialize the state of the button. (The add-in's GetPressed method has not been added yet and will be presented in the next section.) The second function that needs to be added to the Ribbon1 class is a ResetState method that the add-in can call to invalidate the toggle button's current state. Calling this method will cause the ribbon to ask for a re-evaluation of its pressed state. This means another call to GetPressed. Both of these functions are included in Listing 11-5.

Listing 11-5. *The GetPressed Callback*

```
Public Function GetPressed(ByVal control As Office.IRibbonControl) As Boolean
    Return Globals.ThisAddIn.GetPressed()
 End Function
Public Sub ResetState()
      Me.ribbon.InvalidateControl("toggleButton1")
End Sub
```

Additionally, a class at the top of the `Ribbon1.vb` file needs to be uncommented; it allows the application to hook into our ribbon customizations. This class is a partial class of the ThisAddIn class that informs the application that the add-in contains ribbon customizations. VSTO includes a TODO task to remind you to uncomment it.

Lastly, the XML in Listing 11-2 contained a getImage attribute for the toggle button. This attribute allows us to specify a callback in which our code can return a picture to be placed on the button. There is a bit of an issue that .NET managed code and the Office COM applications prefer to work with graphics differently. Specifically, the COM world of Office relies on IPictureDisp objects, whereas in managed code we are provided Image or Bitmap objects. Listing 11-6 is a class that you can add to the end of the Ribbon1.vb file to help with the translations. It relies on the AxHost class, which wraps ActiveX controls for the managed Windows Forms environment.

Listing 11-6. *Translating Images and Icons to IPictureDisp Objects*

```
Friend Class PictureDispMaker
    Inherits System.Windows.Forms.AxHost
Sub New()
    MyBase.New(Nothing)
 End Sub


 Public Shared Function ConvertImage(ByVal image As~
     System.Drawing.Image) As stdole.IPictureDisp
    Return AxHost.GetIPictureDispFromPicture(image)
End Function

Public Shared Function ConvertIcon(ByVal icon As~
     System.Drawing.Icon) As stdole.IPictureDisp
   Return ConvertImage(icon.ToBitmap())
End Function
End Class
```

The GetImage callback method then uses the PictureDispMaker class to convert the image and return it to the application. For this project we selected an icon graphic, share.ico, from the VS 2005 Image Library and embedded it into the project as a resource. Listing 11-7 details the GetImage callback's retrieval of the resource image and its conversion before returning the picture to the Office application. You can read more about adding project resources at the URL mentioned earlier: http://msdn2.microsoft.com/en-us/library/3bka19x4.aspx.

Listing 11-7. *GetImage Callback*

```
Public Function GetImage(ByVal control As Office.IRibbonControl) As~
     stdole.IPictureDisp
   Dim pic As stdole.IPictureDisp = Nothing
   Select Case control.Id
       Case "toggleButton1"
           pic = PictureDispMaker.ConvertIcon(My.Resources.share)
   End Select
   Return pic
End Function
```

Managing the Task-Pane Instances

Since the SaveMessage add-in's task pane is displayed within the Outlook window for reading email messages, there could be several instances of the task pane displayed at the same time. The user would simply have to open two email messages and click our SharePoint Save button in the ribbon in each message window without closing the window. So we need to implement a strategy for keeping track of which task-pane instance belongs to which inspector window. Earlier we defined an ArrayList named mInspectors in the ThisAddIn class. When a user clicks the toggle button in the ribbon, the responding ShowTaskPane method of the add-in will not only create a task pane instance, but also add the current inspector to the mInspectors collection. Since both of these are added at the same time, the task pane and its inspector will always be at the same index within their respective collections. Listing 11-8 details the ShowTaskPane method.

Listing 11-8. *The ShowTaskPane Method*

```
Public Sub ShowTaskPane()
  Dim currInspector As Outlook.Inspector = Me.Application.ActiveInspector
  ctp = Me.CustomTaskPanes.Add(New ucTaskPane(), "Save  to SharePoint",~
currInspector)
  ctp.DockPosition =~
Microsoft.Office.Core.MsoCTPDockPosition.msoCTPDockPositionRight
  ctp.Width = 250
  ctp.Visible = True
  mInspectors.Add(currInspector)
  AddHandler currInspector.Close, AddressOf Window_Close
End Sub
```

Notice that the last line of Listing 11-8 adds an event handler for the Close event of the inspector. We want to intercept two different actions to clean up the task pane and inspector collections properly. The user could click our toggle button again, causing the Remove-TaskPane method to be called. The user could also just close the Outlook window. Regardless of the action, the code in Listing 11-9 gets a reference to the current, active inspector and finds where this inspector is in the mInspectors collection. Once it's found, we can remove the inspector and the task pane (which is at the same position).

Listing 11-9. *Cleaning Up Task Panes*

```
Public Sub RemoveTaskPane()
    Dim currInspector As Outlook.Inspector = Me.Application.ActiveInspector
    CleanUp(currInspector)
End Sub

Private Sub Window_Close()
    Dim currInspector As Outlook.Inspector = Me.Application.ActiveInspector
    CleanUp(currInspector)
End Sub
```

```
Private Sub CleanUp(ByVal activeInspector As Outlook.Inspector)
    Dim i As Integer = 0
    For i = 0 To mInspectors.Count - 1
        Dim item As Outlook.Inspector = CType(mInspectors(i), Outlook.Inspector)
        If (item Is activeInspector) Then
            Me.ribbon.ResetState()
            Me.CustomTaskPanes.RemoveAt(i)
            mInspectors.RemoveAt(i)
        End If
    Next
End Sub
```

This technique makes sure that the task-pane instances are cleaned up when the user hides our task pane or closes the window where one was displayed. Notice the use of the ResetState method we added to the ribbon class earlier. This call makes sure that the ribbon's toggle button is depressed even if the user closes the window without closing our custom task pane. To complete the pressed-state management for this solution, we need to add the Get-Pressed function to the add-in. This function looks through the collected inspectors to see if the current inspector is in the collection. If the inspector is found, the pressed state of the toggle button is set to match the visibility of our corresponding task-pane instance. If a match is not found, the function returns false, setting the toggle button to not be pressed. Listing 11-10 shows this method.

Listing 11-10. *The Add-in's GetPressed Method*

```
Public Function GetPressed() As Boolean
        Dim currInspector As Outlook.Inspector = Me.Application.ActiveInspector
        Dim i As Integer = 0
        For i = 0 To mInspectors.Count - 1
            Dim item As Outlook.Inspector = CType(mInspectors(i), Outlook.Inspector)
            If (item Is currInspector) Then
                Return Me.CustomTaskPanes(i).Visible
            End If
        Next
        Return False
    End Function
```

But how do you know this code works? For testing purposes only, you can add an event handler to trap when the user exits Outlook. The code in Listing 11-11 needs to be placed in the ThisAddIn class. It will be triggered when the user selects Exit from the File menu of Outlook.

Listing 11-11. *Testing to See If the Task Panes Have Been Removed*

```
Private Sub Application_Quit() Handles Application.Quit
    MessageBox.Show(Me.CustomTaskPanes.Count)
End Sub
```

Go ahead and run your project, which will launch Outlook with your add-in loaded. Open a few emails, hide and show the task pane in different windows, and close Outlook through the File/Exit command. The message box will return a zero, confirming that we are cleaning up our object instances.

Retrieving the Document Libraries

The task pane is designed to first ask the user for the URL of the site to which he wants to save the message and/or the attachments. An example of a valid URL is `http://portal.sample.com/SiteDirectory/team1`. When the user clicks the Go button, the task pane works to discover information about the lists and libraries contained in the site. To accomplish this task, the Outlook add-in relies on the GetListCollection method of SharePoint's `lists.asmx` web service. The GetListCollection method returns information about all the lists and libraries in the site. We will make this call using the current user's Windows identity, which is more appropriate within an organization/intranet scenario. To call this method, you will need to add a web reference in the SaveMsgAddin project. Take the following steps to create the web reference:

1. In Visual Studio's Solution Explorer window, right-click the References node of the SaveMsgAddin project and select Add Web Reference.

2. Type in the URL of the meeting workspace with a `_vti_bin/lists.asmx` ending. SharePoint's web services are called by adding the _vti_bin folder on to the end of any site URL. You do not need to worry about which site you select in the development of this solution as long as it is a valid one for the generation of the proxy. The actual URL used during execution will depend on the site the user is trying to save the message to. SharePoint's use of the _vti_bin folder enables the web service call to discover the call's context and return answers specifically to the site referred to by the rest of the URL. So continuing with our example, the URL would be `http://portal.sample.com/SiteDirectory/team1/_vti_bin/lists.asmx`.

3. Click Go. The window below the URL should display a listing of all of the methods in the Lists web service.

4. In the Web reference name text box, change the text to **WSLists**.

5. Click Add Reference.

With the web reference in place, the Go button's click event handler can be coded. Listing 11-12 displays this code.

Listing 11-12. *Retrieving the Site's Lists and Libraries*

```
Private Sub btnGo_Click(ByVal sender As System.Object,~
    ByVal e As System.EventArgs) Handles btnGo.Click
  Me.UseWaitCursor = True
  Dim listService As WSLists.Lists = New WSLists.Lists
  listService.Credentials = System.Net.CredentialCache.DefaultCredentials
  listService.Url = Me.txtURL.Text + "/_vti_bin/lists.asmx"
  AddHandler listService.GetListCollectionCompleted,~
```

```
            AddressOf GetListCollectionCompleted
        listService.GetListCollectionAsync()
    End Sub
```

When the user clicks the Go button, we want to make sure that all the hard work of examining the site does not interfere with the Outlook application's user interface. Therefore, this work will be set up to run on a different thread. To support this background processing, the Go button's event hander first changes the user's cursor to the WaitCursor (typically an hourglass). The web service proxy is then configured to make the call under the user's security context and to access the service through the site URL entered by the user. When the GetListCollection method is called, we call its Async implementation so that the current thread will not wait for a response. Instead, the proxy class will call the GetListCollectionCompleted method of this task pane when it receives its response or an error/timeout occurs. This is controlled by the AddHandler line just before the call.

Once the web service has returned a response to the SaveMessage add-in, our code will execute the GetListCollectionCompleted subroutine. The response from the web service call is a string of XML that includes references to many different namespaces. Therefore this method loads that XML into an XmlDocument object and sets up an XmlNamespaceNavigator so that it can easily search for the information it is looking for. The add-in needs to record any document libraries it finds in the site. The task pane can obtain this information by looking for lists that have a ServerTemplate attribute with a value of 101. This value is a constant representing a document library. The task pane records the title and URL of each library it finds. These attributes will be stored in a LibraryItem class (Listing 11-13), which we added to the end of the task pane code-behind file.

Listing 11-13. *The LibraryItem Class for Storing Discovered Libraries*

```
Public Class LibraryItem
    Private m_name As String
    Private m_url As String
    Public Property Name() As String
        Get
            Return m_name
        End Get
        Set(ByVal value As String)
            m_name = value
        End Set
    End Property

    Public Property Url() As String
        Get
            Return m_url
        End Get
        Set(ByVal value As String)
            m_url = value
        End Set
    End Property
End Class
```

All of the SharePoint list-based information will reside in the XML namespace prefixed by sp. Listing 11-14 shows the XPath query technique for finding the collection of document libraries in the site.

Listing 11-14. *Finding a Site's Document Libraries*

```
Public Sub GetListCollectionCompleted(ByVal sender As Object, ByVal e As~
    WSLists.GetListCollectionCompletedEventArgs)
  Dim ndLists As XmlNode
  ndLists = e.Result
  Dim xmlDoc As XmlDocument = New XmlDocument()
  xmlDoc.LoadXml(ndLists.OuterXml)
  Dim namespaceMgr As XmlNamespaceManager = _
    New XmlNamespaceManager(xmlDoc.NameTable)
  namespaceMgr.AddNamespace(SharePointNamespacePrefix, _
    SharePointNamespaceUri)
  'are there any document libraries
  Dim libNode As XmlNodeList =~
    xmlDoc.SelectNodes("//sp:List[@ServerTemplate='101']", namespaceMgr)
  If (libNode IsNot Nothing AndAlso libNode.Count > 0) Then
    'store the name and url of each doc library
    Dim xmlNode As XmlNode
    For Each xmlNode In libNode
        Dim item As LibraryItem = New LibraryItem
          item.Name = xmlNode.Attributes("Title").InnerText
          item.Url = xmlNode.Attributes("WebFullUrl").InnerText
          Me.siteDocLibraries.Add(item)
    Next
  End If
  Me.UseWaitCursor = False
  'go back to the main thread to continue
  Dim uiContinueDelegate As New UIContinue(AddressOf Me.ListGatherComplete)
  Me.Invoke(uiContinueDelegate)
End Sub
```

At the end of this method, the WaitCursor is turned off and the task pane invokes a delegate referring to the ListGatherComplete method. By using the Me.Invoke() technique, we are returning control to the original thread, leaving the one that performed the background processing. Once in the ListGatherComplete method, the task pane enables the controls in the panel and binds the collection of LibraryItem objects to the combo box. This code is displayed in Listing 11-15.

Listing 11-15. *The ListGatherComplete Method*

```
Public Sub ListGatherComplete()
   Me.lstLibrary.DisplayMember = "Name"
   Me.lstLibrary.DataSource = Me.siteDocLibraries
   Me.pnlDetails.Enabled = True
End Sub
```

Saving the Email Message

Once the user has selected the document library to which she wants to save them email message, she can specify options for saving the message text as well as folder options. The folder options are the radio buttons that allow the user to select if the file should be saved in the root of the library or in an automatically created folder named according to the email's sender or subject. When the Save button is clicked, the event handler in Listing 11-16 retrieves the selected LibraryItem object from the combo box and gets a reference to the current mail item. This provides enough information to pass to a function that will create the folder.

Listing 11-16. *Retrieving User Save Preferences*

```
Private Sub btnSave_Click(ByVal sender As System.Object,~
    ByVal e As System.EventArgs) Handles btnSave.Click
Me.UseWaitCursor = True
Dim item As LibraryItem = CType(Me.lstLibrary.SelectedValue, LibraryItem)
Dim folderUrl As String = String.Empty
Dim currInspector As Outlook.Inspector =
Globals.ThisAddIn.Application.ActiveInspector
Dim message As Outlook.MailItem = CType(currInspector.CurrentItem, Outlook.MailItem)

If (Me.optEmailSender.Checked) Then
    folderUrl = CreateFolder(message.SenderName, item)
ElseIf (Me.optEmailSubject.Checked) Then
    folderUrl = CreateFolder(message.Subject, item)
Else
    'root
    folderUrl = Me.txtURL.Text + item.Url.Substring(0, item.Url.IndexOfAny("/", 1))
End If
```

Notice that the different calls to the CreateFolder function result in a URL being returned. This URL is the complete, fully qualified URL to the place where the attachments are to be stored. In the case of the root of the document library, we parse out the library portion from the default-view URL we obtained earlier.

■**Note** You cannot rely on the name of the library to build its URL; the user may have changed the display name, making it different from the URL name. It is better to parse a returned URL from an examination of the site.

The same Lists web service we used to retrieve the set of libraries in the site can be used to create the folder. This web service has a method named UpdateListItems, which takes an XML string representing update actions to take on the list. In Listing 11-17, the strBatch string variable contains XML to direct the creation of a new folder. For more information on how to update list items visit the following web site:

- How to: Update List Items

    http://msdn2.microsoft.com/en-us/library/ms440289.aspx

Listing 11-17. *Creating the Folder in the Library*

```
Private Function CreateFolder(ByVal folderName As String,~
    ByVal item As LibraryItem) As String
Dim listService As WSLists.Lists = New WSLists.Lists
listService.Credentials = System.Net.CredentialCache.DefaultCredentials
listService.Url = Me.txtURL.Text + "/_vti_bin/lists.asmx"
Dim strBatch As String = "<Method ID='1' Cmd='New'> " + _
        "<Field Name='ID'>New</Field>" + _
        "<Field Name='FSObjType'>1</Field>" + _
        "<Field Name='BaseName'>{0}</Field>" + _
      "</Method>"
Dim xmlDoc As XmlDocument = New System.Xml.XmlDocument()
Dim elBatch As System.Xml.XmlElement = xmlDoc.CreateElement("Batch")
elBatch.SetAttribute("OnError", "Continue")
elBatch.SetAttribute("ListVersion", "0")
elBatch.InnerXml = String.Format(strBatch, folderName)
Dim ndReturn As XmlNode = listService.UpdateListItems(item.Name, elBatch)
```

The response that will be returned from this call is an XmlNode, which is stored in the ndReturn variable in Listing 11-17. It will contain two key pieces of information. The first is an ErrorCode element that details whether the folder was created successfully. We will use this value to identify whether a new folder was actually created or whether the folder we asked for was already there. The string value of 0x8107090d represents the case where a folder with the requested name already existed. The other key piece of information is an attribute of the row element. The ows_EncodedAbsUrl attribute of the response will contain the URL address of the newly created folder that we can use to save the attachments. Listing 11-18 contains the remainder of the CreateFolder function (started in Listing 11-17).

Listing 11-18. *Examining the Response to Creating a Folder*

```
Dim errorCode As String = String.Empty
errorCode = ndReturn.FirstChild.Item("ErrorCode").InnerText
Dim folderUrl As String = String.Empty
If (errorCode = "0x00000000") Then
    'the folder was created successfully
    Dim returnNode As XmlNode = ndReturn.FirstChild.Item("z:row")
    If (returnNode IsNot Nothing) Then
        folderUrl = returnNode.Attributes("ows_EncodedAbsUrl").InnerText
    End If
ElseIf (errorCode = "0x8107090d") Then
    'The folder already existed
    folderUrl = Me.txtURL.Text + item.Url.Substring(0, item.Url.~
```

```
        IndexOfAny("/", 1)) + "/" + folderName
End If
Return folderUrl
End Function
```

The add-in is now ready to save the message and/or attachment files to the specified document library in the SharePoint site. Our add-in will first save the files into the local temp directory and then upload them. The use of the local temp directory is exactly the same technique that Outlook uses when the user double-clicks to open an attachment. Even with the attachments stored locally, the interesting problem is how to upload them. The files are stored on the file system of a client machine, so there is no access to the SharePoint object model bits running on the SharePoint server. Looking through the documentation of web services will also leave you empty-handed because there is no web service for uploading files. To overcome this hurdle we'll rely on an XML-formatted HTTP post to a dll library. This type of invocation is a remote procedure call (RPC) of which there are two types: FrontPage and Windows SharePoint Services. The Windows SharePoint Services RPC calls support methods like exporting, creating, or deleting lists. FrontPage Server Extensions RPC methods include commands such as checking in or out a document, retrieving or saving a document, and applying themes. The "Further Reading" section of this chapter includes URLs that provide a complete list of each type.

Instead of having to develop code to construct the FrontPage RPC calls from scratch, we leveraged a library from a reference application (SharePad) that was once provided on http://www.gotdotnet.com/. The GotDotNet site was once used by the community of Microsoft developers to post utilities, tools, and guidance. At the time of this writing, GotDotNet is being retired. Many of the applications have not found new homes, but similar tools are starting to show up on the newer CodePlex site, http://www.codeplex.com. Since it may be difficult to find where SharePad lands, our code download includes an upgraded version (compiled to the .NET 2.0 Framework) of its FPRPC assembly that encapsulated the logic for FrontPage RPC calls. We did add one line of code to this assembly to use it in the Outlook add-in solution. The line of code is in the StartWebRequest function of the FrontPageRPC class, as it is necessary to pass the current user's security credentials when performing the RPC request. This line of code (see Listing 11-19) is in the C# language since that was the language used in SharePad.

Listing 11-19. *Modified StartWebRequest of FrontPageRPC Class*

```csharp
private HttpWebRequest StartWebRequest(string url,~
        System.Collections.Specialized.NameValueCollection methodData)
{
   HttpWebRequest req = GetHttpWebRequest(url);
   //Added this line here
   req.Credentials = CredentialCache.DefaultCredentials;
   System.IO.Stream reqStream = req.GetRequestStream();
   System.IO.StreamWriter sw = new System.IO.StreamWriter(reqStream);
   AddCollectionData(sw, methodData);
   sw.Flush();
   return req;
}
```

Add this project to your Outlook add-in solution by right-clicking on the SaveMsgAddIn solution node in Visual Studio's Solution Explorer and choosing Add Existing Project. Browse to where you extracted the code download and select the FPRPC.csproj file. With the FPRPC project as part of your Outlook solution, add a reference to it in the SaveMsgAddin project. Use the Projects tab in the Add Reference dialog as shown in Figure 11-5.

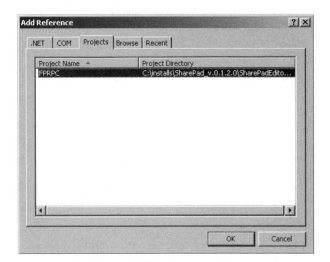

Figure 11-5. *Adding a reference to FPRPC*

With the ability to utilize FrontPage RPCs, the task pane saves the attachments to the local temp directory and uploads them to the site. The upload is accomplished through the Put-Document RPC method. Working with the FPRPC assembly, the Outlook add-in needs to pass in only the desired URL for the file and a FileStream object that has the file open for reading. Listing 11-20 contains this code.

Listing 11-20. *Saving the Attachment Files*

```
Dim path As String = System.Environment.~
    GetEnvironmentVariable("TEMP", EnvironmentVariableTarget.User)
Dim rpc As FrontPageRPC = New FrontPageRPC()
Dim attachmentItem As Outlook.Attachment
For Each attachmentItem In message.Attachments
    attachmentItem.SaveAsFile(path + "\" + attachmentItem.FileName)
    Dim fs As FileStream = File.OpenRead(path + "\" + attachmentItem.FileName)
    rpc.PutDocument(folderUrl + "/" + attachmentItem.FileName, fs)
    fs.Close()
Next
```

The last step is the optional saving of the message. For this example, we save the message as an ordinary text file. This file is saved to the same temporary directory and uploaded using the same technique as for the attachments. Once this action is complete, a task-pane label is set to inform the user that the save was successful. Listing 11-21 concludes the task pane's work.

Listing 11-21. *Saving the Email Message*

```
'save and upload email
If (Me.chkSaveEmail.Checked) Then
    Dim messageFileName As String = message.Subject + ".txt"
    message.SaveAs(path + "\" + messageFileName, Outlook.OlSaveAsType.olTXT)
    Dim fs As FileStream = File.OpenRead(path + "\" + messageFileName)
    rpc.PutDocument(folderUrl + "/" + messageFileName, fs)
    fs.Close()
End If
Me.UseWaitCursor = False
Me.PublishEmailComplete()
End Sub

Public Sub PublishEmailComplete()
    'set complete message
    lblMessage.Text = "The email has been saved successfully."
    lblMessage.Visible = True
    Me.pnlDetails.Enabled = False
End Sub
```

Just running your project will launch Outlook with the completed add-in functionality. Figure 11-6 shows a successful run of this application, storing two attachment documents and the email message to a document library folder named after the message's subject.

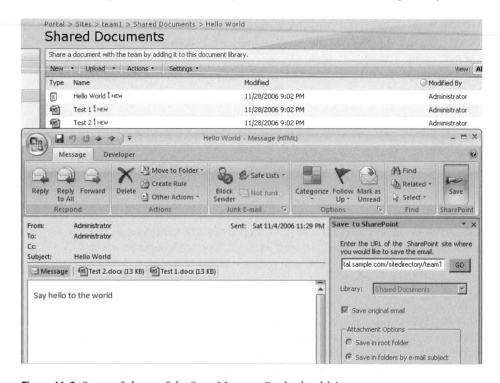

Figure 11-6. *Successful run of the Save Message Outlook add-in*

Important Lessons

The Save Message Outlook add-in incorporated several key techniques that are worth high-lighting, as they could easily be reused in other projects.

Managing task-pane instances: The solution detailed how to manage possible multiple instances of the custom task pane in different Outlook windows. New task panes were created when the user clicked the custom toggle button in the ribbon interface. The solution trapped both the user depressing the toggle button and just a closing of the window to clean up the appropriate task-pane instances.

Discovering a site's lists and libraries: This application interacted with SharePoint to query the site to discover what lists and libraries it contained. This was accomplished through SharePoint's Lists.asmx web service. The GetListCollection method of this web service returned XML that detailed the lists and libraries the site contained. With this XML, the add-in used an XPath query to find all lists of a certain type, filtering based on the ServerTemplate attribute.

Creating a folder in a library: The Save Message add-in also interacted with the Share-Point library to create a folder with either the message's subject or the sender's name. This was accomplished through SharePoint's Lists.asmx web service. The UpdateListItems method received an XML string of commands to perform against the list and returned success or failure notification.

FrontPage RPCs: Uploading documents to a SharePoint library from an external application can be accomplished by creating a FrontPage RPC request. These requests are HTTP posts of XML and binary content to dll files on the SharePoint server. This solution leverages a library in a reference application called SharePad to generate the FrontPage RPC request.

Extension Points

While coding this example, we thought of several variations to the solution that we didn't include because they distracted from the solution's overall objective. We call them out now as extension points since they may be applicable to a specific project you are working on.

Include the option of site provisioning: The solution detailed how to create a folder and upload the files to an existing site, but did not include the option to create a new site. If we used the Create Service FrontPage RPC method and the SiteProvision WSS RPC method, the add-in could include an option to first create a new site.

Add protection against special characters: In our example, we didn't protect ourselves against certain characters that would cause problems. For example, if the message subject included a slash (/) character, this would throw off the folder-creation process. Be on the lookout for troublesome characters such as these: #, %, &, *, {, }, \, :, <, >, ?, /, and +.

Place hyperlinks to the attachments in the mail message: One interesting twist would be to save the Outlook message as HTML and then to modify the HTML to include hyperlinks to the attachments. Since the solution was focused on how to work within Outlook and interact with SharePoint, we didn't see this as a need.

Further Reading

The following links are to resources a reader interested in this chapter's material will find useful:

- SaveAs Method

  http://msdn2.microsoft.com/en-us/library/aa210279(office.11).aspx

- Mike Fitzmaurice's Blog: FrontPage RPCs are Here to Stay, Too

  http://blogs.msdn.com/mikefitz/archive/2005/03/14/395112.aspx

- Windows SharePoint Services RPC Protocol

  http://msdn2.microsoft.com/en-us/library/ms448359.aspx

- FrontPage Server Extensions RPC Protocol

  http://msdn2.microsoft.com/en-us/library/ms443099.aspx

- 2007 Office System Document: Lists of Control IDs

  http://www.microsoft.com/downloads/details.aspx?familyid=
  4329d9e9-4d11-46a5-898d-23e4f331e9ae&displaylang=en

- Customizing the Ribbon in Outlook 2007

  http://msdn2.microsoft.com/en-us/library/ms788199.aspx

CHAPTER 12

■■■

Surfacing Data from Line-of-Business Applications

It is rare to find an organization that has a seamlessly integrated data tier that is uniformly used by the organization's business applications. More common is a set of siloed tools that duplicate data with no obvious authoritative source. Information workers in this type of environment often jump in and out of tools, copying and pasting data from one screen to the next to accomplish their tasks. With SharePoint, the organization is introducing enterprise portals and collaboration workspaces into this environment— and without careful planning, they are increasing the risk of redundant data. SharePoint lists and metadata of documents often need to include values whose source is one of these external applications. In this chapter, we will detail how as a developer you can register an external application so that is data is referenceable in SharePoint using the Business Data Catalog.

But you were expecting this to be an Outlook chapter, right? Integrating SharePoint with the external application is only the beginning. Shouldn't this effort be reusable by other applications? What if we could expose the capability of the Business Data Catalog? Microsoft Outlook is capable of maintaining lots of different types of objects: messages, contacts, tasks, notes, etc. These objects may also have properties whose values are found in the same application you will integrate into SharePoint. Therefore, this chapter will also show you how to build a custom web service that exposes your Business Data Catalog work and present a technique to extend an Outlook form with .NET code to consume it.

Real-World Examples

Almost every organization has data repositories whose values need to be a part of other applications. Obvious examples include a database of customers or products. We have also seen repositories that describe units of the organization, such as divisions, departments, and teams, as popular choices for this type of integration. Having this data referenceable is useful in task-oriented processes, project-management plans, and lists of issues.

We also routinely see the extension of Outlook forms in solutions. Often organizations want to use Outlook as a tool to construct messages that require more metadata than the average email. This data usually is required to enforce routing logic, security, or retention policies. Customer relationship management systems are also built on the fundamental principal of extending the basic message, contact, meeting, or task with more data about its context.

Solution Overview

Data in a line-of-business system is often siloed to its particular application. However, within an organization this data often needs to have greater reach to users who may never even open the application. This is especially true for data elements that are referenced often. Consider documents that require a metadata column specifying the customer or account they were constructed for. Ideally, authors of the document do not have to open the siloed line-of-business (LOB) system to discover these values. Rather, they should be surfaced into the collaboration environment the user is working in.

The first goal of this solution is to detail the framework provided by Microsoft Office SharePoint Server's Business Data Catalog (BDC) for integrating line-of-business applications. The BDC is new to SharePoint and reduces the amount of integration code developers have to write to surface data from external applications. With the previous version of SharePoint, there evolved some common scenarios in which organizations tried to hook in external data. These scenarios focused on surfacing this data through web parts, columns of lists or libraries, and integration with search results. In the past, a developer would write their own code for each application they needed to integrate and that code was specific to one of the scenarios. The premise of the BDC is that the framework can generalize this problem so that developers can spend more time applying the technologies to business processes and less time writing the same code over and over again. Therefore, the BDC abstracts the developer from having to write code and instead focuses on a metadata model where the developer uses an XML application definition to describe the external system. The Business Data Catalog can then use this definition to expose the LOB system's data to web parts or columns of lists or libraries, as well as register the application as a content source for search indexing. This solution will detail the major components of the application definition, showing how it contains connection information, details of the various objects within the system, and relationships between them. Once the application definition is uploaded to the Business Data Catalog, we will demonstrate some of the various ways SharePoint can surface data from the line-of-business system.

Though the BDC provides a framework to integrate a line-of-business application with SharePoint, it doesn't offer any way of exposing this capability to other systems. In other words, if I had another application that wasn't SharePoint, we would have to have a different integration solution. Not leveraging the work we put into the BDC would create multiple paths to the LOB system and could result in a maintenance nightmare since changes would not be confined to a single point. Therefore, this solution includes a custom SharePoint web service that will expose the Business Data Catalog so that other applications can invoke its capability.

To wrap up the solution, we needed a consumer of the web service. Since the context for our solution is customers and the sales people that support them, we thought it natural that this data would also be valuable in Microsoft Outlook. Users in an organization would often have their own personal contacts for different customers. We decided to leverage the integration of the line-of-business system with the Business Data Catalog to allow users to retrieve business contact information for their personal customer contacts. To achieve this, we will extend the Outlook contact form with a new form region. The solution addresses how we can connect managed code to the form, allowing us to call the customer web service and process its results.

Solution Walkthrough

The following section will detail the major elements of the solution and the decisions that were made in coding it. The walkthrough will show you the details of the database we will use as a sample line-of-business application. We will then take you through the details of an XML file that describes this database to the Business Data Catalog. When uploaded to the BDC, this application definition will support surfacing the external data through web parts, search, and list columns. The walkthrough will show you how to implement some of these integration scenarios. Of course, surfacing this data in SharePoint is only half the goal. We also want to expose the features of the BDC so that other applications can take advantage of its integration with the line-of-business system. To expose the BDC, the solution contains a custom web service. For an example consumer of this service, the walkthrough details how to extend the Outlook contact form with a form region. We will show you how this technique allows you to use managed code behind the form region to call the web service, which in turn invokes the BDC to return data out of the line-of-business system.

The Sample LOB Database

For our sample LOB application, we will use a SQL Server 2005 database named Customer-Info. This database stores the list of the organization's customers and the different sales people that are assigned to them. The cardinality of the relationship between customers and sales people is many to many. That means that a single customer could have several sales people assigned and a single sales person is responsible for many different customers. Figure 12-1 is a diagram of the database showing the Customer and SalesPeople tables as well as the table that maintains the relationship.

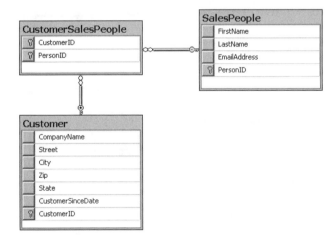

Figure 12-1. *Diagram of the CustomerInfo database*

To set up the database in your environment, copy the mdf and ldf files from the Cus-tomerInfo database to your SQL Server. If you did a default install, SQL Server 2005 is using the following path to store these database files: C:\Program Files\Microsoft SQL Server\ MSSQL.1\MSSQL\Data. Once they are in place, right-click on the Databases node of the Management Studio's Object Explorer and select Attach. In the dialog, click Add and locate the CustomerInfo.mdf file. The default options are fine. Your dialog should look like Figure 12-2. Click OK; the Object Explorer will refresh to include the ProductsTest database. (If you need more help attaching databases in SQL Server 2005, use the steps on MSDN: http://msdn2. microsoft.com/en-us/library/ms190209.aspx.)

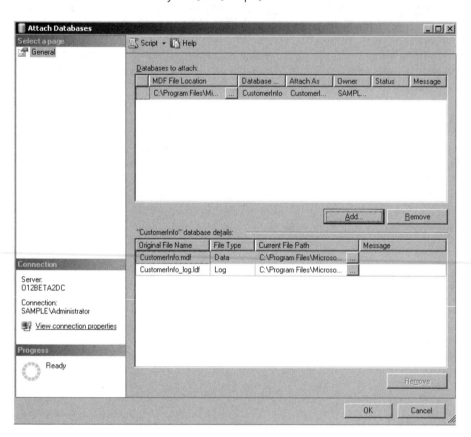

Figure 12-2. *Attaching the ProductsTest database*

The database also includes several stored procedures. The GetCustomers and GetSales-People stored procedures are used for retrieving a specific row of their respective tables or doing a wildcard search. For this reason, each of the procedures can accept a specific ID or a string. For customers the wildcard comparison is against the CompanyName column, whereas for sales people it is against their email address. In each stored procedure, an ID of zero represents an unspecified value. Listing 12-1 shows how these parameters are used in the GetCustomers procedure.

Listing 12-1. *The GetCustomers Stored Procedure*

```
CREATE PROCEDURE [dbo].[GetCustomers]
     @CustomerID int = 0,
     @CompanyName varchar(50) = null
AS
BEGIN
   SET NOCOUNT ON;
   SELECT * FROM Customer
   WHERE (@CustomerID = 0 OR CustomerID = @CustomerID)
   AND (CompanyName LIKE @CompanyName)
END
```

The other stored procedures are GetCustomerPeople and GetCustomerIDs. The Get-CustomerPeople stored procedure returns the set of sales people for a specific customer. GetCustomerIDs simply returns the list of IDs in the Customer table.

While you are in SQL Server's Management Studio, you will want to confirm that the server's security settings are going to support our integration strategy. There are several options for controlling security when tying an application to the Business Data Catalog, which we will elaborate on in the next section. In this solution, we will rely on a model in which the BDC uses a specific account regardless of which user is requesting data. This technique is useful when the data being surfaced does not need to be altered for different security contexts. The account we will use is the domain account for the BDC shared service provider. Confirm that the domain account you use for the shared service provider's application pool has rights to the database. At a minimum, this account will need to execute the database's stored procedures. You can find this identity in Central Administration in SharePoint or in IIS Manager. As shown in Figure 12-3, Central Administration contains this account in the Service Accounts page on the Operations tab.

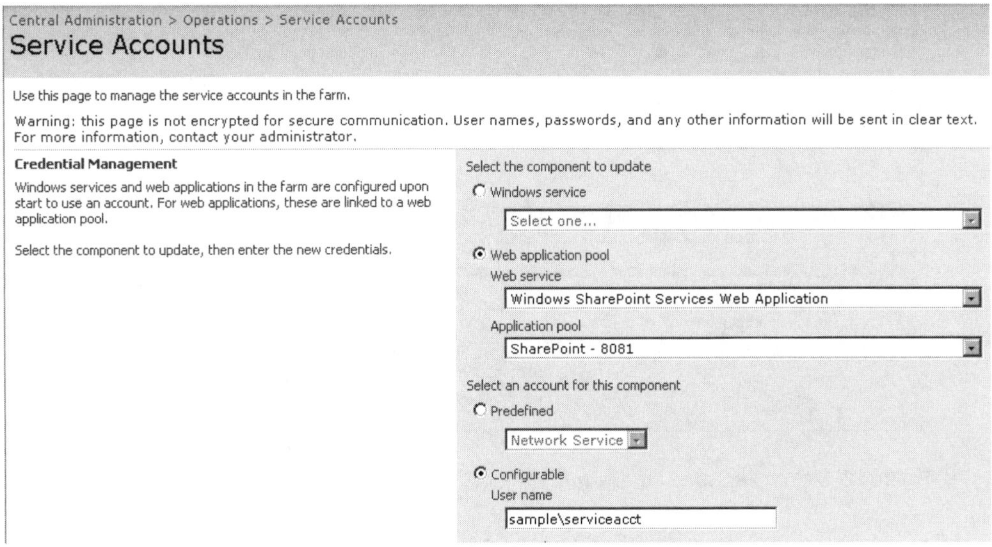

Figure 12-3. *Finding the shared service provider's service credentials*

Constructing the BDC Application Definition

The Business Data Catalog (BDC) provides a framework to integrate external applications into SharePoint so that sites can surface data stored there. To take advantage of this service, the external application must be reachable through an ADO.NET database connection or through web services. There are several supported integration scenarios. These include surfacing the external application in web parts as well as using its data for columns of lists and libraries. The Business Data Catalog also allows you to hook the application into SharePoint's search so it can be crawled by the index server and displayed as search-result items. All of these scenarios are supported without a developer having to introduce new compiled code into the environment. This is an important advantage, as traditionally developers built their own web parts, controls, or protocol handlers to accomplish these tasks in earlier versions of SharePoint. Regardless of the project type, each required custom code to be written, tested, deployed, and maintained. With the BDC, developers can focus on describing the application with an XML file called the *application definition*. This file details how to connect to the external application as well as its different entities, relationships, and methods.

We will begin the solution with an application definition for the CustomerInfo database, which represents our sample line-of-business system. Use the following steps to set up the solution and the project in Visual Studio.

1. Create a New Project in Visual Studio. As shown in Figure 12-4, select the Visual Basic Empty Project template.

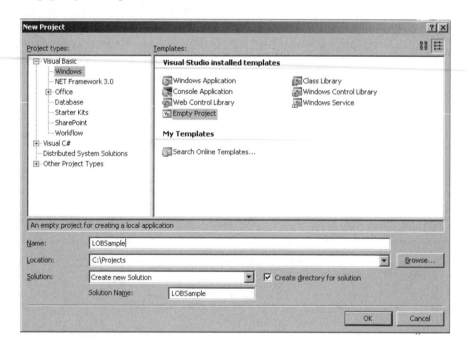

Figure 12-4. *Creating the LOBSample project*

2. Name the solution and project **LOBSample**.

3. Since this project will contain only the application definition XML file, we need to exclude it from the compiler. Right-click on the solution in Visual Studio's Solution Explorer.

4. In the Solution Property Pages dialog, find the Configuration node below Configuration Properties in the tree navigation on the left.

5. Uncheck the check box in the Build column for the LOBSample Project.

6. Click OK.

This chapter will not detail every line of the application definition file, as some sections of it are repetitive. Instead we will describe the major components and their responsibilities. For that reason, you will want to obtain the application definition file from the code download (CustomerApplication.xml) available from the Source Code/Download section of http://apress.com, add it to your LOBSample project, and follow along with the rest of this section. Once the XML file is in your project, you'll want to associate it with the Office Server schema for BDC metadata. You can do this using the Properties window in Visual Studio with the CustomerApplication.xml file selected. Set the Schemas property to point to the bdcmetadata.xsd schema. This file is installed in the C:\Program Files\Microsoft Office Servers\12.0\Bin directory by default.

A BDC application definition describes the external application, including connection information and its entities. An entity is a discrete object stored within the application. In our sample system, the entities are customers and sales people. For each entity, the application definition details the various methods that the BDC can use to interact with it. These interactions are typically different ways of retrieving individual data items or sets of items. Though it is possible to allow the BDC to write data to the external application, such a system could accidentally bypass the application's business logic. Therefore, you should consider carefully the consequences of relating a method to an insert, update, or delete operation. Typically the BDC is about surfacing the external data into SharePoint for it to be viewed and related to other SharePoint objects.

The beginning of the application definition for our CustomerInfo database first defines the external application. As Listing 12-2 shows, this is accomplished with the LobSystem element. The attributes of LobSystem provide a name for the external application, a version number of the definition, and detail that this external application is a database (as opposed to a system exposed through web services). The Properties element informs the BDC that our database management system uses the percent (%) character for wildcard-based queries.

Listing 12-2. *Defining the External Application*

```
<LobSystem
xmlns="http://schemas.microsoft.com/office/2006/03/BusinessDataCatalog"
Type="Database"
Version="1.0.0.0"
Name="CustomerApplication">
<Properties>
   <Property Name="WildcardCharacter" Type="System.String">%</Property>
</Properties>
```

The next section of the file details a specific instance of the application. This provides us the opportunity to detail the connection information on how the BDC will communicate with the database. Within the Properties element of Listing 12-3, you will see the values that usually make up a connection to a SQL Server database.

Listing 12-3. *Connection Information for the External Application*

```
<LobSystemInstances>
<LobSystemInstance Name="CustomerApplicationInstance">
<Properties>
    <Property Name="AuthenticationMode"
                    Type="System.String">RevertToSelf</Property>
    <Property Name="DatabaseAccessProvider"
                    Type="System.String">SqlServer</Property>
    <Property Name="RdbConnection Data Source"
                    Type="System.String">YourSQLServerName</Property>
    <Property Name="RdbConnection Initial Catalog"
                    Type="System.String">CustomerInfo</Property>
    <Property Name="RdbConnection Integrated Security"
                    Type="System.String">SSPI</Property>
    <Property Name="RdbConnection Pooling"
                    Type="System.String">true</Property>
</Properties>
</LobSystemInstance>
</LobSystemInstances>
```

The most interesting property is AuthenticationMode. In this example, we have set its value as RevertToSelf. In this mode, the shared service provider's application pool identity will be used to make the connection to the database regardless of the user. This setting is useful for applications in which you do not need to restrict certain rows of data for different users. This system will return the same data regardless of the SharePoint site user. With this technique, you can still restrict what stored procedures and other database objects this account has access to, and you also gain the benefits of connection pooling since the security context of the connections remains the same. Other possible values for this property include PassThrough, RdbCredentials, and WindowsCredentials. The value of PassThrough refers to the trusted sub-system model, in which the active SharePoint site user's credentials will be used as the security context for the call to the external system. This is the best choice when the external applica-tion needs the security identity of the calling user to return the appropriate results. However, the site's authentication provider will need to be set to Kerberos instead of NTLM for a Win-dows identity to leave the SharePoint server and traverse the network to another resource. The other two modes, RdbCredentials and Windows Credentials, are where the connection is going to be made with some other database credential or Windows account. These modes support relying on SharePoint's Single Sign-On service in both the individual and group modes.

Now that the BDC knows how to connect to the external application, the Entities node details the types of objects it will find there. Listing 12-4 details the beginning of the Customer entity. In this fragment, the CompanyName field is called out to be the title field for the entity. This means that when we display customers, the name of the company will be the field the user clicks on to select a customer, find more details, or perform some other action. The CustomerID field is also set to be the unique identifier for the entity. As in this example, you will usually see the table's primary key used as the entity identifier.

Listing 12-4. *The Customer Entity*

```
<Entity EstimatedInstanceCount="1000" Name="Customer">
<Properties>
    <Property Name="Title"
                    Type="System.String">CompanyName</Property>
</Properties>
<Identifiers>
    <Identifier Name="CustomerID"
                    TypeName="System.Int32" />
</Identifiers>
```

The BDC interacts with an entity through its various methods, which are contained in a Methods element. Listing 12-5 shows the metadata for the GetCustomers method. In this example, the method matches to the database stored procedure you saw earlier in the chapter. Other possibilities include a database SQL query or a web service method. The FilterDescriptors describe the different ways that the BDC will capture user input. The Wildcard filter will find customers whose CompanyName field matches a specified string pattern, such as "starts with Acme". This filter matches our stored procedure's code to find rows using a SQL-like clause against the CompanyName field. The comparison filter will return only rows where the condition is met—and in this case it is used to return a single customer row based on the CustomerID field. The UsedForDisambiguation property specified here designates the filter that should be used to display a list of possible matches.

Listing 12-5. *The GetCustomers Method*

```
<Method Name="GetCustomers">
<Properties>
    <Property Name="RdbCommandText"
                    Type="System.String">GetCustomers</Property>
    <Property Name="RdbCommandType"
                    Type="System.String">StoredProcedure</Property>
</Properties>
<FilterDescriptors>
    <FilterDescriptor Type="Wildcard" Name="CompanyName">
        <Properties>
            <Property Name="UsedForDisambiguation"
                            Type="System.Boolean">true</Property>
        </Properties>
    </FilterDescriptor>
    <FilterDescriptor Type="Comparison" Name="CustomerID">
    </FilterDescriptor>
</FilterDescriptors>
```

The GetCustomers method has two input parameters: CustomerID and CompanyName. The CustomerID is passed in when the system needs to return a specific customer record. Listing 12-6 shows the metadata for the @CustomerID parameter. Notice how this parameter is associated with the CustomerID filter and it is paired with the entity's identifier. This metadata also includes default values for the method instances. Though GetCustomers is a single method, there are two different ways we expect it to be called: The CustomerFinderInstance is when the user is searching for customers by name and the CustomerSpecificFinderInstance is when a specific customer is being recalled based on its ID. When the BDC calls this method, we want to specify default values. Since the CustomerID field is an integer type, we selected a default value of zero. For the @CompanyName parameter, the default value is just a percent (%) character, which would return all customers.

Listing 12-6. *The @CustomerID Input Parameter*

```
<Parameters>
<Parameter Direction="In" Name="@CustomerID">
<TypeDescriptor
        TypeName="System.Int32"
        AssociatedFilter="CustomerID"
        Name="CustomerID"
        IdentifierName="CustomerID">
<DefaultValues>
    <DefaultValue MethodInstanceName="CustomerFinderInstance"
                            Type="System.Int32">0</DefaultValue>
    <DefaultValue MethodInstanceName="CustomerSpecifcFinderInstance"
                            Type="System.Int32">0</DefaultValue>
</DefaultValues>
</TypeDescriptor>
</Parameter>
```

In addition to input parameters, the GetCustomers method has a return parameter specified. This parameter is of type IDataReader and represents the flow of records as a result of our stored procedure's execution. Notice how in Listing 12-7, the return parameter defines the different fields contained in the returned record—including which ones match the entity's identifier.

Listing 12-7. *The Customers Return Parameter*

```
<Parameter Direction="Return" Name="Customers">
<TypeDescriptor
    TypeName="System.Data.IDataReader, System.Data, Version=2.0.3600.0,~
                        Culture=neutral, PublicKeyToken=b77a5c561934e089"
    IsCollection="true" Name="CustomerDataReader">
<TypeDescriptors>
    <TypeDescriptor
```

```
               TypeName="System.Data.IDataRecord, System.Data, Version=2.0.3600.0,~
                            Culture=neutral, PublicKeyToken=b77a5c561934e089"
          Name="CustomerDataRecord">
              <TypeDescriptors>
                  <TypeDescriptor TypeName="System.Int32"
                          IdentifierName="CustomerID" Name="CustomerID">
                  </TypeDescriptor>
                  <TypeDescriptor TypeName="System.String"
                                            Name="CompanyName" />
                  <TypeDescriptor TypeName="System.String"
                                            Name="Street" />
                  <TypeDescriptor TypeName="System.String"
                                            Name="City" />
                  <TypeDescriptor TypeName="System.String"
                                            Name="Zip" />
                  <TypeDescriptor TypeName="System.String"
                                            Name="State" />
                  <TypeDescriptor TypeName="System.DateTime"
                                            Name="CustomerSinceDate" />
              </TypeDescriptors>
          </TypeDescriptor>
      </TypeDescriptors>
      </TypeDescriptor>
</Parameter>
```

Entities within a system can also be related, and the BDC application definition supports this through associations. At the bottom of the CustomerApplication.xml file you will see the metadata in Listing 12-8. This association connects the Customer and SalesPeople entities. The properties of the association detail that the Customer entity is the source in the relationship and that the customer's sales people can be retrieved using the GetCustomerPeople method.

Listing 12-8. *The CustomerToSalesPeople Association*

```
<Associations>
<Association
    AssociationMethodEntityName="Customer"
    AssociationMethodName="GetCustomerPeople"
    AssociationMethodReturnParameterName="SalesPeople"
    Name="CustomerToSalesPeople">
    <SourceEntity Name="Customer"/>
    <DestinationEntity Name="SalesPeople"/>
</Association>
</Associations>
```

■**Note** As you can see, generating the metadata for an external application, even one as simple as this database, can be quite tedious and time-consuming. For this reason, there are several efforts in the community to construct a tool that, when pointed to an external application, can discover and generate this file automatically. At the time of this writing, these tools are just getting started and are not quite granular enough to be a complete solution. However, the momentum here is quite strong and we suspect that writing an application definition by hand will soon be a thing of the past. One particular effort of note is the BDC Meta Man being constructed by Todd S Baginski and Nick Swan:

- BDC Meta Man

  http://www.bdcmetaman.com/default.aspx

Now that we have reviewed the application definition available in the code download, we need to configure the BDC. Before uploading the file, let's confirm the service's security settings.

1. From the Shared Services administration screen, click Business Data Catalog Permissions in the Business Data Catalog group.

2. Since our goal is for all users to be able to access the data in the external application, add your Domain Users group to the permission set, granting those users Execute and Select in Clients rights.

From the Shared Services Administration page, click the Import Application Definition action in the Business Data Catalog group. Browse and upload the CustomerApplication.xml file. Once you've done that, you will be able to view the application using this administration area. Figure 12-5 shows the View Application screen, which contains information about the external application and a list of its entities. Take some time to click through each entity and see how the Business Data Catalog gathered all of the different metadata elements.

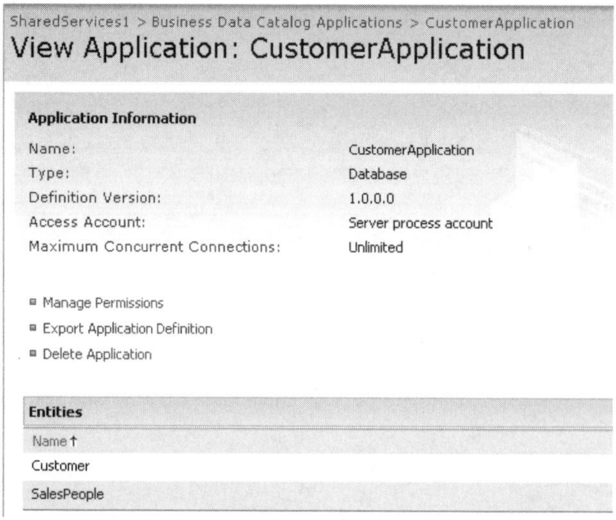

Figure 12-5. *Viewing the CustomerApplication in the BDC*

Configuring the Profile Pages

When you uploaded the application definition file to the Business Data Catalog, the BDC created a `customer.aspx` page as well as a `salespeople.aspx` page. These are profile pages for the entities and they are responsible for the default display of an instance of the entity from the external application. A profile page is viewable by a user when he selects View Profile from anywhere the data is used. These pages also serve the search-integration scenario, as it will be this page the user is directed to when he clicks on a search-result item. You can find the URL to the customer profile page by viewing the customer entity within the BDC administration. The URL will be in the section called Actions and it will have a format like this: `http://o12server:8081/ssp/admin/Content/Customer.aspx?CustomerID={0}`. Note that the server name and port will be different in your environment and should match the web application that hosts the shared service provider.

Notice the {0} in the URL. This is a placeholder that will be filled in by an identifier. In the case of customers, it will be a specific CustomerID. You can view and modify these pages. Use the following steps to customize the `customer.aspx` profile page to also include information about the customer's sales people.

1. In a browser window, navigate to the profile page, replacing the {0} characters with the value **1101**. This identifier is for Sample Inc.

2. From the Site Actions menu, place the page in edit mode. You will notice that there are two web parts already on the page. One is the Business Data Item Builder. This web part is responsible for capturing the identifier query string parameter and providing it to the other web parts on the page through web-part connections. The second web part is a Business Data Item web part, which displays the fields of a specific instance of the entity.

3. Click Add a Web Part in the middle zone of the page.

4. Locate the Business Data grouping of web parts. All of these web parts are capable of surfacing data from the application definition. The advantage here is that these web parts are generic enough to work with any application definition. This is a far better experience then coding all of this work as custom web parts.

5. Add the Business Data Related List web part to the bottom of the middle zone. We will use this web part to also display this customer's sales people.

6. Using the Edit drop-down of the web part, choose to modify its settings.

7. In the web part admin pane, click the Browse button for the Type property. You should be able to select to display SalesPeople from the CustomerApplicationInstance.

8. Be sure to select the CustomerToSalesPeople relationship in the Relationship property directly below the Type setting.

9. Click OK.

10. Using the Edit drop-down of the SalesPeople List web part, connect it to the Customer Details web part. Use GetRelatedItems from Customer Details as the settings of the connection.

11. Click to Exit edit mode.

Your profile page should now look similar to Figure 12-6. Using the settings of the web parts, you can change the toolbars, modify the view to selectively show fields or change their order, or even write your own XSLT for generating the interface. Also try changing the parameter to **1102**, which is the other customer record in the sample database. See how your changes to the profile page apply to all instances of the entity.

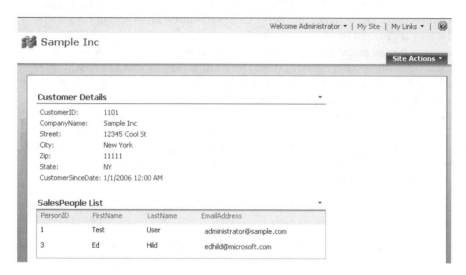

Figure 12-6. *The customer BDC profile page*

Testing in a Team Site

Now that we have an application registered in the Business Data Catalog, we can explore some of the integration scenarios we cited as benefits earlier. Select a team site where you can test some of this functionality. Confirm that the site has the Office SharePoint Server Enterprise Site Features feature enabled. This can be found in Site Settings ➤ Site Features. Without this feature activated, the Business Data Catalog web parts will not be available. Use the following steps to test the Business Data List web part.

1. From the Site Actions menu, place the page in edit mode.

2. Click Add a Web Part in the left zone of the page.

3. Locate the Business Data grouping of web parts.

4. Add the Business Data List web part. We will use this web part to support locating customers.

5. Using the Edit drop-down of the web part, choose to modify its settings.

6. In the web-part admin pane, click the Browse button for the Type property. You should be able to select to display Customer from the CustomerApplicationInstance. This application is made available to any web applications that are relying on the same Shared Service Provider where you uploaded the application definition.

7. Click OK and Exit edit mode.

Notice how this web part exposes the different FilterDescriptors, allowing a user to do a wildcard search based on company name or to retrieve a specific instance given a CustomerID. Perform a wildcard search for companies whose name starts with *s*. Click Retrieve Data. The Sample Inc customer will be included in the search results. Remember that we designated the CompanyName field as the title? The BDC makes that field actionable. Hover over the Sample Inc company name and click the down arrow on the menu that appears. This will display the View Profile action that, when clicked, will take the user to the profile page. Figure 12-7 shows this option.

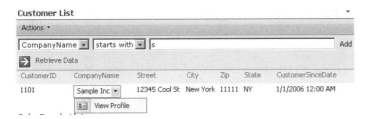

Figure 12-7. *Performing a wildcard search*

The customer and sales people entities can also be used as columns in lists. In the same test site, add a new column to an existing list. Name the column **Customer** and choose Business Data as its type. Notice that you can select the type of entity to map this column to, as well as control which field is to be displayed. Select CompanyName as the field to display and Click OK. Add new items to the list and see how the form interacts with the external application. An important fact about this integration scenario is that the list item copies the values from the external application. This means that if the external application were to change (the company name, for instance), the list item would not reflect that until it was modified or explicitly refreshed with the refresh/update button at the top of the column.

Building the Custom Web Service

At this point in the solution we have integrated the external application into SharePoint. The goal is to expose this integration so that other applications can take advantage of it. To accomplish this, we will build a custom web service that invokes the Business Data Catalog through SharePoint's object model. Use the following steps to add the necessary projects to your solution for the custom web service. If these steps are not granular enough, refer to the web page Walkthrough: Creating a Custom Web Service, mentioned in the "Further Reading" section of this chapter.

1. From Visual Studio's File menu, select to Add a New Web Site project to your solution.

2. Choose ASP.NET Web Service as the project type and replace WebSite1 in the file path to **BDCService**.

3. Delete the Service.vb file in the App_Code folder and the default Service.asmx.

4. Add a new web service BDCService.asmx to this project. This will create the BDCService.asmx and BDCService.vb class files.

5. Now since we want to deploy the code for this web service to the Global Assembly Cache, add another Class Library project to the solution and call it BDCServiceCode.

6. Generate a key and sign this assembly.

7. Remove the default class file from this project and move the BDCService.vb file from the web service's App_Code directory to the class library project.

8. You will need to compile the BDCServiceCode class library project so you can use the sn.exe -T Visual Studio command line technique to retrieve this assembly's public key token. This will be necessary as we have to modify the directive in the BDCService.asmx file so it can find its code-behind, which is now in the separate BDCServiceCode assembly.

9. With the public key token from step 8, change the WebService directive of the BDCService.asmx file to match that of Listing 12-9. Remember to use your public key token.

Listing 12-9. *Setting the Custom Web Service's Directive*

```
<%@ WebService Language="VB"
    Class="BDCServiceCode.BDCService, BDCServiceCode,~
            Version=1.0.0.0, Culture=neutral,~
            PublicKeyToken=9e4c7a60c0679071" %>
```

The BDCService.vb file has exactly one web method, called GetEntitySpecificFinder. You should grab this class file from the code download at http://apress.com; however, we will take you through each section and explain how this method was coded. First, since this class file will be interacting with the BDC object model, we added a reference to the Microsoft.SharePoint.Portal.dll assembly. This assembly should be the first reference listed as Microsoft Office SharePoint Server component in the .NET tab of your Add Reference dialog. Be sure to confirm that the path to this assembly is C:\Program Files\Common Files\Microsoft Shared\web server extensions\12\ISAPI\Microsoft.SharePoint.Portal.dll. Then add the Imports statements in Listing 12-10 for the BDC (formerly named ApplicationRegistry).

Listing 12-10. *The Import Statements for the BDC API*

```
Imports Microsoft.Office.Server.ApplicationRegistry
Imports Microsoft.Office.Server.ApplicationRegistry.Runtime
Imports Microsoft.Office.Server.ApplicationRegistry.Infrastructure
Imports Microsoft.Office.Server.ApplicationRegistry.MetadataModel
```

Notice that we are not naming this method GetCustomer or something specific to the particular application we have registered in the Business Data Catalog. We want this method to be generic and able to return the details of any entity in any external application. All that we require is that the entity supports a SpecificFinder. Therefore, the parameters to this method include the name of the external application, the name of the application instance, the name of the entity, and the input parameter representing the entity instance we want returned. We simplified this signature a bit by assuming that our entities are going to have a single value as an identifier. The GetEntitySpecficFinder will return an XML representation of the entity. In Listing 12-11, you can see this web method's signature and the setup of the return value.

Listing 12-11. *Signature for the GetEntitySpecificFinder Web Service Method*

```
<WebMethod()> _
Public Function GetEntitySpecificFinder(ByVal ApplicationName As String, _
   ByVal ApplicationInstance As String, ByVal EntityName As String, _
   ByVal Parameter As String) As System.Xml.XmlDocument
      Dim returnDocument As XmlDocument = New XmlDocument()
      Dim root As XmlNode = returnDocument.CreateElement("root")
      returnDocument.AppendChild(root)
```

The first block of code in the GetEntitySpecificFinder enumerates through the Business Data Catalog object model to find the requested entity type. This path starts with the name of the application and continues through the application instance and entity name. Once the entity is found, we confirm that it has a SpecificFinder and discover its parameter type. In this example, we are expecting the SpecificFinder to have a single input parameter of type Int32, Guid, or String. Finally, with this information we execute the FindSpecific method, passing in the strongly typed parameter. Listing 12-12 details this section of the method.

Listing 12-12. *Finding the Requested Entity Instance*

```
Dim systemObj As LobSystem = ApplicationRegistry.~
        GetLobSystems()(ApplicationName)
Dim systemInstance As LobSystemInstance =~
        systemObj.GetLobSystemInstances()(ApplicationInstance)
Dim requestedEntity As Entity = systemObj.GetEntities()(EntityName)
If requestedEntity.HasSpecificFinder() Then
   Dim instance As IEntityInstance = Nothing
   Dim paramTypeString = requestedEntity.GetSpecificFinderMethodInstance().~
           GetMethod().GetInputParameters()(0).GetRootTypeDescriptor().TypeName
   Select Case paramTypeString
       Case "System.Int32"
               instance = requestedEntity.FindSpecific(Integer.Parse(Parameter),~
                               systemInstance)
       Case "System.String"
               instance = requestedEntity.FindSpecific(Parameter, systemInstance)
       Case "System.Guid"
               instance = requestedEntity.FindSpecific(New Guid(Parameter),~
                               systemInstance)
   End Select
```

Now that we have found the specific entity instance we are looking for, we add XML element nodes to the return document for each field of the entity. Notice the use of the XmlConvert class in Listing 12-13 in case the name of the property includes characters that need to be encoded to be properly represented in XML. Listing 12-13 shows the loop through the fields collection.

Listing 12-13. *Placing the Entity Instance's Fields into the Response*

```
Dim f As Field = Nothing
For Each f In requestedEntity.GetSpecificFinderView().Fields
    Dim fieldNode As XmlNode = returnDocument.CreateElement(~
            XmlConvert.EncodeName(f.Name))
    Dim txtNode As XmlNode = returnDocument.~
            CreateTextNode(instance(f).ToString())
    fieldNode.AppendChild(txtNode)
    root.AppendChild(fieldNode)
Next
```

In addition to all of the fields of the entity, we also want to return a URL that the external application could follow for more information on the entity instance. For our customer and sales people entities, this would be a URL to the profile pages we configured earlier. Of course, we can't assume that there is a View Profile action even though the BDC creates one by default. Therefore, we will include the URL to the default action in the returned XML. Listing 12-14 shows how we can obtain this value and add it to our return value.

Listing 12-14. *Adding the Default Action URL to the Response*

```
Dim actionNode As XmlNode = returnDocument.CreateElement("Action")
Dim url As String = instance.GetActionUrl(requestedEntity.GetDefaultAction())
Dim actionUrl As XmlNode = returnDocument.CreateTextNode(url)
actionNode.AppendChild(actionUrl)
root.AppendChild(actionNode)
End If
Return returnDocument
End Function
```

Deploying and Testing the Web Service

The custom web service we constructed in the previous section of the chapter needs to be deployed so that it appears in the _vti_bin directory like the other SharePoint web services. The reason for this is that when the web service is called, it needs to find the Business Data Catalog service in the appropriate shared service provider. By deploying it into the _vti_bin directory, the web service will hook into the same context of the web application and therefore have access to that site's shared service provider as configured in Central Administration. The WSS 3.0 SDK (see Walkthrough: Creating a Custom Web Service, mentioned in the "Further Reading" section of this chapter) has detailed steps on how to deploy such a service, including the necessary actions to create ASPX page representations of the web service's disco and WSDL files. We included these in the code download to save you a few steps. Also, don't forget to install the BDCServiceCode.dll assembly into the Global Assembly Cache. This can be as easy as dragging it into the C:\Windows\assembly folder using Windows Explorer.

Included in the code download (available from the Source Code/Download section of http://apress.com) is a WebServiceDriver console test program. This console project includes a web reference to the web service: http://portal.sample.com/_vti_bin/BDCService.asmx. The program issues a call, as shown in Listing 12-15, looking for the Sample Inc customer.

Listing 12-15. *Testing BDCService.asmx*

```
Sub Main()
  Dim service As BDCWebService.BDCService = New~
        BDCWebService.BDCService()
  service.Credentials = System.Net.CredentialCache.DefaultCredentials
  Dim doc As Xml.XmlNode = Nothing
  doc = service.GetEntitySpecificFinder("CustomerApplication",~
        "CustomerApplicationInstance", "Customer", "1101")
  Console.WriteLine(doc.OuterXml)
  Console.ReadLine()
End Sub
```

Building the Outlook Form Region

Users of Outlook interact with several different types of objects, including messages, contacts, tasks, and events. Each of these objects is presented in an Outlook form. It seems as if from the very beginning organizations have wanted to customize, extend, and inject code into these forms. This is largely due to the prominent placement of Outlook. Many users leave it open all day, checking messages and maintaining their calendar. Before Outlook 2007, developers who wanted to customize an Outlook form usually found themselves redesigning the entire form even when all they wanted to do was add a few fields. In older versions of Outlook, these custom forms were deployed centrally on the Exchange server and often took too long to open. Developers also had a difficult time injecting their own code or script for their form. Outlook 2007 introduces a new concept called Form Regions, which brings managed code to Outlook form development.

An Outlook 2007 form-region solution is made up of three main elements. The first is the form region itself, which contains the layout of the form and its controls. The form regions are constructed in Outlook and stored as an Outlook Form Storage (OFS) file. The second element of an Outlook form-region solution is an Outlook add-in that runs code in response to the user interacting with controls on the form region. Lastly, a manifest XML file that Outlook finds through the Windows registry informs the application of which custom assembly should be loaded for the form region and how it is to be displayed.

There are three ways to add a custom Outlook form region. You can append a region to an existing form, replace the first tab page of a built-in form, or completely replace an existing form. Regardless of the approach, Outlook 2007 provides the tools through its Developer ribbon to create the OFS file. Use the following steps to design an Outlook form region that will extend the default Contact form.

1. Open Outlook 2007 and create an empty contact with only a first and last name. Make sure that you have this contact open before continuing.

2. If the Developer tab on the ribbon is not displayed, enable it through Editor Options. This choice is on the "pearl" Office button, which has the Office logo in the top left-hand corner. Simply check the option to Show Developer Tab in the Ribbon.

3. On the developer tab, click the Design a Form control.

4. Select Contact and click Open.

5. From the Form Region control, select New Form Region. Optionally, you can open the form region provided in the code download at http://apress.com. The form region is saved in a file called CustomerContactFormRegion.ofs.

6. The Field chooser should automatically open to the right of the form-design surface. Also open the control toolbox through the button in the ribbon. Figure 12-8 shows the layout that we are going to construct. Details of the controls and their properties appear in the list after the figure.

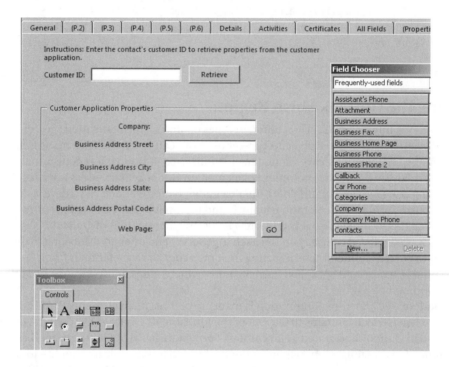

Figure 12-8. *Designing the customer-contact form region*

- The instructions are contained within a label control placed on the form via the toolbox.

- The Customer Application Properties box is a frame control.

- All of the fields on this form already exist within a contact. You can use the field chooser to drag them onto the form's surface. For each field, you get a label as well as a text box.

- The only exception to the text-box rule is the Web Page field. In this case, Outlook places a clickable control. Since we are going to use these controls to assign values to the contact, delete the default control and instead add a text box from the toolbox. The text-box control will be simpler for our code to assign the action URL of the entity to the WebPage field.

- By right-clicking each text box, you can select to set its properties. Use this technique to name the controls: **OlkCustomerID**, **OlkCompany**, **OlkStreet**, **OlkCity**, **OlkState**, **OlkZip**, and **OlkWebPage**. Since you added the web-page text box, use the Value tab of the Properties dialog to associate it with the WebPage field.

- The Retrieve and Go buttons are command buttons from the toolbox. They are named **cmdRetrieve** and **cmdGo**.

The premise behind this customer form region is that users often have contacts stored within Outlook. Some of these contacts may be ones that the user has established within a customer's organization. Instead of making each individual user responsible for maintaining the contact data about the business, our form region will allow them to populate these fields using the CustomerInfo database application we registered with the Business Data Catalog. So the use case is that a user opens a contact item in Outlook and navigates to our region, with the goal of retrieving this information. The user enters the CustomerID of the organization and clicks Retrieve. The Outlook form region communicates with the CustomerInfo database through the customer web service that leverages the Business Data Catalog. When a response is received, the fields are updated and the WebPage property is set to the Customer entity profile page. The Go button here is a convenience since it will open the browser to this page when clicked. With the form region designed, use the Form Region control to save it to an OFS file named CustomerContactFormRegion.ofs.

The form region is served to Outlook through an add-in. Fortunately Visual Studio Tools for Office 2005 SE provides a project template for Outlook 2007 add-ins. In the code download, this project is named CustomerOutlookAddin (in the LOBSample solution). We will not explain every line of code, so please use the code download to follow along. If you want more-detailed instructions that take you through a form region add-in, visit the Walkthrough: Creating an Outlook Form Region site listed in the "Further Reading" section of this chapter.

In the project's directory, we copied the CustomerContactFormRegion.ofs file we created earlier. This file was also added as a project resource through the Resources tab of the project's Properties dialog. See the following URL for help adding embedded resources: http://msdn2.microsoft.com/en-us/library/3bka19x4.aspx. We set a web reference to our custom web service that we developed earlier (http://portal.sample.com/_vti_bin/BDCService.asmx) and added a reference to the Microsoft Forms 2.0 Object Library, which is listed in the COM tab of Visual Studio's Add Reference dialog.

The ThisAddIn class represents the main entry point for the add-in's scope and it is here that you will find the glue that serves up the form region. This class contains the code in Listing 12-16, which is an override of the RequestService function. The Outlook application will call this method to discover the customizations the add-in is hosting. When Outlook is looking to start up any form regions, we will return our own class (FormRegionHelper), which implements the Microsoft.Office.Interop.Outlook.FormRegionStartup interface. Outlook will use this class to interact with the form region, including any custom code we wish to attach to the controls we placed in the layout.

Listing 12-16. *The RequestService Override of the ThisAddIn Class*

```
Protected Overrides Function RequestService(~
    ByVal serviceGuid As System.Guid) As Object
If serviceGuid = GetType(Outlook.FormRegionStartup).GUID Then
   Return New FormRegionHelper()
Else
   Return MyBase.RequestService(serviceGuid)
End If
End Function
```

The FormRegionHelper.vb file contains the class that serves as the code-behind for the form region. Since the add-in returned this class to Outlook for any custom form regions, the first operation we need to support is returning the OFS file that contains the form region's layout and controls. We embedded this as a resource within the assembly; the code in Listing 12-17 shows how it is retrieved as part of the implementation of the GetFormRegion-Storage function. The string value of CustomerContactFormRegion is a value that Outlook is passing in from the information it was given in the Windows registry. We will explore the registry information in the next section of this chapter.

Listing 12-17. *Returning the Form-Region OFS File to Outlook*

```
Public Function GetFormRegionStorage(ByVal FormRegionName As String,~
    ByVal Item As Object, ByVal LCID As Integer,~
    ByVal FormRegionMode As Microsoft.Office.Interop.Outlook.OlFormRegionMode,~
    ByVal FormRegionSize As Microsoft.Office.Interop.Outlook.OlFormRegionSize)~
    As Object Implements~
    Microsoft.Office.Interop.Outlook._FormRegionStartup.GetFormRegionStorage
Application.DoEvents()
Select Case FormRegionName
   Case "CustomerContactFormRegion"
      Dim ofsBytes As Byte()
      ofsBytes = My.Resources.CustomerContactFormRegion
      Return ofsBytes
   Case Else
      Return Nothing
End Select
End Function
```

With the form region's layout served to Outlook, we then want to capture the BeforeForm-RegionShow event so that our managed code has the opportunity to hook into its controls. In the FormRegionHelper class we have variables declared for each of the text boxes and command buttons in the layout. Listing 12-18 shows how during the BeforeFormRegionShow event these variables are assigned references to the appropriate controls.

Listing 12-18. *Setting Up References to the Form Region's Controls*

```
Public Sub BeforeFormRegionShow(ByVal FormRegion As~
    Microsoft.Office.Interop.Outlook.FormRegion) Implements~
    Microsoft.Office.Interop.Outlook._FormRegionStartup.BeforeFormRegionShow
Me.mFormRegion = FormRegion
Me.mUserForm = FormRegion.Form
Try
   OlkCustomerID = mUserForm.Controls.Item("OlkCustomerID")
   cmdRetrieve = mUserForm.Controls.Item("cmdRetrieve")
   OlkCompany = mUserForm.Controls.Item("OlkCompany")
   OlkStreet = mUserForm.Controls.Item("OlkStreet")
   OlkCity = mUserForm.Controls.Item("OlkCity")
   OlkState = mUserForm.Controls.Item("OlkState")
   OlkZip = mUserForm.Controls.Item("OlkZip")
   OlkWebPage = mUserForm.Controls.Item("OlkWebPage")
   cmdGo = mUserForm.Controls.Item("cmdGo")
Catch ex As Exception
   MessageBox.Show(ex.ToString())
End Try
End Sub
```

Since the command buttons were declared with the WithEvents keyword, the Form-RegionHelper class can have event handlers for their Click events. When the cmdRetrieve button is clicked, the code in Listing 12-19 calls our web service, using its asynchronous implementation and passing in the value of the OlkCustomerID text box. Notice that this call is made with the user's currently logged-in credentials. Because of the asynchronous implementation, the GetEntitySpecifiedFinderCompleted method will be invoked once the form region has received a response.

Listing 12-19. *Calling the Custom Web Service*

```
Private Sub cmdRetrieve_Click() Handles cmdRetrieve.Click
Dim service As BDCWebService.BDCService =~
    New BDCWebService.BDCService()
service.Credentials = System.Net.CredentialCache.DefaultCredentials
AddHandler service.GetEntitySpecificFinderCompleted,~
    AddressOf Me.GetEntitySpecificFinderCompleted
service.GetEntitySpecificFinderAsync("CustomerApplication", _
    "CustomerApplicationInstance", "Customer", Me.OlkCustomerID.Text)
End Sub
```

The last step is to process the results. Remember that the custom web service returns the fields and default action URL of the entity in an XML document. Listing 12-20 shows how the GetEntitySpecificFinderCompleted method retrieves some of these values. In each case, the value is obtained using XPath queries.

Listing 12-20. *Example of Processing the Results*

```
Public Sub GetEntitySpecificFinderCompleted(ByVal sender As Object, _
    ByVal e As BDCWebService.GetEntitySpecificFinderCompletedEventArgs)
If (e.Error Is Nothing) Then
    Dim xmlResult As XmlNode = e.Result
    Dim companyName As String = String.Empty
    Dim street As String = String.Empty
    Dim action As String = String.Empty
    companyName = xmlResult.SelectSingleNode("//CompanyName").InnerText
    street = xmlResult.SelectSingleNode("//Street").InnerText
    action = xmlResult.SelectSingleNode("//Action").InnerText
    Me.OlkCompany.Text = companyName
    Me.OlkStreet.Text = street
    Me.OlkWebPage.Text = action
End If
End Sub
```

Deploying the Form Region

For you to run your add-in, you must also build a manifest file that describes the form region for Outlook. This manifest file names the form region, specifies the title that is used in the ribbon when it is displayed, and references the matching add-in. In the Visual Studio project, its Copy to Output Directory property is set to Copy Always so that the manifest file will be located with the assembly. Listing 12-21 shows the contents of manifest.xml.

Listing 12-21. *The Form Region Manifest File*

```
<?xml version="1.0" encoding="utf-8" ?>
<FormRegion xmlns=~
      "http://schemas.microsoft.com/office/outlook/12/formregion.xsd">
  <name>CustomerContactFormRegion</name>
  <title>Customer Application</title>
  <formRegionType>separate</formRegionType>
  <showCompose>true</showCompose>
  <showRead>true</showRead>
  <showPreview>false</showPreview>
  <hidden>true</hidden>
  <addin>CustomerOutlookAddin</addin>
  <version>1.0</version>
</FormRegion>
```

There is one remaining item necessary for your solution to run. We need to provide a method for Outlook to locate the manifest file. Outlook locates form-region manifests through keys in the Windows registry. For this reason, we have included a RegisterFormRegion.reg file in the code download for the project. This file, when double-clicked in Windows Explorer, adds a registry key specifying the location of our manifest file for the Outlook contact form.

Before using this file, you will want to confirm that its path to the manifest file matches your development environment. Listing 12-22 includes the content of this file.

Listing 12-22. *Registering the Form in the Windows Registry*

```
Windows Registry Editor Version 5.00

[HKEY_CURRENT_USER\Software\Microsoft\Office\Outlook\~
    FormRegions\IPM.Contact]
"CustomerContactFormRegion"="C:\\Projects\\LOBSample\\~
    CustomerOutlookAddin\\bin\\Debug\\manifest.xml"
```

Now you should be able to run your solution with the Outlook add-in set as the startup project. Outlook will launch, and if you go to the contact you created earlier, the ribbon will have a Customer Application option in the Show control group. Clicking this button takes you to our form region. Test retrieving the values for customer IDs 1101 and 1102. Figure 12-9 shows the result.

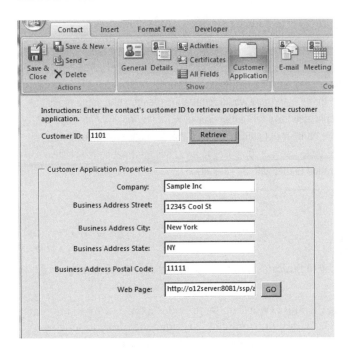

Figure 12-9. *Running the form-region solution*

Notice that if you click back to the general contact form, the values that we are assigning to the fields are persisted. Figure 12-10 shows how the URL of the profile page is correctly displayed; linking this contact to the page constructed by the Business Data Catalog. If you save and close the contact, you can also see these values in the list of all Outlook contacts.

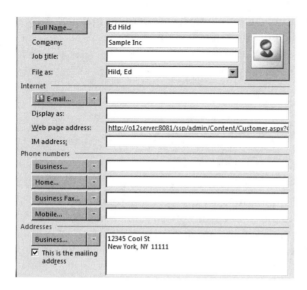

Figure 12-10. *Persisted values in the general contact form*

Note Many of these deployment steps are written for a developer working on a development machine. Making this Outlook form region available to the enterprise would require the creation of a setup project to install the add-in and manifest file. You could also have this setup project write the registry entry, but this might be difficult to maintain across a large number of machines should these values change over time. Another option for the registry entry would be to use a group policy to push this information to your users. With this technique you have a central location to maintain this setting.

Important Lessons

This solution incorporated several key techniques that are worth highlighting, as they could easily be reused in other projects.

The Business Data Catalog: The Business Data Catalog provides a framework to integrate external databases or web services without introducing custom code into your environment. Instead, the application definition file describes the system, and how to connect to it, its entities, and relationships. Once deployed, SharePoint can then surface the external application's data in web parts, lists, and searches.

Custom SharePoint web services: When the SharePoint object model provides access to a feature's API, you can expose that feature to external systems by writing your own custom web service. A SharePoint custom web service has its code deployed to the GAC and the ASMX file deployed to the ISAPI folder so that it is accessible through the _vti_bin directory. This type of deployment allows the web service to access the site context it is being invoked from. There are several steps necessary to properly deploy such a service (see the "Further Reading" section).

Outlook form regions: You can now extend Outlook forms with your own layout and managed code. The layout is constructed using a designer hosted in Outlook, which is then saved as an OFS file. This file is utilized by an Outlook add-in assembly that contains the code that runs in response to the user's interaction with the region's controls. A manifest file and Windows registry entry are required as part of the deployment of the solution.

Extension Point

While coding this example, we thought of a variation to the solution that we didn't incorporate because it distracted from the overall objective of the solution. We call it out now as an extension point since it may be applicable to a specific project you are working on.

Integrating MOSS search: The solution explored the integration scenarios of web parts and list columns supported by the Business Data Catalog, but left out hooking the application into the Search service. In the code download, the Customer entity already has a method named CustomerIDEnumerator, which is required for the search integration. The Enabling Business Data Search URL in the "Further Reading" section provides the steps needed to configure SharePoint search.

Further Reading

The following links are to resources a reader interested in this chapter's material may find useful:

- Business Data Catalog: Overview

  http://msdn2.microsoft.com/en-us/library/ms551230.aspx

- Walkthrough: Creating an Outlook Form Region

  http://msdn2.microsoft.com/en-us/library/aa942741(VS.80).aspx

- Business Data Catalog Samples

  http://msdn2.microsoft.com/en-us/library/aa598181.aspx

- Enabling Business Data Search

  http://msdn2.microsoft.com/en-us/library/ms492695.aspx

- Walkthrough: Creating a Custom Web Service

  http://msdn2.microsoft.com/en-us/library/ms464040.aspx

PART 6

■■■

Microsoft InfoPath Solutions

This section will focus on solutions built around Microsoft InfoPath. In Chapter 13 we focus on the challenges of taking forms to the Web by leveraging the new Forms Server capability of Microsoft Office SharePoint Server 2007. We discuss design concerns in integrating these web-based forms with enterprise systems, as well as demonstrate their flexibility for being hosted in custom applications and web parts. In Chapter 14 we add workflow to the forms processing, showing how to integrate Windows Workflow Foundation. This integration illustrates the ability to incorporate an ad-hoc, human-oriented workflow into an enterprise forms processing strategy.

CHAPTER 13

∎∎∎

Taking InfoPath Forms to the Web

InfoPath, introduced with Office 2003, is an Office application that allows users to quickly create electronic forms that can collect and display business data. These forms can include validation rules and rich formatting, as well as have the ability to read and persist data to XML files and enterprise data sources without requiring extensive development expertise. Most information workers in the enterprise quickly realized InfoPath's value by creating simple solutions that automated the collection of data traditionally collected on paper, such as vacation requests and expense reports, with relative ease. In fact, most of the InfoPath 2003 solutions that exist today are simple departmental email or SharePoint-library-based forms solutions that allow users to collect, route, and store data using familiar desktop tools both online and offline. The next obvious question is, what about the Enterprise? Enterprise forms solutions typically require custom business logic or workflow, and in some cases extend beyond organizational boundaries to people in other departments and even outside the corporation.

These types of solutions, by design, are usually multi-tier and require some amount of customization and integration with line-of-business systems. In InfoPath 2003 you could extend a forms solution using scripting languages, and with the introduction of InfoPath 2003 Service Pack 1 (SP1) managed code in either C# or VB.NET using the InfoPath 2003 Toolkit for Visual Studio .NET. However, the development environment was still challenging, making these types of solutions tedious to construct and even harder to deploy. In fact, this lack of fully integrated Visual Studio development support tended to be a deterrent for the .NET development community. The second-most-talked-about complication was InfoPath 2003's lack of support for the Web: InfoPath 2003 required that a user's computer have InfoPath installed to view or modify the form.

The release of InfoPath 2007 and Visual Studio 2005 Tools for Office Second Edition (VSTO 2005 SE) increases the number of enterprise scenarios that developers can address; these releases introduce a number of new enhancements that make it much more attractive to the enterprise developer, including support for thin clients and the integration of the Visual Studio development environment to build and test solutions. These new capabilities give an organization the tools it needs to construct solutions that can securely extend to users both inside and outside its organizational boundaries, are easier to deploy, and are by design tightly integrated with WSS, MOSS 2007, and ASP.NET 2.0. In this chapter we will demonstrate how to construct a forms solution that takes advantage of these new enterprise forms capabilities.

Real-World Examples

There are many scenarios that have benefited from InfoPath allowing users to fill out forms both on and offline. An example is an expense report that needs to be filled out offline by a remote sales executive and later submitted on the corporate network or Internet using a web service. The real value of InfoPath 2007 is its ability to let you design a form once and then extend it to the Web, allowing users outside an organization or those without the InfoPath client to use the same forms solution. This increases the value of InfoPath—it gives organizations the ability to manage a process over the Internet or the extranet and to touch data stored in line-of-business applications in a thick- or thin-client deployment scenario, both online and offline. We can fill out credit applications, submit our taxes, and even apply for bank loans on the Internet today. These forms can be simple and contain a few data points, or be more complex, such as an IRS tax form. Most of the site types we've mentioned are traditionally built as a custom web application that persists the data we enter to a back-end database, beginning some type of workflow inside the organization. Such applications usually require a significant amount of custom code and are difficult to manage when business requirements change.

Let's take a deeper look at a typical expense-reporting workflow. Most expense reports are filled out by the employee and then submitted for approval to one or more supervisors. Once approved, the expense information updates a back-end enterprise resource-planning application and other line-of-business systems, resulting in payment to the employee. We can now build an expense form that is available in a thick or thin client and that, when saved, persists the data to a SharePoint 2007 forms library. There a workflow process is started automatically to route the document to the appropriate management for approval. Once the document is approved, that same workflow could update the line-of-business applications.

In a perfect world we would have a common toolset that is robust enough to create multi-tier forms solutions for both the Web and thick client, and that is flexible enough to adapt to an organization's changing requirements without our having to redevelop the entire solution. That's where InfoPath 2007 and Windows Workflow Foundation come in. InfoPath gives you a set of tools to build, test, and deploy forms for the enterprise. The toolset is built on top of the .NET platform, allowing developers to focus on the business process instead of the basic forms-development tasks. Windows Workflow Foundation, covered in Chapter 14, integrates the capability to route the data to the appropriate person and/or application for processing.

Solution Overview

In this chapter we'll show you how to build a forms solution that allows users to view and fill out a form while working in a web browser or the InfoPath client application and then persist that data to a SQL Server database in a similar fashion to the expense-report scenario we described in the "Real-World Examples" section. The form in this chapter will collect data about a bank's loan application. Most forms solutions require some ad-hoc workflow. In this chapter we will focus exclusively on the InfoPath piece of the solution. Chapter 14 will introduce a forms workflow in a similar scenario to complete the concept. You do not need to complete this solution to code the one in Chapter 14; however, since this chapter focuses on the form, it does spend more time discussing the form's construction and integration strategies with enterprise systems.

The form itself is very straightforward and contains nine data elements, which we will create manually, as its data source. In this solution we will use Visual Studio.NET so that we can incorporate managed code into the solution and take advantage of Visual Studio's design environment to build, test, debug, and deploy InfoPath forms just as you would any other .NET application. We will create the form solution using Visual Studio .NET and VSTO 2005 SE using the InfoPath project template. We will also create an InfoPath form template part that we will use as the standard header. This is a new capability in InfoPath 2007 that allows you to create template parts that can be used in multiple forms and then modified once to cascade the change throughout the forms that use it. Once we've created the form we will create a web service that saves the loan-application data to a SQL Server database. Lastly, we'll link that web service to the form's submittal functionality.

The thin-client capabilities we need for this solution are exposed through SharePoint 2007 Forms Server, which is built on top of the WSS and ASP.NET 2.0 platform. During the development process, we will discuss how to debug and test the multi-tier functionality as well as deploy the finished solution to Office Forms Server 2007. We will deploy the form as a centrally managed form in MOSS 2007 under Central Admin ➤ Application Management ➤ Manage Form Templates. This will create a content type that we can use in a library to add, edit, and delete loan applications in that library. We will also create a custom ASP.NET 2.0 application under the root of the `portal.sample.com` web application to host the loan-application form. The application will consist of one ASPX page called `default.aspx` and will host a control (XMLFormViewer) that ships with Office Forms Server 2007 to display the forms in our application. This web page will access the centrally stored template and store the user's data in a SQL Server database using the web service. Finally, we will demonstrate the reusability of this form by hosting it inside a web part.

Solution Walkthrough

In this solution walkthrough we will discuss how to build, test, and deploy a three-tier InfoPath solution. The three tiers will consist of an InfoPath form exposed via the Web, a web service, and a SQL Server database. The walkthrough will cover the construction of four projects. The first is a simple InfoPath form project that contains a single form. The second project is the web service that calls a stored procedure in the SQL Server database. We will also add a new ASP.NET page to the root of the web application to host the form in a custom web page. Throughout the walkthrough we will discuss how we deal with the challenges of multi-tier data access and authentication, as well as the integration of managed code to extend the solution. The final project added to the solution will demonstrate how to build a custom web application that can host the web form, allowing us to take advantage of InfoPath's design-once toolset from within our own ASP.NET applications.

Understanding the Cross-Domain and Multi-Hop Problems

You need to think about two things when building forms that are deployed to the Web: server connections that cross domains, and the multi-hop problem. Let's look at the cross-domain issue first. A cross-domain connection request occurs when you make a request from one domain to another. For example, the form we are creating will live on `http://portal.sample.com` and the web service we are creating will live on `http://localhost`. When the web form makes the request to the web service, you want to make sure that the correct credentials are supplied, but you also want to make sure that that user is allowed to make a cross-domain request. InfoPath supplies the credentials automatically when you make a request to a web service from within the InfoPath client application. However, the form we are going to build will be web-enabled and when we debug it within Visual Studio, it will prompt us for permission before calling the web service. The real issue appears when you view the same form in a web browser. HTTP is a stateless protocol and doesn't have the ability to stop the form's execution automatically to prompt the user. To handle this and other security-related issues, InfoPath 2007 implements an enhanced administrative security model. The basic premise behind the model is that administrators need a more granular level of control over the forms that are deployed and the data sources those forms access at both the Web and site-collection level. The other driving factor is the introduction of web-enabled forms. To learn more about the administrative enhancements, you can review the InfoPath team's blog referenced in the "Further Reading" section at the end of this chapter.

In this chapter we will focus on two new concepts: a UDC data connection and the three new security modes that are imposed on web-enabled forms (restricted, full-trust, and domain). Restricted templates cannot be run on a server. Full-trust templates, however, have no restrictions and require administrator approval to run on the server. Our example and all templates containing managed code require full trust. Domain templates follow the Internet Explorer security model and, when executed, prompt you for permission before trying to make the cross-domain connection. You can control access to cross-domain connections at the administrator level and can even turn them off completely. You can also allow the administrator of the site collection or farm to control permission to data sources through the management of data connections contained in Universal Data Connection version 2 (UDC V2) files.

UDC files store the connection information for a data source in an XML file that lives in the SharePoint server's content database. Because the connection information lives outside the InfoPath 2007 template, you can do things like share connection settings between forms and change the connection settings of a form without modifying the form itself. This is a great tool to use when you have to migrate a form from a test to a production data source. The UDC files are managed using the Manage Data Connection File page in the Application Management section of the SharePoint Central Administration site or in a data connections library in a SharePoint site. The InfoPath template retrieves the connection settings at run time from the data-connections library using the URL for the root of the site collection where the form was opened. In our example we create a fully trusted form that requires administrator approval. Form templates that are not admin-approved and fully trusted require that all cross-domain connection settings be stored in a UDC file in a data-connections library. In our example we are going to create a UDC connection to the web service.

This is where the multi-hop problem comes into play. Most web applications in IIS rely on the NTLM protocol for authentication. NTLM authentication supports or trusts second-hand evidence about the identity of a user but cannot trust any handshake past that. When you load a form inside the InfoPath client application, the application has firsthand evidence of who you are. You logged onto your workstation and launched the application under that identity. As Figure 13-1 shows, the form can then make requests to data sources directly or through a web service, which would then have second-hand evidence of your identity with hops 1 and 2. A *hop* refers to the transfer of data between tiers—in this case the desktop, web server, and database. When a user accesses an InfoPath form from the Web, she launches a web browser

using the first-hand evidence then passes that evidence to the web form. The web form then tries to access the web service but can't because the chain of evidence is third-hand, as shown in Figure 13-1 in the hops from 3 to 4 to 2.

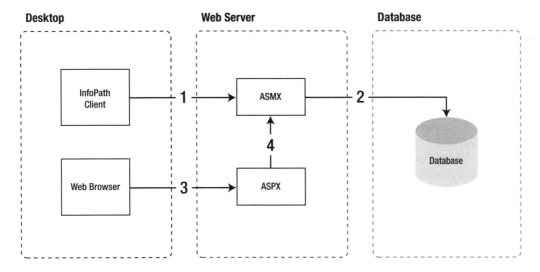

Figure 13-1. *An illustration of the multi-hop problem*

There are a number of ways of deal with the multi-hop problem in forms services, and if you've worked with multi-tier web applications in the past you should be familiar with much of what we will discuss in the following paragraphs. At each tier we will need to decide how we want to configure secure access. In Figure 13-1 we have three tiers: the web page, the web service, and the database. In a perfect world we would want to use Windows Integrated Security and Kerberos to pass credentials through all three tiers, but this isn't always possible—especially if the form needs to be accessed in an Internet scenario. We could also implement an Office Single Sign-on (SSO) infrastructure. The following is a list of the most common security architectures:

- Anonymous connections

- HTTP basic authentication

- Kerberos

- Office Single Sign-on

- Web service proxy

The first three in the list are probably the most common and are used regularly to secure access to .NET web applications and .NET web services. Anonymous connections allow you to basically turn off the authentication requirement. In our example we could set anonymous user access on for both the web form and web service, basically bypassing the problem at the third tier. When the web service makes the connection to the database, we would provide the connection string containing the user ID and password in inline code. This is definitely not the most secure way to do things, but is very useful during development.

HTTP basic authentication is slightly more secure and allows you to prompt the user for credentials when she makes a request to view the web form. The credentials are passed in clear text or digest form to the web server, usually over an SSL connection. The web server then has primary evidence of the user's identity so it can now pass that identity to the web service without breaking the NTLM evidence-chain rule. By default SharePoint uses Windows Integrated Security authentication, but you can set up IIS to use basic authentication. This is a fairly simple way to allow Internet access to web forms. You could also use the ASP.NET authentication-provider model to allow access in this scenario.

Kerberos authentication allows the delegation of credentials across multiple tiers, unlike NTLM, and is the preferred method for solving the three-tier problem. However, this works only for solutions that are deployed in a domain environment running a post-Win2K Windows version as its operating system and has replaced NTLM with Kerberos as its standard authentication protocol.

There are also two options available with SharePoint 2007 called Office Single Sign-on (SSO) and web service proxy. Single Sign-on allows system administrators to store username-password pairs in an encrypted data store as an SSO application definition. Applications running on the server can then make requests to the SSO service using the SSO application ID to retrieve the pairs to log on to Windows and make a trusted data connection to a data source. The web service proxy, when turned on, can forward the user's associated SharePoint identity to the web service. The username is passed in the SOAP header using WS-Security.

In our example we'll start by turning on anonymous access to the web service, and the database connection information will be stored in an ASP.NET config file during development. From there we will add a UDC file that contains the connection information to the web service. This will allow us to impersonate the user credentials required to access the web service, eliminating one of the evidence hops. The web service call will be made with second-hand evidence of the user's identity, allowing it to pass NTLM checks. The web service and the SQL Server database will be modified to use Windows Integrated Security authentication to accept that identity.

Note Our goal here is not to decide how to best secure access to a web form or a SQL Server database. Security architecture decisions are always a tradeoff based on many different factors. We are simply trying to demonstrate how you can use common-practice techniques to secure a web-enabled InfoPath 2007 forms solution.

Creating the InfoPath Solution

The Visual Studio solution we are going to create will contain three projects, the first of which is the InfoPath project. You create this project like you would any other: by opening Visual Studio and selecting the File ➤ New Project menu item. In the dialog that appears you should notice an Office node under the Visual Basic Language node. Expand that node and select the InfoPath Form Template option as shown in Figure 13-2.

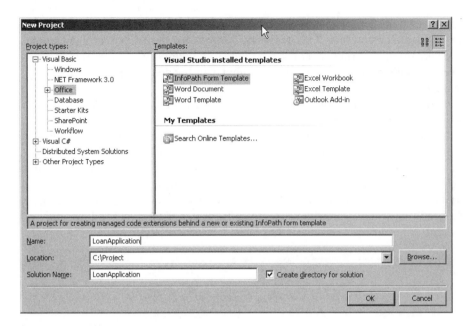

Figure 13-2. *Creating the InfoPath project*

Next you'll see a dialog named Design a Form Template; it asks you to select the data source for the template and whether you would like the template to be web-enabled. For our solution you are going to keep the default values (blank for the data source and yes for the web) and if you want to match the code in the download available from the Source Code/ Download section of http://apress.com, name the solution **LoanApplication**. You will also notice an option called Template Part. Template parts allow you to create reusable components that you can insert into multiple InfoPath forms. We are going to create a template part for the form header later in this section.

When the project opens in Visual Studio, you should see a solution named LoanApplication with an InfoPath project named LoanApplication. The InfoPath project should contain a number of files built automatically and visible in the Solution Explorer. The folder named InfoPath Form Template contains the InfoPath form itself (manifest.xsf), which should also be open in the visual designer; the schema for the project myschema.xsd; some sample data; and a sample view. The code-behind or managed code for the form is located in the InfoPath Form Code folder, which contains the formcode.vb file that we will be adding code to later.

Before we begin to build the form, let's create a template part for the form header. Template parts are new in InfoPath 2007 and can be used in multiple forms, giving us the ability to modify it once and have the changes cascade to any templates that reference it. You design template parts just as you would any other form; the only difference is that some of the form-design features are disabled. For example, you cannot have code associated with a template part, so if you were to construct a new template part project in Visual Studio, the programming menu would be disabled. If this part were used in multiple forms and we wanted to change it, we would simply modify the template part—not each individual form that uses the part. This is similar to how we used to use custom controls in InfoPath 2003 SP1. SP1 introduced custom controls; however, the controls had to be ActiveX controls and be safe for scripting and initialization. Template parts are much easier to create and even easier to use. Our template part contains only layout for the header; however, template parts can be much more complex, containing controls, schemas, rules, and calculations. We can create a template part in Visual Studio or by using the InfoPath client. Our header is going to contain only layout, so we will use the client.

To create the header template part, open InfoPath 2007. In the Getting Started dialog box that appears, select the Design a Form Template link. In the next dialog select the Template Part radio button. This dialog is identical to the one you saw when you created the InfoPath project in Visual Studio. You should then see two data-source options: blank and XML or Schema. Keep the default value blank and make sure the Enable Browser-Compatible Features check box is checked. The form we created earlier is web-enabled, which requires that any template part it uses also be available via the Web. The template part in this solution consists of a simple table and some text, which you can add in the designer. Figure 13-3 shows the header we created.

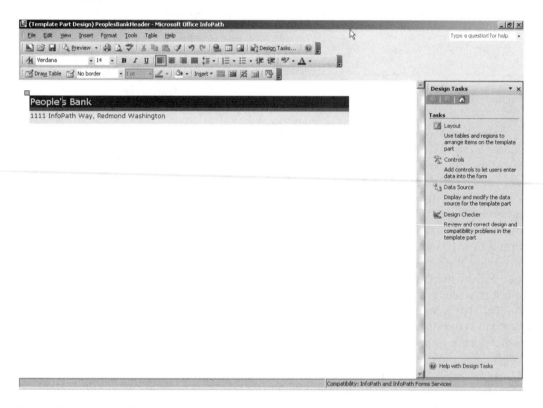

Figure 13-3. *Creating the InfoPath template part for the header*

A *template part* is a new type of InfoPath solution that has an .xtp extension instead of an .xsn extension when you save it. Once you have finished your header template part, save the template as an .xtp file.

To use the template part in our loan application, go back to your Visual Studio project and navigate to the designer for the form. Open the Visual Studio toolbox and right click anywhere in the General section. In the drop-down menu that appears, select Choose Items. In the dialog select the Add button. This will begin the Add Custom Control wizard. In the first step of the wizard, choose the Template Part radio button and then select the .xtp file you just created. The header template should now appear in the Visual Studio toolbox. To add the header to the LoanApplication project, drag the control onto the design surface in Visual Studio.

The form we are creating will collect information about the individual applying for a loan. First we need to define the data source for the data we are collecting. We could have started from an existing XML schema or database schema, but in this scenario we are going to create the data source at design time. To do this, navigate to the InfoPath designer in Visual Studio by selecting the manifest.xsf file in the Solution Explorer (if it's not already open). In the Solution Explorer's Design Tasks tab, select the Design Tasks tab and choose Data Source. In the Data Source tab use the following steps to create the data source for the form:

1. Right-click Myfield and rename the group **LoanApp**.

2. Right-click on LoanApp and select the Add Menu option in the dialog that appears.

3. Add SSN as a field element under LoanApp with a data type of String.

4. Follow these same steps to add the remaining fields, displayed in this list:

    FirstName—String

    LastName—String

    Street—String

    City—String

    State—String

    Zip—String

    Income—Decimal

    Loan Amt—Decimal

Once you have finished creating the data source, select the root node LoanApp and drag it just below the header template part on the form-designer surface. In the pop-up menu that appears, select the Controls in Layout option. Your form and solution should now look like Figure 13-4.

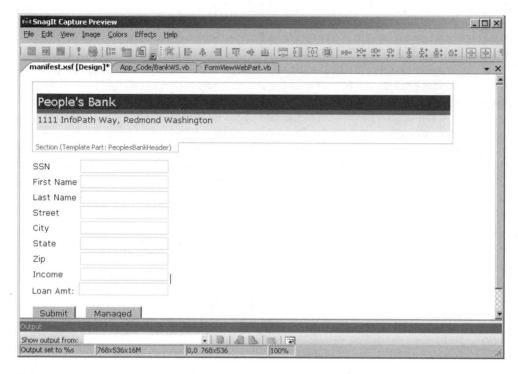

Figure 13-4. *The LoanApplication form with data sources*

Setting Up the Database—LoanData

For our LoanApplication form, we will use a SQL Server 2005 database named LoanData. This database stores the loan-application details for each loan application. The code download (available in the Source Code/Download section of http://apress.com) includes the database files, which you can attach to your development box by using SQL Server Management Studio. Figure 13-5 is a diagram of the database that shows the LoanApps table.

Figure 13-5. *Diagram of the LoanData database*

This database also includes a stored procedure. The InsertLoanApp stored procedure saves loan-application data to the LoanApps table. For this reason, the stored procedure accepts each of the LoanApps table's fields as parameters. Listing 13-1 details this procedure.

Listing 13-1. *The InsertLoanApp Stored Procedure*

```
CREATE PROCEDURE [dbo].[InsertLoanApp]
      @SSN [nvarchar](11) = null,
      @FirstName [nvarchar](50) = null,
      @LastName [nvarchar](50) = null,
      @Street [nvarchar](50) = null,
      @City [nvarchar](50) = null,
      @State [char] (2)= null,
      @Zip [nchar](50) = null,
      @Income [numeric]= 0
AS
BEGIN
SET NOCOUNT ON;

INSERT INTO [LoanData].[dbo].[LoanApps]
          ([SSN]
          ,[FirstName]
          ,[LastName]
          ,[Street]
          ,[City]
          ,[State]
          ,[Zip]
          ,[Income])
     VALUES
          (@SSN,
           @FirstName,
           @LastName
           @Street,
           @City,
           @State,
           @Zip,
           @Income)
END
```

To set up the database in your environment, copy the MDF and LDF files of the LoanData database to your SQL Server. If you did a default install, SQL Server 2005 will use the following path to store these database files: `C:\Program Files\Microsoft SQL Server\MSSQL.1\MSSQL\Data`. Once they are in place, right-click on the Databases node of the Management Studio's Object Explorer and select Attach. In the dialog, click Add and locate the `LoanData.mdf` file. The default options are fine. Click OK; the Object Explorer will refresh to include the LoanData database. If you need more help attaching databases in SQL Server 2005, use the following steps on MSDN:

- How to: Attach a Database (SQL Server Management Studio)

  http://msdn2.microsoft.com/en-us/library/ms190209.aspx

Creating the Web Service

To update the database we just attached, we will need to create a web service. We can create this ASP.NET web service as its own Visual Studio solution or add it to the solution with the other projects in this chapter. Here we'll add it to the solution by using the following steps:

1. From Visual Studio's File menu, select Add ➤ New Web Site.

2. Select the ASP.NET Web Service project template.

3. Make sure that the Location drop-down is set to HTTP and that Language is set to VB.NET.

4. Specify the URL as http://localhost/BankWS.

5. Click OK.

When you add the project to the solution, Visual Studio will add the default file Service.asmx to the project. It will also add a file named Service.vb in the App_Code directory. Delete both of these and add a new ASP.NET web-service item named BankWS.asmx. The corresponding code file in the App_Code folder will be added for you. The web service we are creating needs to be able to accept the XML data from a data connection in the InfoPath form. There are several ways we can accomplish this; a common way is to create a public class that mirrors the structure of the schema we are using in the LoanApplication InfoPath form and expose it as the input to our web service. The creation of the class can be automated using the Visual Studio's xsd.exe tool. To create the class, launch a VS.NET command prompt by navigating to Start ➤ All Programs ➤ Microsoft Visual Studio .Net 2005 ➤ Visual Studio .Net Tools ➤ Visual Studio .Net 2005 Command Prompt. From there navigate to the directory that stores the myschema.xsd file for the InfoPath solution. In our case this was the c:\Project\ LoanApplication\LoanApplication\Infopath\form template directory. The file that we need access to, myschema.xsd, will be locked if the InfoPath solution is loaded, so either unload the solution or copy myschema.xsd to another location. At the command prompt type the following: **xsd.exe myschema.xsd /classes /l:vb**. You should now have a class file named myschema.vb in that directory that contains a Loan class we'll use as the input parameter for the web service. Once you've created the class file, add it to the BankWS web service App_Code directory. Listing 13-2 details portions of the Loan class we just created. Many of the properties are too redundant to list completely.

Listing 13-2. *Loan Class*

```
Option Strict Off
Option Explicit On

Imports System.Xml.Serialization
```

```
'''<remarks/>
<System.CodeDom.Compiler.GeneratedCodeAttribute("xsd", "2.0.50727.42"), _
 System.SerializableAttribute(), _
 System.Diagnostics.DebuggerStepThroughAttribute(), _
 System.ComponentModel.DesignerCategoryAttribute("code"), _
 System.Xml.Serialization.XmlTypeAttribute(AnonymousType:=true), _
 System.Xml.Serialization.XmlRootAttribute([Namespace]:="http://~
schemas.microsoft.com/office/infopath/2003/myXSD/~
2007-01-21T17:56:39", IsNullable:=false)> _
Partial Public Class Loan
    Private sSNField As String
    Private firstNameField As String
    Private lastNameField As String
    Private streetField As String
    Private cityField As String
    Private stateField As String
    Private zipField As String
    Private incomeField As System.Nullable(Of Double)
    Private incomeFieldSpecified As Boolean
    Private loanAmtField As System.Nullable(Of Double)
    Private loanAmtFieldSpecified As Boolean
    Private anyAttrField() As System.Xml.XmlAttribute

    '''<remarks/>
    Public Property SSN() As String
        Get
            Return Me.sSNField
        End Get
        Set
            Me.sSNField = value
        End Set
    End Property

    '''<remarks/>
    Public Property FirstName() As String
        Get
            Return Me.firstNameField
        End Get
        Set
            Me.firstNameField = value
        End Set
    End Property

    '''<remarks/>
    Public Property LastName() As String
        Get
            Return Me.lastNameField
        End Get
```

```
        Set
            Me.lastNameField = value
        End Set
    End Property


    '… some properties removed; see code download for complete list


    '''<remarks/>
    <System.Xml.Serialization.XmlElementAttribute~
(IsNullable:=true)> _
    Public Property Income() As System.Nullable(Of Double)
        Get
            Return Me.incomeField
        End Get
        Set
            Me.incomeField = value
        End Set
    End Property


    '''<remarks/>
    <System.Xml.Serialization.XmlIgnoreAttribute()> _
    Public Property IncomeSpecified() As Boolean
        Get
            Return Me.incomeFieldSpecified
        End Get
        Set
            Me.incomeFieldSpecified = value
        End Set
    End Property


    '… some properties removed; see code download for complete list


    '''<remarks/>
    <System.Xml.Serialization.XmlAnyAttributeAttribute()> _
    Public Property AnyAttr() As System.Xml.XmlAttribute()
        Get
            Return Me.anyAttrField
        End Get
        Set
            Me.anyAttrField = value
        End Set
    End Property
End Class
```

The web service has a single public function named AddLoanApp that accepts our typed
Loan class. The method uses ADO.NET to create a connection to the database we created earlier and call a stored procedure with the values stored in the Loan class. To keep things simple
we have included the database connection string, which contains the user ID and password,

in the web configuration file. Listing 13-3 displays the code for the web service. We included only enough code in Listing 13-3 to show a few of the passed parameters; use the code download (available at http://apress.com) for a complete listing.

Listing 13-3. *The Web-Service Method for Inserting a Record into the LoanData Database*

```
<WebMethod()> _
Imports System.Web
Imports System.Web.Services
Imports System.Web.Services.Protocols
Imports System.Xml
Imports System.Data.Sql
Imports System.Data.SqlClient

<WebService(Namespace:="http://tempuri.org/")> _
<WebServiceBinding(ConformsTo:=WsiProfiles.BasicProfile1_1)> _
<Global.Microsoft.VisualBasic.CompilerServices.~
    DesignerGenerated()>

Public Class BankWS
    Inherits System.Web.Services.WebService

    <WebMethod()> Sub AddLoanApp(ByVal Loan As Loan)
        Dim retVal As Double
        Dim conn As SqlConnection = Nothing
        Try
            Dim config As System.Configuration.Configuration
            config = System.Web.Configuration.~
WebConfigurationManager.OpenWebConfiguration("/LoanWS")
            Dim connString As _ System.Configuration.ConnectionStringSettings
            connString = _config.ConnectionStrings.ConnectionStrings("LoanApp")

            conn = New SqlConnection(connString.~
                    ConnectionString)
            Dim cmd As SqlCommand = New SqlCommand()
            cmd.Connection = conn
            cmd.CommandType = Data.CommandType.~
                            StoredProcedure
            cmd.CommandText = "InsertLoanApp"

            Dim param1 As SqlParameter = New SqlParameter()
            param1.DbType = SqlDbType.VarChar
            param1.Direction = Data.ParameterDirection.Input
            param1.IsNullable = True
            param1.ParameterName = "@SSN"
            param1.Size = 50
            param1.Value = Loan.SSN
            cmd.Parameters.Add(param1)
```

```
        Dim param2 As SqlParameter = New SqlParameter()
        param2.DbType = SqlDbType.VarChar
        param2.Direction = Data.ParameterDirectin.Input
        param2.IsNullable = True
        param2.ParameterName = "@FirstName"
        param2.Size = 50
        param2.Value = Loan.FirstName
        cmd.Parameters.Add(param2)

        '… some parameters removed; see code download for complete list

        Dim param9 As SqlParameter = New SqlParameter()
        Param9.DbType = SqlDbType.Float
        Param9.Direction = Data.ParameterDirection.Input
        Param9.IsNullable = True
        Param9.ParameterName = "@LoanAmt"
        Param9.Value = Loan.LoanAmt
        cmd.Parameters.Add(param9)

        conn.Open()
        retVal = cmd.ExecuteScalar()
        conn.Close()

    Catch ex As Exception
        Throw (ex)
    Finally
        If (conn IsNot Nothing AndAlso conn.State <> Data.~
        ConnectionState.Closed) Then
            conn.Close()
        End If
    End Try
End Sub

End Class
```

You can view the web service by right-clicking on the BankWS.asmx file and selecting View in Browser. This will cause Visual Studio's local web server to run and a browser window will be opened to the web service. You can't really use this page to test the web service because complex type parameters are not supported in this view; also notice that the URL is a specific port off of localhost. Remember this port—we will need this information to set up the data connection to the web service in the InfoPath form. In a production environment the web service would be hosted on a production IIS web server and this port name would be specific to your server name. Since you can't use the Visual Studio autogenerated interface to test the web service, we have included a simple Windows form application called WSTestApp in the code download available on the Apress web site. You can use this Windows form to test the web service, including its connection to the stored procedure. Make sure to update the web reference in the WSTestApp to match the port in your development environment.

Connecting the Form to the Web Service

Creating a data connection to a web service in an InfoPath form is fairly straightforward; however, if the form is web-enabled you need to consider a few things before you deploy it to a Forms Server. Before we tackle that challenge, let's create the data connection to the web service in the Visual Studio development environment and test the form in the InfoPath client application. Connecting an InfoPath form to a web service in VS.NET does not follow the traditional procedures for adding a web reference. To connect the InfoPath Submit action follow these steps:

1. Open the `manifest.xsf` file in the Visual Studio Project Explorer.

2. From the form designer, open the toolbox and drag a button onto the design surface just below the fields we added earlier.

3. Click the button you just added; in the Button Properties dialog that appears, set the Action drop-down to Submit. The Submit Options button will appear. Press it to modify the Submit behavior.

4. In the Submit Options dialog that appears check the Allow Users to Submit this Form check box and in the Send Form to a Single Destination drop-down select Web Service.

5. To create the web-service connection select the Add button in the dialog to begin the Data Connection wizard.

6. In the Web Service Details dialog of the wizard, enter **http://localhost/BankWS/ BankWS.asmx?WSDL**, as shown in Figure 13-6. Then click Next. Your port may be different and is dependent on your web-server environment.

7. In the dialog that appears select the AddLoanApp operation and click Next.

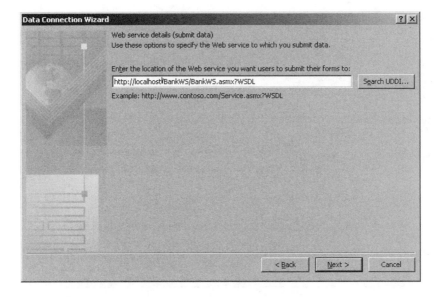

Figure 13-6. *The Data Connection Web Service Details dialog*

308 CHAPTER 13 ■ TAKING INFOPATH FORMS TO THE WEB

To set the parameters, select the button next to the Field or Group options; in the dialog that appears, highlight the Loan group, as in Figure 13-7.

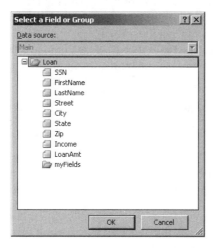

Figure 13-7. *Setting the parameters*

9. Keep the remaining defaults in the Data Connection dialog, as shown in Figure 13-8, and click Next.

10. Name the connection **WS Submit** and click Finish.

11. Click OK to save the connection and then choose Apply in the Button Properties dialog to save the properties for the button.

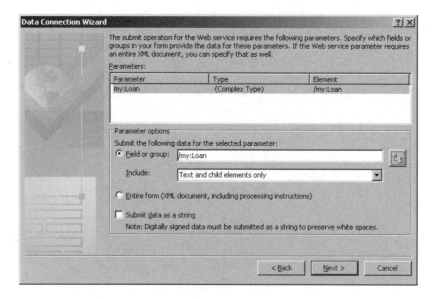

Figure 13-8. *Field or Group options selection*

We are now ready to test the connection to the web service in debug mode. Save the solution, then press F5 to begin debugging. We haven't added any managed code manually at this point, but we can run the form from within Visual Studio to test it prior to deploying it to the Office Forms Server. The form should appear within InfoPath, as shown in Figure 13-9 (the Managed button will be added later in this chapter).

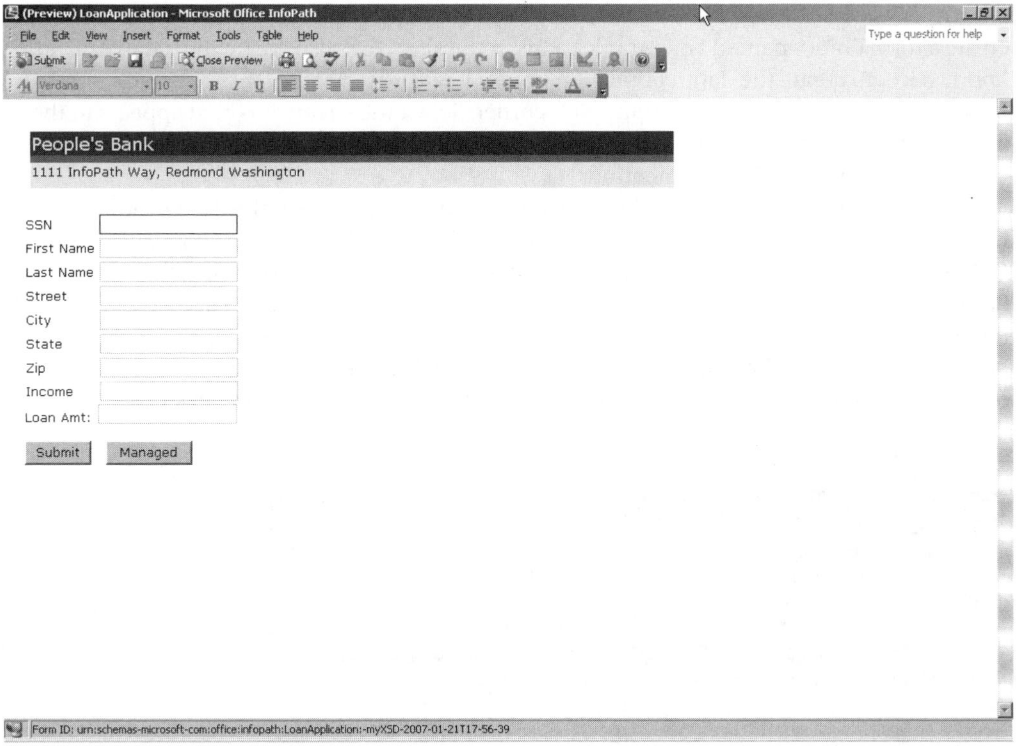

Figure 13-9. *The LoanApplication form in InfoPath*

The database is not configured with a primary key and requires only a Social Security number; enter some data and press the Submit button. The form will display a Microsoft InfoPath Security Notice asking you if you want to connect to the data source—in this case the web service. Select Yes; a second window should appear shortly to tell you that your submittal was successful.

The form in our example will be deployed to Office Forms Server. To achieve the same results seen in the InfoPath client, we need to check for web compatibility and configure a UDC connection on the server for the web service. We also need to enable cross-domain access for InfoPath Forms Services. To check for web compatibility open the manifest.xsf file and navigate to the Design Tasks tab in the Project Explorer. Next select the Design Checker and click Change Compatibility Settings. In the dialog that appears, enter the URL for the Office Forms Server in our example: http://portal.sample.com. Make sure the Browser Compatibility check box is checked. Click OK and then the Refresh button. Any compatibility issues that need to be resolved before the form can be published will appear in the dialog.

To enable cross-domain access go to SharePoint Central Admin and switch to the Application Management tab. Underneath InfoPath Forms Services choose Configure InfoPath Forms Services and check Allow Cross Domain Access for User Templates. To create the UDC connection we need to create a data-connection library in a site collection. When we deploy the form to the Forms Server it will use this connection information to talk to the web service.

To demonstrate the use of the form in SharePoint 2007 we also need to create a form library. This example uses the web site called http://portal.sample.com. To test our form we'll create a form library named LoanApplications in the site. We'll also create the data-connection library here. To create the data-connection library navigate to http://portal.sample.com and select the Documents link in the upper-left corner. Select the Create link that appears in the upper-right corner of the page. Select the Data Connection Library option under Libraries and name the library **BankDataConnections**.

To create the data connection in the form we need to navigate to the design view of the LoanApplication form and click the Submit button. In the dialog that appears, select Submit Options and then click Manage on the WS Submit data connection. Next click the Convert button and enter the URL http://portal.sample.com/bankdataconnections/LoanApp.udcx in the URL field, as shown in Figure 13-10. Click OK, keeping the Relative to Site Collection option checked. Save the changes and exit out of the submit button settings. If you navigate back to the library, you'll see this data connection was saved there. We are now ready to publish the form.

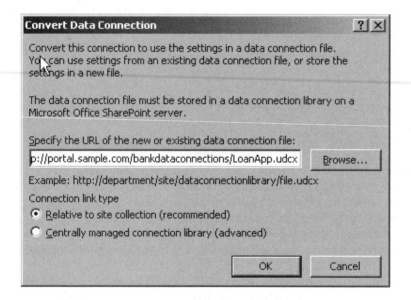

Figure 13-10. *Entering the data-connection library's URL*

Deploying the Template to Office Forms Server

Publishing a form to Office Forms Server involves a number of steps. You must first publish the InfoPath template to a SharePoint library using the Publish option in Visual Studio's Solution Explorer. In the "Debugging and Testing Managed Code in Visual Studio" section later in this chapter we'll add managed code to our form, meaning it can be deployed only as a fully trusted form and must be approved by an administrator. Because it must be approved by an administrator, you have to upload the form using the SharePoint Central Administration page and then activate it to a site collection. Once it's activated it creates a new content type for the template automatically. To use the form, we will create a form library that allows multiple content types, and we'll specify the LoanApplication as the default content type. When we create a new document, the template will be rendered in the browser. The detailed steps to accomplish this are provided in the following sections.

Publishing the InfoPath Template

1. Right-click the form project in the VS.NET Solution Explorer. In the pop-up menu that appears, select Publish.

2. In the dialog that appears, select the To a SharePoint Server with InfoPath Forms Server radio button and click Next.

3. Select the LoanApplication forms project in the Visual Studio Project Explorer and right-click, selecting the Publish menu option.

4. Enter the `http://portal.sample.com` as the URL and click Next.

5. Check the Enable This Form to Be Filled Out by Using a Browser check box and click Next. (If the check box is grayed out make sure you have enabled enterprise features on all web sites in the site collection.)

6. Enter the file location where you would like to save the template that's ready to be uploaded to SharePoint.

Uploading the Template to Office Forms Server

1. Launch the SharePoint Central Admin page and select the Application Management tab.

2. From the InfoPath Forms Services section select the Manage Form Templates link and click Upload Form Template.

3. Click the Browse button and navigate to the file location where you published the form.

4. Highlight the form and click Open and then Upload.

5. If the template loads successfully a page will notify you that it has been uploaded successfully.

6. Navigate back to the Manage Form Templates page, select the uploaded template and select Activate to Site Collection.

7. In the page that displays select the `http:portal.sample.com` web and root site collection and click OK.

8. Once the activation has completed you can create the form library and associate the content type created for the template to that site.

Associating the Template with a Form Library

1. Navigate to `http://portal.sample.com` and select the Create button to create a new forms library.

2. Under the Libraries category select Form and name the library **Loan Applications**.

3. From the Settings button, choose the Form Library Settings and then select the Advanced Settings.

4. Select Yes for the Allow Management of Content Types option and click OK.

5. Under the Content Types options click Add from Existing Site Content Types and select Loan Application. Click OK.

6. This should return you to the Form Library Settings page. Select the Advanced Settings. In the Browser Enabled Document Settings dialog (Figure 13-11) select the Display as a Web Page radio button. If you have InfoPath installed on the client, this will force the form to display in a browser instead of the InfoPath client so that we can test the form in a web browser.

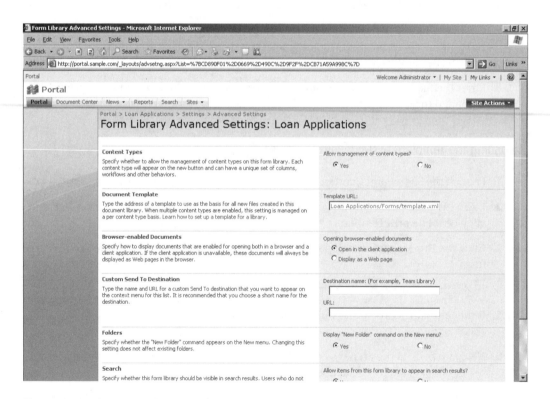

Figure 13-11. *The Form Library browser-enabled configuration*

Debugging and Testing Managed Code in Visual Studio

Before we can debug our template we must add some managed code to the form. We'll add a second button to our example's form to execute some VB.NET code. The code in this example demonstrates how to talk to objects on the form. To add the button to the form, open the LoanApplication form solution in Visual Studio and then open the InfoPath template designer for the form. From the toolbox drag and drop a new button onto the design surface next to the Submit button we added earlier, and then double-click on the new button. In the dialog that appears, change the label to **Managed** and the name to **btnManaged** and then select the Edit Code button. You should now be in the code-behind `FormCode.vb` for the LoanApplication InfoPath template. Clicking the Edit Code button created a new event handler for a subroutine, named btn_Managed_Clicked. Listing 13-14 shows the code we will add to this subroutine.

Listing 13-4. *Managed Code*

```vb
Imports Microsoft.Office.InfoPath
Imports System
Imports System.Xml
Imports System.Xml.XPath

Namespace LoanApplication
    Public Class FormCode
        Private Sub InternalStartup(ByVal sender As Object, ByVal e As EventArgs)_
 Handles Me.Startup
            AddHandler EventManager.XmlEvents("/my:Loan/my:myFields").~
            Changed, AddressOf myFields_Changed
            AddHandler DirectCast(EventManager.ControlEvents~
            ("btn_Managed"), ButtonEvent).Clicked, AddressOf _
            btn_Managed_Clicked
        End Sub

        Public Sub myFields_Changed(ByVal sender As Object, _
ByVal e As XmlEventArgs)
            ' Write your code here to change the main data source.
        End Sub

        Public Sub btn_Managed_Clicked(ByVal sender As Object, _
ByVal e As ClickedEventArgs)
            Dim root, user As System.Xml.XPath.XPathNavigator
            root = Me.MainDataSource.CreateNavigator
            user = root.SelectSingleNode("/my:Loan/my:FirstName", _
                Me.NamespaceManager)
            user.SetValue("Hi Susie")

        End Sub
    End Class
End Namespaced
```

Visual Studio generates most of the code automatically for you. The code in the subroutine btn_Managed_Clicked creates an instance of XPathNavigator and assigns the data source to the object. From there we find the FirstName field in the form and write some text to it to demonstrate how to communicate with the objects on the form from within the code. To deploy the form we follow the same steps we did previously by publishing the form to a file location and then uploading it to the Office Forms Server using the SharePoint Central Administration Site. To upload an update to the form, simply select the Upload button on the Managed Form Templates page of Application Management. The form will automatically upload and reactivate itself in the site collection. You have the option when redeploying to specify whether you want users currently in the form to be able to finish with that form before the new form is used, or whether you want the current form-filling sessions to be terminated automatically.

Once you have uploaded the form, navigate to the Loan Applications form library we created earlier and select the Loan Application menu option from the New menu. The form should appear in the web browser with the new Managed button. To debug the form, we need to attach the Visual Studio debugger to the w3wp.exe process that corresponds to the web application and set a breakpoint in the code-behind for the button. To attach Visual Studio to a worker process, you first need to discover which IIS worker process corresponds to the portal.sample.com SharePoint web application we are using to host this form. In your environment, you may have more than one IIS worker process. This is especially true if you have deployed SharePoint's Shared Service Provider to a dedicated web application or if you simply have other IIS web sites on the machine.

For help selecting the right worker process, run the following command from a command prompt: c:\windows\system32\iisapp.vbs. This script will list the process IDs (PIDs) and App-PoolIds for the IIS worker processes. The AppPoolId should help you determine which worker process is your MOSS web application; the corresponding PID is displayed in Visual Studio's Attach to Process dialog. With the process ID, you can then use Visual Studio's Attach to Process command and connect to the appropriate IIS worker process. To do this open the LoanApplication project and select Debug ➤ Attach to Process. In the dialog that appears, select the w3wp.exe process and click Attach. The Attach to Process dialog is displayed in Figure 13-12.

Then double-click the Managed button and select Edit Code. To set the breakpoint, press F9 on any line of code in the event handler. You are now ready to debug the form. Navigate back to the web browser and click the Managed button in the web form. You should now be in the debugger, stepping through the code just as you would any other .NET web-based application.

Integrating Security and SSO

Earlier in the chapter we discussed the multi-hop problem and how we would solve the security issues associated with multi-tier access. Up to this point our solution has used Windows Integrated Security to access the InfoPath form and anonymous access at the web service tier that used the database connection configuration information stored in the ASP.NET config file to access the stored procedure. In a production environment you would want to lock down the security even more. There are several ways to do this, but we'll discuss only three.

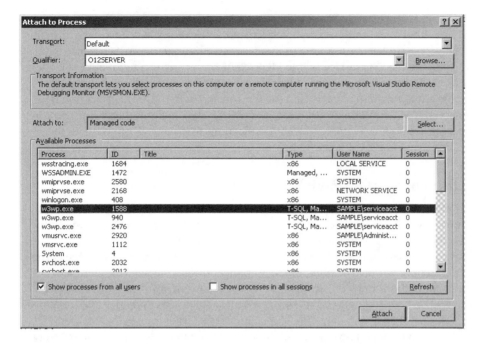

Figure 13-12. *Attaching Visual Studio to the w3wp.exe worker processes*

Let's start at the database tier. To guarantee that only authorized users that have rights to add loan applications and to take advantage of connection pooling, we created a single Windows user named LoanApp that represents all users that have the right to add a loan application to the database. We then gave that user access to the database and execute rights on the stored procedure in SQL Server 2005. In the web service we removed the code that pulled the connection information from the config file and set the connection string to use Windows Integrated Security. We then restricted access to the BankWS.asmx page so that only users who have the security context of the LoanApp user can access the web service. When the web service opens the connection, it will employ the LoanApp user to gain access to the database.

The web-form tier is quite flexible when it comes to the number of ways you can secure it. You could use ASP.NET 2.0's forms authentication to allow users to authenticate using a non-domain identity and then impersonate the LoanApp users for calls to the web service. You can also modify the UDC XML data connection and add the code in Listing 13-5 to it to simulate the impersonation of the LoanApp user. Be careful to remove this when moving into production, as the UDC file is stored in plain text.

Listing 13-5. *Authentication Code Block for a UDC File*

```
<udc:Authentication>
        <udc:UseExplicit CredentialType="NTLM">
                <udc:UserId>myusername</udc:UserId>
                <udc:Password>mypassword</udc:Password>
        </udc:UseExplicit>
</udc:Authentication>
```

SharePoint's Enterprise Single Sign-on Service is also an option. When you created the UDC connection, InfoPath automatically created an authentication block inside the XML file, similar to what you see in Listing 13-5 except that it's preconfigured to use SSO. To use SSO you need to configure the SSO service on the MOSS 2007 server and create a new application that has the user_id/password pair required for the web form. Additionally, you'll need to uncomment the authentication block within the file and add both the SSO application ID and the CredentialType. The configuration of SSO in MOSS 2007 requires many configuration steps. Please refer to InfoPath Team Blog: Data Connections in Browser Forms URL in the "Further Reading" section for guidance.

Hosting the Form in ASP.NET

Up to this point you've built an InfoPath 2007 form, deployed it to a Office Forms Server, and used the form to save data to a SQL database and to create documents in a SharePoint library. Everything we have done up to this point, from the end user's perspective, has been in the context of SharePoint 2007 or WSS 3.0. But what if we want to take advantage of Office Forms Server capabilities from within a custom ASP.NET application? Do we need to reference the template from within the context of a form library? Absolutely not. InfoPath Forms Services ships with an ASP.NET control named XmlFormViewer that allows us to render an InfoPath 2007 from inside an ASP.NET web page. Take for example the form we just created, Loan Application.xsn. We developed this form and then deployed it to the Forms Server as a fully trusted template requiring administrator approval because it contained managed code. We then approved the form and activated it to the portal.sample.com site collection, which created a content type that we attached to a form library. However, we can access this same template from within the XmlFormViewer ASP.NET control in a custom ASP.NET web page. To accomplish this the ASP.NET page that contains the control must live in the same web application as the deployed InfoPath form. In our example that means it must live off the root of http://portal.sample.com. The easiest way to do this is to open the Internet Information Services (IIS) manager and determine the actual file location of the portal.sample.com site. From there you can open the site inside Visual Studio and add a new page that will host the control. This control uses the template's URL to render it at run time. In our example the URL is http://portal.sample.com/formservertemplates/Loan%20Application.xsn.

To build an ASP.NET 2.0 page that contains the form, follow these steps:

1. Open the IIS manager and navigate to the server where you have installed SharePoint 2007 (in our case, O12Server).

2. Navigate to the Web Sites folder under that sever and find the site for your web application, as shown in Figure 13-13.

3. Copy the file location to the clipboard.

4. Open the LoanApplication Visual Studio .NET solution, right-click on the solution, and select Add Existing Web Site from the Add drop-down menu.

5. In the dialog that appears copy the file location from the clipboard, minus the web.config at the end, as displayed in Figure 13-14.

6. In the Project Explorer for the site, add a folder called **ViewLoanApp**.

7. Right-click on that folder and add a new web form called ViewLoanApp.aspx.

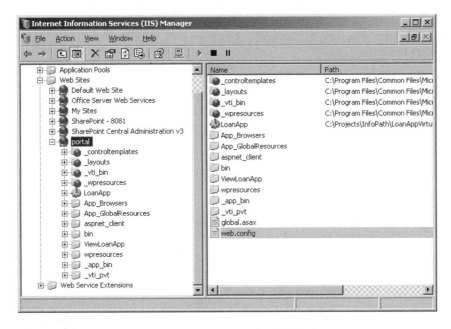

Figure 13-13. *Locating the SharePoint 2007 web-application root*

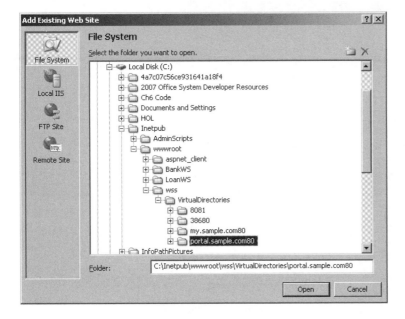

Figure 13-14. *File location of portal.sample.com*

Next we need to add the XMLFormViewer ASP.NET control to the Visual Studio.NET tool-box, drag and drop it onto the design surface, and then set the URL to the `Loan Application.xsn` InfoPath template:

1. From the Visual Studio.NET designer, navigate to the toolbox's General section, right-click, and select Choose Items. In the dialog that appears, browse to `c:\Program Files\ Microsoft Office Servers\12.0\Bin` and select `Microsoft.Office.InfoPath.Server. dll`. This will add the XMLFormViewer control to the toolbox.

2. Drag and drop the XMLFormViewer control onto the ASP.NET design surface.

3. Set the property XsnLocation property for the control to `http://portal.sample.com/ formservertemplates/Loan%20Application.xsn`.

4. Open Internet Explorer and browse to `http://portal.sample.com/ViewLoanApp/ viewloanapp.aspx`.

The form should now appear like Figure 13-15 in the browser.

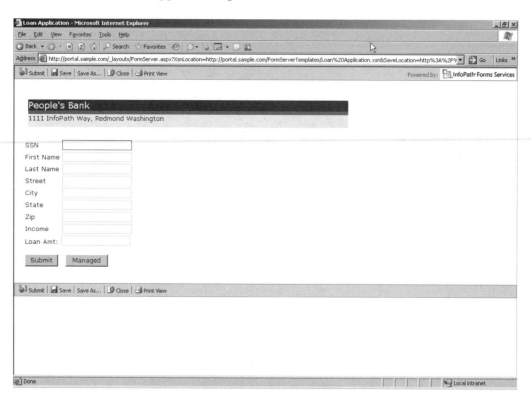

Figure 13-15. *Custom ASP.NET page displaying the InfoPath form*

■**Note** Notice the default header and footer on the rendered InfoPath form. You can turn one or both of these off by setting properties in the XMLFormViewer control. You can also customize the look and feel of the form by including the control with other ASP.NET controls and custom-formatting them just as you would in a typical custom ASP application. For example, you could easily add an additional control to the page to read the contents of a WSS 3.0 library.

Web-Part Hosting

If we can host InfoPath forms inside an ASP.NET custom web page, the obvious next question is whether we can also host them inside a web part. Probably the most interesting part about solving this problem is that the XMLFormViewer control we used in the web page is actually a web part. However, it is not one you would want to register as a safe control and simply drag into a SharePoint zone. This is because it really wants to be on a page by itself and not one of many on the SharePoint site. To make it behave in a web-part zone of a SharePoint page as well as to add support for web-part connections, we wrapped it in a custom web part. (For more information about creating your own web parts, see Chapter 10.) Listing 13-6 presents the code for the XMLFormViewer wrapper.

Listing 13-6. *FormView Web Part for InfoPath Forms*

```
Imports System.Web.UI.WebControls.WebParts
Imports System.Web.UI.WebControls
Imports Microsoft.SharePoint
Imports Microsoft.SharePoint.WebControls
Imports Microsoft.Office.InfoPath.Server.Controls
Imports System.Xml

Public Class FormViewWebPart
    Inherits System.Web.UI.WebControls.WebParts.WebPart

    Const defaultXmlLocation = ""

    Private m_xmlLocation As String = defaultXmlLocation
    Private WithEvents m_xmlFormView As XmlFormView
    Private m_errorMessage As String = String.Empty


    <WebBrowsable(), Personalizable(PersonalizationScope.User), _
WebDisplayName("XMLLocation"), WebDescription("URL of web-enabled ~
InfoPath form")> _
    Public Property XMLLocation() As String
        Get
            Return m_xmlLocation
        End Get
```

```vbnet
            Set(ByVal value As String)
                m_xmlLocation = value
            End Set
        End Property



    Protected Overrides Sub RenderContents(ByVal writer As System.Web.~
UI.HtmlTextWriter)
        Me.EnsureChildControls()

        If m_errorMessage <> String.Empty Then
            writer.Write(m_errorMessage)
        Else
            If (Me.m_xmlLocation.Length > 0) Then
                m_xmlFormView.XmlLocation = m_xmlLocation
                m_xmlFormView.DataBind()
                m_xmlFormView.Visible = True
            End If

            MyBase.RenderContents(writer)
        End If
    End Sub

    Protected Overrides Sub CreateChildControls()
        MyBase.CreateChildControls()
        m_xmlFormView = New XmlFormView()
        m_xmlFormView.Visible = False
        Me.Controls.Add(Me.m_xmlFormView)
        m_xmlFormView.EditingStatus = XmlFormView.EditingState.Editing

    End Sub

    <ConnectionConsumer("XMLLocation")> _
    Public Sub GetConnectionInterface(ByVal providerPart As IWebPartField)
        Dim callback As FieldCallback = New FieldCallback(AddressOf Me.~
                                    ReceiveField)
        providerPart.GetFieldValue(callback)
    End Sub

    Public Sub ReceiveField(ByVal field As Object)
        Me.EnsureChildControls()
        If (field IsNot Nothing) Then
            Me.m_xmlLocation = CType(field, String)
        End If

    End Sub

End Class
```

The web part we created is a consumer and expects to receive the location of the InfoPath XML file from another source. The web part is strongly named and signed so that it can be installed in the GAC. Install the web part by registering it in the GAC or by coping it into the bin directory of your web application (http:\\inetpub\wws\VirtualDirectories\portal. sample.com80\bin). Register it as a safe control in the web.config file. Then go to the Site Collections Web Part Gallery and add the web part. To place the web part on a page, go to the AllItems page of the form library itself. Then connect the web part to the web part that lists all of the form instances. As the connection is established, specify the binding to be on the Document URL column. Now you'll be able to preview each form instance on the same page as the list of form instances, as shown in Figure 13-16.

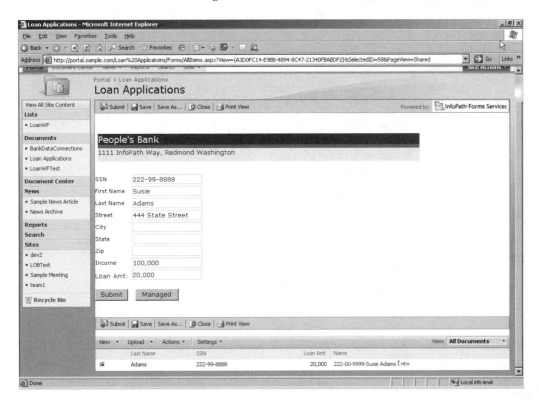

Figure 13-16. *Using the FormViewer web part with the list of form instances*

Extension Points

While coding this example we thought of two variations to the solution that we didn't incorporate because they distracted from the overall objective of the solution. We call them out now as extension points since they may be applicable to a specific project you are working on.

Use ASP.NET 2.0's forms authentication provider: Because Office Forms Server sits on top of ASP.NET 2.0, you can easily use ASP.NET 2.0's forms-based authentication provider or substitute your own authentication provider.

Rendering the form in a custom ASP.NET page: Our custom ASP.NET page was very simplistic. Events that are fired by the XMLFormViewer control can be trapped, allowing you to read and write data bi-directionally between the form and the web page.

Further Reading

The following links are to resources a reader interested in this chapter's material will find useful:

- Developing Solutions with Microsoft InfoPath

  http://msdn.microsoft.com/library/default.asp?url=/library/en-us/~
  odc_ip2003_bk/html/officeinfopathdevelopingsolutionsch7.asp

- InfoPath Team Blog: Data Connections in Browser Forms

  http://blogs.msdn.com/infopath/archive/2006/10/02/~
  Data-Connections-in-Browser-Forms.aspx

- Write Custom WebParts for SharePoint 2007

  http://www.codeguru.com/csharp/.net/net_asp/webforms/article.php/c12293/

- Writing Custom Webparts for SharePoint 2007

  http://blah.winsmarts.com/2006/05/14/writing-custom-webparts-for-
  sharepoint-2007.aspx

CHAPTER 14

■ ■ ■

Incorporating Workflow into Forms Processing

In the previous chapter we discussed how InfoPath 2007 and SharePoint Forms Server 2007 allow developers to quickly create enterprise forms solutions that can be deployed to a user desktop and to the Web, giving information workers the ability to work both online and offline as well as in a thin-client setting. In this chapter we are going to build on that concept by introducing the ability to automate the business processes that these solutions typically feed. When we think of business-process automation we usually associate it with some type of workflow. There are three basic types of workflow: application-oriented or structured, human-oriented or ad-hoc, and those that span both. Historically Microsoft has had a somewhat disjointed workflow story with several different implementations in several different products, many of which overlapped; this made it difficult for developers to choose the right technology for the task at hand. Take for example the workflow capabilities exposed in Exchange 2003 and those in BizTalk Server. Exchange gives power users the ability to construct ad-hoc email-based workflow. BizTalk Server provides the ability for developers to construct highly scalable, declarative, rules-based workflow and introduces a framework for developing human-oriented workflow—called Human Workflow Services (HWS). To solve this problem Microsoft developed a workflow platform called Windows Workflow Foundation (WF). Built on the .NET Framework 3.0 (WinFX) namespace, it provides a workflow engine and a Visual Studio .NET visual designer that for the first time gives developers a common programming model, engine, and set of tools to build workflow applications of any type in a consistent manner on the Windows platform. The release of WF also provides a common platform for Microsoft to build its own products on—for example, Microsoft Office 2007 now has support for WF workflows in its clients and Microsoft Office SharePoint Server 2007 ships with several standard workflows.

In the previous chapter we discussed how InfoPath and Forms Server combine to provide a compelling electronic forms strategy. Using this approach, an organization can move its paper forms to the Web and integrate its line-of-business (LOB) applications. This type of solution is very effective at getting data into an enterprise application; however, the problem is more complicated. The InfoPath solution did not account for any process other than the input of the form's data. In most offices, complementary processes exist before the data ever touches a line-of-business application. These processes could include a required series of approvals or a need to capture additional information from other users before continuing. The processes are often ad-hoc and human-oriented—there is not necessarily a prescribed, fixed set of steps. Today most of this activity may take place through email or by passing a paper form around. In this chapter we will detail how, as a developer, you can construct a solution that incorporates SharePoint's workflow capabilities into an organization's forms-processing strategy.

Real-World Examples

There are many scenarios that benefit from the combination of forms and workflow. We mentioned an expense report in the previous chapter. Most expense reports are filled out by the employee and then submitted for approval to one or more supervisors. The approval route may be different based on the type or the amount of the expense. Once approved, the expense information updates a back-end ERP application and other LOB systems, resulting in payment to the employee. The selection of line-of-business applications to update may also depend on data in the form. Another popular example of forms-based workflow is incident-management systems. When an incident or event is observed, a form is completed. That form's data is then routed to different individuals or organizations and eventually reaches a state where it is ready to be captured in a LOB system. Like the forms solutions that typically feed these types of processes, these workflows are usually custom-built for each unique process and require a significant amount of time to develop and maintain. But not all workflows are this complicated; there are simple office workflows that occur during a typical workday—for example, the sign-off by a supervisor on a purchase order. Wouldn't it be nice if the information worker could attach an approval workflow to this type of common office document? Now that there is a common framework in place, this is possible.

The Windows Workflow Foundation (WF) architecture provides a framework and set of building-block services that can be used by a WF engine to execute the workflow. The workflow engine consists of an implementation of each of these services and a host container application. WF ships with an ASP.NET host and a base set of services, and developers have the ability to create their own. Microsoft Office SharePoint Server 2007 also provides a WF host and its own implementation of the WF services. Office 2007 provides a layer of abstraction on top of SharePoint's WF implementation, allowing client applications like Microsoft Word and Excel to leverage these services so that information workers can easily integrate workflow into their daily activities without having to write custom code. Users can utilize the standard workflow templates that ship with SharePoint or build customized workflows using the SharePoint Designer. The SharePoint Designer provides an intuitive user interface for nondevelopers to construct simple workflows from a predefined set of SharePoint WF actions and does not allow you to add any custom .NET code. In this chapter we will use Visual Studio .NET to construct a SharePoint workflow that requires custom code. The workflow will route form data created with an InfoPath form to a user for approval.

Solution Overview

In this chapter you'll learn to build a SharePoint workflow that automates a human-oriented approval process. We will automate the approval process that a loan application might have to go through before it is accepted by a bank. The Forms Server solution from Chapter 13 consisted of an InfoPath web-enabled form that allowed users to submit the application data to a web service that updated a SQL database. In the real world you might want to execute some type of business process to automate the steps required to approve the loan application prior to storing the data in the database. We will not build on the solution in Chapter 13, but we will use the same database and web service that we used there. You can easily add a workflow to Chapter 13's solution, but for the purposes of this chapter we are going to create and use a stand-alone InfoPath test form to begin the workflow. Figure 14-1 displays the simple approval workflow we are going to create.

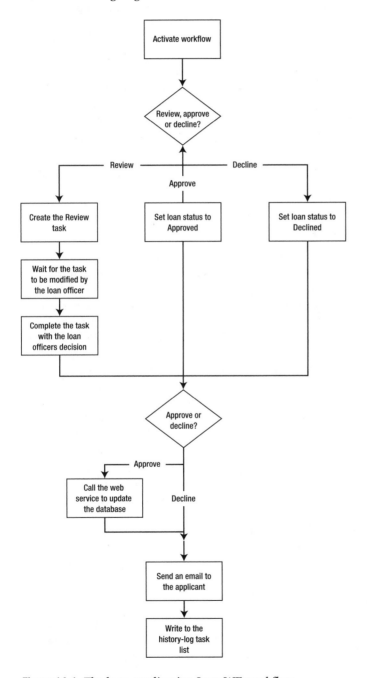

Figure 14-1. *The loan application LoanWF workflow*

The workflow begins by reading four properties that have been promoted by the InfoPath form when the form is published: LastName, FirstName, LoanAmt, and Income. If the loan amount is greater than one million dollars or the income ratio (income to loan amount) is less than .3 and greater than .2 then it must be approved by a loan officer. The workflow will create a new task in a SharePoint task list for the loan officer. Creating the task will automatically email the loan officer a link to the task. The loan officer can either click that link or go directly to the task list to review it. A custom task form for the approval task will allow the loan officer to view the loan-application data and then either approve or reject the application when he reviews the task. If the loan application is approved it will continue through the workflow, calling the web service to insert a record into a SQL Server database. The last two steps in the workflow send a confirmation or rejection email to the applicant and log the current status of the workflow to a history list that tracks milestones throughout the workflow process.

A loan application can also be approved or rejected without human intervention. If the ratio of loan amount to income is above .3 or the loan amount is less than one million dollars then the loan is automatically approved. If neither of those conditions is meet, the loan is automatically rejected. In these cases the workflow follows the same process for approval and rejection, sending an email to the applicant to notify him in either case.

Solution Walkthrough

In this section we will discuss how to build, test, and deploy a SharePoint sequential workflow that automates an approval process. The process begins by saving an instance of an InfoPath form to a SharePoint forms library, so the first thing we'll do is create a new InfoPath test form and publish it to a SharePoint forms library. This form will allow us to create new instances of a loan application to start the workflow. Then we will create the workflow VS.NET project called LoanWP using the Windows Workflow SharePoint Sequential Workflow project template. This template is available to you when you install the Windows Workflow Visual Studio.NET add-in and the Enterprise Content Management (ECM) starter kit which is included in the MOSS SDK. We will also create a custom task form. You can create custom task forms using InfoPath or ASP.NET; we are going to use InfoPath. The loan officer will use our form to view the SharePoint task that's created when a loan application requires approval. The form is very simple and contains four fields (LastName, SSN, LoanAmt, and Income) and two buttons (Approve and Reject). To associate the form with the workflow we will modify a few of the configuration files that the project template creates automatically. Once we have completed the workflow development we will publish the solution as a SharePoint feature and activate it. After the workflow feature is activated in the site collection we will configure a forms library to execute the workflow when a new document is added.

Throughout this walkthrough we will discuss the challenges of automating business processes using SharePoint's workflow capabilities and best practices for configuring SharePoint 2007 workflows.

Understanding Workflow in SharePoint

SharePoint's workflow capabilities are built on top of the Windows Workflow Foundation and the tools it provides in the Visual Studio.NET add-in and the ECM starter kit. This ECM starter kit allows developers to visually construct workflows from predefined activities developed specifically for SharePoint on the WF platform. You can author WF workflows using the VS.NET graphical tool, which generates XOML, custom code, or a combination of both. For the purposes of this chapter we are going to focus on using the graphical designer in Visual Studio .NET. The designer is installed with the WF add-in for Visual Studio. The SharePoint-specific activities are added when you install the ECM starter kit.

Before you begin building a workflow solution you need to understand some basics about WF and how SharePoint has implemented it. Let's begin with the basics of WF. WF consists of a framework, a runtime engine, and set of service components that must run within a host application. (WF provides the runtime engine and the developer must provide the host application for it to run in.) The runtime can be hosted in any .NET process and WF ships with an ASP.NET host example. The runtime services run in the host application and provide help to the runtime engine. SharePoint provides a custom host implementation that was designed for human-oriented office workflows. (Figure 14-2 shows a diagram of SharePoint's WF architecture.) SharePoint's host is part of Windows SharePoint Services 3.0 (WSS v3) and provides custom implementations of transaction, persistence, notification, messaging, tracking, and role services for workflows that run in its context.

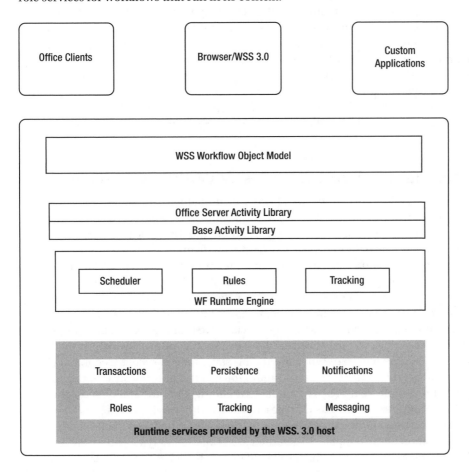

Figure 14-2. *WF SharePoint architecture*

A workflow is a container that consists of a group of activities. Activities are units of work that accomplish some action. Windows Workflow Foundation ships with a base activity library that is visible in the Tools menu in Visual Studio .NET, and you can also construct your own. Not all of the activities that ship with WF are available to SharePoint workflows; however, the ECM toolkit provides activities that are specific to SharePoint. Activities are then organized to form a workflow, which is referred to as a *schedule*. When a workflow runs, the WF runtime engine executes these activities in the host container. WF supports two workflow styles— sequential and state-machine—and workflow schedules can consist of any combination of the two. Sequential workflows execute the activities in some predefined sequence and are best suited for structured workflows. State-machine workflows are very ad-hoc and execute the activities based on the particular state of an activity as they are executed.

WSS v3 provides workflow capabilities through an implementation of a WF host container. To better understand exactly what services the host container provides, let's look at what the runtime engine and runtime services provide. The WF runtime engine manages workflow execution and allows workflows to remain active for long periods of time. Runtime services provide core services like transaction management and persistence to the runtime engine. When you author a WSS 3.0 workflow, WSS is the host for the workflow. So the runtime provides the core set of services that every workflow traditionally needs: sequencing, state management, tracking, and transaction support. It also serves as the state machine responsible for loading and unloading workflow templates and managing the state of all running workflow instances. The WSS 3.0 host replaces the pluggable services that are included with WF with its own implementation of them. The services provided include transactions, persistence, notifications, roles, tracking, and messaging (as Figure 14-2 shows). The WSS 3.0 implementation also exposes the functionality of WF and the runtime engine through the WSS 3.0 object model.

Understanding How WSS 3.0 Processes Workflow Activities

You need to know several terms to understand WSS 3.0's implementation of workflow. Three of the most important are templates, instances, and associations. A *template* is a definition of a workflow that contains a list of forms used in the workflow and the name of the workflow assembly. The template is usually deployed as a SharePoint feature. It's stored in the central repository for the site collection—just like many other features, but as a type of workflow manifest. *Associations* connect a template to a particular SharePoint list or content type and store information such as whether the workflow template should be started automatically, what lists the tasks and workflow history should be stored in, and other parameters such as who the default approvers are. A list or content type can have multiple associations for the same template. For example, you may need to run two different approval workflows on documents in the same document library. When a workflow starts for a particular document or item, you are creating an *instance* of the association. You can run only one instance of an association at a time for a single item. When a workflow is running it has the ability to use the SharePoint object model to create tasks that are associated with activities in the workflow. This is how the human-oriented interaction with the workflow is accomplished. While you're configuring the association of the template to a particular list or content type, you define which task list will hold workflow tasks and which will hold history list data. The tasks are generated by a workflow and give users the ability to interact with a running business process. These task lists are normal SharePoint task lists; however, they are also mapped to a workflow association.

The only remaining thing to talk about is the concept of *modifications*. SharePoint workflow modifications allow you to modify the workflow execution while it is in process. Our example will not demonstrate this capability; if you would like to learn more please refer to the "How to: Access Contact Data in Workflow Initiation and Modification Forms" URL in the "Further Reading" section of this chapter.

Now that you understand some of the terminology, you should know how SharePoint actually processes a workflow. When SharePoint starts a workflow it will continue processing that workflow until it reaches an event that requires it to wait for a response. In most cases this is the Create Task activity. At that point SharePoint will persist the current state of all activities in the workflow to the content database. This action is referred to as the workflow *dehydrating* itself. More specifically, the workflow is removing itself from memory. (This is similar to the way BizTalk Server processes its workflows; it also persists the state to a database dehydrating it.) The workflow will *rehydrate* (or retrieve the current state of the workflow) from the content database when an event occurs (such as Task Complete) to continue processing the workflow. This improves the servers' overall performance by allowing more long-running workflows to run simultaneously. If a workflow is waiting for a response, it simply dehydrates, removing itself from memory until it is ready to wake up.

Creating the LoanWF Test Environment

To test the workflow you need to be able to create and save an XML file to a forms library that complies with the Loan XML schema that is used to call the web service in our example. To do this we will create a forms library and an InfoPath form. To create the forms library navigate to your site-collection's home page and select the Documents link. Under All Site Content select the Create button. Under the Libraries column select Form Library, name the library **LoanWFTest**, keep the defaults, and click the Create button.

Next you need to create an InfoPath form for the loan application. The XML schema for the InfoPath form can be found in the `LoanWF\starterfiles` directory of the code download for this chapter (available from the Source Code/Download section of `http://apress.com`) and is named `myschema.xml`. You can create the InfoPath form by following these steps:

1. Open InfoPath and select to design a new blank template from an XML file or schema. In the dialog that appears select the `myschema.xsd` file and click OK.

2. Navigate to the Data Source pane in the Design Tasks panel and drag and drop the Loan tree node onto the forms design surface. In the pop-up menu that appears, select the Section with Controls option.

3. Add a button control below the fields on the design surface and then right-click the button and select the Button properties menu option.

4. In the dialog that appears, change the action to Submit and click the Submit Options button.

5. Select the Allow Users to Submit This Form check box, and in the Send the Form to a Single Destination drop-down select the SharePoint Document Library option.

6. Click the Advanced button, and in the After Submit drop-down select Close Form.

7. Click the Add button to add a new data connection. The new data connection will save the form to the forms library we created at `http://portal.sample.com/LoanWFTest`.

8. Enter the URL of the forms library and select the Last Name field as the unique name for the document when it is saved. Then name and save the connection and apply the changes to the Submit button.

9. Save the form to a local file location by selecting the File menu's Save As menu option and name the file **TestForm**.

10. Publish the form to the LoanWFTest forms library we created. To do this select File ➤ Publish. In the dialog that appears, select to publish it to a SharePoint server and click Next.

11. Enter the location of the SharePoint server (in our case it is `http://portal.sample.com`) and click Next. In the dialog that appears keep the defaults and click Next; this will allow us to publish the form to the LoanWFTest library. Then select LoanWFTest from the list of available libraries and click Next.

12. In the dialog that appears click the Add button to add four fields: SSN, LastName, LoanAmt, and Income. This will promote the fields so that we can use them in the workflow and the forms library.

13. Click Next and then the Publish button to publish the test form to the LoanWFTest library.

If you navigate to the LoanWFTest forms library and select the New Document menu option the form we just created should open and allow you to save documents to the library. `TestForm.xsn` should look like Figure 14-3. Figure 14-4 displays the LoanWFTest forms library.

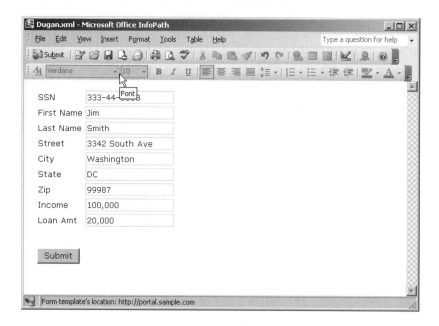

Figure 14-3. *The TestForm InfoPath form*

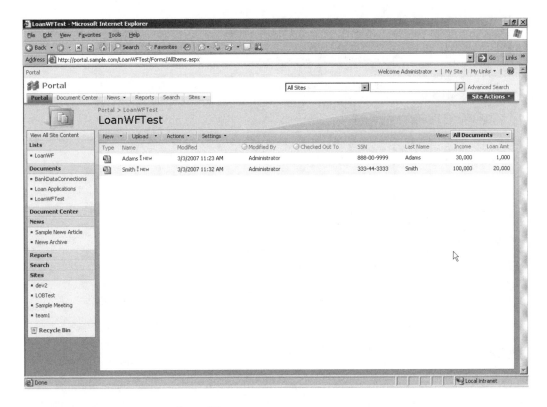

Figure 14-4. *The LoanWFTest forms library*

Creating the Workflow Template

The Visual Studio solution we are going to create will contain one project and reference a web service that we will call to update the Loan database. To create the project, open Visual Studio and select File ➤ New Project. In the dialog that appears expand the SharePoint node under the Visual Basic Language node. Select the SharePoint Server Sequential Workflow Library option as shown in Figure 14-5.

Once the project is created you will notice that the template automatically includes a directory named Deployment Files. The Deployment Files directory contains two directories (FeatureFiles and ProductionDeployment) and a batch file named `PostBuildActions.bat`. The Features directory contains two XML files: `feature.xml` and `workflow.xml`. These template files contain configuration information that is used to deploy the workflow as a SharePoint feature. We will be modifying both of these a little later. The `PostBuildActions.bat` file will run automatically when the project is built. This file deploys and activates the workflow feature on a SharePoint site collection so that we do not have to do it manually. The last file, named `workflow1.vb` in the LoanWF root directory, is the workflow template. To begin, rename the `workflow1.vb` file to `LoanWF.vb` by right-clicking on `workflow1.vb` and selecting Rename.

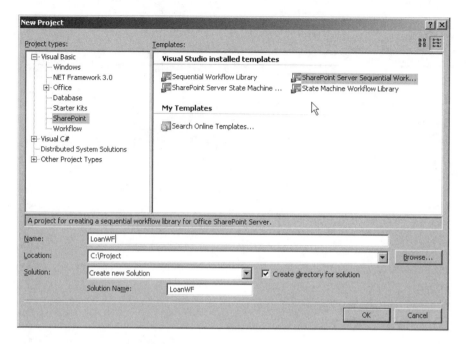

Figure 14-5. *Creating the LoanWF workflow project*

Next we need to add activities to the workflow. To do this open LoanWF.vb by double-clicking on it in the Solution Explorer. The workflow designer that opens contains one activity named onWorkflowActivated1, as displayed in Figure 14-6. The red exclamation point in the upper-right corner of the activity is a designer hint that appears when properties are not configured correctly on that activity.

The workflow we are creating will need to retrieve four data fields from the InfoPath form that started the workflow. The workflow can read these fields because InfoPath promoted them when the form was deployed and they are configured in the Loan Applications forms library as properties. The workflow reads these properties from the SharePoint list-item object to access them. Before we add any activities to the workflow we need to add a few lines of code to define member variables so that we can compute the income-to-loan-amount ratio and store the email message text that we will use later in the workflow. We also need to add some code to help us work with tasks and properties before and after the task is completed. To add code to the code-behind for the workflow, right-click on the WorkflowActivated activity in the workflow designer. In the pop-up menu that appears select Add Handlers. Then reselect the WorkflowActivated activity and right-click again, but this time select the View Code menu option to open the code-behind file for the workflow. Listing 14-1 displays the code you need to add.

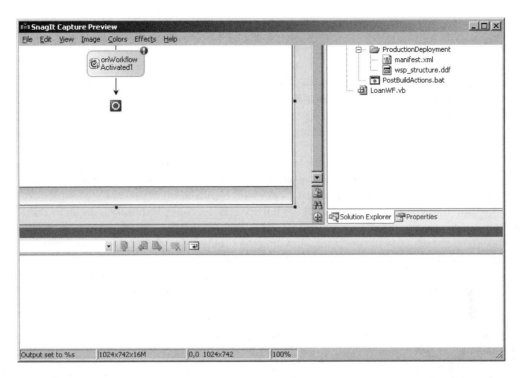

Figure 14-6. *The LoanWF workflow*

Listing 14-1. *The LoanWF Class*

```vb
Public Class LoanWF
    Inherits SharePointSequentialWorkflowActivity
    Public Sub New()
        MyBase.New()
        InitializeComponent()
    End Sub
    Public workflowProperties As SPWorkflowActivationProperties = _
        New Microsoft.SharePoint.Workflow.SPWorkflowActivationProperties

    Public dblLoanAmt As Double
    Public dblIncome As Double
    Public dblLoanRatio As Double
    Public strMailMessage As String
    Public taskStatus As String
    Public historyStatus As String

    Private Sub onWorkflowActivated1_Invoked(ByVal sender As System.~
        Object, ByVal e As System.Workflow.Activities.ExternalDataEventArgs)
        dblLoanAmt = Double.Parse(workflowProperties.Item("Loan Amt").ToString)
        dblIncome = Double.Parse(workflowProperties.Item("Income").ToString)
```

```
            dblLoanRatio = dblIncome / dblLoanAmt
    End Sub
End Class
```

When the InfoPath form was published to the SharePoint Forms Library, properties were promoted so that they were visible to the library. The code in the onWorkflowActiviated1_ Invoked event reads the InfoPath forms promoted properties using SharePoint's API. The public property dblLoanRatio will be used later in the workflow to determine whether a loan officer needs to approve the loan.

Next drag the ifElse activity from the Windows Workflow Foundation section of the toolbar and drop it beneath the OneWorkflowActivated1 activity. This ifElse activity will have three branches, two of which are created automatically when you add the shape to the designer. To add the third branch right-click on the ifElse activity and select the Add Branch menu option. Before we add any additional code to the workflow let's place all the activity shapes we need for our ifElse activity onto the designer. First drag the CreateTask activity located under the SharePoint Workflow section of the toolbar into the leftmost branch of ifElse. Place the OnTaskChanged activity followed by the CompleteTask activity under CreateTask. Then drag a Code activity from the Windows Workflow section of the toolbar onto the remaining two ifElse branches. Your workflow schedule should look like the one in Figure 14-7.

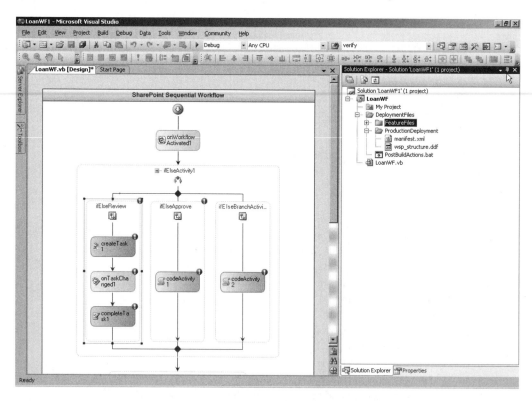

Figure 14-7. *The ifElse activity*

The red exclamation points on each of the shapes tell us that some activity properties need to be set. Let's start by selecting the OnWorkflowActivated activity in the designer. Right-click on it and select Properties. When we changed the name of the workflow to LoanWF we invalidated a few properties that we now need to update. Set both the CorrelationToken property and the OwnerActivityName property under it to **LoanWF**. To do this select the Cor-relationToken; you should see the OwnerActivtyName property. In the drop-down you'll see LoanWF as an option. The CorrelationToken tells the workflow engine which instance of an association to rehydrate when it is removed from memory. You will need to set this on every activity that could cause the state of the schedule to be persisted to a database. We also need to modify the WorkflowProperties to point to the LoanWF workflow properties. The workflow properties tell the activity which workflow object instance it belongs to. To do this, select the ellipsis in the Workflow Properties text box. In the dialog that appears select workflowProper-ties under LoanWF, as in Figure 14-8. The red exclamation point should no longer be visible on this activity.

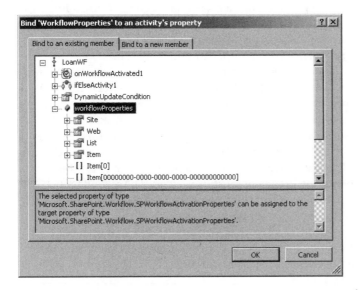

Figure 14-8. *Setting the workflow properties*

Next we need to configure the properties for the first branch of the ifElse activity. The first branch will execute if the loan-amount-to-income ratio (named dblLoanRatio and calculated when the workflow begins) is less than or equal to .3 and greater than .2 and if the loan amount is greater than or equal to one million dollars. Click on the red exclamation point and pull down the drop-down. It should say that no condition has been set. Selecting the red exclamation point will take you to the Condition property for the activity. In the Condition drop-down select the Declarative Rule option. A plus sign should now appear next to the Condition property. In the Condition Name field enter **Review**. Then select the ellipsis in the Condition Expression field. In the dialog that appears enter the condition as displayed in Figure 14-9.

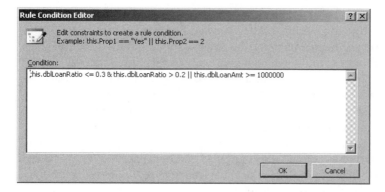

Figure 14-9. *Setting theReview ifElse condition*

Next we need to set the Correlation property for the Create Task activity. Correlation tokens help the WF runtime determine which instance of a workflow to rehydrate when a task is complete or when an event occurs that rehydrates an instance of a workflow. We are going to create a new task token and then set the taskToken property for the CreateTask, TaskChanged, and TaskCompleted activities to it. To create the task token select the CreateTask activity's red exclamation point. In the Properties window for the CreateTask activity enter **taskToken**. A plus sign should appear next to the CorrelationToken property. Drill down on the Correlation-Token property and set OwnerActivityName to LoanWF. Next select the OnTaskChanged activity and navigate to its properties. Set its correlationToken property to taskToken and do the same for the CompleteTask activity. The final step for this branch of the ifElse is to give it a name. Select the branch itself and navigate to its properties. Name the branch **ifElseReview**.

Next we need to configure the second branch of the ifElse activity. The second branch will execute if the loan amount is less than one million dollars and the loan-to-income ratio is greater than .3. Select the red exclamation point for the branch and navigate to its properties. In the drop-down for the Condition property select the Declarative Rule Condition menu option. Name the condition **Approve** and then select the ellipsis in the Condition field. In the dialog that appears enter the condition text as displayed in Figure 14-10. The last branch in the ifElse activity does not have a condition.

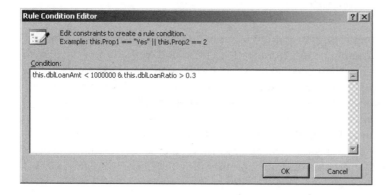

Figure 14-10. *Setting the Approve ifElse condition*

Next we need to add a line of code to each of the Code activities in the Approve ifElse branch and in the third branch of the ifElse activity (named ifElseBranchActivity3). To do this select the Code activity and navigate to its properties. Name the Code activity in the Approve ifElse branch **codeApproved**, and name the Code activity in the third branch **codeDeclined**. Then right-click the codeApproved activity. In the drop-down select the Generate Handlers option. This will take you to the code block that will execute for this activity. Repeat the same steps for the codeDeclined activity and enter the code as displayed in Listing 14-2.

Listing 14-2. *The codeApproved and codeDeclined Code*

```
Private Sub codeApproved_ExecuteCode(ByVal sender As System.Object, _
ByVal e As System.EventArgs)
        strMailMessage = "Your loan has been approved!"
        historyStatus = "Approved"
End Sub

Private Sub codeDeclined_ExecuteCode(ByVal sender As System.Object, _
ByVal e As System.EventArgs)
        strMailMessage = "Your loan has been declined!"
        historyStatus = "Rejected"
End Sub
```

We are now ready to add some code to the ifElseReview branch tasks. First let's rename the task activities. Select the CreateTask activity and navigate to its properties. Change its name to **createReviewTask**. Then change the onTaskChanged activity to **onTaskReview-Changed** and the completeTask activity to **completeReviewTask**. Before we begin to add code to the activities, we need to add a few public members to our code-behind, as shown in Listing 14-3. These public members are declared in the LoanWF class prior to the onWork-flowActivated1_Invoked subroutine.

Listing 14-3. *Adding the Tasks' Public Properties*

```
Public taskIDField As System.Guid = Nothing
    Public taskPropertiesField As SPWorkflowTaskProperties ~
= New Microsoft.SharePoint.Workflow.SPWorkflowTaskProperties
    Public beforeProperties As SPWorkflowTaskProperties ~
= New Microsoft.SharePoint.Workflow.SPWorkflowTaskProperties
    Public afterProperties As SPWorkflowTaskProperties ~
= New Microsoft.SharePoint.Workflow.SPWorkflowTaskProperties
```

Next we need to add the code for each of the task activities. Right-click on the createRe-viewTask activity and select the Generate Handler menu option. In the code-behind for this method enter the code displayed in Listing 14-4 right below the other public properties we created earlier.

Listing 14-4. *The createReviewTask Code*

```
taskIDField = Guid.NewGuid()
taskPropertiesField.AssignedTo = "sample\susiea"
taskPropertiesField.TaskType = 0
taskPropertiesField.Description = "Please approve or reject a loan for _
        $" + workflowProperties.Item("Loan Amt").ToString
taskPropertiesField.DueDate = DateTime.Today.AddDays(7)
taskPropertiesField.Title = "Loan Approval for: " + workflowProperties.~
        Item("Last Name").ToString + "-" + workflowProperties.Item("SSN").ToString
taskPropertiesField.ExtendedProperties("SSN") = workflowProperties.~
        Item("SSN")
taskPropertiesField.ExtendedProperties("LoanAmt") = workflowProperties.~
        Item("Loan Amt")
taskPropertiesField.ExtendedProperties("Income") = workflowProperties.~
        Item("Income")
taskPropertiesField.ExtendedProperties("Name") = workflowProperties.~
        Item("Last Name")
```

When a task is created you must create a unique identifier for the task by assigning the taskIDField to the GUID in the first line of code. Then we set the standard task property for AssignedTo to sample\susiea, a user we created in our sample domain who will act as the loan officer and approver in the example. Next we set the Description and Title properties and then retrieve the loan-application information from the promoted properties on the SharePoint list. In the end we want to pass these properties to a custom-task InfoPath form that we will create. To do this we add them to the task's extended properties.

Next we need to add the code for the onTaskReviewChanged activity. When the workflow is executed it will create the task and then dehydrate and wait for the task to change. When the loan officer approves or rejects the task, the workflow will rehydrate and execute this activity. To create the handler for this activity, select it in the workflow designer and right-click. In the menu that appears, select the Generate Handler option and enter the code shown in Listing 14-5.

Listing 14-5. *The onTaskReviewChanged Code*

```
taskStatus = afterProperties.ExtendedProperties("TaskStatus").ToString()
```

Finally, we need to add some code to the handler for the completeReviewTask activity using the same method we used for the onTaskReviewChanged activity. Listing 14-6 displays the code for the handler. We will use these properties later in the workflow to send an email message and write to the history log.

Listing 14-6. *The completeReviewTask Code*

```
        If taskStatus = "Approved" Then
            strMailMessage = "Your loan has been approved!"
            historyStatus = "Approved"
```

```
Else
    strMailMessage = "Your loan has been rejected!"
    historyStatus = "Rejected"
End If
```

Even though we do not have any more red exclamation points on our visual designer we need to configure a few more properties on the task activities. In Listing 14-4 we created some public properties for the taskIDField and task properties. We need to set the properties in the task activities to these values so that they will execute on the right task. To do this select the createReviewTask activity and navigate to its properties. In the TaskId property field select the ellipsis; in the dialog that appears select the LoanWF taskIDField as shown in Figure 14-11.

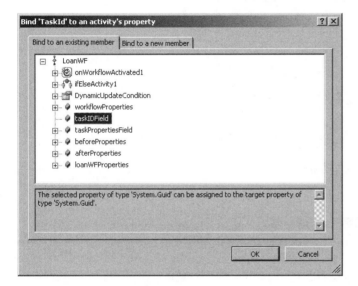

Figure 14-11. *Setting the taskID for the CreateTask Activity*

Do the same for the TaskProperties field, except this time select LoanWF taskProperties-Field in the dialog box. Then repeat the steps you completed in the preceding paragraph and set the TaskId property as we just did in the onTaskReviewChanged activity and the completeReviewTask activity. We also need to set the beforeProperties and afterProperties on the onTaskReviewChanged activity to the beforeProperties and afterProperties public variables we created earlier.

Up to this point we have reviewed the loan to determine if it needs to be approved by a loan officer; if it did we assigned a task to that loan officer. Now we need to add a few additional shapes to act on the approval or rejection. Start by dragging an ifElse activity from the toolbar directly below the existing ifElse activity.

If the loan application was approved we will submit the application data to a web service, adding a new record to the loan database. The web service we are going to call was created in Chapter 13 and was hosted in the default IIS web site. In this chapter we are going to create a new web site for the web service outside the default web site that is installed with IIS. We decided to do this to avoid any issues that might arise from reusing an IIS site that was managed by SharePoint. To create the web site open the IIS administration console, select the Web

Sites node on the server, and right-click. In the dialog that appears, name the site **BankWS** and click Next. You need to also create a host header so that you can keep the site on the same port. In our example, we named the host header service.sample.com, as shown in Figures 14-12 and 14-13.

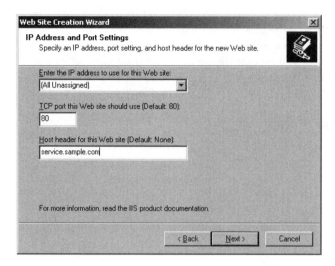

Figure 14-12. *Creating the BankWS web site*

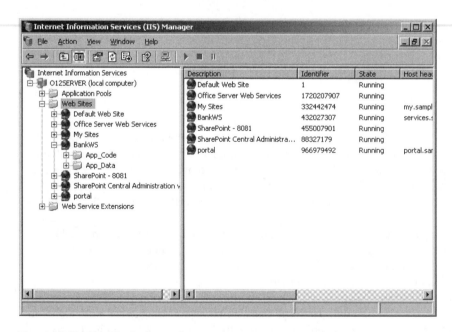

Figure 14-13. *The IIS configuration*

The code for the BankWS site and the associated database that it updates are included in the dialog and explained in detail in Chapter 13 and they are available in the code download at http://apress.com. To call the web service from the workflow you need to drag the invokeWebService activity onto the ifElseBranchActivity4 branch of the ifElse activity. When you drag the invokeWebService shape onto the designer, a dialog box will ask you to enter the URL of the web service you want to call. Enter http://services.sample.com/bankWS.asmx into URL field. Change the Web Reference Name to **BankWS** and press the Add Reference button. Then navigate to the properties for the activity and change the Method Name property to **AddLoanApp**. We then need to set the loan property so that we can pass data to the web service. To do this we need to first create an instance of the loan object and populate it with data from the loan application. The code to do this will be located in the handler for the invokeWebService we just added. To create the handler right-click on the invokeWebService activity in the designer and select the Generate Handlers menu option. Enter the code shown in Listing 14-7 into the invokeWebServiceActivity1_invoking subroutine.

Listing 14-7. *Setting the Loan Object Properties*

```
loanapp = New BankWS.Loan
loanapp.SSN = workflowProperties.Item("SSN").ToString
loanapp.LastName = workflowProperties.Item("Last Name")
loanapp.LoanAmt = workflowProperties.Item("Loan Amt")
loanapp.Income = workflowProperties.Item("Income")
```

Then navigate to the properties for the invokeWebService activity and set the Loan parameter to the LoanWF loanapp object you just created. To finish this ifElse activity we need to add a condition to check whether the loan was approved. Navigate to the properties for the ifElse activity, name the condition **IfApproved**, and select Declarative Rule for the type of condition. Select the ellipsis for the rule and enter **this.historyStatus==“Approved”** into the Rule Condition Editor.

We have two more shapes to add to our workflow. The first is a sendMail activity. We are adding this one to send an email message to the loan applicant to let him know whether the loan was approved. Drag the sendMail shape directly below the last ifElse activity we added (named ifElseActivity2) and the logToHistory directly below that. Then navigate to the properties for the sendMail activity and set its correlation token to **workflowToken**. Select the variable strMailMessage for the Body property and set the Subject to **Loan Request**. In the To property enter the applicant's email address. In our example it is edhild@sample.com. This would typically be a dynamically filled property, but for simplicity we hard-coded it.

The last shape is a logToHistory activity that will write the outcome of the workflow to the history task list. For the logToHistory activity set the History Outcome property to the historyStatus field we created earlier and set the user to the workflowproperties.OriginatorUser.ID field.

Adding Error Handling

All good developers account for error handling, and developing workflows should be no different. To trap and log errors in our example we are going to use the built-in fault-handling capabilities within the Windows Workflow Foundation designer. To add an error handler to the schedule we just created, right-click anywhere in the background of the schedule and select the View Fault Handlers menu option. This will bring up the Workflow Exceptions design surface. We need to add two activities to this part of the schedule—a FaultHandler from the Windows Workflow section of the toolbox and the logToHistoryList activity—as shown in Figure 14-14. This will allow us to trap all errors that occur during the processing of the workflow and write the error description to the workflow history list.

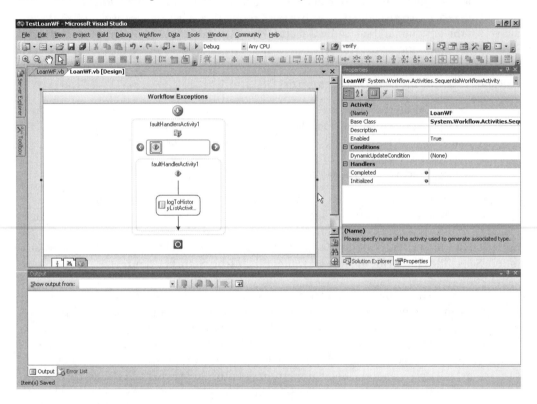

Figure 14-14. *Adding activities to the workflow exceptions*

Drag the fault handler into the FaultHandlers activity and set its FaultType property to System.Exception by clicking the ellipsis in the FaultType property as shown in Figure 14-15.

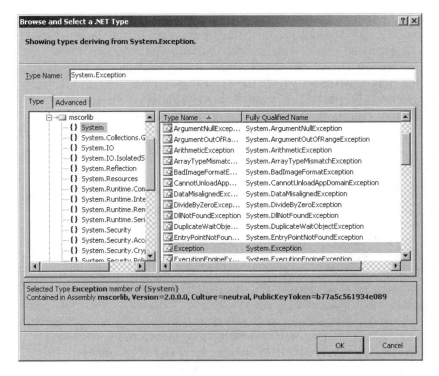

Figure 14-15. *Setting the FaultType property*

Then drag the logToHistoryList activity directly under it and navigate to its properties. Set the HistoryOutcome property to the text Error, and set the HistoryDescription to fault-HandlerActivity1.Fault.Message, as in Figure 14-16.

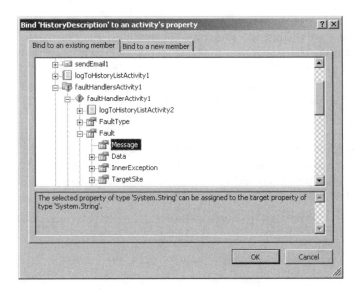

Figure 14-16. *Setting the HistoryDescription property*

At this point we have completed the development of the workflow schedule. We are now ready to strongly name and sign the assembly and build the workflow. To sign the assembly select the project in the Solution Explorer and right-click, selecting the Properties menu option. Navigate to the Signing tab and click the Sign the Assembly check box. In the Select Strong Name Assembly drop-down select New. In the dialog that appears name the file **LoanWF** and uncheck Protect My File with a Password. To build the assembly select the project in the Solution Explorer, right-click, and select the Build menu option. We now need to create the custom task form that will allow the loan officer to approve or reject the loan.

Creating the Custom Task Form

Custom forms give you the ability to collect information at various predetermined times in a workflow. There are three types of forms: association and initialization forms, modification forms, and task forms. Association and initialization forms are displayed to users before the workflow begins and allow a user to do things like set parameters for the workflow. Modification forms give users the ability to modify the parameters of a running workflow. Task forms give you the ability to replace the default task-form interface with a custom form. In our example the workflow is started automatically when a document is saved to the forms library, so we will not be implementing an association and initialization form; we are not giving users the ability to modify the workflow in process, so there is also no need to implement the modification form. If you would like to learn more about these two types of forms and how to implement them, please see the "Further Reading" section at the end of this chapter.

The workflow we just built creates a task in a SharePoint task list. The task is assigned to the loan officer (susiea@sample.com) so that she can approve or reject the loan application. When you create tasks in SharePoint you typically edit those tasks using the default SharePoint task interface that is linked to the default task content type. By default all SharePoint tasks are assigned a content type. You can specify a new content type for a workflow task, which allows you to customize the task-editing experience by creating custom forms that are assigned to that content type.

The task we created in the workflow asks a user to approve or decline the loan. To allow the loan officer to make this decision we will need to pass some information about the loan to the custom task form and then pass the task status back to the workflow after the task is complete so that it can finish processing. The task form we are going to create is an InfoPath form named `CustomApprovalTask.xsn`. To create the form open InfoPath and select the Design a Form Template menu option. In the Design a New Form Template dialog select the Blank Form Template option and make sure the Enable Browser-Compatible Features check box is checked.

The first thing we need to do is add a data source that will track the status of the task and allow us to send that status back to the workflow. To create this data source select the Data Source option in the Design Tasks panel and add a new field below myfields named **taskStatus**, as shown in Figure 14-17, by right-clicking on myfields and selecting Add.

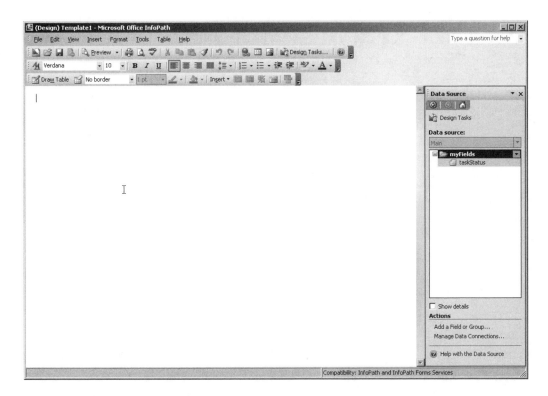

Figure 14-17. *Creating the task-form data source*

Next we need to add a secondary data source to receive the data from the workflow. Windows SharePoint Services always passes the task XML to the form as a secondary data source. The default schema for that XML file requires that all fields begin with ows_. In our example we are going to pass four fields. Listing 14-8 shows the schema for our inbound secondary data source. Copy this XML to a new file named ItemMetaData.xml so that you can use it to define the secondary data source.

Listing 14-8. *The Default Task XML Schema*

```
<z:row xmlns:z="#RowsetSchema" ows_SSN="" ows_Name="" ows_Income="" ows_LoanAmt=""/>
```

To create the secondary data source in the InfoPath select Data Connections from the Tools menu. In the dialog that appears, select Add. Then select the Create a New Connection To and the Receive options and click Next. In the XML data-field details dialog, enter the path of the ItemMetaData.xml file you just created and click Next. Keep the Include the Data as a Resource File radio button checked and click Next and Finish and close the Data Connections dialog. Your drop-down for the data sources should now contain a secondary data source named ItemMetaData, as shown in Figure 14-18.

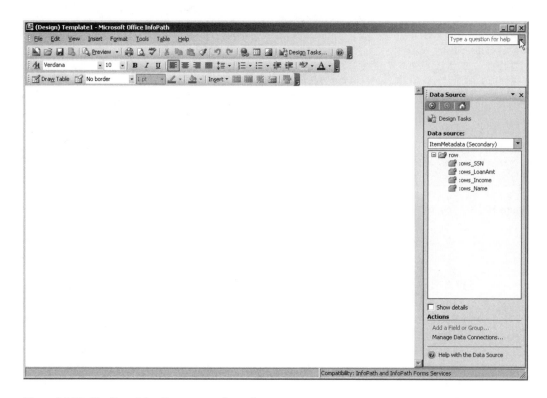

Figure 14-18. *The ItemMetaData secondary data source*

Now we need to add the metadata fields to the form and add buttons for Approve and Reject. To add the fields to the form, highlight them one by one in the data source and drag them onto the design surface. Then select Design Tasks in the Data Source panel, select controls, and add two buttons below the fields. Right-click the first button and change its label to **Approve** and the other to **Reject**. Before we modify the button actions we need to add one more data source that will allow us to submit the taskStatus back to the workflow. To do this select Tools ➤ Data Connections. In the dialog that appears, click the Add button. Select Create a New Connection and Submit, then click Next. Then select the To Hosting Environment option for the How Do You Want to Submit Your Data radio button and click Next. Leave the name of the connection as Submit, click Finish, and then close the Data Connections dialog.

If a loan officer approves a loan application we want to set the status of the taskStatus field to Approve, submit the taskStatus back to the workflow, and close the form. To do this we need to configure the rules for the Approve button. Select the Approve button and right-click. In the menu that appears select Button Properties and then Rules. We are going to add one rule with three conditions that will execute in sequence. To create the rule click Add and then Add Action. In the dialog that appears select the Set a Fields Value in the Action drop-down. In the Field text box select taskStatus and in the Value textbox enter **Approve** as displayed in Figure 14-19.

Figure 14-19. *Creating the Approve button action*

Next add two more actions. In the first new action select Submit Using a Data Connection in the Action drop-down and select the Submit data connection. In the second select Close This Form in the Action drop-down, save the rule, and apply the changes to the button. We also need to add rules and actions to the Reject button using the exact same steps—except this time set the taskStatus field's value to **Reject**.

The custom task form is now complete. To use this form in our workflow we need to save the form locally (for our example, we saved it to c:\project\LoanWF). Then publish the form to the Deployment\FeatureFiles directory in the LoanWF project structure. The InfoPath solution is automatically published to SharePoint when the workflow feature is deployed. The form must also have a security designation of Domain. To set the security for the form, navigate to the Tools menu and select Forms Options. In the dialog that appears select Security and Trust and uncheck Automatically Determine Security Level then select Domain. To save the form, select File ➤ Save As. To deploy the form to the Features project directory, select the File menu's Publish option and select the To Network File Location radio button in the dialog that appears. Click Next, browse to the FeatureFiles directory under the DeploymentFiles directory for the LoanWF project, name the file **CustomApprovalTask**, and click OK. Click Next and remove the alternate access path's text.

■**Caution** You must remove the alternate path's text to use the task form. If you do not, the feature will deploy but when you try to open a task it will tell you that the form is closed.

Click Next; a pop-up window will tell you that you cleared the access path. Ignore the warning and click OK. Then click Publish and Close. The form should now look like the one in Figure 14-20.

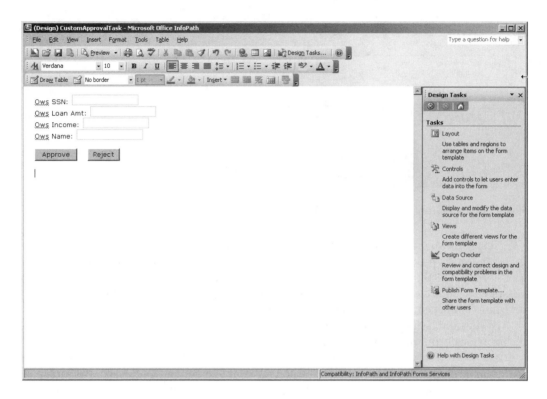

Figure 14-20. *The CustomApprovalTask InfoPath form*

Deploying the Workflow

We are now ready to deploy the workflow and link it to a forms library. But before we can deploy the workflow we need to modify a few of the deployment files associated with the project and modify the project's post-build events so that the PostBuildActions.bat file will install the workflow feature. We need to complete the following steps, one of which we have already done:

1. Compile the workflow as a strongly named assembly (already completed).

2. Modify the feature.xml file to add a reference to CustomTaskForm.xsn.

3. Modify the workflow.xml file.

4. Modify the PostBuildActions.bat file so that it will deploy to http://portal. sample.com instead of http://localhost.

Let's begin by modifying feature.xml. Open the feature.xml file, located in the DeploymentFiles directory in Visual Studio. The SharePoint ECM starter kit installs code snippets that will help you add the appropriate elements to this file. Right-click below the text and select Insert Snippet. In the pop-up menu that appears select Windows SharePoint Services Workflow ➤ Feature.xml. In general you need to replace the highlighted placeholder text with information for the workflow project. For our solution you need to create a new GUID using the Tools ➤ Create GUID menu option in VS.NET and place it in the Feature Id property and then add two additional lines of code in the Properties section to let the feature know it has a custom task form. Listing 14-9 displays the code for `feature.xml`.

Listing 14-9. *The feature.xml File*

```
<?xml version="1.0" encoding="utf-8"?>
<!-- _lcid="1033" _version="12.0.3111" _dal="1" -->
<!-- _LocalBinding -->


<Feature  Id="E1D7B274-1A46-41f8-B74D-CE91923AB414"
                  Title="LoanWF"
                  Description="Loan Approval Process Workflow"
                  Version="12.0.0.0"
                  Scope="Site"
                  ReceiverAssembly="Microsoft.Office.Workflow.Feature, ~
Version=12.0.0.0, Culture=neutral, PublicKeyToken=71e9bce111e9429c"
                  ReceiverClass="Microsoft.Office.Workflow.Feature. ~
WorkflowFeatureReceiver"
                  xmlns="http://schemas.microsoft.com/sharepoint/">
          <ElementManifests>
            <ElementManifest Location="workflow.xml" />
            <ElementFile Location="CustomApprovalTask.xsn"/>
          </ElementManifests>
          <Properties>
            <Property Key="GloballyAvailable" Value="true" />
<!-- if you don't have forms, use *.xsn -->
<Property Key="RegisterForms" Value="*.xsn" /></Properties>
</Feature>
```

Next we need to modify the `workflow.xml` file. Open the file in VS.NET and right-click as we did in the `feature.xml` file to add the snippet, but this time select the `workflow.xml` snippet. Again we need to change the highlighted text for our workflow project. Follow these steps to modify the file:

1. Change the Name property to **LoanWF**.

2. Change the Description property to **Loan Approval**.

3. Generate a new GUID to uniquely identify the workflow using the VS.NET Tools ➤ New GUID tool and update the Id property in the file.

4. Add a new entry in the MetaData section to identify the custom task form. This entry requires the unique uniform resource name (URN) for the task form we created. To find the URN open the `CustomTaskForm.xsn` in design mode and select File ➤ Properties.

5. Copy the Id field for the template into the <Task0_FromURN> tag.

6. Open the Visual Studio command prompt from the Start menu and navigate to the bin directory for the project: `loanwf\bin`. Type **sn.exe –T loanwf.dll** to retrieve the public key token for the assembly and then use that key to update the PublicKeyToken property.

Listing 14-10 displays the `workflow.xml` file for the LoanWF project.

Listing 14-10. *The workflow.xml File*

```xml
<?xml version="1.0" encoding="utf-8" ?>
<!-- _lcid="1033" _version="12.0.3015" _dal="1"    -->
<!-- _LocalBinding    -->
<Elements xmlns="http://schemas.microsoft.com/sharepoint/">
  <Workflow
       Name="LoanWF"
       Description="Loan Approval WF"
       Id="9669DDA8-9AC9-4afa-9166-F1CE3FD094A1"
       CodeBesideClass="LoanWF.LoanWF"
       CodeBesideAssembly="LoanWF, Version=1.0.0.0, Culture=neutral, ~
    PublicKeyToken=33700a147ac96049"
       TaskListContentTypeId="0x01080100C9C9515DE4E24001905074~
F980F93160"
       StatusUrl="_layouts/WrkStat.aspx"
       AssociationUrl="_layouts/CstWrkflIP.aspx"
       InstantiationUrl="_layouts/IniWrkflIP.aspx"
       ModificationUrl="_layouts/ModWrkflIP.aspx">

    <Categories/>
    <MetaData>
          <Task0_FormURN>urn:schemas-microsoft-com:office:infopath: ~
CustomApprovalTask:-myXSD-2007-03-03T17-04-55</Task0_FormURN>
      <StatusPageUrl>_layouts/WrkStat.aspx</StatusPageUrl>
    </MetaData>
  </Workflow>
</Elements>
```

The final thing we need to do before we build and deploy our solution is modify the build events for the project. To do this right-click the project in the Solution Explorer. Select the Properties menu option, navigate to the Compile tab, and click the Build Events button at the bottom of the page. In the dialog that appears click the Edit Post Build button and change NODEPLOY to DEPLOY. The `PostBuildActions.bat` file also needs to be modified to point to the SharePoint server location that we want to deploy to; in our case this is `http://portal.sample.com`. The batch file currently points to `http://localhost`, so open `PostbuildActions.bat` and replace all instances of `http://localhost` with the proper server location.

You are now ready to build and deploy the workflow solution. Select Build ➤ Build Solution to compile the workflow assembly, and then run the `PostBuildActions.bat` file. The batch file will complete the following tasks automatically:

1. Add the workflow assembly to the global assembly cache (GAC).

2. Create a new Features directory named `c:\Program Files\Common Files\Microsoft Shared\web server extensions\12\Template\Features\LoanWF` and copy the `feature.xml`, `workflow.xml`, and `CustomTaskForm.xsn` files into it.

3. Deactivate and uninstall the feature if it was previously installed.

4. Install and activate the feature.

5. Reset IIS.

Attaching the Workflow to a Forms Library

Earlier in this chapter we created a forms library named LoanWFTest and published an InfoPath template to it. Now we need to modify the settings for that forms library so that the LoanWF workflow will start automatically when a new loan-application document is saved to it. Before we configure the library settings, we need to create a new task list in the site collection to hold the tasks for the loan officer. To do this, navigate to the home page of the site collection—in our example its `http://portal.sample.com`—and select the Lists link. On the Lists page click the Create button. Then select the Tasks link under the Tracking heading. Name the list **LoanWF**, and in its List Settings admin area select the option to Send E-mail When Ownership Is Assigned. When a task is created this will send an email automatically to whomever the task was assigned. The email will contain a link to the task. In this case the task will be assigned to susiea@sample.com.

To connect the LoanWF forms library to the workflow, navigate to the Site Collection home page and open the LoanWF library. Select Settings ➤ Forms Library Settings, and under the Permissions and Management category select the Workflow Settings link. Then set the properties in the page as in Table 14-1 and click Next. (You can follow the same steps to connect the workflow to the Loan Applications forms library from Chapter 13.)

Table 14-1. *Workflow Settings Properties*

Property	Setting
Workflow	LoanWF
Name	LoanWF
Task List	LoanWF
History List	New History List
Start Options	Start This Workflow When a New Item Is Created

When you save the settings the workflow history list is created automatically and named the same as the workflow plus the word *History*. In our example the history list's name will be LoanWF History. You are now ready to test the workflow.

■**Note** Each time you deploy a new version of the workflow feature you will need to go back to the forms library and rebind it to the workflow.

Testing and Debugging the Workflow

To test the workflow, navigate back to the LoanWF forms library and select New ➤ New Document. The InfoPath TestForm we created earlier should open in the InfoPath client. Fill out the data in the form, making sure that that loan-to-income ratio requires approval, and press the Submit button. This will create a new .xml file in the document library and begin the workflow. Close the InfoPath client; you should see the document with the status of the workflow showing In Progress, as in Figure 14-21.

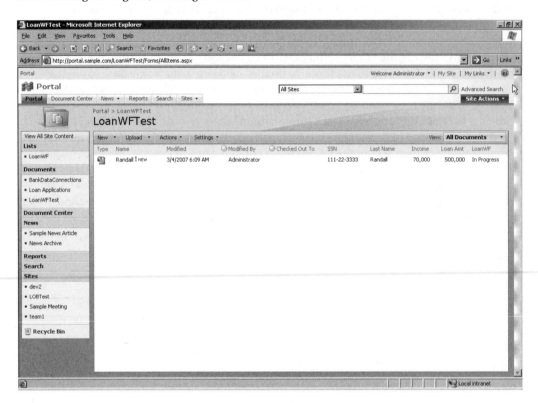

Figure 14-21. *The LoanWFTest forms library with a running workflow*

At this point an email has been sent to the loan officer susiea@sample.com and a task has been created to review the application. You can navigate to the task by either clicking on the link in the email or by going directly to the task in the LoanWF task list. When you click on the task the CustomTaskForm InfoPath form should appear for you to use to approve or reject the application. If you approve the application the form will close. The workflow will then wake up and continue processing.

To debug the workflow you need to attach the Visual Studio debugger to the w3wp.exe process your SharePoint web application is using and set a break point in the code-behind for one of the activity event handlers. To attach Visual Studio to a worker process, you first need to discover which process corresponds with the portal.sample.com instance we are using. Typing **IISAPP /a** in a command window will return you a list of the IIS application pools and the corresponding process IDs. From this list, it should be easy for you to identify the correct process

ID. With the process ID, you can then use Visual Studio's Attach to Process command and connect to the appropriate IIS worker process. To do this open the LoanWF project and select the Debug ➤ Attach to Process menu option. In the dialog that appears select the `w3wp.exe` process shown in the window. You will also want to use the Select button next to the Attach To prompt to designate that you are interested in debugging Workflow code. With both of these items configured, click OK.

Extension Points

While coding this example, we thought of two variations to the solution that we didn't incorporate because they distracted from the overall objective of the solution. We call them out now as extension points since they may be applicable to a specific project you are working on.

Create and use multiple custom task forms in a single workflow: Our workflow example was very simple and contained only a single task. Most workflows, however, will be much more complex and require multiple tasks and corresponding custom task forms. You can use these multiple task forms by numbering the task forms in the `feature.xml` file. You can also create separate task forms for editing or viewing a task.

Modify the workflow while it is running: In many scenarios you may want to give process administrators the ability to modify the parameters of a workflow at runtime. You can do this using modification forms. For more details on modification forms, see the "Further Reading" section.

Further Reading

The following links are to resources a reader interested in this chapter's material may find useful:

- Introducing Microsoft Windows Workflow Foundation: An Early Look

  http://msdn2.microsoft.com/en-us/library/aa480215.aspx

- How to: Access Contact Data in Workflow Initiation and Modification Forms

  http://msdn2.microsoft.com/en-us/library/ms517395.aspx

- Windows Workflow Foundation

  http://msdn2.microsoft.com/en-us/netframework/aa663328.aspx

- Workflow Development in Visual Studio 2005

  http://msdn2.microsoft.com/en-us/library/ms461324.aspx

PART 7

■■■

Conclusion

This section will revisit the vision of developers leveraging the Office system as a platform. It will recap common themes of the solutions in this book and provide insight into how to determine whether these techniques make sense for your project. It will also highlight some new tools that seek to further reduce the complexity of this book's solutions. Lastly, this section will look at the road ahead as the Office development platform matures.

CHAPTER 15

■■■

Realizing the Vision

Today many organizations lose productivity because their workers find it difficult to find, use, and share the information they need. Software developers build solutions to try to reduce this loss. However, by not incorporating their applications into tools familiar to the user, they can often increase user workload.

Consider a solution that helps educators generate and track student learning plans. A developer may read the requirements for standardization, compliance, and promotion of best practices, and as a result deliver a Windows application that provides the teachers with a wizard that stores the plans in a central database. This solution would standardize the plans and provide a vehicle for enforcing regulations for how frequently they are reviewed and updated. By using a wizard approach, the application breaks the plan into sections, providing thought-provoking instructions and best practices for each area. A school system could reasonably expect the application to not only meet their goals for standardization, but also to increase the quality of the plans' content.

However, many solutions are capable of *increasing* the user's workload. After the deployment of new systems, users must be overwhelmed with the value proposition to be motivated to adjust their behaviors. Even if an organization sets the policy that all plans are to be constructed the new way, the teachers are just as likely to continue to use their old document templates to construct plans and then copy/paste their contents into the wizard tool to be compliant. This bypasses the best practices and instructions the wizard provided and reduces the likelihood that there will be a change in the quality of the plans. More importantly, it increases the amount of time teachers spend working on each plan.

One of the reasons for the increased user workload is that applications often don't provide a familiar environment. Continuing with our teaching example, imagine that the teachers were comfortable with Microsoft Word. Developers today quickly limit the architecture options for their solutions to either the Web or Windows. Developers also need to view Office as a development platform. Microsoft Word, Excel, Outlook, and PowerPoint have been on users' desktops for over a decade and have a well-established connection, level of comfort, and adoption rate. Instead of building a new application that is separate from Office, the developers in the teaching example should have extended Microsoft Word to incorporate the new application's requirements. By developing with Office, what was once viewed as a separate, siloed system that requires special training can instead be viewed as just a new feature of a familiar tool.

This example application could now be developed within Microsoft Word. An add-in could use a task pane to display the best practices and instructions sensitive to the user's position in the document. By using the Open XML file format as well as Word's support for XML schemas, the plan document could easily be parsed into the central database. Going one step farther, SharePoint could provide search services across the repository, versioning of the plans, and a workflow system for approvals. Such a solution would meet the goals of the school system without removing users from the tool they had always used to maintain the plans.

Viewing SharePoint as a Set of Services

From reading this book, you would think that we look at the world through SharePoint-coated glasses, that every customer we talk to hears the word SharePoint in the answer, and that we recommend every solution be built on top of it. The funny thing is that most customers are eager to have their application "built on top of SharePoint" without really understanding what SharePoint has to offer. When working with customers, the challenge is to get them to quantify the SharePoint services that their application needs. Simply porting an ASP.NET application to SharePoint does not justify the cost if it does not provide any additional functionality.

In this vein, we'd like to highlight the various services that SharePoint provides. When considering your applications, use these lists and ask yourself, What does my solution need? Even if there are services your application can leverage, consider how much custom developing this feature would cost you versus the product's cost. Are there any future advantages? In other words, by tying yourself with the product, will your solution benefit from the product enhancements over time? Table 15-1 includes some of the important services in Windows SharePoint Services; Table 15-2 details additional services provided by Microsoft Office SharePoint Server.

Table 15-1. *Services Offered by Windows SharePoint Services v3*

Service	Description
Team sites	WSS is best viewed as a provisioning engine that can create web-based workspaces for teams of users to execute share information. Often these sites represent an instance of a business process. In addition to using the out-of-the-box site templates, you can create your own that contain the necessary functionality for the team.
Document libraries	Document libraries provide storage containers for files, including support for item-level security, versioning, and metadata.
Lists	Lists are a large component of WSS and can provide features to your application such as calendars, tasks, and discussion threads. Their flexibility makes them great for storing rows of information; however, they are more difficult to use in a highly relational system.
Workflow	WSS hosts Windows Workflow Foundation. Though it comes with no workflows, you can create your own with SharePoint Designer or VS.NET. This allows you to leverage the workflow engine without having to implement it in a hosting application. SharePoint's implementation includes user interfaces for interacting with the workflow, including tasks and auditing.
Web parts	You can build web parts with just ASP.NET 2.0. However, WSS provides many of them out of the box and generates one for each of your lists and libraries.
Search	WSS provides a search engine that allows users to search within the site for information.

Service	Description
RSS	WSS lists and libraries can easily be set up to be RSS providers. This supports site content being pulled and aggregated into other RSS viewers, such as Internet Explorer, Windows Vista gadgets, and Outlook 2007.
Alerts	WSS provides an alerting structure for users to sign up for notifications about changes to items or new items being added to a list or library.

Table 15-2. *Services Offered by Microsoft Office SharePoint Server 2007*

Service	Description
Single Sign-on	Single Sign-on in MOSS provides developers a solution for securely storing alternate credentials for users to external applications.
Enterprise search	MOSS includes the enterprise search service which supports the indexing of content both inside and outside of SharePoint. This can include source such as file shares, web sites, Exchange public folders, and custom database or web-service applications through the use of the Business Data Catalog.
Web content management	The web content management features of MOSS allow users to maintain HTML portions of site pages with restrictions so that they are forced to comply with an organization's style guidelines.
Records management	Records management is about applying retention policies for content so that they can be reviewed or removed when they expire. This service within MOSS also includes labeling and bar-coding functionality to link physical documents to the electronic ones.
Excel Services	Excel Services can provide many different types of services. It can be used as a calculation engine or a data-visualization service. It also helps the distribution of spreadsheet-driven processes.
Forms services	MOSS forms services provide new features to Microsoft's electronic forms strategy. To a developer, this service can decouple the data-entry mechanism from a custom application, allowing the organization to support the form UI. The forms can now be displayed in thin/web or thick/InfoPath interfaces.
Personalization and dashboards	MOSS includes the ability to personalize its interface to specific audiences or user roles.
My Sites	The My Sites of MOSS provide a personal dashboard for users to maintain their own workspace. In addition, they can serve as profile pages. Powering the My Sites is a user-profile store whose fields can be populated from Active Directory, other applications, or the users themselves. This profile directory is also available through a web service, making it accessible to custom applications.
Integration	The Business Data Catalog service of MOSS rapidly integrates applications into SharePoint. With an XML application definition, the BDC can surface the applications' data into search results, web parts, and columns of lists.
Data connection libraries	Data connection libraries allow you to publish the necessary connection information to an external source as a single file. Using this file, the users can then reuse this information to visualize data in spreadsheets or incorporate it into forms.

A Real-World Example

Here's a real-world example of evaluating whether a solution should be built on top of Share-Point. An RFP (request for proposal) that once came across my desk asked for a solution to be built that allowed teams of lawyers to share information regarding cases they were working on. Each case included content like a shared calendar, documents, contact information, and other lists. This likely sounds like an obvious SharePoint opportunity; however, there were no requirements about it being a web-based solution. In fact, the customer envisioned the solution as a desktop tool so that the lawyers could take the content to court with them. In building the response, I didn't want our developers to have to build an entire structure that stored the documents as well as construct features to provide security, versioning, and metadata. So we proposed SharePoint as a server, and a smart-client application that interacted with it. Each case would get its own team site even though at no point were the users ever going to see its web interface. They would simply select which case they wanted to work on and we would pull the site content into a local data store for the application. This allowed us to propose a shorter development time for the application, as well as a lower cost. Not only did we win, but during the follow-up requirements confirmation additional requests were made. The requests included allowing the lawyers' assistants to search across all cases for information, and for users outside their organization to have access to the information, but not by installing the tool. As you can guess, it was a good thing that we had SharePoint in the design. None of these changes were difficult because SharePoint provided the enterprise search service and could be set up to support an extranet web-based scenario.

Tools to Support the Development Environment

As the Office development platform continues to mature, so will its tools. Visual Studio Tools for Office has undergone an incredible transformation, increasing the number of different types of solutions that can be built as well as reducing the amount of code it takes to build them. To conclude this book, we would like to highlight a few of the additional development tools that are going to make a huge impact on Office-based solutions.

SharePoint Solution Generator

The SharePoint Solution Generator is a tool that is included in the Windows SharePoint Services extensions for Visual Studio (covered later). Even though it is included within a larger package, its promise is so great that it is worth dedicating time to. The SharePoint Solution Generator is capable of capturing an existing list or site as a definition. We used this tool for exactly this purpose as part of the solution in Chapter 5. This capability reduces the amount of work developers will do in the depths of schema.xml and onet.xml files. Instead of having to know how to code these by hand, a developer can create an instance of what he is trying to define and run this tool to capture it as a definition. Once in this format, it can be deployed to the file system of the front-end servers, providing new site and list types to the SharePoint environment. Figure 15-1 includes a screen shot of this tool. The tool is included in the WSS Extensions package:

- Windows SharePoint Services 3.0 Tools: Visual Studio 2005 Extensions

  ```
  http://www.microsoft.com/downloads/details.aspx?~
  FamilyID=19f21e5e-b715-4f0c-b959-8c6dcbdc1057&DisplayLang=en
  ```

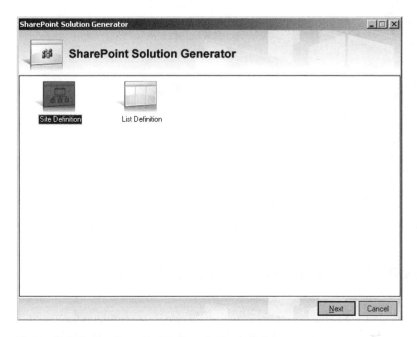

Figure 15-1. *Capturing existing lists as list definitions*

Enterprise Content Management Starter Kit

This toolkit is included in the download of the MOSS SDK. A major emphasis of this starter kit is the development of workflows that will be hosted in SharePoint. Therefore, the kit includes workflow activities, custom reports, and more than a dozen sample workflow projects. These go beyond the set provided by the extensions for Windows Workflow Foundation and show a developer SharePoint-specific workflow techniques. The workflows cover the simple Hello World sequential workflow, multistage workflows, confidential approvals, group approvals, and many more. We used these workflow elements in Chapter 14. Figure 15-2 shows a Share-Point sequential workflow project with the toolbox of activities open on the left. This starter kit can be downloaded here:

- SharePoint Server 2007 SDK: Software Development Kit and Enterprise Content Management Starter Kit

  ```
  http://www.microsoft.com/downloads/details.aspx?~
  familyid=6D94E307-67D9-41AC-B2D6-0074D6286FA9&displaylang=en
  ```

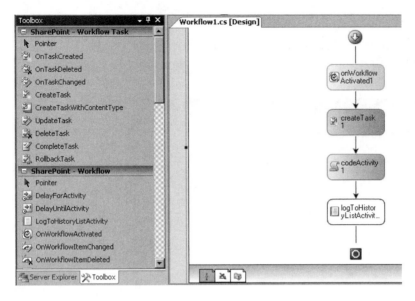

Figure 15-2. *Building a SharePoint workflow with the Enterprise Content Management starter kit*

Windows SharePoint Services 3.0 Tools: Visual Studio Extensions

This tool provides developers with SharePoint-specific project and item templates for Visual Studio. Among these are templates for web parts, site and list definitions, custom fields, and content types. It can be obtained from `http://www.microsoft.com/downloads/details.aspx?FamilyID=19f21e5e-b715-4f0c-b959-8c6dcbdc1057&DisplayLang=en`. Figure 15-3 shows Visual Studio's new project dialog with these templates installed.

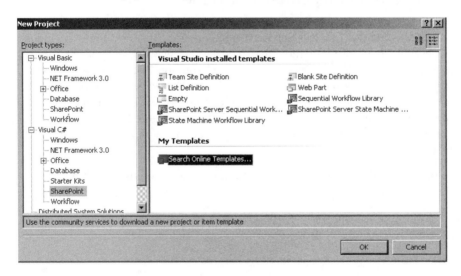

Figure 15-3. *New project types provided by WSS extensions for VS.NET*

Business Data Catalog Application Definition Generators

The Business Data Catalog feature of Microsoft Office SharePoint Server dramatically reduces the amount of code a developer has to write to integrate an external application. Through the creation of an XML application definition, the developer is able to surface the external application's data through web parts, search, and columns of lists. There is an additional benefit: This approach does not introduce any new compiled code written by the developer into the SharePoint environment. Though there is no compiled code, it still takes some time to generate the XML application definition. There are several efforts in the community to reduce even this effort for developers:

- BDC Meta Man

  `http://www.bdcmetaman.com/default.aspx`

- BDCGenerator

  `http://weblog.vb-tech.com/nick/archive/2006/08/30/1750.aspx`

Looking Ahead

The future is bright for the types of solutions included in this book. The next release of Visual Studio, code-named Orcas, will have the greatest impact on your ability to build solutions on top of the Office platform. It includes the next version of Visual Studio Tools for Office. This release is still a Community Technology Preview (CTP) at the time of this writing, but the features are already impressive. Included in the January CTP is support for document-level projects for Microsoft Word and Excel 2007. Design-time support is added for Word's content controls, and Outlook form regions get a major face lift. To read more about what is coming, keep up with the VSTO team blog. Specifically you can preview some of the help topics for this release at the following URL:

- Microsoft Visual Studio Tools for the Microsoft Office System

  `http://blogs.msdn.com/vsto2/archive/2007/01/15/~`
  `help-topics-in-the-visual-studio-code-name-orcas-january-ctp.aspx`

The team has also made a virtual-image development environment available for you to test-drive.

Microsoft itself sees the value of Office as a development platform. The company has classified these types of solutions as Office Business Applications and has set up a portal on MSDN:

- Office Business Applications Developer Portal

  `http://msdn2.microsoft.com/en-us/office/aa905528.aspx`

The portal contains a wide variety of content, including case studies, background material, and guidance for using Office as a development platform. On their team blog (`http://blogs.msdn.com/oba/`), the developers discuss line-of-business interoperability (LOBi) for Office SharePoint Server. The yet-to-be-released LOBi extension is a set of services that provides a framework around MOSS for developers to integrate external applications with Microsoft

Office. Though this extension will not be available until Office 14, it shows the prominence of Office in Microsoft's vision of integration.

As we've discussed, a major reason for developing on top of the Office platform is the connection and comfort level users have with its applications. With the release of Office 2007, Microsoft has decided to provide a no-cost, royalty-free license of the Office UI. This means that other software vendors will be able to incorporate the Office look and feel into their own products. This promises to open the flood gates for component developers to release controls that allow you to reuse elements of the Office UI in your own custom applications. Imagine dragging a ribbon control onto your own Windows Forms applications. That vision is not far from being a reality. You can read more about Office UI licensing here:

- Office UI Licensing

  ```
  http://msdn2.microsoft.com/en-us/office/aa973809.aspx
  ```

A Thank-You

This book set an ambitious goal of introducing Microsoft Office as a solution platform for developers. We made our case by examining common problems that we see with customers on a routine basis. Hopefully a few of these problems sounded familiar. The best developers are ones with a lot of experience and a wide set of tools that they can apply to new problems. By reading this book, we hope you have learned from some of our experiences and gained a few new tools. By no means do we think this story is complete; this platform is still new and the community is still exploring ways to leverage it. If you made it to this page of the book (and just didn't flip to the end!), we appreciate your time. We challenge you to extend the techniques we've covered to apply them for your customers. Please share your experiences as we have so that this development platform evolves and matures. We will continue to have this conversation. Follow along through Ed Hild's blog, where he discusses new ways to build solutions with Microsoft Office, SharePoint, and .NET code:

- edhild's WebLog

  ```
  http://blogs.msdn.com/edhild
  ```

Index

forums.apress.com

JOIN THE APRESS FORUMS AND BE PART OF OUR COMMUNITY. You'll find discussions that cover topics of interest to IT professionals, programmers, and enthusiasts just like you. If you post a query to one of our forums, you can expect that some of the best minds in the business—especially Apress authors, who all write with *The Expert's Voice*™—will chime in to help you. Why not aim to become one of our most valuable participants (MVPs) and win cool stuff? Here's a sampling of what you'll find:

DATABASES
Data drives everything.

Share information, exchange ideas, and discuss any database programming or administration issues.

INTERNET TECHNOLOGIES AND NETWORKING
Try living without plumbing (and eventually IPv6).

Talk about networking topics including protocols, design, administration, wireless, wired, storage, backup, certifications, trends, and new technologies.

JAVA
We've come a long way from the old Oak tree.

Hang out and discuss Java in whatever flavor you choose: J2SE, J2EE, J2ME, Jakarta, and so on.

MAC OS X
All about the Zen of OS X.

OS X is both the present and the future for Mac apps. Make suggestions, offer up ideas, or boast about your new hardware.

OPEN SOURCE
Source code is good; understanding (open) source is better.

Discuss open source technologies and related topics such as PHP, MySQL, Linux, Perl, Apache, Python, and more.

PROGRAMMING/BUSINESS
Unfortunately, it is.

Talk about the Apress line of books that cover software methodology, best practices, and how programmers interact with the "suits."

WEB DEVELOPMENT/DESIGN
Ugly doesn't cut it anymore, and CGI is absurd.

Help is in sight for your site. Find design solutions for your projects and get ideas for building an interactive Web site.

SECURITY
Lots of bad guys out there—the good guys need help.

Discuss computer and network security issues here. Just don't let anyone else know the answers!

TECHNOLOGY IN ACTION
Cool things. Fun things.

It's after hours. It's time to play. Whether you're into LEGO® MINDSTORMS™ or turning an old PC into a DVR, this is where technology turns into fun.

WINDOWS
No defenestration here.

Ask questions about all aspects of Windows programming, get help on Microsoft technologies covered in Apress books, or provide feedback on any Apress Windows book.

HOW TO PARTICIPATE:
Go to the Apress Forums site at **http://forums.apress.com/**.
Click the New User link.

You Need the Companion eBook

Your purchase of this book entitles you to buy the companion PDF-version eBook for only $10. Take the weightless companion with you anywhere.

We believe this Apress title will prove so indispensable that you'll want to carry it with you everywhere, which is why we are offering the companion eBook (in PDF format) for $10 to customers who purchase this book now. Convenient and fully searchable, the PDF version of any content-rich, page-heavy Apress book makes a valuable addition to your programming library. You can easily find and copy code—or perform examples by quickly toggling between instructions and the application. Even simultaneously tackling a donut, diet soda, and complex code becomes simplified with hands-free eBooks!

Once you purchase your book, getting the $10 companion eBook is simple:

❶ Visit **www.apress.com/promo/tendollars/**.

❷ Complete a basic registration form to receive a randomly generated question about this title.

❸ Answer the question correctly in 60 seconds, and you will receive a promotional code to redeem for the $10.00 eBook.

2560 Ninth Street • Suite 219 • Berkeley, CA 94710

eBookshop

THE EXPERT'S VOICE™

Offer valid through 11/07.